Helping the Good Shepherd

Medicine, Science, and Religion in Historical Context
Ronald L. Numbers, *Consulting Editor*

Helping the Good Shepherd

Pastoral Counselors in a Psychotherapeutic Culture
1925–1975

SUSAN E. MYERS-SHIRK

The Johns Hopkins University Press

Baltimore

© 2009 The Johns Hopkins University Press
All rights reserved. Published 2009
Printed in the United States of America on acid-free paper
9 8 7 6 5 4 3 2 1

The Johns Hopkins University Press
2715 North Charles Street
Baltimore, Maryland 21218-4363
www.press.jhu.edu

Much of chapter 8 appeared in "To Be Fully Human: U.S. Protestant Psychotherapeutic Culture and the Subversion of the Domestic Ideal, 1945–1965," *Journal of Women's History* 12, no. 1 (2000): 112–136, © Indiana University Press, and is reprinted, in slightly altered form, by permission of The Johns Hopkins University Press.

Library of Congress Cataloging-in-Publication Data
Myers-Shirk, Susan E., 1958–
  Helping the Good Shepherd : pastoral counselors in a psychotherapeutic culture, 1925–1975 / Susan E. Myers-Shirk.
    p. cm.
  Includes bibliographical references and index.
  ISBN-13: 978-0-8018-9047-5 (hardcover : alk. paper)
  ISBN-10: 0-8018-9047-0 (hardcover : alk. paper)
    1. Pastoral counseling—United States—History—20th century.
2. Liberalism—Religious aspects—Protestant churches—History—
20th century. 3. United States—Church history—20th century. I. Title.
  BV4012.2.M94 2009
  253.50973'0904—dc22   2008021240

A catalog record for this book is available from the British Library.

Special discounts are available for bulk purchases of this book. For more information, please contact Special Sales at 410-516-6936 or specialsales@press.jhu.edu.

The Johns Hopkins University Press uses environmentally friendly book materials, including recycled text paper that is composed of at least 30 percent post-consumer waste, whenever possible. All of our book papers are acid-free, and our jackets and covers are printed on paper with recycled content.

For

Stephanie Jo Myers, 1968–1990

CONTENTS

ACKNOWLEDGMENTS

As the setting for one of her Peter Wimsey mysteries, *Gaudy Night*, Dorothy Sayers chose an imaginary women's college at Oxford University. Sayers was familiar with the scholarly life and created a character named Miss Lydgate who had spent a good bit of her academic life writing a history of prosody—repeatedly revising and editing her prose and checking—and rechecking—her facts. Her colleagues finally wrested the manuscript from her and carried it off to the publisher, despite Miss Lydgate's protest "about a footnote on page 97." I am somewhat in Miss Lydgate's situation; only through the intervention of friends, family, and colleagues has this work made its way to the light of publication. As a result, I have a rather long list of people to thank and acknowledge.

In its original incarnation, this book was a dissertation, and so I want to acknowledge the help and direction given me early in my career by my dissertation director, Sally McMurry, my committee chair, Isabel F. Knight, and committee members Anne Rose and Judith Van Herik, all at Penn State University. My fellow graduate students and dear friends Su-Ya Chang and Bill Blair, and Bill's wife, Mary Anne, played a critical role in those early years. Once I arrived at Middle Tennessee State University, the Women's Work Group in the History Department took up where my graduate school mentors and friends had left off. I owe a deep debt of gratitude to Yuan-ling Chao, Martha Harroun Foster, Gina Hames, Mary Hoffschwelle, Jan Leone, Rebecca Cawood McIntyre, and Amy Sayward, who have challenged me intellectually and encouraged and prodded me at various points along the way.

I have also been extremely fortunate in the funding I have received for this project. First, while the manuscript was still a dissertation, I received a fellowship from the University of Chicago Divinity School Congregational History Project. Two grants, an MTSU Faculty Research and Creativity Activity Grant and assistance from the Louisville Institute for the

Study of Protestantism and American Culture, allowed me to begin revisions in the summer of 1995. In 1997 the Pew Program in Religion and American History at Yale University, directed by Harry S. Stout and Jon Butler, funded a year of work on the project. In the same year, I spent a semester at the Center for the Study of American Religion at Princeton University. I am especially grateful to CSAR director Robert Wuthnow for his encouragement and useful direction and to the fellows that year, Rebecca Kneale Gould, Bernadette McCauley, and Ann Taves, who offered me friendship and wise counsel. Cynthia Eller likewise offered support and encouragement, and she skillfully edited the manuscript at a point when I needed some inspiration to continue.

At the midpoint of the project, Rodney Hunter encouraged me to continue, and he gave me the opportunity to present my work to his students at Emory University's School of Theology. Hunter's *Dictionary of Pastoral Care and Counseling* was indispensable, as was the considerable help I received from staff at Emory University's Pitts Theology Library. The archival work I completed there expanded on the work I had done earlier at Harvard Divinity School's Andover-Harvard Theological Library, where the staff were also extremely helpful. A portion of this manuscript was published in the *Journal of Women's History* in Spring 2000, and I am grateful to Leila J. Rupp, the journal's editor at the time, who understood that this work was not just about religion and psychology but also fundamentally about gender. My thanks go to John McGowan and Allen Dunn, who allowed me to participate in the 2001 NEH Summer Institute on Literature and Values in Chapel Hill and who, along with other members of the seminar, especially Miriam Kalman Friedman, encouraged me to think in new ways about this project. Most recently, the Tennessee Pastoral Care Association, Hospice Alive in Nashville, and the Pastoral Counseling Centers of Tennessee, Inc., have given me a place to present the work as it neared publication and, hence, an opportunity to keep the work fresh.

I am especially indebted to Ronald Numbers, the series editor of the Johns Hopkins University Press series Medicine, Science, and Religion in Historical Context, who, having asked me what I was working on, really listened when I answered and then found a place for this book in that series. Many thanks go also to Johns Hopkins University Press editor Jacqueline Wehmueller, who so graciously and kindly helped me navigate an unfamiliar process, and to Anne Whitmore, who so carefully and thoroughly copyedited the manuscript.

As long as this process has taken, it has nevertheless been rewarding. I have met good people, read interesting books, and spent time thinking about things that matter. During my graduate studies of Enlightenment Europe, the question of the relationship between science and religion first caught my attention. When I shifted my focus to American culture, E. Brooks Holifield's *A History of Pastoral Care* helped me understand pastoral counseling as the starting point for examining the intersection of science, religion, and liberal thought. I value Holifield's contribution and see my own work in continuity with his.

Throughout this process, my family's support has been unwavering. My parents, Nelson and Faith Myers, and my husband's parents, Ernest and June Shirk, as well as my sisters, their husbands and children, and my husband's brother, sister-in-law, and nephews, have been a tremendous source of encouragement, even when my work seemed to have no clear relevance to their lives.

I first learned about pastoral counseling nearly three decades ago when, as an undergraduate history major at a small, Christian liberal arts college, I decided to take a pastoral counseling class as an elective—in order to be close to a boy, who happened to be a Bible major. As a feminist, I should perhaps deplore such behavior, but since that boy has for all the subsequent years of my life loved, encouraged, and, where necessary, nagged me, as well as generally made sure I had everything I could want or need, I must dedicate this book to him, David Shirk, with all my love and gratitude. There would be no book without him.

Helping the Good Shepherd

Introduction

"The Deeper Our Religious Faith the More We Feel the Need of
Science to Free Us of Sicknesses Which Hamper Spiritual Growth."
—SUBTITLE OF "THE HARD CORE OF COUNSELING,"
PASTORAL PSYCHOLOGY, APRIL 1950

ON A COLD AND SNOWY evening in the middle of the nineteenth century, "Mrs. E" trudged the half-mile from her house to the home of
her minister, Ichabod Spencer, pastor of Brooklyn's Second Presbyterian
Church. The story of that visit has survived because, unlike most of his
nineteenth-century counterparts, Spencer kept detailed records of each
of the private conversations he had with his parishioners. He later published those accounts in a two-volume set entitled *A Pastor's Sketches:
Or, Conversations with Anxious Inquirers Respecting the Way of Salvation*. In the second volume, Spencer included the story of Mrs. E under
the title "The Stormy Night: Or, Perseverance."[1] Comparing this story to
one recounted below about a twentieth-century pastoral counselor illustrates a fundamental shift in American religious life—a shift in how
Americans thought about the authority and purpose of the clergy, the
purview of science, and the nature of moral decision making.

Like most of the people who came to see Spencer, Mrs. E wished to be
"saved." The subtitle of the sketch, "Perseverance," derived from Mrs.
E's dogged determination to settle the matter of her soul's salvation,
which led her to visit her pastor's home almost every Sabbath evening for
nearly two years. Mrs. E's case illustrates Spencer's style of pastoral counseling especially well. Spencer applied himself energetically to the task
of securing Mrs. E's eternal salvation and, by his own account, brought
all the weight of his ministerial office to bear on Mrs. E's recalcitrant conscience. He addressed his reluctant and tearful parishioner "time after
time" with Bible in hand and by virtue of his position as a "minister of

God." While he stressed the "unbounded love" of God and the "kindness of Christ," he also "demanded her heart's faith and instant submission to divine authority" and besieged "her mind, her conscience, her heart" with the "threatenings" and "promises of God."[2] In the published account of his meetings with Mrs. E, Spencer admitted that on a number of occasions he nearly gave up on her. At one point, he even acknowledged to her his surprise that she had walked alone through blowing, drifting snow to talk with him—a sentiment shared by her husband, who was not a believer. According to Spencer, Mrs. E's persistence was rewarded: she eventually found peace and "Christian hope," as did her husband, in part because of his wife's willingness to brave the storm in search of salvation.[3]

Mrs. E later told Spencer that his surprise at seeing her on that stormy night temporarily discouraged her, especially since escape from the "hailstones and coals of fire" he had described in his sermon seemed so much more important to her than avoiding a winter storm.[4] She asserted, however, that Spencer's refusal to give up on her made her unwilling to give up on "trying to be saved."[5] Both in his description of Mrs. E's situation and throughout his book of "sketches," Spencer downplayed his own contribution and instead stressed the importance of the work of the Holy Spirit in bringing about salvation. But he also saw the use of his ministerial authority as central to his ministerial task. He saw himself as obligated to use the weight of his office to urge the sinner on to repentance.

A little over a century later in the winter of 1957, "Anne Vick" sought counsel from a Disciples of Christ minister named Lowell Colston who served at a counseling center in the city of Chicago. Colston, too, kept a record of his counseling sessions, but for reasons that differed significantly from those of Ichabod Spencer and with goals, methods, and a style of counseling that differed dramatically. Unlike Mrs. E, who came to her pastor seeking salvation, Mrs. Vick came to the counseling center seeking help with a specific problem—an abusive husband. At the time she came for counseling, Anne Vick had left her husband and home in the suburbs and moved to the city with her small son to live with her sister while she decided whether to seek a divorce.[6] Vick had not worked outside her home since her marriage, and the thought of striking out on her own intimidated her. Mrs. Vick was a tall, heavy-set woman and spent some of her counseling sessions talking about the difficulties she had encountered in her life, even as a child, because of her size. The majority of her counseling sessions, however, she devoted to talking about her relationship to her husband. She described how he belittled her in front of her friends, criticized her in everything she did so that she could "make [herself] perfect," told her she was "neurotic," and would sometimes become so angry he would strike her.[7] After one of their fights, he had admitted that he felt like killing her. Colston listened patiently, repeating, summarizing, reflecting back to Mrs. Vick everything she said, and allowing her to sort through her concerns. Still, Mrs. Vick hesitated to divorce her husband. In the process of describing her problem to Colston, however, she became convinced that she could not tolerate her husband's verbal and physical abuse and that her only solution was to leave him permanently.

In early summer, still apparently unsettled about what to do, Mrs. Vick terminated the counseling sessions and asked Colston to telephone her at the end of the summer to ask whether she thought she needed more counseling. When Colston did call her several months later, she declined further counseling and told him that "she had been surprised and pleased" to discover that she had been able to go through with the divorce. Throughout the fifteen counseling sessions with Mrs. Vick, Colston never offered advice or direction, electing instead to allow Vick to choose the direction of each session and to revisit each issue as often as she desired. Neither Colston nor Mrs. Vick ever mentioned salvation or any explicitly religious issues. In a written summary of the counseling sessions published in a book entitled *The Context of Pastoral Counseling* (1961), Colston remarked that he wished Mrs. Vick had gained greater "insight" into herself from counseling and that the marriage could have been preserved, but he reaffirmed Mrs. Vick's right to make her own choices.[8]

The differences between Spencer and Colston are striking. Perhaps most notably, Colston appeared to have no inclination to exercise any ministerial authority or to make any moral judgments, while Spencer did both with fervor, enthusiasm, and conviction. Understanding the context in which Colston wrote and practiced helps explain the shift. Colston was part of a twentieth-century movement among Protestant ministers who combined their theology with theories and methods they had borrowed from the social sciences in order to imagine a new way of relating to their parishioners, first through something called clinical pastoral education (CPE), in the 1920s, and later through pastoral counseling. They saw themselves engaged in an attempt to understand the relationship between science and religion and to apply the lessons they learned from their studies to their pastoral practice.

The Meaning and Importance of Science

For pastoral counselors and clinical pastoral educators, the meaning of "science" varied according to context and changed over time. It generally signified a cluster of related disciplines that included psychology, psychoanalysis, psychiatry, and medicine, as well as social sciences, such as anthropology and social work. The meaning of "religion" varied, too, and most often referred to pastoral practice but could also mean anything from rituals and beliefs to systematic theology. In its simplest form, talking about the intersection of religion and science was code for talking about what happened when clergy incorporated the principles and practices of the psychological disciplines into parish practice.

Colston based his approach to counseling on the methods of psychologist Carl Rogers and saw what he was doing as a contribution to integrating science and religion. Carl Rogers had established the counseling center where Colston counseled Mrs. Vick, at the University of Chicago in 1945 when he became a faculty member in the University of Chicago's Department of Psychology.[9] Rogers's theories and methods played a pivotal role in the way many clergy approached counseling at the midcentury. Although Rogers later in life downplayed his religious roots, he had much in common with the clergy who self-identified as pastoral counselors. He had grown up in a religiously conservative home in the Midwest and had once planned a career as a missionary. After beginning studies for a degree at Union Theological Seminary in New York City, he decided to transfer to Teachers College of Columbia University to study psychology. From there, he went to Rochester, New York, to serve as director of the Child Study Department at the Society for the Prevention of Cruelty to Children and was later director of the Rochester Guidance Center.[10] His experiences prompted him to develop a new counseling method, which he referred to initially as "non-directive," then later as "client-centered," and finally as "person-centered."[11] In Rogerian therapy, therapists declined to offer advice or guidance and instead attempted to create a warm, loving therapeutic relationship in which counselees sorted out their problems for themselves and made their own decisions. Rogers, along with psychologists Gordon Allport, Rollo May, and Abraham Maslow, helped to found the humanistic or "third force" psychology movement of the twentieth century.

During his years in Chicago, Rogers focused on demonstrating the effectiveness of client-centered therapy through a number of scientific studies. His concern with establishing scientifically the effectiveness of therapy was a response to the general bias against applied psychology that he perceived among his peers. Academic or scientific psychology was dominated by psychologists who considered tests conducted in laboratories to be pure science and who looked with suspicion on the clinical practice of psychology, including psychological testing, counseling, and psychotherapy. Rogers's interest in research and in establishing an empirical basis for his counseling method provides another point of connection with Colston. Colston's counseling with Mrs. Vick was part of a two-year social scientific study that he and colleague Seward Hiltner conducted to measure the effectiveness of pastoral counseling.

With the aim of demonstrating the scientific validity of pastoral counseling, Hiltner and Colston designed a study similar to those constructed by Rogers. As part of the study, Colston held counseling sessions in two different Chicago settings, the Bryn Mawr Community Church and the Counseling Center of the University of Chicago. Hiltner and Colston worked from the premise that Colston's "basic approach and method" of pastoral counseling would not change even if the setting did, and, thus, the variable in effectiveness would be the context, not the counselor.[12] Colston and Hiltner chose the participants for their study from a group of volunteers who had sought counseling either at the church or at the center and who agreed to participate in the research.[13] Intending that the two cohorts be roughly equivalent, they attempted to "match" participants from the church to participants at the center in factors such as sex, age, "social background," and "educational achievement."[14] At the outset, they planned to administer three tests at three points during the study—once immediately prior to counseling, once immediately upon termination of counseling, and a third time six months after the termination of counseling. For their tests, they chose the Thematic Apperception Test (TAT), the Butler-Haigh Adjustment-through-Self-Concept Test, and a third test composed of portions of several interrelated tests that were intended to measure social attitudes, including ethnocentrism, religious conventionalism, and traditional family ideology.[15] They also asked participants to evaluate the "degree of progress" they thought they had made during the course of counseling.

Several of the participants never took the postcounseling test or the six-month follow-up test, but Colston and Hiltner argued that they could nevertheless draw some conclusions about the significance of context in pastoral counseling from the data. They concluded that the church setting had given Colston a "slight edge," although they conceded that the difference in the progress made by counselees in the two settings was not "significant statistically."[16] They felt that they could, in good conscience, reassure clergy that being a minister was at least not a disadvantage to those who chose to take up counseling.

The fascination with science illustrated by the Hiltner/Colston study had wide-ranging implications for pastoral counseling theory and practice. Most important was the way in which questions about moral reasoning and the clergy's moral authority moved to the center of their professional discourse. Rogers's method did not allow for giving advice, direction, or guidance, which was territory traditionally claimed by clergy. Much of the talk about science at the time underlined the importance of objectivity and maintaining a critical distance from one's subject of study, which raised questions about how ministers could promote ethical standards and simultaneously remain objective.[17] As pastoral counselors engaged the literature and theories of the social and behavioral sciences, difficult questions about truth and how truth ought to be determined and about right and wrong and who ought to decide what constituted moral and ethical behavior inevitably arose. It is here, I argue, that we find the historical significance of the pastoral counseling movement. Early pastoral counselors are important not so much for their original theories of counseling or their influence on American psychology but for the way they addressed questions about right and wrong and for the insight they give us into the moral sensibility of twentieth-century liberal Protestants.[18]

The Meaning of "Liberal" and "Moral Sensibility"

In choosing pastoral counselors and clinical pastoral educators as a beginning point for examining the liberal moral sensibility, I am making certain assumptions about the meaning of "liberal." It is a word notoriously difficult to define. While recognizing that liberal Christians of the period from 1925 to 1975 were diverse in their beliefs, I think it is still possible to formulate a working definition of "liberal" as it applied to them. In general, I consider these pastoral counselors and clinical educators to be liberal because many of them saw the task of finding a rapprochement between religion and science as one of the most important duties facing the clergy in the twentieth century.[19] They came from Protestant denominations that had led the way in the embrace of science. Early pastoral counselors and clinical pastoral educators counted among their numbers Presbyterians, Episcopalians, Methodists, Disciples of Christ, and Congregationalists. There is obviously much more to the definition of Christian liberals than attraction to scientific pursuits, but I am working from the premise that their fascination with science was formative. In addition, "liberal" must be understood on a continuum, as a term that is defined in relation to other terms, not as something static or essentialist. For instance, Mennonites, Southern Baptists, and Evangelical Lutherans were early and active participants in both clinical pastoral education and pastoral counseling. In other social and historical circumstances, all three might be considered conservative. The point here is not to discard the term "liberal" in referring to them but to think of liberalism as an intellectual and moral framework that led to a particular set of actions and a way of thinking in the middle years of the twentieth century.

I employ the phrase "moral sensibility" as shorthand for referring to a cluster of ideas, attitudes, values, and beliefs regarding the nature of right and wrong. In doing so, I deviate a bit from the historical meaning of the word "sensibility." Historically, sensibility was associated almost exclusively with emotions. One of the most famous examples is Jane Austen's Marianne in *Sense and Sensibility*, who seemed to feel everything more deeply than anyone else. Austen described Marianne's excess of sensibility this way: "She was sensible and clever, but eager in everything; her sorrows, her joys, could have no moderation. She was generous, amiable, interesting: she was every thing but prudent."[20] In the psychology of the seventeenth and eighteenth centuries, "sensibility" was defined in terms of emotions and affections and believed to be best moderated and governed by the will.[21] In contrast, I use the term "moral sensibility" in a way that incorporates both the world of the intellect and ideas (theology, philosophy, and psychology) and the world of attitudes and values that sometimes are grounded more firmly in emotion and intuition than in rational thought.[22]

I am not the first to use the phrase "moral sensibility," although perhaps among the first to apply it to liberal thought and to think about it historically.[23] I argue that moral sensibility encompasses those clearly identifiable principles and values that come to the forefront to govern moral reasoning when individuals are faced with a moral choice. I do not use the term "moral sensibility" in a particularly rigid way. That is, I do not assume that all Democrats share a liberal moral sensibility or that all Republicans share a conservative moral sensibility. I do not assume that evangelical or fundamentalist Christians necessarily share a conservative moral sensibility or that "mainline" Protestants share a liberal moral sensibility. To complicate matters further, I do not assume that all folks who share a particular moral sensibility will always come to the same conclusions regarding any given moral dilemma.

Why Studying the Liberal Moral Sensibility Is Important

And yet, if we recognize the existence of a liberal moral sensibility and, by extension, its opposite, a conservative moral sensibility, some of the broader trends in American political and cultural life begin to make sense. This approach provides an explanatory framework for some of the most heated debates of the late twentieth and early twenty-first centuries. For the framework to be useful and workable, it must be understood that neither of these categories is pure; both have been located on a continuum in which those in the middle have moved fairly easily back and forth between liberal and conservative moral reasoning while those on the far ends have felt like those at the other end are speaking a foreign language. Debates between liberals and conservatives in the United States in the late twentieth century illustrate the extent to which those on the ends of the spectrum have dominated public rhetoric and the subsequent consequences for public discourse. The debates were characterized not only by extraordinary rancor but also by the assumption on the part of conservatives generally and religious conservatives particularly that they had a natural and incontestable claim to the moral high ground. Conservative Christians claimed biblical authority and made clear, assumedly unambiguous, assertions about truth and morality; and in doing so, they made values central to a great deal of political discussion. They merged religious and political conservatism in unprecedented ways. For some Christian conservatives, the line was so clear that to be Christian was to vote Republican, because Democrats or liberals were seen as having no values. Whatever their reasons, historians, pundits, and cultural critics did little to challenge this view.

Seeing liberals as devoid of moral values juxtaposes "Godless liberals" with God-fearing conservatives and erases not only religious liberals but also nonreligious conservatives from the political landscape. It is also historically inaccurate, narrowing the definition of values and obscuring generations of social activism by religious liberals—Jewish, Catholic, and Protestant—who were driven by ethical concerns. I argue that a more complete grasp of the history of the values of religious liberals is necessary to understanding contemporary American political rhetoric and having a broader and more accurate conception of American liberalism and history.

Liberal Christianity and the Social Gospel Movement

Twentieth-century religious liberalism should be understood as a continuation of the Progressive and Social Gospel movements. The Social Gospel, as defined by historians C. Howard Hopkins and later by Robert T. Handy, was a response to the poverty and injustice spawned by urbanization and industrialization.[24] According to Wendy Edwards and Carolyn Gifford, editors of *Gender and the Social Gospel* (2003), the understanding of the Social Gospel advanced by Hopkins and Handy is still "widely accepted." According to this interpretation, "social gospelers perceived themselves to be acting on divine mandate as they marshaled public opinion, the tools of social science, and the power of the democratic political process in efforts to reconstruct society and its institutions, from the local to the global level, according to Christian ethical principles."[25] While a rich and growing literature on the nature, meaning, and constituents of Social Gospel activism has flourished in recent years, most of those accounts end with World War I.

Many historians argue that after World War I, the Social Gospel movement ended and liberal Christianity declined and lost authority as a result of capitulation to science, as part of the larger trend toward secularization.[26] Critics in the 1920s and 1930s, such as conservative Christians who rejected liberal theology and modernist understandings of scripture, helped to establish this narrative. Theologian J. Gresham Machen in his book *Christianity and Liberalism* (1923) argued that "naturalistic" Christianity had so completely accommodated science that it could no longer be considered Christianity.[27] At the same time, liberal Christians turned a sharp and not very sympathetic eye on their own beliefs and practices. For instance, Reinhold Niebuhr, whom many consider the foremost liberal theologian of the twentieth century, sharply criticized liberal Christians for their overly optimistic view of human nature, which was a legacy of both the Progressive era and their embrace of psychology.[28] In the early 1960s, Philip Rieff argued in *The Triumph of the Therapeutic* that, in the course of the twentieth century, liberal Christians had allowed a secular, therapeutic culture to usurp the power and authority of Christian culture.

I argue that efforts of clinical pastoral educators and pastoral counselors to engage the principles of science should not be interpreted as evidence of secularization or as an indication of the decline of liberal Christianity but as evidence of their eagerness to find some middle ground between the two worlds they saw as most important and relevant. To see engagement with science as secularization implies that adopting the principles of science necessitates a move away from a kind of Christianity that is somehow more pure or true or right. The argument for secularization has lost much of its force in recent years with the resurgence of religious sentiment beginning in the 1990s. Most of the new scholarship, however, has focused on fundamentalist and evangelical Christianity, which has not had the same kind of problematic relationship to science. The question of secularization needs to be reframed in the context of religious liberalism.

In this book, I attempt to address the question of secularization in two ways. First, I follow the argument of some of the newer work on the

Social Gospel that suggests that the time line for religious liberalism needs to be revised and extended well beyond World War I and that the religiously progressive ideas upon which twentieth-century liberal religious thought was built prospered in the 1920s and 1930s.[29] I argue that the clergy who attempted to unite their theology with the knowledge of the rapidly growing social sciences represented a continuation of the aims of Progressive reform and the Social Gospel. Where their predecessors sought to affect society by changing social institutions, these clergy sought to change society through work with individuals. Second, I shift the focus away from whether liberal Christianity is true or right or somehow adulterated by psychology and instead focus on that point of intersection between psychology and religion where moral questions became most pressing and from that point examine the moral sensibility of liberal Christians. I work from the premise that accepting the truth of psychological principles does not lead to an erosion of values.

Why Look at Pastoral Counselors?

Three factors make early pastoral counselors an ideal starting point for making my case regarding the liberal moral sensibility. First, because they saw themselves as engaged in scientific endeavor, they took copious notes and kept extensive records. As a result they left a remarkable paper trail. They published hundreds of books and pamphlets on the theory and method of counseling as well as two professional journals, *Pastoral Psychology* and *Journal of Pastoral Care*, that provided a venue for discussion of a wide variety of topics of interest to chaplains and pastoral counselors. In addition, the national records for the Association for Clinical Pastoral Education offer a rich source of unpublished materials relevant to both pastoral counseling and clinical pastoral education.

Second, because they were clergy, they were intensely concerned about moral and ethical issues. They viewed it as their obligation, especially initially, to offer moral guidance; but that conflicted, as they saw it, with their concurrent commitment to scientific objectivity and, later, with their embrace of the counseling theory and practice promoted by Carl Rogers. A significant portion of their published and unpublished writings revolve around questions concerning the moral reasoning and practices of their parishioners and their own moral authority. As they struggled with these questions, they maintained a running dialogue both with professionals in related disciplines and with their parishioners. Determining the exact numbers of parish ministers (as opposed to theologians or seminary professors) who read about and experimented with counseling is difficult, but their presence, especially in the journal *Pastoral Psychology*, is pronounced. Some, like H. Walter Yoder and Roy Burkhart, established counseling programs in their churches. Others, like Russell Becker and Seward Hiltner, offered counseling at the church they attended while teaching in seminaries. Still other parish ministers contributed articles to the journals, sent letters to the editor, and submitted questions about psychology and counseling to the "Readers' Forum" and the "Consultation Clinic," two regular features in *Pastoral Psychology*. The effect is unique. The discussion in their publications is simultaneously religious and secular, popular and intellectual, practical and theoretical. Moreover, several of the most important figures published extensively over several decades, allowing us to map change in their theory and practice over time very effectively. The result, in fact, is a map of the religious liberal moral sensibility, but a map that is also useful for thinking about liberalism generally.

Third, their relationship with their female parishioners ended up shaping their thinking on moral reasoning and so allows us to understand the implications of gender for the liberal moral sensibility. The numerical dominance of women in the history of Protestant denominations, and their complicated relationship to their ministers, has been well documented for the nineteenth century and early twentieth century.[30] More remains to be done. This book adds another piece to the puzzle of that relationship. I argue that the question of gender ran as a persistent thread through pastoral counselors' discussions of moral reasoning. Male pastoral counselors were concerned about what their female parishioners wanted and needed and, as I argue later, attempted to incorporate what they perceived as the perspective of women into their moral theory. What is ironic is how little room they allowed for women in the professional hierarchy of either clinical pastoral education or pastoral counseling. A handful of the leaders of the two movements could identify women who had played a formative role in their professional development. Others were willing to work with women from related professions such as social work, anthropology, or psychology. Still others made an explicit argument for women's equality. But most pastoral counselors resisted the idea of women clergy in the parish ministry. More troubling is the almost total silence about sexual impropriety in the relationship between counseling pastors and their counselees, until very recently. And yet, their willingness to incorporate women's perspective was significant.

How the Liberal Moral Sensibility Changed

In this book, then, I document the changing nature of the liberal moral sensibility in the twentieth century by examining the ongoing conversation among psychologically sophisticated Protestant clergy. At its height during the midcentury, this sensibility—shaped by the encounter between religion and science as well as by the interaction with their parishioners—encompassed a dedication to relieving human suffering, an embrace of personal autonomy and individual freedom as primary values, and a belief in the therapeutic value of loving, compassionate relationships. Pastoral counseling literature allows us to trace the changing nature of that sensibility and the shift from an earlier emphasis on adjustment, social control, and moral uplift to an emphasis on personal autonomy and loving relationships.

To illustrate this shift, I begin by examining the work of Anton Boisen, who attempted to document the relationship between religion and mental illness and who, in the 1920s, established one of the first programs to teach clergy and religious workers the scientific study of religion. These clinical pastoral education programs were seedbeds for the later pastoral counseling movement, which emphasized the marriage of psychology and religion for therapeutic purposes. All three, Boisen, clinical pastoral education, and early pastoral counseling, were firmly grounded in Progressive values. Influenced by the events of World War II—particularly the spread of fascism—and following the lead of psychologist Carl Rogers, pastoral counselors emphasized an ethic of autonomy and the importance of achieving one's "potentialities." In doing so, they embraced a more personalized and generalized definition of freedom than did prewar counselors. Such seemingly unregulated personal freedom had its dangers, however, and female parishioners in particular resisted. Pastoral counselors, attempting to respond to their female parishioners and to address their own concerns about the selfishness of an ethic of autonomy, turned to the theology of Martin Buber and Paul Tillich to articulate an ethic of relationships intended to mitigate the effects of too much personal autonomy.

The story of pastoral counselors highlights the origins of the great divide between the liberal moral sensibility and the conservative moral sensibility. Early in the 1950s, pastoral counselors began to argue specifically for women's autonomy and equality using the language of rights. In doing so, they failed, as has liberalism generally, to understand the political implications of the ethic of relationships and to understand the extent to which the ethic of relationships formed a basis for political engagement and virtue ethics. The emergence of evangelical Christian counseling in the late 1960s and early 1970s underscored this failure. Evangelical psychologists criticized pastoral counselors and secular psychologists for their emphasis on autonomy and their disregard for biblical revelation, feeling that these practices resulted in a failure to offer any grounds for ethics. From that point, the liberal and conservative moral sensibilities diverged dramatically. By the mid-1990s, neither side could recognize the moral and ethical principles that guided the other.

How This Book Is Organized

To tell this story I have divided the book into three sections. The first section—composed of chapters 1, 2, and 3—covers the period up to World War II, when liberal clergy sought most eagerly to appropriate the principles of science. This section focuses on three distinct but related phenomena: Anton Boisen's scientific study of religion, the clinical pastoral education movement, and early pastoral counseling. There is quite a bit of overlap in that Boisen played a key role in the founding of CPE and many early pastoral counselors enrolled in clinical pastoral training programs, in some cases actually studying with Boisen. Taken together, these subjects illustrate some aspects of the liberal moral sensibility. The second section—chapters 4 and 5—examines the pivotal point during the World War II years when that sensibility changed substantively and pastoral counselors embraced Rogerian therapy as their primary method of counseling. Chapter 5 focuses on the immediate postwar era, when the pastoral counseling movement grew substantially and pastoral counselors explored the importance of individual psychological autonomy.

The third section—chapters 6, 7, and 8—focuses on specific aspects of counseling in the decade of the 1950s and on the way in which pastoral counselors attempted to reconcile the tensions between the individual's freedom and the obligation to community that Rogerian therapy seemed to create. These chapters explore further changes in the liberal moral sensibility and the implications of those changes for ministerial professional identity, for women, and for liberalism generally. The last section— chapters 9, 10, and 11—focuses on the resolution for pastoral counselors of many of their philosophical tensions by their return to theological language to reframe their professional identity and the introduction of a critique launched by neoevangelical and evangelical Christians who were dissatisfied with that resolution.

Exploring the theories and methods of early evangelical counselors helps to highlight the points of tension between a liberal and a conservative moral sensibility and brings us around again to the central point of this book: that how we answer questions about the nature of truth and the meaning of right and wrong has implications for our politics that are wide ranging and fundamental. Recognizing the way in which moral sensibility figures in decision making illuminates and explains the shifting alliances, unlikely bedfellows, and surprising twists and turns of American politics and culture in the late twentieth and early twenty-first centuries. Historian James Kloppenberg has argued that the study of history can contribute to democratic politics by giving us examples of good democratic practices. In this case, history can help us understand why contemporary Americans are having so much trouble talking civilly to one another.[31]

CHAPTER ONE

Anton Boisen and the Scientific Study
of Religion

I replied . . . that sanity in itself is not an end in life. The end of
life is to solve important problems and to contribute in some way
to human welfare, and if there is even a chance that such an end
could best be accomplished by going through Hell for a while, no
man worthy of the name would hesitate for an instant.

—ANTON BOISEN, AUGUST 25, 1921

IN NOVEMBER OF 1935, Anton Boisen suffered his fourth major psychotic episode and ended up hospitalized through mid-December.[1]
Between two earlier episodes, Boisen had joined with an eclectic mix of
medical doctors, psychiatrists, Protestant ministers, and social welfare
workers to establish a new program in ministerial education called clinical pastoral education (CPE). In 1925 Boisen had begun a summer training program for religious workers in which they could learn "scientific"
methods for the study of the relationship between religion and mental
illness. In Boisen's model programs at Worcester State Hospital in Massachusetts and Elgin State Hospital near Chicago, theological students
designed and participated in recreational activities for the patients, published a weekly newsletter, conducted a patient orchestra and choir, and
organized baseball teams and picnics on the lawn. As Boisen intended,
the students used those encounters to observe patient behavior and draw
conclusions about how religious experience figured in mental illness.

The work and life of Anton Boisen illustrate the basic principles of the
liberal moral sensibility in the first quarter of the twentieth century. Boisen self-identified as a liberal and lived out his professional life in the
context of a network of Progressive reformers, social science profession-

als, and liberal Christians. At one point, he declared himself to be a "disciple" of liberal clergyman Harry Emerson Fosdick.[2] He embraced the fundamental importance of science, believed in the possibility of the transformation of human beings through moral striving, and stressed the importance of making some kind of contribution to the social good. Boisen's interest in the scientific study of religion was piqued early in his life and was fostered by his personal experience of mental illness; it remained a commitment throughout his life.

In his research he returned frequently to certain basic themes that had first occurred to him during a psychotic episode. This group of ideas included the belief that there were two kinds of mental illness, one "organic" and the other "functional." By "organic illness" Boisen meant a disease of the body. By "functional illness" he meant a "disease of the soul" or of the mind. Boisen argued that functional mental illness was potentially "constructive" or "problem-solving," analogous to the way fever in the human body works to cure illness. Functional illness was caused by "inner disharmony" brought on by a perception of personal failure. As a result of his research conducted at Worcester and Elgin, Boisen concluded that the content of functional mental illness was consistent across the population. Functional mental illness included delusions of grandeur and a sense of impending doom. According to Boisen, the person who suffered a functional mental illness had much in common with some of the world's greatest religious figures, such as Jesus, George Fox—a key figure in the founding of the Society of Friends—and the Apostle Paul. Most important, both to Boisen's theory and to his mental health, was his conviction that the best "solutions" to emotional disturbances helped others in some way. Boisen's work challenged the idea that mentally ill people were depraved, a view articulated most fully in the early nineteenth century but one that persisted into the early twentieth century. In fact, he seemed to be arguing that the individual who suffered from functional mental illness was actually the most sensitive in moral and ethical matters. Boisen's life and work provide one example of the confluence of science and religion in the early twentieth century, and his ideas provided the starting point for much that came later in clinical pastoral education and pastoral counseling.

The Meaning of Scientific Method

Boisen's choice to pursue the study of religion through science was logical given his intellectual context. He shared the prevailing assumptions about the importance of a scientific method in the study of human behavior. Early in his career he had studied with religious educator George Albert Coe at Union Theological Seminary; Coe had, in turn, been influenced by William James. Both these men placed a premium on the scientific method of study. In many ways there was a straight intellectual line from James to Boisen. William James's *Varieties of Religious Experience* advanced the same interest in the scientific observation of religious experience that governed Boisen's research. Boisen went to Union specifically for the purpose of studying the psychology of religion and was disappointed to find that James's work received little attention in theological education at that point.[3]

Scholars and professionals in many disciplines wanted to show the scientific validity of their field of study and its likeness to the natural sciences. So, while talk about the "scientific method" or the meaning of science may not have characterized the natural or "hard" sciences in this era, it dominated in the social sciences. As historian Dorothy Ross has pointed out in *The Origins of American Social Science* (1991), the scientific method became an end in itself for social scientists in the years between the world wars.[4] Most social scientists did not agree on the meaning of science or the scientific method, but the question generated endless discussion. In an attempt to address the question of scientific method, the Committee on Scientific Method in the Social Sciences, a subcommittee of the Social Science Research Council, compiled an 824-page tome exploring the scientific method from almost every perspective, with chapters on economics, politics, law, sociology, social work, psychology, archaeology, history, and anthropology.[5]

Boisen had a specific definition of science and the scientific method that guided his research. In 1944 he opened his seminar in psychopathology for clinical pastoral trainees at Elgin State Hospital with a discussion session titled "Scientific Method in the Study of Human Nature" in which he outlined those views. Boisen's discussion notes indicate that he drew on John Dewey's *Logic, The Theory of Inquiry* (1938), E. A. Burtt's *Principles and Problems of Right Thinking* (1928), A. D. Ritchie's *Scien-*

tific Method (1923), and Stuart Rice's mammoth compilation *Methods in Social Science* (1931). Based on Dewey, Boisen defined science as the effort to "organize human experience by the classification of facts," recognizing the "sequence and relative significance" of those facts and subjecting scientific "generalizations to rigid tests." Boisen elaborated on that definition using Dewey's steps in reflective thinking. Dewey's fifth step in reflective thinking, paraphrased by Boisen, was "observation and experimentation designed to test [hypotheses] by empirical fact." It was this fifth step that Boisen claimed in the name of Dewey as the "distinguishing characteristic of modern science."

According to Boisen, eight "scientific principles" further governed the use of the scientific method, whether in the natural or the social sciences: empiricism ("scientific reasoning proceeds from the concrete to the abstract"); objectivity (the elimination of bias); continuity ("new phenomena are explained in terms of previous observations"); particularity ("the field of inquiry must be limited and the problem clearly defined"); universality ("the aim of all scientific work is to discover relationships that are universally valid"); provisionality ("all . . . findings are tentative and subject to revision"); economy (the simplest explanation is the best); and disinterestedness ("the desire to find the truth must be supreme"). While adhering to these principles, Boisen contended, the scientist also relied on three "scientific procedures": "controlled experimentation," "naturalistic observation" and "statistical studies."

Boisen argued further that, for social scientists, controlled experimentation was not an option, since the complexity of human beings made the control of variables impossible. He likewise found statistical methods of limited value and instead focused on "naturalistic observation" as the primary tool of the social scientist—governed, of course, by the eight scientific principles. He observed, too, that the social worker and the "minister of religion" were in a particularly good position as "participant observers" to document the role of values in the lives of human beings.

Boisen shared the view of the first generation of social scientists that scientific study ought to change society for the better. Historian Mark Smith argues that the first generation of social scientists saw the scientific method as means to both control and improve society.[6] Smith contends, in addition, that the second generation of social scientists, as part of the process of professionalization and the institutionalization of social science in universities and foundations, stressed objectivity as a means to avoid professional penalties for activist scholarship.[7] Perhaps Boisen was feeling the pressure of that second generation of scholars who stressed "objectivity" and were moving toward the notion of "value-free" science, because he pointed out that the scientific method did not preclude an interest in ethical or moral values. In fact, he wanted to use the scientific method as he defined it to study human values. He argued that this endeavor was as legitimate a subject for scientific study as "chemistry or physics."[8]

In the late 1930s, Boisen wrote an article about Pentecostal practice that illustrates the interplay he perceived among science, religion, and social justice. In the article, which was published in the journal *Psychiatry* and titled "Economic Distress and Religious Experience," Boisen described the rising incidence of "holy roller," by which he meant Pentecostal, sects. He compared the religious experience of this sect to mental illness, arguing that much of what Pentecostals did and believed had much in common with what mentally ill people did and believed. He asserted that the social and "constructive" aspects of religious experience made it different from mental illness, noting that religious experience brought people into fellowship and community, while mental illness isolated its victims. His observations about the negative aspects of Pentecostalism, however, reveal Boisen's liberal moral sensibility. He was willing to concede that parts of Pentecostal experience might be constructive, but he described most Pentecostal beliefs and practices as "dangerous," "eccentric," and "regressive." For one thing, he saw Pentecostals as lacking social vision. He observed, "There is in their message nothing which goes to the heart of the problems of this sick and suffering world. . . . They have no social vision, no promise of social salvation except that which is to come miraculously when the Lord returns in glory." According to Boisen, Pentecostals also suffered from an exceptionally narrow world view. In fact, he described their view of the universe as "diminutive," so "tiny" that it had "no room for all that we have been finding out about stars and atoms and plan[e]ts and men." In other words, it was a world view that left no room for science and it discoveries. For Boisen this was unthinkable. He viewed science as the tool for advancing a social vision, and his social vision derived its meaning and purpose from his religious beliefs.[9]

Early Life and Mental Illness

The circumstances of Boisen's early life and his subsequent mental illness spurred his interest in the scientific study of religion and contributed to his theories about the connections among science, religion, and a social vision. To some extent, all scholars and scientists find that their research agendas are driven by their personal experiences, but this was especially true for Boisen. He did not want to believe that his mental illness was organic or physiological and thus, by the medical standards of the time, incurable. Nor did he wish to believe that he was somehow morally degenerate or corrupt—the other possible explanation for his illness. He spent a lifetime arguing the opposite, using the language and methods of science to do so. This intimate connection between Boisen's personal struggles and his intellectual life makes his biography central to understanding his contribution to the study of science and religion.

Boisen told the story of his mental illness in two places. The first was the introduction to a book published in 1936. In the book, *Exploration of the Inner World*, Boisen laid out many of his basic principles. He admitted in the preface to a subsequent reprint that the first edition of the book had been finished even as the last of his psychotic episodes was rapidly approaching. In any case, in the first chapter of the 1936 edition, he described his illness as an introduction to the theoretical work that followed. In 1960, shortly before his death, Boisen published a more detailed account of his illness, describing his life both before and after the illness. This second work, *Out of the Depths*, was strictly biographical, but the familiar themes first laid out in *Exploration of the Inner World* were very much visible.[10]

Boisen's interest in the systematic study of both religion and mental illness was entirely consistent with his early experience. His story began in Indiana, where he grew up in a deeply religious and well-educated family. Boisen's father, Hermann Boisen, taught modern languages at Indiana University in Bloomington; his grandfather, Theophilus Wylie, taught natural philosophy; and his uncle, Brown Wylie, taught chemistry. Even

Boisen's mother was well educated, having graduated from a female seminary and been one of the first female undergraduates to enroll at Indiana University, where she studied for a year before leaving to marry Boisen's father.[11] His mother's family, in particular, maintained an intense loyalty and commitment to the Presbyterian Church and its ways. After the death of Boisen's father from a heart attack, in 1881, Boisen, his mother, and his sister went to live with his grandfather, who, in addition to his responsibilities at the university, served as pastor of the New Side Reformed Presbyterian Church. Boisen remembered his grandfather as a "faithful Scotch-Irish Covenanter" who was strict but not unreasonable. At the same time, Boisen also recalled compulsory church attendance, daily family prayers, and strict rules for Sabbath keeping.[12] In other words, he grew up in an environment where there was no ostensible conflict between religion and scholarship.

Boisen never rebelled against the ties of church and family. Upon graduation from high school, he enrolled at Indiana University. After his graduation from college, unable to settle upon a career, he spent some time taking graduate classes at the university and serving as a French tutor there and a part-time high school teacher. During these years he first encountered a problem that would cause him recurring difficulties: he struggled with what he saw as overwhelming—and unacceptable—sexual desires and urges. The struggle was resolved, at least temporarily, with what he described as a "spontaneous religious conversion" on Easter of 1898.[13] In the wake of this experience, he decided to follow his father's interest in nature and the outdoors and pursue a career in the U.S. Forest Service.[14]

Although Boisen explicitly declared his liberal affiliation in his scholarly work, there is a sense in which he was part of the Progressive community without being fully aware of the extent of his involvement. For one thing, the Forest Service was in many ways the quintessential expression of liberal reform. He was also connected to the Young Men's Christian Association, worked for the Presbyterian Mission Board, and attended Union Theological Seminary, all flagship organizations of liberal Protestant culture. Shortly after making his decision to enter the Forest Service, Boisen met a woman who substantially changed the course of his life. Alice Batchelder, employed by the Young Women's Christian Association, ended up having a profound effect on Boisen's career and his spiritual wellbeing. After meeting Alice, Boisen felt "called" to the ministry, in part, he admitted, because he hoped it would allow him to join her in religious work. Throughout this period, Boisen continued in his forestry career; but he was hovering near psychosis, apparently because of Alice's refusal to accept him and his profession of love.[15] It was with Alice's encouragement that Boisen had enrolled in Union Theological Seminary and, upon graduation in 1911, pursued a pulpit. Initially unsuccessful in securing a church, he took up survey work in Missouri and later in other areas of the mid-South for the Presbyterian Board of Missions. He described his work as "a fine introduction to sociology and economics," more evidence of the way in which a particular scholarly and scientific mind-set permeated religious organizations involved in reform at the time.[16]

Having secured a pastorate, he discovered that he was, at best, a mediocre parish minister.[17] After serving with the Overseas YMCA during World War I, he came back to the United States with an invitation to do more survey work, this time for the Interchurch World Movement. Both the YMCA and the Interchurch World Movement (IWM) are good examples of the Progressive network to which Boisen belonged. Both had their roots in religious liberal reform. Though historians have tended to treat it as a secular phenomenon, the YMCA served as a missionary outlet for liberal Christians and supporters of the Social Gospel in the early twentieth century. The Interchurch World Movement emerged after World War I as a short-lived liberal Protestant ecumenical movement. Participants in the IWM relied on the methods of sociology and social work to document American religion through survey work. As one of their projects, the movement's members worked for social justice for industrial workers. Outspoken support of the 1919 steel strike resulted in the demise of the IWM.

Anticipating the collapse of the movement, Boisen left North Dakota, where he had been doing survey work, and renewed his search for a parish, meanwhile working temporarily in the IWM office in New York City.[18] Throughout these years, his relationship with Alice had been tumultuous and his mental health precarious. Every time she agreed to see him or correspond with him regularly, he imagined that she might be inclined to return his affections. He wanted a parish because Alice wanted that for him, but also, he hoped to be able to propose to her and believed he needed a parish with a reasonable income in order to do so.[19]

Late in 1920, after almost eighteen years of unrequited loved, Boisen seems to have acknowledged finally that Alice did not want him. The result was the first of three psychotic breaks that resulted in hospitalization. Two of the three episodes seem to have been directly precipitated by events in his relationship to Alice. What Alice thought of all this is unclear. The only known accounts of the relationship are from Boisen's perspective, so it is difficult to determine the exact nature of their relationship. Perhaps Alice had turned him away years before and he simply could not accept it. In any case, this first episode marked the beginning of his intellectual productivity. It was from this point that Boisen began to think about the ideas that would become the central themes in his work.

While a patient at Westboro Psychopathic Hospital, in Westboro, Massachusetts, Boisen discovered the inadequacy of most therapeutic techniques of the time. In his memoir, he recalled spending a fair amount of time on the "disturbed ward," where he was subjected to beatings by staff who were angry with him because he insisted on going to the "tub-room" and demanded to be put in the tubs in place of one of his fellow "inmates." Medical professionals of the era considered the baths therapeutic, but Boisen recalled seeing them as punishment and so offered himself as a sacrifice for his friends. In any case, the attendants gave Boisen a very thorough beating, what they called "the old bughouse knockout."[20]

Boisen recounted that his most important moment on the "disturbed ward" was when he realized that his perception was skewed. Images of the moon were central to his delusion, and one night he thought he saw a cross in the moon (the cross representing suffering) and concluded that this was some "dire portent." But several nights later he discovered that when he changed his position, the cross disappeared because he was no longer viewing the moon through the wire screening that covered the window. He recovered rapidly after this discovery and was moved within a week to the convalescent ward. Boisen concluded that the beatings he had received actually made him more violent and that when he finally started to get well it was not because of any "treatment" he had received or as a result of the physical abuse but because he had allowed "*the faith-*

ful carrying through of the delusion itself" (Boisen's emphasis). He believed that the delusion should be allowed to play itself out until the patient was able to see an alternative explanation for the events in his or her
life, and that treatment of the body (like the hydrotherapeutic baths)
would have little effect, since the patient's mind was sick, not his or her
body.[21]

Newly released from the disturbed ward, Boisen began to think more
carefully about the nature of his illness. Almost immediately, he became
convinced that it was necessary to distinguish between "cerebral" disease
and mental disorder (he later referred to this as a distinction between
organic and functional illness).[22] In the former, the illness resulted from
the disease of a bodily organ—the brain—and, in the latter, the mental
processes were somehow disturbed. The distinction Boisen insisted upon
making between organic and functional mental illness cost him dearly in
social and professional support, but he was adamant on the subject.
Among American psychiatrists at the time of Boisen's hospitalization,
the organic view (that mental illness had a physiological basis) prevailed.
This distinction would turn out to be critical not only for Boisen but also
for colleagues who later became interested in counseling and psychotherapy. For most medical doctors of the time, Freud notwithstanding,
functional illness referred to mental illness for which no organic or physiological cause could be determined. These doctors argued that one could
not conclude that such mental illness was psychogenic, only that the
cause would be found eventually and that it would be discovered to be
physiological in origin. The view that treating the body was tantamount
to treating the mind persisted, especially among psychiatrists who
worked with institutionalized populations.[23] As a result, American psychiatrists continued to privilege somatic cures, such as electroshock therapy, hydrotherapy, and drug therapy.

But Boisen recalled noticing that his fellow patients were apparently
in good physical health. As he observed them he was struck by an intuition: "It came over me in a flash that if inner conflicts like that which
Paul describes in the famous passage in the seventh chapter of Romans
can have happy solutions, as the church has always believed, there must
also be unhappy solutions which thus far the church has ignored. It came
to me that what I was being faced with in the hospital was the unhappy
solutions."[24] He concluded that if what he was seeing was not rooted in

organic causes, there was a good chance that at least some of his peers had been hospitalized with religious or spiritual problems they had failed to resolve.

Boisen decided that his own illness, diagnosed as "catatonic dementia praecox" (also, then as now, referred to as schizophrenia), belonged in the category of functional illness.[25] In several pivotal works published in the 1930s, Boisen developed his ideas more thoroughly, identifying two different groups within the category of dementia praecox. He argued that some people fell ill as a result of "malignant character tendencies such as easy pleasure-taking and aimless drifting and concealment in its various forms."[26] Here Boisen was describing a familiar nineteenth-century image—individuals suffering from serious character flaws. They lied and cheated and indulged in all of the petty vices that nineteenth-century reformers found objectionable. In this view, mental illness resulted from the progressive degeneration of the character. In this line of reasoning, Boisen resembled those contemporaries of his who would have identified their work as "the cure of souls" and who drew a fairly straight line from immoral behavior to mental illness, or, put another way, from sin to sickness. But Boisen identified another kind of dementia praecox that he found more interesting from the religious perspective. He argued that this second group did not exhibit "malignant features" and that, in these cases, the "emotional disturbances" these individuals experienced should be seen as akin to "fever or inflammation in the physical organism." In the same way that fever was the body's attempt to fight off illness, emotional disturbances were the mind's attempt to heal itself.[27] Elsewhere, Boisen described this type of schizophrenia as the individual's "attempt at reconstruction [of the personality]" in response to the emotional distress brought on by "an intolerable sense of inner disharmony and of personal failure."[28]

The idea that mental illness resulted not from moral failure but from the individual's perception of failure was crucial to Boisen's intellectual construct. For anyone with even a passing knowledge of Freud, the idea that unnecessary guilt spawns mental illness will sound familiar. But Boisen resisted association with Freud and, instead, insisted that he owed his intellectual debt to American psychologists. Drawing on the work of George Herbert Mead, Boisen argued that language was crucial to understanding both schizophrenia and the construction of a conscience, because language was central to the construction of personality. Boisen did not use the word "identity," but to a large extent that was what he was describing. He observed, "Language is the distinctive basis of not only human social organization, but also of the structure of personality."[29] Further, Boisen argued that personality was shaped by interaction with "the generalized other,"a term he took from Mead, and "the particular rôle [the individual] assumes as his own."[30] He posited that individuals grow by assimilating new material: "These materials, in the case of personality, are the stuff of experience, and it is assimilated by discovering relationships between it and organized experience. This involves the use of language."[31]

So, what did all of this have to do with the construction of conscience and the perception of moral failure? In the process of conversation both with others and with the self, claimed Boisen, the individual "is able to build up within himself an inner organization, a conscience, by which his conduct may be determined not by outward compulsion, but by inner self-direction."[32] Boisen, drawing heavily on Mead, argued that individuals saw themselves through the eyes of other members in the group and judged themselves accordingly: "Conduct is thus determined by self-criticism which is at the same time social criticism[,] and the system of values is dependent upon and a function of social relationships."[33] All of this, in Boisen's view, was possible only because of language.

At the same time, Boisen conceded the importance of "feeling and intuition," which preceded language. He concluded that the schizophrenic's problems arose because he or she had accepted the authority of the generalized other and then had failed to live up to those standards, usually because of a failure to control certain "instinctual tendencies."[34] Again, this resembles Freudian theory, with feeling and intuition being roughly equivalent to the realm of the unconscious and "instinctual tendencies" similar to Freud's instincts or drives. But Boisen resisted recognizing Freud's contribution, asserting that Mead's "generalized other" was the same thing as Freud's superego and predated it.[35] Boisen also rejected the idea that instinctual tendencies were "unconscious" and insisted that they were only unarticulated ("not put into words"). According to Boisen, unresolved guilt feelings in the schizophrenic led to anxiety and eventually fragmentation of the personality. He was arguing that the method some people used to deal with guilt made them sick, not sinful. It was in the midst of the moral struggle to be a better person that the individual was overcome by illness.

At the time of his first hospitalization, Boisen had not yet worked out all the details of his theory; but a kernel of the idea was there, and his newly discovered convictions about the nature of mental illness and its "functional" character initially caused a problem. At Christmas of 1920, he was planning a visit to his mother; but hospital staff denied the visit because Boisen happened to mention his ideas to one of his doctors, who took immediate exception to Boisen's views on the etiology of mental illness. In a letter to Boisen's friend Fred Eastman, the Westboro superintendent noted that "[Boisen] still believes that the experience through which he has been passing is part of a plan which has been laid out for him and that he has not suffered any mental illness. This mistaken idea is sufficient to tell us that he is still in need of hospital treatment."[36]

His convalescence continued in January and February of 1921, and Boisen became ever more convinced that, as he wrote in the letter to his mother, "in many of its forms, insanity . . . is a religious rather than a medical problem."[37] He also became convinced that he was going to spend his life exploring the exact nature of the relationship between religious experience and mental illness. He was still, however, not well. After arranging, with the help of his good friend Fred Eastman, to transfer from Westboro to Bloomingdale, in White Plains, New York, but before the transfer had taken place, Boisen suffered another psychotic break. In retrospect, he believed it was brought on by a fear that at Bloomingdale he would be subjected to psychoanalytic treatment—something he feared greatly. In any case, he remained at Westboro and spent ten more weeks on the "disturbed ward."[38]

About ten days after his transfer to the convalescent ward, Boisen began to realize that he was just as unhappy with the treatment plan on the convalescent ward as he had been on the more intensive ward. He then took it upon himself, as a patient, to transform life at Westboro. In July of 1921 he wrote a memo to hospital staff describing in some detail the deficiencies of the Westboro program for those who were at the convalescent stage of their illness. He observed that the patients had little to do besides ruminate and think "gloomy thoughts." He inventoried the amusements available to patients—a Victrola, a set of checkers, and a few books and magazines—all of which were locked away from the patients. He recommended and implemented Fourth of July and Labor Day programs and took up the job of hospital photographer. He even began a survey of the facility similar to the surveys he had conducted earlier in his life in rural churches.[39] As a result of his experience, he began to think about further seminary education that would allow him to explore more carefully the connections he saw between religion and mental illness.

Clinical Pastoral Education

Even before his release from Westboro, Boisen began to contact people he thought would be receptive to his venture. First, he renewed his relationship with George Albert Coe at Union Theological Seminary. Coe was receptive, but he did not necessarily agree with Boisen's view of mental illness. In a letter of September 1921, Coe indicated that he thought that the origins of mental illness could be found in "the physiological." He wished Boisen the best and encouraged him to continue his newfound work as a photographer.[40] Boisen also contacted Elwood Worcester at Emmanuel Church in Boston, from whom he received a much more sympathetic response—a response he had good reason to expect.

Worcester had gained national prominence for establishing a clinic with his fellow minister Samuel McComb at their church, in November of 1906. Initially, the clinic enjoyed the support of important members of the medical and academic community, including Harvard's James Jackson Putnam. As historian Eric Caplan describes the program, it "consisted of three mutually reinforcing elements: a medical clinic where physicians provided free weekly examinations; a weekly health class . . . [with lectures] on a variety of issues relating to physical, mental, and spiritual health; and private sessions during which the minister employed psychotherapy."[41] The psychotherapy practiced by Worcester and McComb was a form of suggestion used to relieve a wide variety of symptoms and complaints ranging from neurasthenia and neurosis to alcoholism and hysteria.[42] But Worcester was only permitted to meet with those patients who had first been declared by medical doctors to be free of any disease that might have an organic or physiological origin.

The activities at Emmanuel Church gained national attention. Elwood

Worcester published a number of popular works that fostered interest in the movement. In addition to articles in *The Ladies Home Journal,* Worcester coauthored, with McComb and medical doctor Isador H. Coriat, a book that described the principles and practices of the Emmanuel Movement. The book, *Religion and Medicine: The Moral Control of Nervous Disorders* (1908), included chapters on the origins of nervousness, the principles of suggestion, and the application of those principles in psychotherapy. In regard to the practice of suggestion, the book's authors observed, "The most important fact which has yet been discovered in regard to the subconscious mind is that it is suggestible, i.e., it is subject to moral influence and direction."[43] The application of suggestion involved substituting positive thoughts for negative thoughts. In their chapter on fear and worry, they advised:

> Morbid thoughts can be driven out only by other and healthy ones. Substitute for the fear the thought of some duty not yet achieved, or the thought of the Divine presence which is near us alike in our going out and in our coming in. Cultivate that condition of mind which, conscious of God's fatherly regard, feels safe in His hands, and is willing to meet good or evil as He wills it. In a word, re-educate yourself, morally and spiritually. Summon the forces of your nature against this debasing fear, and through prayer, through obedience to law moral and law physiological, through concentration on some enterprise that carries you beyond your petty interests, win back the gift of self-control which is the secret of every life worth living.[44]

As the clinic and the movement flourished and seemed poised on the verge of extraordinary growth, some medical doctors reasserted the physiological ground of all illness and, therefore, their exclusive right to practice psychotherapy. Boisen was not at all interested in psychotherapy, but he *was* interested in demonstrating his idea that at least some mental illness was functional rather than organic. He rightly assumed that Worcester would offer a sympathetic ear. And, indeed, Worcester became somewhat of an advocate for Boisen in his release from Westboro. Boisen met with Worcester for a series of interviews conducted over a period of six months, and the two commenced a correspondence that lasted until Worcester died in 1940.[45]

Boisen's greatest patron was another of the original Emmanuel Movement supporters, Richard C. Cabot. The two men met after Boisen was released from the hospital in January of 1922 and enrolled at Andover Theological School and Harvard Graduate School to study the psychology of religion. He began his studies by taking Cabot's social ethics course.[46] Cabot shared and encouraged Boisen's interest in the relationship between medicine and religion even though he disagreed with Boisen's understanding of the etiology of mental illness. The subject later became a serious point of contention between the two. At least initially, Cabot seemed willing to overlook the differences. An influential medical doctor from an old, respected, and progressive Boston family, Cabot had already made his mark both in his own discipline and in the field of social work, cooperating with Ida Cannon to establish one of the first medical social work programs in the United States, at Massachusetts General Hospital. He had been one of the early supporters of Worcester's Emmanuel Movement but had later withdrawn that support. Boisen probably should have seen that reversal as a warning, but he welcomed Cabot as an advocate.

With Cabot's assistance, Boisen secured a position as chaplain at Worcester State Hospital, near Boston, so that he could continue his research on the connection between religion and psychology.[47] The chief of medicine at Worcester was William Bryan, a medical doctor who had a reputation for open-mindedness and for innovative techniques if he thought they might benefit his patients. Once Boisen was established at Worcester, Cabot sent a few of his students to Boisen to inquire about summer jobs at Worcester. This, in turn, inspired Boisen to design summer training sessions for theological students. The same year Boisen taught his first summer school, 1925, Cabot published "A Plea for a Clinical Year in the Course of Theological Study."[48] The clinical training programs Boisen established, first at Worcester State Hospital and later at Elgin State in Illinois, reflected his interest in the scientific study of religion. In fact, he and friend Arthur Holt, who took a position at Chicago Theological Seminary at about the same time that Boisen went to Worcester, both believed that seminaries "had been failing to make use of scientific method in the study of present-day religious experience."[49] And both, according to Boisen, took up their respective positions hoping to change theological education. Boisen welcomed religious workers generally, not just theological students, because he saw them all as potential scientists of religion, and he planned to use the training programs to further his own research agenda and to train the next generation of social scientists.

The idea of offering a clinical training for theology students gained momentum. To administer the growing program, Boisen, along with a small group of medical doctors and theologians with similar interests, cofounded the Council for the Clinical Training of Theological Students (CCTTS) early in 1930. Boisen's cofounders included Richard Cabot, who served as first president of the council, and Philip Guiles, an Andover-Newton seminary professor and Boisen student, who served as its first executive secretary. The new council members appointed Helen Flanders Dunbar as director. Dunbar was one of the first graduates of the summer program at Worcester. When she first met Boisen, she was midway through her divinity studies at Union Theological Seminary and pursuing simultaneously a degree from Columbia University in medieval literature and another from Yale Medical School.[50] Intensely loyal to Boisen, she shared his views on the etiology of mental illness and played a key role in the council's development.

Whatever similarities the first council members shared, there were subtle but important differences in their educational goals. Boisen made his goals clear in a lecture he gave in the morning session of the first annual meeting of the council. In his lecture, entitled "Our Objectives," Boisen articulated his view of clinical education. He outlined a program intended to teach religious workers about mental illness and give them the skills they needed to work as peers and colleagues of medical workers. He called worries that his program would produce "pseudo-psychiatrists" ill founded, pointing out that his students' focus on the connection between religion and mental illness would give them a distinctive role. Moreover, he assured his listeners that he saw both his own task and that of his students as primarily theological. He expected that clinically trained ministers and other religious workers would, as a result of their work with mentally ill patients, draw conclusions about what he called "spiritual laws" and reflect upon the theological implications of those laws. Also, he imagined the growth of a "scientific" theology. Using the language of the scientific method, he talked admiringly about the possibility of long-term studies that might result in "a body of tested facts" regarding the relationship between religion and health. With equal enthusiasm, he described the importance of "accurate observation" and careful recordkeeping as means to a "more conscious and intelligent [religion] capable of verification and transmission." The idea that the scientific method could be applied profitably to the study of religious experience guided all that Boisen did.[51]

Boisen understood that his students needed to begin by acquiring basic information about "disorders of the personality" in order to make the intellectual connections he envisioned. Thus, his program in the summer of 1930 at Worcester devoted about half of all the sessions to describing various types of psychosocial disorder; included, for instance, were sessions on "The Anxiety Reaction," "Despair," and "Problem Children." A handful of sessions, such as one titled "The Problem of Sin and Salvation," sought to address explicitly the connections between religion and mental health.[52]

In addition, Boisen intended that clinical pastoral education should prepare ministers to meet a need that he believed the liberal churches had failed to address. Early in his career Boisen published an article on this topic, and he raised it again in his autobiography. The liberal churches, he argued, had failed to offer an "authoritative message of salvation." Instead, they had focused on "bringing in the kingdom of God" and had turned the "sick of soul" over to the medical doctors. As Boisen saw it, they were attempting to explain their "ancient faith" in "modern" terms but were "failing to go forward in the task of exploring the field which was distinctively their own." As a result, he concluded, the fundamentalist churches stepped into the void, offering revivals and "saving souls." Boisen intended clinical pastoral education to give parish ministers the skills that would allow them to diagnose and treat human suffering— that was his message of salvation, one that he believed was better than the relief offered by a revival experience.[53]

To teach his students the skills he thought they would need, Boisen required trainees to serve either as ward attendants or research assistants. In addition, the students maintained a musical program (an orchestra and singing sessions twice a week in the chapel as well as taking the singing program to the wards twice a week) and an athletic program (softball and hiking) and published both a weekly news sheet and an annual hospital pictorial album. At least one student, Carroll Wise, worked on the "research wards" working for the Research Service of the hospital and helping with "observations." All students wrote observations on a group of patients, wrote up a report on a case assigned to them, and presented the report in seminar. Boisen wanted his students to learn as much as possible from studying "the living human document."[54]

Boisen's second psychotic break ended his relationship with Cabot and precipitated his move from Worcester to Elgin State Hospital in Elgin, Illinois. The episode occurred in November of 1930, even as Boisen's work with clinical pastoral education was thriving.[55] Boisen believed that it was at this point that his views about mental illness became "abhorrent" to Cabot, who insisted, with Guiles's concurrence, that Boisen not be involved in training at Worcester that summer.[56] It appears that Boisen acquiesced to the prohibition but stayed on for another year at Worcester to work on a research project with the assistance of Geneva Dye before moving to Elgin in April of 1932. Carroll Wise, an exceptionally adept theological student whom Boisen mentioned in his first annual report, went on to assume the supervisory position at Worcester when Boisen made the move to Elgin. Wise ended up playing an important role in CPE and pastoral counseling.

Boisen interpreted the move to Elgin as serendipitous. He had ties to Chicago Theological Seminary and, at least in retrospect, saw Chicago as the center of American theological education. To be located at Elgin, where he could establish a new program along the lines of the original Worcester program and could teach at Chicago Theological Seminary where he had been a research associate since 1925, seemed propitious.[57] More to the point, Alice Batchelder lived in Chicago, and she agreed to meet him occasionally downtown for dinner or the opera. So, what had appeared at first to be a difficult situation turned in Boisen's favor, at least from his point of view.

At Elgin, Boisen implemented all of his most cherished goals. Upon his arrival, he found himself at cross purposes with the recreational director, who provided patients with "amusements" but not enough involvement in activities to suit Boisen. He apparently won that argument, because subsequent years at Elgin saw a whole slate of new recreational activities, including softball, volleyball, bowling, play festivals, and separate sports programs for women, including rhythmic dancing. Among the educational activities offered by Boisen and his theological students to encourage patient participation were weekly talent shows, special classes for convalescent catatonics, a "news sheet" distributed to the patients twice per week, a choir, and an orchestra. In addition, Boisen and his students offered a mental health conference for patients who wanted to learn more about mental illness through the use of case histories and a small newspaper called "The Hospital Interpreter" issued to families of patients.

Boisen was most proud of the changes he made in the religious services at Elgin. Before his arrival, services were conducted on Sunday afternoons at 1:30 under the direction of visiting ministers from the community along with a pianist and a guest vocalist and with about 70 in attendance. He moved the services to Sunday morning, doubled the amount of music, introduced a new hymnal, and added an orchestral prelude and postlude. Attendance jumped to 170. Boisen argued that changes in the hymnal were especially critical, since some traditional hymns were not suitable for individuals suffering from mental illness. As he pointed out in his autobiography, "Of the fifteen psalms [in the hymnal then being used], six were of the imprecatory type, with all too many references to 'enemies,' and of the hymns some were actually disturbing. The classic example was the well-known hymn, 'O Christian, dost thou see them?' a hymn which evokes all the hallucinations, and calls for action besides."[58]

Boisen had good reason to be sensitive to these issues. He had still not escaped his own recurring illness. His final psychotic episode occurred in November of 1935 when he learned that Alice was terminally ill from cancer. He remained hospitalized until some weeks after her death in December.[59] After Alice's death, Boisen never suffered another psychotic episode, although he lived for another thirty years. He spent the rest of his life exploring the significance of his mental illness by studying the mental illness of others and demonstrating that the mentally ill person was not necessarily physiologically ill, incurable, nor morally corrupt.

The Morally Sensitive Individual and the Liberal Ideal

In order to make his case that the functionally ill were the most morally sensitive individuals, Boisen focused his research on functional illness and on demonstrating its similarities to the difficulties suffered by some of Christianity's most important figures. While Boisen's theories differed substantially from those of many psychologists, medical doctors, and theologians of the day, his moral sensibility was liberal to the extent that he emphasized the importance of the will and moral striving and celebrated the possibility of individual transformation and of contribution to the social good. Like Mead, Dewey, and James, he placed the individual in a social matrix and recognized the importance of adjusting to that matrix in the interest of the good of the community.

From Boisen's perspective, the delusions shared by the functionally mentally ill were an important element in understanding mental illness and the moral character of those who fell ill. In a 1932 article, Boisen recounted the case of a fifty-two-year-old man named "Oscar N" and others who suffered from schizophrenia, or dementia praecox. He argued that not only did these patients who had the same illness all have delusions but, most important, that the content of those delusions was consistent across the population. Oscar interpreted his experiences as "manifestations of the superpersonal": he believed God was talking to him. He also saw himself as dead or about to die, leading to a concurrent belief that it was necessary for him to sacrifice himself for his family through suicide. He believed that a great world change was about to occur, that he would play an important part in that world change, and that he had been reincarnated over a period of 2000 years. These same ideas, Boisen claimed, were expressed by other patients with dementia praecox and had, in fact, figured in his own mental illness. Delusions that involved saving the world were characteristic not of individuals who were suffering a moral degeneracy but who, in fact, were morally sensitive. According to Boisen, their willingness to sacrifice and suffer for others set them apart from other mentally ill individuals.[60]

In his 1936 *Exploration of the Inner World*, Boisen developed many of the ideas he had addressed in discussing the case of Oscar N. He again based his conclusions on observations of patients who had been diagnosed with dementia praecox. Boisen's exploration of the spiritual lives of the mentally ill was part of a larger study begun at Worcester in 1927 and directed by Roy G. Hoskins, on the faculty of Harvard Medical School and editor of the *Journal of Endocrinology*. Hoskins focused on the "physiological" aspect of the investigation but allowed Boisen to explore the "behavior and ideation" of the 173 subjects in the study, of which Oscar N was one.[61] The course of treatment prescribed by Hoskins and his colleagues included "glandular medication" and a combination of psychiatric care and recreational and occupational therapy. As part of the study, patients were periodically graded, and their grades were posted as a means to provide incentives for getting well.[62]

For his part of the study, Boisen developed a list of questions that he used to interview the first 80 subjects in the study. He also used a ward observation form that he had developed for his CPE students to use while they were working as attendants on the wards, and he relied on his students, using these same forms, to collect information for the research project.[63] Boisen admitted freely that part of his goal was to show that his own experience of mental illness was not "an isolated one." He hypothesized that dementia praecox could "be explained in terms of the disorganization of the inner world consequent upon the upsetting of the foundations upon which the critical judgments are made and that, as such, it [a particular kind of dementia praecox] is closely related to certain types of religious experience."[64] To explain the conclusions he had drawn from the study, Boisen used one extensive case study, that of Albert W, as a starting point for examining the remaining cases. He described the nature of the illness and identified "causative factors" such as heredity, intelligence, early influences, health, and "life situation," which included "social relations," like how well the patient interacted with family and friends; "sex adjustments," such as whether the patient engaged in homosexual behavior or masturbation; and "vocational adjustments," like whether the patient had been frustrated or successful in achieving his career goals.[65] He also documented the patients' behavior, or "reactive patterns," and the "content" of their thought, or "ideation." Boisen concluded that how patients reacted to their illness was a good predictor of recovery. Those who experienced an acute onset of the illness accompanied by a reaction of panic, but who also had an attitude of "frankness and self-blame," as well as evidence of a marked "religious concern," had the best chance of recovery. In contrast, among those patients with "certain malignant character tendencies," given to "drift-ing" and "concealment," evidencing "surly and bitter attitudes," and showing "little religious concern," recovery was rare. For the former group, "psychoses are essentially problem-solving experiences" similar to "certain types of religious experience." The psychosis, Boisen argued, allowed the patient's personality to disintegrate and then, given the right attitudes, to reintegrate or reorganize.[66]

To underline the moral character of the individual who was function-ally ill, Boisen pointed out that many of the same delusions were shared by some of the most important religious figures of the previous several centuries. In *Exploration of the Inner World,* in a chapter entitled "Some Successful Explorers," Boisen examined the religious experience of some famous Christians, including George Fox, founder of the Society of Friends, Fox's contemporary John Bunyan, author of a widely read clas-sic in Christian devotional literature, *Pilgrim's Progress,* and the Apostle Paul. From Boisen's perspective, each of these important figures in the history of Christianity had episodes in his life in which, if he had been under the care of a doctor, he might have been diagnosed as mentally ill. Boisen described his patient Albert W and the Quaker founder Fox as "fellow travelers in that little-known country."[67] Drawing on Fox's ac-count of his life written while he was imprisoned for his beliefs, Boisen made a case for the similarities between Albert W's delusions and those of Fox. Like Albert W, Fox experienced a sense of impending doom, saw himself as a key figure in resisting the powers of evil, and believed him-self to be a "recipient of direct revelation from God." As with Albert W and Boisen, the precipitating event for his "disturbance" was relatively minor, but Boisen saw Fox's response as an indication of his moral sen-sitivity. Fox's response to the episode was constructive; he made an ear-nest effort "which enabled him to bring order and even something of beauty out of the chaos": Fox helped to establish a vibrant religious movement that had thrived into the twentieth century.[68]

Boisen went on to analyze the stories of John Bunyan, Emmanuel Swedenborg, the Old Testament prophets Ezekiel and Jeremiah, and the Apostle Paul, in each case trying to show how mental disturbances could result in much good, both for the individual and for society generally. In telling these stories, he was attempting to prove not only that mental ill-ness could be transformed into something socially useful, but that some of the people who suffered from mental illness were the most morally sensitive. He noted, "Common to all our men of religious genius has been the presence of a will to righteousness and moral achievement."[69] Boisen's attempt to apply the scientific method in studying the intersection of religion and mental illness was also an attempt to affirm the value of moral striving and to make his own contribution to a better society. In doing this, he epitomized the liberal moral sensibility.

While it would be unfair to describe Boisen's ideas as static, it is true that his intellectual work was founded on a number of key principles that changed very little in the course of his career. His idea that human beings were essentially moral beings who could strive for something better even when they were ill and who, when they did fall ill, did so because of their better moral nature, was truly original and entirely consistent with a Progressive perspective. Boisen's ideas about how to help the mentally ill were also consistent with these basic principles. He worked to create an environment where the reintegration of the personality could occur and sought to provide mentally ill people with the information they needed to get better, through his scientific study of religion. His intention in providing clinical training to ministers and other religious workers was that they too would help to create the necessary environment for healing to occur and that they would do so by joining him in "the study of living human documents" to "discover the laws of the spiritual life applicable to all of us."[70] Boisen did not talk about social change the way a Progressive reformer might have, but he did think of individuals as located within a social matrix and with social obligations to make that society better. Such a theory had, potentially, wide-ranging implications for society. Boisen did not envision, at any point, that psychotherapy would be a part of the work of either clergy or other religious workers. So when, as is discussed in the next chapter, his colleagues who had helped him found the Council for the Clinical Training of Theological Students began to develop training programs that differed substantially from his original vision—including training students in the basics of pastoral counseling—he was deeply distressed.

CHAPTER TWO

The Methodology of Clinical
Pastoral Education

If the [minister] is to be restored to his place in the populace which
has imbibed deeply of the scientific method, he must drink at the
same well.

—HELEN FLANDERS DUNBAR, EXECUTIVE DIRECTOR,

COUNCIL FOR THE CLINICAL TRAINING

OF THEOLOGICAL STUDENTS, 1930

THE NUMBERS OF clinical training programs for seminary students
grew steadily in the years after Anton Boisen and his colleagues
formed the Council for the Clinical Training of Theological Students in
1930. Some of the programs followed Boisen's model for training and his
emphasis on the "mental" hospital, but the council also began to establish training programs in other settings, including general hospitals, prisons, and social agencies such as the Judge Baker Guidance Center, a child
guidance clinic.[1] For each program, the council established a collaborative relationship with a hospital or social agency and assigned a council-
trained theological supervisor to the program. Many times, although not
always, the theological supervisor was also the hospital chaplain or was
employed by the agency in some similar capacity. In the early years, the
council offered training during summer term only. During the academic
year, Helen Flanders Dunbar, the first director of the council, advertised
clinical pastoral education in seminaries, collected applications for the
summer training programs, and assigned students to them.[2] In the early
years, almost all students lived on or near the program site, worked half-
days in the wards or offices of the hospital, clinic, or agency to which
they were assigned, and received some kind of financial support funded

by donations from patrons and provided by the council in the form of room and board. The early programs were small, admitting between four and seven students annually. Of those students, the majority were white, male, and mainline Protestant, although not exclusively so. A substantial portion of both supervisors and trainees believed that the clinical training experience would make the students better and more effective ministers or religious workers.

The summer program at Massachusetts General Hospital (MGH), administered by hospital chaplain and theological supervisor, Russell Dicks, provides a good example of how most of the earliest programs worked. Dicks had trained at Worcester with Boisen and had been invited to MGH by Richard Cabot, who in the early years paid Dicks's salary. The program in medical social work that Cabot had established earlier, in cooperation with Ida Cannon, made MGH ideal for the sort of collaborative effort early clinical educators envisioned. Seven students enrolled for training at MGH in the summer of 1934. They represented four mainline denominations—Episcopal, Presbyterian, Methodist, and (American) Baptist—and four theological schools—General Theological Seminary and Union Theological Seminary, both in New York; Episcopal Theological Seminary in Cambridge, Massachusetts; and Crozer Theological Seminary in Pennsylvania. Funding for the program came from local patrons, including, again, Richard Cabot. During the first four weeks of the twelve-week program, the students worked half-days as orderlies on the hospital wards and spent the remainder of the day observing in the outpatient department, attending seminars, visiting patients, and reading. Students devoted the last eight weeks exclusively to more patient visitation, reading, and seminars. At the close of his annual report, Dicks, reflecting on the purpose and value of clinical training, noted that "nothing happens in the General Hospital that does not happen outside." Dicks saw the hospital as a microcosm in which the students could observe all of the kinds of problems that humans might potentially encounter. He went on to comment on the role of religion and the purpose of CPE in this context: "Does religion have anything to contribute to the individual facing those experiences? We assume it does. It is our task during the summer to help the students discover what it is and how they go about bringing the forces of religion into play in such situations."[3]

Both the structure and the goals of the summer program at MGH suggest that the medical doctors, social workers, and clergy who joined Anton Boisen in founding the CCTTS to oversee clinical pastoral education programs almost immediately began to envision something different from Boisen's social scientific study of religion. At least some of them found his particular brand of moralism and his occasional bouts with psychosis embarrassing and exasperating. Nevertheless, they did not discount his contribution. Carroll Wise, who had studied with Boisen at Worcester and taken over the program there when Boisen moved to Elgin, recalled Boisen's enormous creativity, noting that the clinical training movement was "the child of that creativity."[4] At the time, however, most of the early clinical educators were much more concerned with what they saw as the decline of the Protestant ministry and the concurrent rise of the "scientific" disciplines, including medicine, psychiatry, and social welfare. The CPE founders responded by attempting to negotiate a strategic alliance with other professionals in the very disciplines that posed the greatest threat to ministerial authority and the most likely competition for their parishioners' loyalty and obedience. Although it was professionally advantageous for them to cultivate such alliances, most of the founders also seemed to be genuinely convinced that many Americans were suffering great emotional distress and that their ministers were failing to help them relieve that suffering, because they were inadequately prepared to do so.

The CPE pioneers suggested that the solution to declining ministerial prestige was to make ministers more effective. By "effective" they meant better able to prevent and alleviate "the infirmities of mankind."[5] They argued that ministers needed training similar in some ways to that of doctors and social workers, who were also in the business of relieving human suffering and who seemed to enjoy much greater prestige. Professional training for doctors and social workers in the 1920s and 1930s relied on clinical (that is, bedside) observation of the patient or client and discussion of case studies, an approach that CPE founders viewed as more "scientific" because it required careful observation, detailed recordkeeping, and systematic analysis of the data collected. They intended clinical pastoral education to mirror the training offered in related disciplines.

In addition, CPE placed a special emphasis on the minister's unique contribution to health and healing. Understanding that their association with doctors, social workers, and other health care professionals could hurt them as well as help them, early CPE advocates recommended dividing the responsibility for the study and care of human beings' mental and physical health among medical doctors, psychiatrists, psychologists, social workers, and ministers, who could then cooperate without threatening one another's sphere of action. Their training programs reflected their interest in cooperating with a broad spectrum of health care and social service professionals. Clinical pastoral education, with its mix of medical, psychiatric, and theological knowledge, had some unintended results too. The use of the interview—first as a tool to collect scientific data, later as a tool to practice skills they would need in the parish, and finally as a therapeutic tool for solving patients' problems—made CPE programs the unintended starting point for a boom in pastoral counseling by giving young clergy their first opportunity to counsel.

As Boisen's work does, clinical pastoral education richly illustrates the prewar liberal moral sensibility, but with significant differences. Like Boisen, his colleagues believed that science and the methods associated with science could transform the world, but where Boisen was engaged in a scientific study of religion and religious experience, his colleagues sought a scientific study of human nature in relation to the work of clergy. Boisen assumed in a general way that the knowledge he accumulated would be helpful in alleviating suffering and that activities similar to occupational therapy would create the right environment for healing. In contrast, his colleagues sought specifically to apply the clinical knowledge they collected to pastoral practice. Boisen's primary and best site for scientifically studying religion was the psychiatric hospital, but for many of his peers, general hospitals, child guidance clinics, and prisons served their purposes equally well. Clinical educators' pragmatism and their seemingly limitless faith in the possibilities of professional expertise fitted very well with a Progressive and Social Gospel vision.

Early Troubles

In the early years of clinical pastoral education, the goals and direction of the programs were shaped primarily by Boisen and a handful of his friends, colleagues, and supporters. Anton Boisen, Richard Cabot, Philip Guiles, and Helen Flanders Dunbar had founded the Council for the

Clinical Training of Theological Students to facilitate the growth of new CPE programs, but the fledging organization quickly ran into trouble. While all of Boisen's cofounders, as well as the first generation of theological supervisors, shared his enthusiasm, they did not necessarily share his priorities. Ideological differences about the nature and purpose of clinical training created deep divisions in the movement in its early years. For one thing, training parish ministers quickly became the priority, which was ironic, since among Cabot, Dunbar, and Guiles only Guiles had ever served in a parish. To complicate matters further, each of the founders brought a strong will and a personal agenda to his or her efforts to establish a new kind of ministerial training. The agendas of the other founders, as much as Boisen's agenda, determined the final shape of CPE. The result was a stormy and tumultuous beginning for the organization.[6] Almost immediately, personal and ideological differences came to the forefront in the council. By 1934, the original CCTTS had broken into two distinct factions. The one known as the "New England group" included Guiles and Cabot. Dunbar moved CCTTS headquarters to New York and in 1938 renamed the organization the Council for Clinical Training (CCT).

A variety of factors drove the founders apart. Carroll Wise offered the most convincing explanation for the early divisions. In the early 1960s, Wise was president of the board of CCT, a member of the faculty at Garrett Theological School, and one of the most influential theorists of the pastoral counseling movement. In the early 1930s, Wise had found himself in the thick of the founders' battles. At the time, a he was a young clergyman who had come to Worcester in the late 1920s to study with Boisen before taking up a parish ministry, but he ended up as chaplain at Worcester Hospital after Boisen's breakdown. As Wise recalled it, the heart of the split between the New York and Boston branches of the council was a disagreement regarding the etiology of mental illness. Cabot and Guiles shared the conviction that all mental illness was caused by organic or physiological factors that could be treated with drugs or somatic therapies—a view shared at the time by the majority of American medical doctors. Boisen and Dunbar, on the other hand, believed that psychological factors could contribute to mental illness in some cases—that mental illness could be psychogenic or, in the terms Boisen embraced, functional.[7] Most pernicious of all, however, in the view of

Cabot and Guiles, was Dunbar's embrace of Freudian theory. It seems odd that this would be a problem for Guiles, since, according to Wise, he had recently become a "devotee" of psychoanalysis.

This apparent paradox is easily explainable, however. While ideology was extremely important in shaping the movement, other factors were also at work—most of them personal. For instance, although Boisen disagreed with Dunbar on a great many issues intellectually—he was steadfastly anti-Freudian—he remained personally loyal to their friendship. Similarly, Cabot's professional choices were influenced by his personal estimate of Boisen. It was no accident that the split in the council occurred shortly after Boisen was hospitalized for his second psychotic break. Finally, and probably most significantly, Guiles and Dunbar were locked in an ongoing power struggle for ideological and administrative control of the council. As Wise remembered her, Dunbar "was a woman of very superior abilities and training, and she would not bow to any man. Even though she was only five feet tall, she had a way of making men defer to her." Equally problematic, from Wise's point of view, was Guiles inability to defer to Dunbar "simply because of the nature of his personality."[8] Cabot, who was loyal to Guiles, apparently simply did not like Dunbar.[9]

Part of the hostility directed at Dunbar came because she was a woman, or, more specifically, a woman who did not know her place. Women played an important and influential role in world of Progressive reform. But even that world was hierarchical and drew clear lines with regard to the roles of men and women. Cabot had worked successfully with female social workers to establish the medical social work program at Massachusetts General Hospital and continued to maintain good working relationships with other professional women. But social work was considered an appropriate realm for women and did not challenge the social hierarchy. Dunbar, in contrast, had earned multiple advanced degrees in fields where men dominated—theology (Union Theological Seminary, B.D., 1927), philosophy (Columbia University, Ph.D., 1929), and medicine (Yale University, M.D., 1930). It probably did not help that she was not especially easy to get along with and apparently engaged in none of the behavior necessary at the time to soothe male egos.[10]

In any case, the split in the council created two separate ideological streams. Under Dunbar's direction, the branch of the council that she established in New York grew rapidly between 1932 and 1941. In 1935 Dunbar appointed recent seminary graduate Seward Hiltner, who later became a pivotal figure in the pastoral counseling movement, as executive secretary of the council. Hiltner had trained with Donald Beatty in a council-administered program in Pittsburgh during the summers of 1932 and 1933. He and Dunbar shared responsibility for tremendous growth in the programs. During his three years as executive secretary, Hiltner recruited students from twenty-seven seminaries that had not previously sent students for training.[11] The council worked independently of the seminaries but obviously relied on them to provide students. Meanwhile, the number and kind of programs expanded. The 1937 catalogue advertised summer programs at a variety of locations and facilities, among them the New Jersey State Hospital, the Judge Baker Guidance Center in Massachusetts, and the United States Industrial Reformatory in Chillicothe, Ohio.[12] Responsibility for directing the New York council shifted in 1936 to Robert Brinkman, a psychoanalytically trained minister. Dunbar became less involved in the council in the late 1930s, choosing to devote herself more fully to researching and writing about psychosomatic medicine, serving as founding editor of the *Journal of Psychosomatic Medicine*, and building a private practice.[13]

In the meantime, the second stream of CPE also prospered. The New England group, under Guiles and Cabot, had reorganized as the Theological Schools' Committee on Clinical Training. The new organization reflected the belief of the committee that clinical training ought to be under the control of theological schools, and, as a result, it consisted of representatives from Andover Newton Theological School, Harvard Divinity School, and Episcopal Theological School, all clustered in the Boston area. The New England group's approach contrasted to that of the New York council in which programs were free-standing, without formal affiliation with seminaries. Like their counterparts in New York, the New England group organized summer courses in clinical training at local hospitals. By the time of the first national conference on clinical training in 1944, the New England group, with a much expanded membership, had formally incorporated as the Institute of Pastoral Care (IPC).

A third ideological stream developed independently of the other two. Predating Boisen's first summer training program at Worcester, the third group placed less stress on hospital training, even though a medical doctor played a crucial role. Physician William S. Keller established a summer program in Cincinnati at an Episcopal seminary called Bexley Hall.[14] The Summer School at Bexley Hall, which in 1925 became the Cincinnati Summer School in Social Work for Theological Students and Junior Clergy, placed seminary students in "general casework programs." Administrators of the Bexley Hall program argued that social service programs exposed students to problems that were similar to those found in the parish.[15] Occasionally, Bexley Hall students did their training in "specialized programs" or institutional settings, such as family welfare offices, juvenile courts, hospitals, and in union or management personnel programs in industry.[16] Between 1923 and 1936, Bexley Hall summer school administrators aimed their programs at seminary students on summer break. In 1935 the Summer School became the Graduate School of Applied Religion and came under the direction of Joseph Fletcher. Between 1936 and 1943 the program expanded to offer curriculum during the winter months to seminary graduates. Those who completed four quarters of the program were awarded a graduate degree in "applied religion." As an increasing number of seminaries offered clinical courses of their own under the auspices of either the Council for Clinical Training or the Institute of Pastoral Care, and as clergy enlisted in the armed forces, enrollments at the graduate school declined. In 1944, when Fletcher moved to the Episcopal Theological School in Cambridge, Massachusetts, the graduate program from Bexley Hall moved with him, and at that point it became part of the IPC. Fletcher gained national prominence after World War II for his controversial work in the field of bioethics as well as for his theory of "situation ethics."[17]

For years after the split in the CCTTS, conventional wisdom among clinical pastoral educators identified the New York group as Freudian and the New England group as pastoral. There was some truth in this distinction. CCT leaders Dunbar, Hiltner, and Brinkman probably were more sympathetic to Freudian theories than just about anybody else in the movement. And, undoubtedly, the IPC leaders kept a much greater focus on the parish minister, as their close relationship with theological schools might suggest. At the same time, both groups continued to adhere to certain basic principles. Both groups stressed the importance of the scientific method (by which they meant the case study method), hospital or field experience, teaching ministers skills that they could use effectively in the parish, and cooperating with other professionals, including psychologists, psychiatrists, medical doctors, and social workers. And if the CCT placed more trainees in psychiatric hospitals while IPC turned more often to general hospitals, the fundamental differences were, in reality, negligible.

CPE Programs, the Case Study Method, and Science

In order to encourage interprofessional cooperation (and achieve their goal of enhancing ministerial prestige), CPE leaders pursued several important strategies. First, they emphasized the common ground they shared with doctors and social workers and designed their programs accordingly, accenting the extent to which they were all involved in a scientific endeavor. Second, they sought the support of health care and social service professionals, stressing the importance of cooperation in the interest of the patient's physical and mental health. From their outset, CPE programs bore a strong resemblance in structure to the training of both medical and social work professionals.[18] The resemblance was intentional. To underline the links of clinically trained ministers to medical doctors and social workers and to the scientific method, most early CPE educators designed programs that required significant amounts of patient contact and observation, taught students the fundamentals of meticulous note taking and recordkeeping, and relied on the case study method as the primary teaching tool. The extent to which the case study could be considered scientific was hotly debated by contemporaries, but at least some social science professionals considered it so.[19]

In one sense, CPE programs in the 1930s remained true to Boisen's vision of the minister as a scientist of religion and to his idea that knowledge about human personality was accumulated most effectively not through the reading of books but through a study of "the living human document." Most programs gave students extensive opportunity for patient contact. For instance, students who enrolled in the CPE program at Worcester State Hospital (a psychiatric hospital) in the summer of 1935 spent the first two weeks assisting on the wards and familiarizing themselves with the routine of the hospital. At the end of those two weeks, they were assigned four or five patients to follow closely. They were expected to spend some part of each day with those patients, during which time they accompanied them on walks or to the swimming pool or they simply engaged them in conversation.[20] Programs varied according to the inclinations of the supervisor and the needs of the program. Those that followed most closely the model established by Boisen at Elgin State Hospital tended to place a greater emphasis on recreation programs. At Rhode Island State Hospital in the summer of 1932, under the direction of theological supervisor Alexander Dodd, students organized baseball games and beach parties, published a hospital newspaper, orchestrated a Fourth of July celebration, and arranged a trip to the state fair for hospital inmates.[21]

At the same time, the needs of the program dictated the kind of patient contact. At Franklin School, for instance, students in the summer of 1933 had direct responsibility for the daily activities of their charges. Franklin was a school for children with behavior problems that included "truancy, stealing, destructiveness, pugnacity, temper-tantrums, and all kinds of negativism."[22] Theology students served as staff and so were responsible for getting the children out of bed in the morning, putting them to bed at night, taking them swimming, accompanying them to meals, and participating in storytelling and play groups. In other words, their contact with patients was, of necessity, much more tied to the daily rhythms of the institution.[23] Massachusetts General Hospital offered a different type of patient contact. At MGH in the summer of 1933, theological students spent half-days working on the wards and then devoted the other half of the day to serving in outpatient clinics, including neurological, psychiatric, and children's cardiac clinics. Students spent a significant amount of time simply observing but at times were put to work in the clinic setting. One student recalled a morning spent at the well baby clinic at the Pennsylvania Hospital in Philadelphia. It was his duty to "page the babies" when it was their turn to be examined by the doctor.[24] Students enrolled in the summer program offered at Syracuse Psychopathic Hospital in 1932 worked in the social service department and, in addition to working on the wards, were required to visit and interview friends and family of patients at their home or place of employment.[25] At Judge Baker Guidance Center, students interviewed boys and girls who were patients and their family members and served as "big brothers" or probation officers for the boys.[26]

While clinical educators stressed the fundamental importance of frequent contacts with patients, they did not intend those contacts to be casual. Rather, as part of their attempt to promote the scientific study of religion and the use of the scientific method, they insisted that patient contact be carefully documented through some sort of note taking or recordkeeping. At Worcester in 1935, for example, students were required to take extensive notes regarding their encounter with patients, recalling as much as possible of any conversation and analyzing any changes in patient behavior.[27] But the nature of note taking varied. Programs like the one at Worcester that focused on helping seminarians to understand mental illness tended to follow the format and priorities of the conventional medical case study. In programs where social workers played an important role, not surprisingly, students followed the format and priorities of the social work case study.

Eventually, the CCTTS moved to standardize note taking in council-sponsored programs. They were not entirely successful, because, of course, case study format had to fit the needs of the program, but certain shared priorities emerged. One such format, devised in the late 1930s and apparently intended for use in a boy's school, divided the case history into three parts. The first section provided a guideline for collecting a personal history of the patient. The opening paragraph was supposed to list the salient characteristics of the patient: age, race, sex, education, occupation, religion, and the reason for commitment. Ideally, the remainder of the first section traced the patient's personal history and included a description of the patient's family and their social, cultural, and economic status, the patient's childhood and adolescent development, and personal "adjustments" both current and in the past with regard to sex, family, and to vocational, social, and religious matters.

Determining the nature of the patient's adjustment required eliciting a wealth of information from either the patient or the patient's family and friends. In order to ascertain, for instance, the patient's "sex adjustment," the theological student was supposed to determine whether the patient had an "attachment or antagonism for either parent," what the patient's attitude was toward the opposite sex and toward sex in general, and what sort of "love affairs" and "sex experience" the patient had encountered in the course of his or her life. In fact, learning about the patient's "adjustments" required a range of questions that covered every aspect of the patient's life, from reading habits and preferences in movies to work habits and patterns of church attendance.

Part two of the case study documented the current "personal characteristics" of the patient under categories labeled "state of consciousness," "field of attention," "mood," "speech," "intellectual functions," "general behavior," and "content of thought." On this last, the student was supposed to describe very specifically how the patient thought about "personal responsibility," "religious concerns," and "erotic involvement." While the first two sections were expected to be wholly descriptive, the last section was intended for interpreting the information that had been collected. Theology students were encouraged to make judgments about the emotional and mental state of the patient and to suggest a diagnosis, a prognosis, and a plan of treatment. This appropriation of medical terminology suggests the extent to which clinical educators were indebted to the medical model.[28]

Regardless of their format, however, these student-generated notes provided the starting point for the systematic analysis of the information the students had collected. In general, that analysis occurred in the context of either case seminars or individual conferences with the student's theological supervisor, the patient's supervising physician, or social work personnel. This meant that, in addition to the time students spent with patients on the wards, they were required to spend a significant number of hours in seminars, usually in the evenings. At Elgin State in 1933, for instance, students attended twenty-two evening sessions in the course of a term, each about two hours long.[29] Most of the programs devoted at least one evening session a week—and typically more—to discussion of case studies. In that context, students examined either sample case studies provided by the theological supervisor or the cases to which they were currently assigned.[30] In the summer of 1933, when Seward Hiltner was in his second summer of CPE with Donald Beatty at Mayview, he spent the summer interviewing newly admitted patients to build "a library of teaching case records."[31] At Greystone Park State Hospital in New Jersey in the summer of 1934, students devoted about a quarter of their seminar time to case studies that illustrated specific types of illness or explored the lives of religious figures such as John Bunyan and George Fox.[32]

In many programs, students were also required to attend hospital staff meetings where, again, case material played a central role.[33] In most programs, too, the students met weekly with the theological supervisor and, whenever possible, met individually with medical personnel or social work staff to discuss the cases that had been assigned to them. Weekly meetings seemed to be the ideal, although at least one supervisor was willing to admit that things did not always go as planned. In his report on CPE at Rochester State Hospital in New York in the summer of 1939, Leonard Edmonds acknowledged that he had had trouble "following through" on his weekly supervisor-student meetings and recommended that the meetings be scheduled for some time other than Saturday morning. Edmonds also admitted that, while he had required his students to write at least five case analyses to be submitted by the end of the twelve week period, at least two of his students completed only two; one student had "trouble with interviewing" and the other could not type.[34]

Interprofessional Alliances

Early clinical educators frequently compared the experience of the minister in clinical training programs with the internship served by medical doctors.[35] The CPE founders failed to recognize the flaw in their own reasoning. Doctors were trained in the hospital because eventually they practiced their profession in the hospital. Social workers were trained in social work clinics because eventually they practiced in those clinics. Most ministers who pursued clinical training, however, ended up in a parish. Moreover, it was the express purpose of most CPE supervisors to train ministers for parish work.[36] Had clinical pastoral educators wished to create a truly parallel training situation, they would have conducted the training of their students in parish settings. But, because clinical educators really intended to encourage what they saw as a strategic alliance between ministers and health care professionals, they emphasized the applicability of institutional experience for the parish minister.

CPE educators developed an institutional structure that encouraged interprofessional alliances. The boards of governors of the CCTTS and its successor groups always included medical doctors, as did the roster of council members.[37] While individuals who served as members or associate members played only an advisory role in council affairs, the board of governors had decision-making power. Its members were drawn in part from CPE graduates but also from organizations such as the Association for Psychosomatic Medicine, the New York Academy of Medicine, and the Commission for Mental Hygiene. The council did not neglect its obligations to the traditional power structure of American Protestantism: its board members were also drawn from the Federal Council of Churches (which in 1950 became the National Council of Churches) and the American Association of Theological Schools. Board members included familiar figures such as prominent liberal clergy: Henry Knox Sherrill, Episcopal bishop and later president of the National Council of Churches; Henry Sloane Coffin, the president of Union Theological Seminary; and Harry Emerson Fosdick, the popular and outspoken pastor of the Riverside Church in New York City.[38]

The CPE program structure encouraged strategic interprofessional alliances. Most programs, in addition to discussion sessions led by the theological supervisor, included a full slate of lectures by physicians, psychiatrists, psychologists, and social workers and, in some cases, field trips to local agencies.[39] This teaching method allowed CPE educators to advance one of their most important goals—teaching young ministers the value of "cooperating" with other professionals to relieve human suffering whether it be mental, emotional, physical, or social. Their understanding of cooperation derived from their understanding of the healthy human being. They believed that human experience had to be viewed both in its constituent pieces—spiritual, physical, emotional, social—and as a whole, to be treated through the cooperation of specialists. And within this model of cooperative healing, the minister played a crucial role.

Clinical educators believed that in order to cooperate with others who were engaged in healing, clergy needed to know certain basic information about what the other professions were doing. It made sense to them to ask specialists in these fields—psychiatry, medicine, and social work—to provide that information. At Greystone Park in 1934, roughly half of the seminars were offered by staff from the hospital and the mental hygiene clinic. Dr. Arthur Garfield Lane, hospital staff psychiatrist, presented a sixteen-lecture series titled "The Biological Approach to Mental Disorder." Herbert Barry, also affiliated with the hospital and a professor of psychology at Tufts University, presented five additional lectures. In addition, theological students were invited to attend lectures presented by the hospital's mental hygiene department for its own staff.[40]

In some senses, CPE supervisors were also teaching cooperation by modeling the correct behavior. Theological students who studied at Greystone saw in the example of their theological supervisor, Robert Brinkman, someone who actively cultivated alliances with the medical staff. The program at Massachusetts General Hospital exhibited a similar integration. In the summer of 1933, the theological supervisor, Russell Dicks, cooperated closely with Ida M. Cannon, the director of social services at MGH, to develop a lecture series presented by doctors, social workers, psychiatrists, the hospital librarian, and the chief of occupational therapy. MGH even permitted one of its social workers, Helen Snow, to serve as a consultant to the theological supervisor. In addition, Snow offered lectures on techniques for interviewing and writing social histories.[41]

The information provided by fellow professionals had a specific purpose. Theological supervisors wanted their students to be able to refer their parishioners to other professionals whenever necessary. To effectively refer, parish ministers needed to have enough information about human personality to intervene at the proper moment and recognize what sort of care the person needed. As a result, CPE programs offered seminars such as "The Laboratory's Contribution to Our Understanding of Human Personality," "The Inadequate Personalities (Simple and Hebephrenic)," "Psychoneurotic Individuals," and "A Case of Multiple Personality."[42] Even programs that were not devoted to the treatment of the mentally ill made certain that their students were introduced to the basics of human personality, through lectures such as "The Physiological Basis for Emotions," and "Neurotics as Met in Everyday Life."[43]

Clinical educators assumed that if they gave their students the proper information during their training, once in the parish they would be able to identify incipient illness or suffering and be able to refer to the appropriate professional. Their beliefs about referral reflected their understanding of illness. First, they saw illness as something that occurred on a continuum. Second, they saw emotional, physical, social, and spiritual suffering as something that could be clearly defined and separated. In other words, they believed it was possible to identify the parishioner's particular kind of suffering and refer appropriately. Knowing when to refer was important because early intervention, they argued, could prevent the most egregious manifestations of illness. From the perspective of theological supervisors, then, being able to make distinctions between normal and abnormal or healthy and sick was crucial if the minister expected to cooperate effectively to relieve human suffering. The theological supervisor at the Franklin School in the summer of 1933 reported with apparent satisfaction the comments on the program offered by one of his students. This student indicated that CPE training had helped him to distinguish between "mildly difficult behavior and a definite neurosis" and to understand the importance of early intervention for the success of psychiatric treatment.[44] Robert Brinkman, the theological supervisor at Greystone Park State Hospital saw the "problem of recognizing and treating these situations before they become extreme as the chief pastoral function of the minister."[45]

In addition, CPE supervisors argued that their students needed to have an equally clear grasp of the resources available: students needed to know not only *when* to refer but to *whom*. In the early years, students typically learned primarily about the resources available within the institution where they had enrolled for training. Eventually, in light of their concern about cooperation, CPE educators offered students a broader base of information about community resources. During the summer of 1934, Massachusetts General Hospital scheduled field trips to McLean Hospital, Massachusetts Eye and Ear Clinic, the Judge Baker Guidance Center, and Boston Psychopathic Hospital.[46] In the summer of 1936, in a program designed by supervisors Seward Hiltner and Richard Parker, theological students at Pennsylvania Hospital learned about a variety of social agencies through lectures from representatives of the Child Guidance Clinic, the Lutheran City Mission, and the Family Society and field trips to the Housing Association, the Franklin Nursery School, and the Department for Mental and Nervous Diseases.[47]

The Unique Contribution of the Clergy

When clinical educators adopted the medical model for training and emphasized professional cooperation and referral, they risked subordinating the role of the clergy and the theological perspective. To avoid this pitfall, they had to make a case for the unique contribution of the clergy to health and mental healing. Fortunately, they were not alone in their efforts to do so. CPE was part of a larger movement among liberal Protestants of the period who were attempting to make an explicit connection between Protestantism and healing, whether physical or mental. In the late nineteenth and early twentieth centuries, as psychology, psychiatry, and psychoanalysis gained prominence and respect, the attempts to delineate the relationship of religion and health became more numerous. Mary Baker Eddy promoted the principles of Christian Science, drawing primarily on a Protestant audience and promising that the mind could heal the body, even as any number of New Thought or "mind cure" movements flourished. Within the mainstream Protestant community, religious educators began to teach the principles of mental hygiene to their seminary students. Worcester's Emmanuel Movement was located at the confluence of the mind cure movement and mainstream Protestantism. Some denominations, such as the Lutheran Church of America, instituted the practice of supplying their community hospitals with chaplains to visit the sick. Boisen was probably the first chaplain employed full time by an American psychiatric hospital, in order to address the spiritual needs of the mentally ill. Harry Emerson Fosdick and John Sutherland Bonnell, through their radio broadcasts, reached wide audiences with the message of psychology's importance for religion. Several ministers, including Bonnell, even published works using the terms "pastoral psychology" or "pastoral psychiatry" in the titles.[48] And by 1937, Norman Vincent Peale and psychiatrist Smiley Blanton had established the Religio-Psychiatric Clinic at the Marble Collegiate Church in New York.[49]

Clinical pastoral educators could be distinguished from other Protestants by their attempts to control and disseminate systematically knowledge about the relationship between religion and health. Their plan to develop schools where they could produce generation after generation of psychologically trained ministers suggests that the founders had a grasp of the bigger picture. They certainly were not the only ones thinking about how to revamp ministerial education.[50] They were the only ones, however, who shared a common understanding of the strategic importance of professional alliances and of locating ministers in a newly developing matrix of professional culture.[51] In this context, CPE leaders stressed the unique role of the clergy on the health care team. Supervisors and their students envisioned cooperation as something more than a one-way sharing of information in which medical and social work professionals supplied information to theological supervisors and their students. CPE supervisors thought that cooperation ought to include working together with medical and social work professionals in the treatment of patients and clients. Clinical pastoral educators delighted in pointing out cases where the medical doctor, psychiatrist, or social welfare worker had asked for the assistance of the theological student or supervisor. Carroll Wise, in his 1935 report on the Worcester program, included a description of Robert Beaven's experience. Beaven, a theological student enrolled in the Worcester program, played an integral part in the recovery of a catatonic patient at the hospital. Beaven's involvement, which included swimming, tennis, and daily walks with the patient, came at the request of one of the hospital psychiatrists, who believed that his young patient needed the companionship of someone who was close to the same age and shared his interests.[52]

CPE supervisors argued that clergy belonged on the health care team as equals because they brought unique "resources" for the purpose of health and healing. They pointed to research in psychosomatic medicine that suggested that patients who were calm, happy, and relaxed tolerated surgery with fewer ill-effects. Seward Hiltner claimed that the "quiet spirit" enhanced physical healing and could be evoked by the minister's traditional tools. And, carrying the medical metaphor a bit further, he noted, "Prayer, meditation, the Bible, other literature, listening, quietness, understanding—these are as real as pills and sometimes more helpful."[53]

For many educators, one of the most important aspects of the information available in the clinical setting was its implications for parish practice. As one supervisor observed, clinical training was intended to teach ministers how to deal with "ordinary people in their own parishes."[54] To that end, clinical educators devoted significant numbers of lectures, case seminars, and supervisor-student conferences to an examination of "pastoral technique."

For most CPE supervisors the heart of pastoral technique was "therapeutic friendship." One supervisor, Rothe Hilger, remarked in his 1933 annual report that learning to be a "friend" to boys and girls was one of the primary objectives of the Judge Baker Guidance Center training program.[55] Russell Dicks, too, in his 1933 report suggested that students both observed and "befriended" patients.[56] Clinical pastoral educators in the mid-1930s, increasingly stressed the importance of the quality of the friendship shared by ministers and their parishioners. In 1934, Carroll Wise identified as one of his program goals at Worcester that the theological student would ultimately recognize the importance of a "relationship of understanding and confidence between the minister and the persons with whom he is working."[57] By 1935 Wise made an even more explicit connection between friendship and the pastorate, equating the theological student's "capacity for real friendship" with the "capacity to be a pastor." Wise saw it as his responsibility to teach his students how to be an "intelligent and understanding friend" as well as the "attitudes and techniques for dealing with others."[58] The idea that theological students served as "friends" to the patients persisted in new programs, such as the one established at Pennsylvania Hospital in the summer of 1936.[59]

The Interview

If clinical educators viewed therapeutic friendship as the heart of pastoral practice, they saw "patient listening" as the heart of therapeutic friendship. In his 1934 annual report for Greystone Park, supervisor Robert Brinkman described the high value he placed on teaching his students the importance of "daily friendly conversations and cultivated listening."[60] The mid-1930s saw increased efforts to use the student-patient interview as a tool for teaching student ministers how to listen well. To improve their listening skills, CCT trainees studied a small number of patients intensively, not just through case studies or observation, but through interviews. Typically, trainees interviewed the patients at least five times per week for at least one hour per interview. At the end of each day, the trainee prepared written reports that included a description of each interview, its content, an interpretation of the interview, and an evaluation of the trainee-patient relationship. Interviews gave students a chance to scrutinize their own behavior in the encounter.

Some theological supervisors used the verbatim method developed by Russell Dicks at Massachusetts General to facilitate his own work with patients in a general hospital setting. In the verbatim approach, students prepared a detailed written preliminary plan prior to each interview.

After each visit, they recorded as much of the interview as they could remember, verbatim, on the right-hand two-thirds of a sheet of paper, leaving the left third of the page for the instructor's comments. Dicks argued that recordkeeping disciplined ministers and allowed them to examine their own behavior in a variety of circumstances.[61]

Some CPE supervisors submitted sample "verbatims" with their annual reports, and one, in particular, illustrates how they used the method to hone the student's listening skills. In the verbatim, the student detailed his encounter with a thirty-four-year-old, divorced woman who had been hospitalized to receive radiological treatments for cancer. The theological supervisor wrote comments in the margin that focused on the student's listening skills. At one point, when the student refrained from interrupting Mrs. P, the lack of interruption allowed Mrs. P to introduce an idea the supervisor believed she would not have expressed had the student not waited: after commenting on how "dull" she was to talk to, Mrs. P paused and then said, "Don't you believe that all the hell that there is we make for ourselves?" At another point, however, when Mrs. P said, "Do you think God punishes us directly?" the student launched into a theological explanation of sin. The supervisor commented, "Here you should have listened. You don't know where her 'growing edge' is. You risk missing her completely."[62] The supervisor also commented on the student's use of prayer and scripture. When the student failed to cite in his verbatim the scripture he had used in his encounter with Mrs. P, the supervisor admonished him and compared the oversight to the doctor who used medicine but did not make a note of what kind of medicine.[63] In general, the supervisor judged the several encounters between the student and Mrs. P a success, because the student had established such "rapport" with Mrs. P that in the fifth interview she "poured out her heart" to him.[64] The supervisor noted that the theological problems Mrs. P presented were just the sort the student might expect to encounter in the parish and that his clinical experience had prepared him to handle those kinds of problems should he encounter them again.

By the end of the 1930s a subtle but important shift had begun to occur in the use of the interview in clinical pastoral education. Whereas initially CPE supervisors had required their students to conduct and record interviews in order to collect data and hone their listening skills, increasingly supervisors and their students viewed the interview as a therapeutic tool, a development perhaps presaged by the tendency to compare prayer to pills. Again, a sample verbatim illustrates the changes in the training process. In this case, the student conducted a series of interviews with a seventy-year-old widow named "Mrs. E" who had been hospitalized for a broken hip. As required, the student completed a verbatim report in which he analyzed his encounter with the patient. Unlike earlier students, however, he studied the verbatim in order to ascertain the patient's needs and what he could do for her, rather than to examine his own listening technique. As a result, at the end of each interview, he wrote a summary of the conversation, attempting to identify Mrs. E's needs, and suggested a plan to meet those needs.

The comments from the supervisor primarily addressed the trainee's phrasing in his replies to Mrs. E, suggesting ways in which it could have been more effective. For instance, when the patient described her pipe-smoking roommate and excused the behavior because the woman was lonely, the trainee responded with a "yes," affirming Mrs. E's assessment of the situation. The supervisor suggested that the trainee could have said, "We often overlook difficulties if by so doing we give pleasure to another." In his summary from the first day, the student attempted to determine the reasons for Mrs. E's reluctance to leave the hospital. He concluded that she needed confidence and that he ought to help her gain it. He also decided that she had not confided completely in him and that he ought to focus on discovering any additional problems that might be "weighing on her mind."[65] After the second interview, the trainee drew many of the same conclusions. He wondered, too, if he ought to be more aggressive in offering positive suggestions that would help her to adjust to going home. After the third interview, the trainee worried that he had failed: Mrs. E seemed just as reluctant as ever to go home. The student engaged in an ongoing struggle to identify his "task" in the relationship and finally decided he should just continue being her friend.

Although this student remained within the framework of therapeutic friendship promoted so vigorously by CPE supervisors in the mid-1930s, his experience is an example of the changes regarding the purpose of interviewing that had begun to occur in clinical pastoral education. The changes were subtle but important. The growing interest in using the interview itself as a therapeutic tool eventually caught on in most of the helping professions. CPE shared with its professional allies a commitment to Progressive ideals, including applying the principles of science and establishing professional standards, in the belief that practitioners of their professions could thereby better relieve human suffering. CPE supervisors did manage to carve out a niche for themselves and their graduates among these professionals, by emphasizing a trained minister's ability to make appropriate referrals but also to make a unique contribution through the use of religious resources, therapeutic friendship, and patient listening. CPE supervisors were wary, however, of the interview's becoming the means to relieve suffering rather than a tool for training or collecting data. The interview, or "counseling," as it was increasingly referred to, rapidly gained popularity as a therapeutic mechanism, and clinical educators were not at all sure that they wanted to see that happen, because they feared that doctors, protective of their territory, would withdraw their support of CPE. At the same time, while most theological supervisors disavowed any intention of training clergy to be counselors, their methods probably did as much as anything to fuel the enthusiasm of young clergy for what was now being called "pastoral counseling."

The Minds of Moralists

Every personality problem is a moral problem.
—ROLLO MAY, *THE ART OF COUNSELING*, 1939

I N THE 1930s a growing number of clergy became interested in offering counseling to their parishioners. Whether they were graduates of clinical pastoral education programs or learned about counseling from the books, sermons, and radio programs of men such as Harry Emerson Fosdick, John Sutherland Bonnell, or Norman Vincent Peale, clergy from a wide spectrum of Protestant denominations began to view therapeutic interviewing, that is, counseling, as an important part of their ministerial obligations. The fascination with counseling was not limited to clergy. Many of their CPE allies, including psychiatrists, psychologists, social workers, and guidance and vocational counselors, likewise had begun to claim the interview as an important therapeutic element.

In some ways counseling and its first cousin, psychotherapy, were the quintessential expressions of the liberal moral sensibility as it developed after World War I. Pastoral counselors, many of whom were graduates of clinical pastoral education programs and some of whom had studied with Anton Boisen, brought to the counseling session a familiar set of ideals and principles that included a belief in the centrality of science and the scientific method, the necessity of alleviating human suffering, and the efficacy of professional expertise. Unlike either Boisen or most of the CPE founders, however, ministers who identified themselves as pastoral counselors saw the personal interview as the critical therapeutic element. And where Boisen and the CPE founders had sought to study, describe, and document the relationship between religion and health, pastoral counselors sought to apply that research, specifically in the context of the interview, where the individual could, by talking, be transformed. In addition, pastoral counselors believed that the transformation occurred not just by talking but as a result of the guidance, advice, and direction ministers offered by virtue of their moral authority. Change required a strenuous moral effort and the support of the minister, and the result was mental health. Pastoral counseling emerged in a competitive environment in which all of the professionals interested in claiming counseling or psychotherapy as their purview shared a common Progressive heritage and set of liberal assumptions. Pastoral counselors claimed counseling as a legitimate endeavor for their profession because they believed mental health had moral implications. The theory and practice of Anton Boisen, clinical pastoral educators, and pastoral counselors illustrate how the liberal moral sensibility played out in the interwar period.

The Progressive Context of Counseling

The Progressive impulse—the desire to remake American society through application of science and professional expertise—in tandem with the Social Gospel did as much as anything to stimulate the interest in both psychotherapy and counseling. Typically, historians have seen the therapeutic turn as evidence of colossal social selfishness and the end of Progressive reform. In the early 1960s, sociologist Philip Rieff argued that it also signaled the end of community. But early psychotherapists and counselors saw themselves remaking society, no less than earlier reformers had, but doing so through changing one life at a time. Transformed individuals would transform society, or so the reasoning went.

Psychiatrists, clinically trained ministers, psychologists, social workers, and professional educators owed the growth of their disciplines to the Progressive impulse, and each in the 1930s moved steadily toward embracing the personal interview, or counseling, as one of their primary tools. Both counseling and psychotherapy played pivotal roles in the construction of a professional identity for a variety of professionals claiming one or the other as their exclusive territory, even as the boundaries between professions remained fluid and the claims contested. Most counselors were careful to distinguish counseling from psychotherapy—and for good reason. By the 1930s American psychiatrists and psychoanalysts had, through a series of strategic moves, laid claim to the realm of psychotherapy. The definitions are slippery and ill-defined—both by contemporaries and by historians—but, generally speaking, psychotherapy referred to psychical or nonsomatic treatments such as suggestion, hypnosis, or psychoanalysis used for the purpose of healing mental illness.

One of the earliest examples of psychotherapy was the Emmanuel Movement, the movement established by Protestant ministers Elwood Worcester (Boisen's mentor) and his associate Samuel McComb. Worcester and McComb's psychotherapeutic clinic, one of the first in the country, was established in Boston in 1906. It had the support of the leading lights of the Boston medical community, but its therapy was nonsomatic and nonmedical. Initially, no one anticipated a conflict, but by 1910 hardly a trace of the movement remained. Historian Eric Caplan, who argues convincingly that the Emmanuel Movement was a victim of its own success, contends that most psychiatrists and neurologists had relied almost exclusively on somatic therapies and had assumed physiological or organic cause for mental illness. They had, in fact, distanced themselves from psychological healing because of the extent to which those activities were associated with a popular, nonscientific "mind cure" movement. At the turn of the twentieth century, however, some psychiatrists and neurologists had begun to entertain the possibility of a psychological explanation for some mental illness, or at least that some symptoms could be explained in terms of psychical factors. From this perspective, Worcester's program seemed both legitimate and innocuous. Patients were under the care of both medical doctors and ministers, attended weekly classes where they heard lectures given by doctors, psychologists, and ministers about mental health issues, and, assuming the doctor had found no organic cause for their illness, attended psychotherapy sessions with Worcester or McComb that consisted, to a large extent, of using the methods of suggestion.[1] As the movement gained national prominence, medical doctors, fearing a loss of territory to clergy, reasserted their claim to psychotherapy, sometimes in quite belligerent terms.[2]

After Freud's visit to the United States in 1909, and just as the Emmanuel Movement was unraveling, psychoanalysis gained ground steadily as the psychotherapeutic technique of choice. In the United States, psychiatrists and psychoanalysts made common cause early in the century; and by midcentury it was typical here, in contrast to European practice, that psychoanalysts were also medical doctors, further tightening the grip that psychiatric medicine had on psychotherapy.[3] As

Caplan has pointed out, in pursuing this alliance, American psychiatrists intended to close off the practice of psychotherapy to other professions, which they managed to do, but only temporarily. Claiming psychotherapy as the province of their profession was important for psychiatrists because of the extent to which it expanded their territory beyond the asylum and the mental institution, giving them jurisdiction over a population of noninstitutionalized, sick but curable persons. And, in the context of the Progressive belief that society could be transformed through the judicious application of scientifically based expertise, psychotherapy offered psychiatrists and psychoanalysts a role in that transformation. Their affiliation with the mental hygiene movement further highlighted psychiatrists' potential contribution to building a better world. The mental hygiene movement was founded by Clifford Beers, who, like Anton Boisen, had spent a number of years institutionalized for mental illness. The movement focused on encouraging good mental hygiene as a means to avoiding mental illness. The founding of mental hygiene clinics gave psychiatrists a much broader base and more prominent role in promoting mental health.[4]

By the mid-1930s, psychotherapy had, at least temporarily, been claimed by the medical profession as its province. The situation with regard to counseling was far less settled. Among the other professional groups seeking to establish counseling as part of their repertoire were psychologists, who saw counseling as a natural extension of their work in applied psychology. Counseling was, after all, based on psychological principles. Scientific psychology, from the time the first laboratory was established by Wilhelm Wundt in Leipzig in 1880, had been dominated by the theories and methods of experimental psychology. But, as with psychiatry, Progressive reform had made the application of psychology to social problems more pressing. The realm of applied psychology developed first in the area of mental testing, which was intended to measure everything from intelligence to vocational aptitude and which led to the formation of clinics intended primarily for administering those tests. The anti-Progressive nature of much of this testing is notorious—intelligence testing to limit immigration being the most prominent example. Progressive psychologists, however, had high hopes for the potential of psychology to improve the quality of life for the next generation of immigrants and working-class people and, increasingly, for upwardly mobile middle

Americans, too. These psychologists grew ever more impatient with the apparent irrelevance of experimental psychology with regard to practical matters. For psychologists, it was a short step from testing to offering counsel based on that testing.

Psychologists also were increasingly employed in a variety of settings, including psychiatric hospitals and clinics, mental hygiene clinics, and general hospitals and outpatient clinics, and educational institutions and juvenile courts. In these settings psychologists frequently worked on teams of specialists which included psychiatrists, social workers, and clergy. In addition to offering mental testing, psychologists sometimes engaged patients in psychotherapy while working under the supervision of medical doctors. This combination of testing and providing therapy predisposed psychologists to see both psychotherapy and counseling as important elements of their professional practice, despite psychiatrists' claims to the contrary. Carl Rogers spent the decade of the 1930s at the Rochester Child Guidance Clinic in Rochester, New York, working as part of a medical team and growing increasingly dissatisfied with both the experimental emphasis of his fellow psychologists and the limitations placed on psychologists by the medical profession.

Psychiatric social work followed a similar path. Probably no profession was as completely a product of the Progressive impulse as social work. Originating in the work of volunteers for private charities, social work was professionalized in the first several decades of the twentieth century, as those interested in social work found professional opportunities in many of the same venues that employed psychologists and CPE trainees and graduates. These early social workers provided follow-up care for newly released patients and inmates and helped clients address an assortment of problems, such as finding adequate housing or securing a job. They worked from the assumption that recovering from mental or physical illness or succeeding in school and avoiding juvenile delinquency required the right environment.

Given the aura of respect that surrounded the sciences and the rapid professionalization in other disciplines, social workers sought to place their profession on what they viewed as a scientific basis. Like clinical pastoral educators, they were inveterate recordkeepers and the client interview and case study were central to their endeavor. And as with CPE, the conjunction of social work with the medical profession generated new areas of expertise and professional authority. Psychiatric social work was one of those areas, and two of the earliest collaborators in the field were psychologist Augusta Bronner and neurologist William Healy, both of whom started out at Chicago's Juvenile Psychopathic Institute in 1909 and then in 1917 moved to the Judge Baker Foundation (known as the Judge Baker Guidance Center after 1930), the site of a CPE program. Another important location for early psychiatric social work was at Massachusetts General Hospital, where James Jackson Putnam instituted a special division of social service for mental patients, headed up by his wife, who was a social worker.[5] Medical social work had been originated at Massachusetts General the year before as the collaborative effort of Richard Cabot and Ida M. Cannon. In the 1920s, Cabot and Cannon turned their attention to encouraging and supporting clinical pastoral education. Medical social work, whether psychiatric or general, relied on the notion, shared by clinical pastoral education and clinical psychology at the time, that its practitioners were part of a medical team and provided a service that differed fundamentally from the services offered by other members of the team.

During the 1920s and 1930s, social workers in psychiatric hospitals or clinics increasingly found themselves engaging in a new kind of interview. In ways that mirrored changes that occurred in clinical pastoral education, the interview was acquiring a therapeutic purpose, intended less for the collection of information or data—although that continued to be important—than for helping the individual to work out his or her problems. The psychiatric social worker continued to see the manipulation of the social environment as important, but personality problems increasingly became the focus of the interview.[6]

A fourth professional group played an important role in the early development of counseling. This was a loosely constituted group of educational professionals that included teachers, vocational guidance professionals, and "student personnel workers" (college counselors). This group originated in the vocational education and vocational guidance movements of the late nineteenth and early twentieth century as part of the Progressive response to industrialization and in the context of perceived problems with juvenile delinquency. In 1910 the first National Vocational Guidance Association meeting brought together a wide variety of professionals, representatives of social agencies, and public officials, including social psychologist George Herbert Mead. Mead, whose ideas were essential to Anton Boisen as he developed his theories about mental illness, had helped to institute vocational education and guidance programs in Chicago schools.[7] The 1920s saw the establishment of a vocational guidance clinic at the University of Pennsylvania, a testing facility at the University of Minnesota, and growing numbers of vocational counselors in colleges. There was clearly overlap here with psychology, since much of the vocational testing was done by psychologists. At the same time, not all guidance professionals were psychologists.

Ministers saw themselves as one group among several with a legitimate claim to the realm of counseling, although, having been so thoroughly rebuffed by psychiatrists and psychoanalysts at the time of the Emmanuel Movement, they were careful to disclaim any desire to be psychotherapists. At least some of their fellow professionals acknowledged the legitimacy of pastoral counseling. To one observer it seemed that ministers had no choice. In a 1943 article in which she compared counseling offered by social workers with pastoral counseling, social worker Alice McCabe observed that circumstances had required that clergy reexamine their roles as counselors. McCabe argued that in the past people had turned to the church for counsel but that, as the "sciences and the professions developed," the church had been forced either to "withdraw from one of its previous activities [counseling], or to integrate scientific findings into the field of religion."[8] McCabe approved of the decision to integrate science in part because she understood pastoral counseling as something fundamentally different from the counseling that social workers did. She was convinced that pastoral counselors' interest in religious principles and "right and wrong" distinguished them from other types of counselors.

McCabe's analysis was accurate. Ministerial counseling in the 1930s did consist largely of offering advice or guidance for the purpose of helping counselees to solve specific problems and to strengthen the will in the interest of making wise choices. Wise choices were understood in terms of adjustment to social convention, pursuit of achievable and socially determined moral standards, and perpetuation of Protestant mores. But pastoral counselors' conviction regarding the legitimacy of their task came not only from what they perceived as their historic claim to the field but also from their assumption that moral behavior was intimately linked to mental health. They worked from the assumption that when moral standards were restored and maintained, mental health ensued. They did not always agree on exactly how moral behavior affected mental health, but they did agree that it played a pivotal role.

The number of ministers who engaged in modern pastoral counseling prior to World War II was quite small, and the number who published on the topic even smaller. It is possible, nonetheless, to make some general claims about the theory and practice of counseling prior to the 1940s and to explore how that theory and practice illustrates the liberal moral sensibility. Methods were eclectic but generally focused on creating a friendly, therapeutic relationship characterized by kindness and genuine concern. For the most part, early pastoral counseling addressed the conscious choices, wishes, and decisions of a fundamentally healthy (or recovering) population as opposed to one that had been institutionalized or diagnosed as mentally ill. At the same time, early ministerial counselors were expected to be aware of psychodynamics even though they did not engage in psychotherapy. Among ministers who wrote about counseling, there was an emerging consensus regarding the goals and strategies of counseling, even when they used very different words to describe their work. Some envisioned themselves engaged in "pastoral psychiatry" or "pastoral psychotherapy," while others referred to "counseling" or the "personal interview."[9] When it came to counseling goals prior to the war, some ministers talked of helping their counselees achieve "maturity," while others encouraged "growth" or "adjustment." The war would change therapeutic goals, as will be described in chapter 4.

Some of these differences derived from the kind of training each minister had pursued. It is surprising, given the emphasis pastoral counselors placed on professional expertise, that until 1965 there was no standardized, commonly agreed upon professional training for pastoral counselors. Some counselors, like Rollo May, who had studied with Alfred Adler in Vienna, sought specialized training. Others, like John Sutherland Bonnell, whose father administered a hospital on Prince Edward Island, learned by observing. Still others learned how to counsel from endless hours spent writing verbatims or case studies to be submitted to CPE supervisors and in the seminars that were part of their CPE training. Eventually, some pastoral counselors sought formal degrees in clinical psychology to augment their seminary education. In the 1930s, however, few, if any, of the degree programs in clinical psychology offered training in counseling. The lack of standardized training in counseling characterized all of the counseling disciplines at the time.

Ministerial counseling, like other kinds, was rooted in Progressive era reform, but it was also connected to the Social Gospel. An emphasis on counseling was consistent with Protestant thinking that placed a premium on individual salvation and religious experience. In fact, ministers saw a logical connection between what they were already doing as clergy and the kind of counseling they did based on psychological principles. For them, their work with individuals was just as much intended to bring in the Kingdom of God through relieving emotional suffering as was settlement house work through relieving social suffering. Ultimately, their counseling practice exhibited the liberal assumption that the world could be remade through the principles of psychological science and the efforts of trained professionals and through the strenuous moral effort of individuals.

Pastoral Counseling Theory

One of the most important early works on counseling was written by Rollo May. May's work and early career illustrate not only some of the most important points of early counseling theory and practice but also the interdisciplinary nature of the activity, the fluidity of professional categories, and the shared heritage of the counseling disciplines. May published his seminal work on counseling in 1939, even though his experience and training at that point were rather limited. He went on to earn a Ph.D. in clinical psychology at Columbia University in 1949. Later, along with Carl Rogers, Gordon Allport, and Abraham Maslow, he played a pivotal role in establishing the new field of humanistic psychology and is better known as a psychologist than a minister. In the late 1930s, however, May differed little in background, education, and experience from his ministerial peers. The product of a Protestant, small-town, midwestern environment, he graduated from Oberlin College in the 1930s and then spent three years in Greece teaching English. While abroad, he traveled to Vienna to study with Alfred Adler, a key contributor to modern personality theory. After returning to the United States, he served as student advisor for undergraduates at Michigan State College, in the mid-1930s. From there he went on to earn a master's degree in divinity from Union Theological Seminary and spent a summer in clinical pastoral education. He subsequently sought ordination as a Congregationalist minister and, in 1938, accepted a position as a minister at a New Jersey church.[10]

In the introduction to his book, May claimed that he had found himself called on repeatedly to offer counsel, despite his lack of formal training; so he addressed his book to all professionals who, like himself, found themselves engaged in counseling by virtue of their position rather than their training. This was the exact cohort of ministers, teachers, social workers, and psychologists who were exploring the theories, methods, and practice of counseling and were finding themselves forced to define what they were doing in contrast to psychotherapy.

Most counselors in the 1930s, (religious and otherwise) saw the act of giving advice or guidance as the very essence of counseling. In his introduction to May's book, psychologist Harry Bone, who ended up acting as friend and consultant to a number of fledgling pastoral counselors, expressed this perspective in his description of counseling as "the practice of helping by advice, counsel, guidance, sympathy, and encouragement, both informally (friend to friend) and professionally (priest to communicant, doctor to patient, teacher to pupil)."[11] This tendency to see counseling as a kind of friendship in which the counselor gave advice was pronounced among the clinically trained who were predisposed to think in these terms as a result of their experience in CPE programs.

More to the point, most early counselors believed that they offered advice in the interest of helping the counselee solve a specific problem rather than for the purposes of healing mental illness. The problems that counselees presented to their pastors varied widely. In the early counseling literature, however, pastoral counselors tended to group those problems according to what they perceived as the most important identifying characteristic of the problem. As a result, all the variety of human problems were frequently assigned to one or more of a handful of categories, most often, fear, anxiety, feelings of inferiority, guilt, sex, child rearing, physical illness, or religious problems. Ministers' attempts to categorize their counselees' problems relied partly on the psychological literature (including psychoanalytic) of the day and partly on the ministerial tradition. Ministers had, historically, visited the sick and counseled with their parishioners who had spiritual problems. Fear and guilt were familiar ministerial territory, but much of what early pastoral counselors had to say about these topics was filtered through their new understanding of psychological principles.

Rollo May's account of "George B" is a good example of the way early counselors used psychological principles to interpret a counselee's problem. George came to May complaining of "a general unhappiness in college."[12] George, in May's judgment, suffered from nervousness, tension, and sleeplessness and displayed an attempt to dominate those around him by "reforming" them; he complained that his girlfriend was too frivolous, his roommate took too long getting ready for bed, his athletic coaches drank beer, and that the college Christian group was not active enough.[13] May observed that George was on his way toward neurosis or a "nervous breakdown." As May saw it, George did not need medical attention, but he did need to address, with the aid of a counselor, what May described as his "personality difficulties" if he expected to solve his problems.

May concluded that George suffered from "exaggerated ambition" fed by an inferiority complex. From May's perspective, George's inferiority complex originated in his birth order; he was the second child and his older sibling was a sister who had attended the same college and was quite successful. According to May, second children, especially boys with an older female sibling, were exceptionally prone to developing exaggerated ambition. May argued that George's critical attitude and reforming zeal came from a desire to put his own ego on top, as a means to satisfy his ambition for success. Over a period of several months, May helped George to recognize his personality flaws (although May was not clear on how he accomplished this). Ultimately, George overcame his inferiority complex by becoming more involved in school activities. Once he became more involved and began to enjoy a measure of success in his social life and receive praise from his peers, his need to criticize others decreased. In May's view, when George confronted his inferiority complex, his other problems were solved.

The kinds of problems that ministers emphasized when they wrote about counseling depended on their background, training, and reading. Since the field of psychotherapy, much less counseling, was in no way standardized in the 1930s, ministers' attempts to conceptualize their counselees' problems frequently relied on fairly eclectic sets of theories and practices. For instance, May's fascination with the inferiority complex probably came from the time he spent studying Alfred Adler, who, when he broke with Freud, developed his own theory of personality, one that relied heavily on an understanding of the inferiority complex as crucial. On the other hand, May also drew on the writings of at least four other highly influential thinkers, (all of whom were Europeans)— Sigmund Freud, Carl Jung, Otto Rank, and Fritz Kunkel. Kunkel is probably the least-known of the three. He wrote a book called *Let's Be Normal!* (1929) that pastoral counselors seemed to have found appealing, given that it appeared in a number of pastoral counseling bibliographies.

Presbyterian minister John Sutherland Bonnell was among those who cited Kunkel, but his background and training differed from May's in important ways; while there were some similarities in the way he understood his parishioners' problems, there were also important differences. Bonnell, much more than May, was rooted in the Protestant "cure of souls" tradition. That is, he saw his duties as a counselor in terms of his duty as a pastor to address the spiritual needs of his parishioners. On the other hand, although he had not participated in a clinical training program, he had personal experiences that mirrored those of the clinically trained minister. Bonnell was a Canadian who spent the latter half of his adult life in New York City as pastor of the Fifth Avenue Presbyterian Church, beginning in 1935. In addition to publishing a book on counseling titled *Pastoral Psychiatry* (1938), which was one of the earliest attempts to deal systematically with the minister's work as counselor, Bonnell broadcast a radio program called "National Vespers" from Radio City Music Hall in New York City for nearly thirty years. He saw himself as engaged in "the cure of souls," by which he meant alleviating human emotional suffering by using the "personal interview," or, as he titled his book, "pastoral psychiatry."

Beginning at about age ten, Bonnell had spent weekends on Prince Edward Island with his father, who served as supervisor of Falconwood Hospital, an institution for the mentally ill. Bonnell's father was not a medical doctor, but he was responsible for the daily operation of the hospital, which required a great deal of interaction with the patients. The younger Bonnell grew up observing his father's methods for dealing with patients and modeled his own behavior on that of his father. In 1910, at the age of seventeen, he became an attendant, or nurse's aide, at the hospital, and stayed in the position for a couple of years. His duties were similar to those assumed by trainees in the clinical pastoral education programs of the 1920s and '30s. He even attended lectures presented to the nurses by the medical superintendent.[14] Bonnell then went on to serve in World War I, complete a divinity degree in Nova Scotia, and work in several Canadian parishes before arriving in New York City at the age of forty-two.

The book he published shortly after beginning his pastorate in New York gives a good indication of how he conceptualized his task as counselor. He began by establishing that his work was primarily spiritual in nature. He distinguished his own task from that of the physician or psychiatrist, contending, "My resources and goals are primarily spiritual"; and he underlined the extent to which his task was to aid God in the solving of problems: "I seek God's help with the problem at hand."[15] At the same time, he emphasized the importance for the minister of being well read in psychology and psychiatry. His views echoed those of May in that he saw his primary task as problem solving, but they diverged from May in that he placed a much higher value on the minister's obligation to serve as spiritual counselor.

Bonnell pointed out that it was not necessarily easy to persuade parishioners to admit that they had a problem. The real challenge, then, for the minister was "to be alert to human need," so as not to miss the opportunity to help individuals with their problems. Bonnell cited an example from his own experience of how careful listening could make a difference. He told the story of a young man who was a newspaper reporter working on an article about clergy who offered personal counseling. When the reporter called for an appointment to see Bonnell, he presented himself as someone in need of counseling. Upon arrival, he admitted that he had made the appointment under false pretenses and really just wanted to interview Bonnell for the newspaper article. Bonnell, however, concluded that the young man really did have something else on his mind; so when the interview was finished and the reporter rose to leave, Bonnell invited him to stay, asking him if he was happy in his job as a reporter. When the young man assented, Bonnell pressed, "But are you really happy within?" The young man responded by pouring out his heart. According to Bonnell, the young man then found both

God and an answer to a problem that before the interview he had believed was "beyond solution."[16]

In the rest of his book, Bonnell laid out a series of other problems that he believed were just as susceptible to solution through the ministrations of the psychologically minded pastor. Included among them were fear, feelings of inferiority, sexual difficulties, child rearing, guilt, and physical illness. To describe those problems, he moved easily between the language of religion and the language of psychology, because, for Bonnell, the line between spiritual problems and psychological problems was fuzzy. For instance, in a chapter titled "Humiliation and Pride," Bonnell proposed that the religious term "humiliation" was synonymous with the psychological term "inferiority." The solution, he thought, was to cease comparing oneself to others (the source of both humiliation and pride) and to submit oneself instead to the judgment of God. Bonnell offered as an example the case of "Mr. Blain," an actor who came to see Bonnell after hearing his radio program. Mr. Blain suffered from intense feelings of "inadequacy and unworthiness." After a bit of conversation, Bonnell told Blain he would have to give up comparing himself to others, and he pointed Blain to the Bible (Galatians 6:3, 4), telling him that God "rates you according to the measure in which you utilize the powers that He has given you—not according to what you are or will be, but by what you might be."[17]

Bonnell explained to Blain that when he submitted himself to God's judgment he would have to let go of his false pride and in doing so would become a "perfectly normal" man and would be susceptible to neither pride nor humiliation because he would no longer be concerned about comparisons between himself and others. This was, in Bonnell's view, true Christian humility. The actor indicated his willingness to submit himself to God's judgment, and the interview ended in prayer to that effect. As in the case of the young man described by Rollo May whose problems resolved after he addressed his inferiority complex, Bonnell's Mr. Blain found his life completely transformed. He wrote to Bonnell several weeks after the interviews and said, "My life is altogether different and I'm sure that it will continue so."[18]

At the heart of this kind of counseling was a particular notion of human nature. It was rooted in an early-twentieth-century Progressive ideal that had been shaped by the philosophies of William James and

John Dewey. Most early pastoral counselors maintained a cheerful optimism regarding the capacity of human beings to make wise choices. The fly in the ointment was Freudian theory. Freud's theories raised the specter of powerful unconscious drives that subverted the human will and made human freedom of choice problematic. Most pastoral counselors were reluctant to dismiss Freud out of hand, recognizing the enormous influence he wielded among American psychiatrists, but they were equally reluctant to let go of the idea that human beings had a free will that could be exerted in the interest of right, good, or wise choices. As they saw it, it was this ability to choose that distinguished human beings from the animals, transforming them into moral beings. When Rollo May claimed, "every personality problem is a moral problem," he was expressing the view common among early pastoral counselors that *any* problem in which individuals could exercise their wills was a moral problem and that, because personality problems could be solved by an exercise of the will, they, too, were moral problems. In the view of many ministers, Freud's claim that human beings were at the mercy of unconscious drives over which they had no control undermined the possibility of moral action. It was important for the clergy to maintain their view of human freedom, because they considered morality their particular realm of expertise and, hence, their entrée into counseling.

As a strategy intended to help them to avoid what they perceived as the excesses of orthodox Freudians, most pastoral counselors remained resolutely eclectic in their methods and theories, acknowledging the existence of unconscious drives while privileging the power of the human will as a means of protecting their own notions of moral and ethical responsibility. To do so they relied much more heavily on the emerging field of social psychology than on psychoanalysis, psychiatry, or academic psychology. Perhaps none of the early pastoral counselors so clearly illustrates this view as does Charles Holman. Like Bonnell, Holman came from the cure of souls tradition and wrote one of the early treatises on the subject; his was entitled *The Cure of Souls: A Socio-Psychological Approach,* published in 1932. He then elaborated on some of those ideas in a book published in the late 1930s titled *The Religion of a Healthy Mind.* In both books he portrayed human beings as fully capable of choosing between right and wrong. Holman asserted that human beings were capable of establishing a "hierarchy of values" and of choosing those values "consciously" and "rationally."[19] In Holman's view, the fully integrated "personality" or "soul" (and he used those two terms interchangeably) was the one "who, to a large extent, consciously chooses his way. He creates his own hierarchy of values. He selects the aspects of experience to which he will pay attention. He is self-directive."[20] Holman argued that the struggle to make good choices was itself a moral struggle and that each individual could and, indeed should, "take himself in hand."[21]

It was not that Holman did not recognize the possible influence of unconscious drives. It was more that he did not want to reduce human beings to a single desire, such as hunger or sex, a shortcoming he attributed to Freud and his followers. In his discussion of human desires, Holman relied much more on American psychologists, such as John Dewey and his ideas about the importance of the social group in shaping human behavior, William James and his theory regarding the formation of "habits," and the social psychologists who referred to "the wish" (referring to a complex bundle of traits including drives, urges, impulses, and hungers to which our values have become attached) rather than "the drive" or "the instinct," which Holman saw as an oversimplification. In Holman's opinion, the framework used by Dewey, James, and their colleagues allowed for a more complex understanding of human behavior.

Holman did describe Freud's theory of the unconscious in some detail but observed that some psychologists did not believe that the unconscious actually existed. Holman conceded that, at the very least, human beings had a tendency to avoid anything unpleasant and to push it to the edge of consciousness. He concluded that, even if unconscious drives did exist, they did not have to be determinative nor did human beings have to be subject to their own cowardice. It was, in Holman's view, possible to free oneself from unconscious forces and from one's habit of avoiding reality, through a strengthening of the will (rather than through the psychoanalysis that Freud would have recommended).[22] Holman recommended a number of strategies for strengthening the will including maintaining physical and mental health, pursuing a broad range of "worthy" interests, paying attention to the consequences of one's actions, and pursuing "suitable" fellowship with other Christians. He noted, too, that ministers could contribute to strengthening of their parishioners' wills by reminding them that "in their upward striving effort" they "share the will and purpose of God."[23]

The strengthening of the will was to occur, of course, in the interest of making good or wise choices, which raises a question: What constituted a "good" or "wise" choice? Even a cursory reading of books and pamphlets from the 1930s suggests that pastoral counselors defined "good" choices in terms of conventional white, middle-class, Protestant morality. As a rule, pastoral counselors discouraged premarital sex, adultery, being or taking a mistress, lying, and stealing. Charles Holman, strongly influenced by the Social Gospel, occasionally reminded his readers that economic sins were as egregious as sexual sins—that American society had an obligation to its poor and dispossessed—but, for the most part, pastoral counselors focused on individual indiscretions rather than social ills. Unlike their contemporaries in the holiness and fundamentalist movements, pastoral counselors did not view drinking, dancing, or smoking as especially offensive, although occasionally, probably in deference to their Social Gospel roots, they made a nod in the direction of temperance.

It made sense that Protestant ministers would promote Protestant morality, especially with regard to sexuality. They were themselves, for the most part, the product of white, middle-class, Protestant families. But it also made sense because pastoral counselors were convinced that choosing to live an immoral life resulted in emotional distress. Charles Holman, for instance, concluded that failure to make a conscious effort to strengthen the will and make wise choices could result in a whole host of difficulties, ranging from fear, worry, and instability to nervous breakdown and utter defeat. Holman offered as an example the story of the young man who had, during his college days, indulged in drugs, drink, and illicit sex. Holman argued that because the young man gradually cared less and less for the opinion of others and increasingly only about his gratification, he eventually ended up on the streets "panhandling." Holman contended that many people who had given up the fight to save themselves—had given up moral effort or attempts to strengthen their will—had ended up in the insane asylum.[24] This was similar to Boisen's argument regarding functional mental illness—that some mental illness did result from a progressive degradation of the will.

For early pastoral counselors, the worst effects of an immoral life could only be avoided by confession and repentance. Refusing to confess a sin was as sure a path to emotional ruin as the refusal to make a moral effort. John Sutherland Bonnell devoted a chapter to illustrating the ways in which refusing to confess a sin could lead to emotional distress. He began with the story of a woman, a German immigrant, who had come to see him suffering from intense anxiety. She had been to see at least twenty doctors in the preceding three years and had spent the last twelve months attending a free psychiatric clinic before coming to see Bonnell. The woman suffered from a large number of phobias. She feared that her sister would tell her husband's Jewish employers that they were German and that her husband would lose his job as a result. She feared her own death and that of her husband. She suffered palpitations when the doorbell or the telephone rang and was a virtual prisoner in her home, unable to use public transportation or even to go out for a short walk. She was meticulously honest, worrying about small details such as whether she had been accurate to the minute when telling someone the time of day. Her husband had converted to Christianity, and, when confessing past sins, had admitted to her that he had been unfaithful. As a result, her anxiety had increased. Eventually, Bonnell uncovered the illicit affair the woman had engaged in with her brother-in-law, who had since died. According to Bonnell, once the woman had fully confessed and accepted God's forgiveness, she was completely cured of her fears and her relationships with her husband and her sister were restored.[25]

Bonnell believed firmly in the emotionally debilitating effects of unconfessed sin, and, using a story similar to the one Holman told about the young man who ended up on the streets panhandling, he argued that it was possible to reach a point of no return. This story was of a woman who came to see him suffering intense anxiety as a result of her decision to conceal from her husband the son she had given birth to before she married him. For twenty years she had kept the secret from her husband while maintaining a correspondence with her son through a third party in order to keep her identity and whereabouts hidden from her son. By the time she came to see Bonnell, she had begun to suffer episodes of psychosis and paranoia, believing that someone in Hollywood knew her story and was weaving it into the movies they made. She believed, too, that songs she heard on the radio incorporated her story and that strangers on the bus were talking about what she had done. According to Bonnell, she was unable to accept forgiveness because she had waited too long to make her confession and "the repressed sense of guilt had done irreparable damage to her mind." In the end, she was institutionalized.[26]

Goals of Early Pastoral Counseling

If an immoral life could cause emotional distress and in some cases psychosis, as pastoral counselors believed, then a moral life could contribute to mental health. Pastoral counselors did not agree, however, on exactly what constituted a moral life, what it meant to be mentally healthy, or how the two were connected, only that they somehow were. They used a variety of terms to describe mental health, including "maturity," "growth," and "adjustment." While these terms did not mean precisely the same thing, they were intimately related and they shaped the goals of much early counseling, or interviewing.

Holman talked most often of "adjustment," arguing that in order to become "free, wholesome, complete persons," human beings had to go through a "constant process of adjustment to changing life-situations," and he concluded that "ineffective, inadequate adjustment spells sickness of soul."[27] In the best adjustments (as opposed to maladjustments) the individual would "face the facts" and deal with life's situations "wisely and purposively."[28] Other early counselors stressed the ability to grow as a marker of and contributor to health, both physical and mental. Richard Cabot, Anton Boisen's mentor, and Russell Dicks, who, together with Cabot, oversaw the development of the clinical pastoral education program at Massachusetts General Hospital and had developed the verbatim as part of the training program there, accented the importance of growth. Their definition of growth had much in common with Holman's ideas about adjustment and self-realization. Earlier, Cabot had played a vital role in establishing hospital social workers as a part of the medical team at Massachusetts General and envisioned something similar for ministers. Cabot had a fairly hierarchical understanding of the relationship among medical doctors, social workers, and ministers, and he expected that social workers and ministers would answer to the authority of the doctor. He also dismissed Freud's theories entirely, as well as any functional understanding of mental illness (a stance which had led to his break in the early 1930s with Boisen and Dunbar). In Cabot's view, the cause of mental illness was organic or physiological—something that could be cured with drugs or with somatic therapies. As a result, he had little patience with psychological therapies and even less with ministers who engaged in any kind of psychological counseling. Instead, he argued that ministers should bring the resources of their tradition to the hospital to facilitate healing and "growth." Despite Cabot's objections to ministerial counseling, his ideas about the clergy's obligations to sick people played a pivotal role in the early thinking of both clinical educators and pastoral counselors.

By growth, Cabot meant something quite specific, and he outlined his views on the connection between religion and growth in a 1934 article titled "Spiritual Ministrations to the Sick." Cabot argued that the minister's job was to meet the spiritual needs of the hospitalized patient by finding that person's "growing edge" and fostering growth.[29] Cabot's metaphor of the "growing edge" was taken from biology. Biologists had discovered that it was possible to grow human tissue in a laboratory in the same way that it was possible to grow fungus or bacteria, and that it was possible to see the "growing edge" of that tissue under a microscope.[30] From there, Cabot argued that each person was a child of God and, as a result, had within him or herself a "general plan of development" that he or she was meant to follow. Cabot asserted that the people following the plan could be recognized because they were "growing more and more intimate with God, as a basis for intimacy with everything else in the universe."[31] The minister's job was to provide an environment in which growth could occur. To accomplish this end, Cabot argued, the minister had to find the patient's growing edge by "good listening" and then "nourish" growth by encouraging love for others, learning (about virtually anything), enjoyment of beauty (music, literature, drama), and service to others.[32] For Cabot, the opposite of growth was a slide into loneliness, fear of death, and a bitter and grudging spirit.[33] A "good" choice in this framework was anything that facilitated growth or "intimacy with the divine spirit of the world."[34]

Cabot and Dicks elaborated on these themes and refined their definition of growth in *The Art of Ministering to the Sick*, the book they published together in 1936. In this book they defined growth in terms of what it was not, maintaining that it was not simply "enlargement," (i.e., getting bigger) or simply changing. Growth sometimes involved letting go of attitudes or beliefs from childhood. It always required that the individual "not turn away from reality." The concern with facing reality echoes Holman's claim that proper adjustment required facing life's problems realistically. In addition, Cabot and Dicks argued that growth never led to self-destructive attitudes or behavior. If an individual had become increasingly bad tempered or deceitful, he or she was not growing.

Cabot and Dicks emphasized the importance of the human will and the ability of human beings to choose—in this case, to choose growth. Of course, the ability to choose made growth a moral issue. Cabot had not fully conceptualized the opposite of growth in his early writings, but in *The Art of Ministering to the Sick*, he and Dicks argued that the opposite of growth was "degeneration." Degeneration resulted from "a refusal to grow," which Cabot and Dicks described as a "mixture of laziness and self-deceit" that was "the essence of evil in the moral sense. Growth . . . connotes all that is morally good and all that is morally good must appear as growth."[35] Cabot and Dicks claimed growth as the "ethical absolute" and argued that growth was achieved through "love, learning, beauty, service, and suffering well borne." They defined the "good life" as "growing, *not toward a goal but in powers* [emphasis in original] such as sympathy, courage, honesty, perspective, tenacity, knowledge."[36] Posing a hypothetical challenge to their own position, they asked whether their definition of growth had anything to do with religious or spiritual growth. Their response was that the best evidence of a truly religious life was not necessarily found in right doctrine or the proper use of Christian terminology but in a "certain quality of thought and action" in which the individual grew in the powers they had listed.[37] According to Cabot and Dicks, these individuals sought to "do the will of our Father," even if they did not articulate that goal in specifically Christian terms, and gave evidence of a "will to learn, to treat men as men and not as means, and to kill self-deceit."[38] The minister's opportunity during times of illness was to encourage through spiritual resources this kind of growth.

For Dicks and Cabot the moral act was choosing growth. The choice for growth was a choice for health. And no figure played a greater role in growth than the minister. While Dicks and Cabot may have taken a less direct route in connecting the moral life and mental health, they, as much as Holman or Bonnell or May, saw a causal relationship between the moral life and mental health and granted religion a key role in fostering both. Early pastoral counselors were a little messy in their use of language, but the implication was clear: morally upright people who led spiritually rich Christian lives were growing, mature, and well-adjusted, mentally healthy individuals. These convictions about the connection among mental health, morality, and religion led to a more complicated understanding of salvation. This expanded understanding of their duty toward their charges was what distinguished the religious counseling in the 1930s from that which the clergy had always done. With a few notable exceptions, counselors in the previous century had focused primarily on the state of the counselee's soul and its potential for life after death and had relied on psychology only as it related to the goal of securing the parishioner's salvation. In contrast, twentieth-century pastoral counselors cared as much about saving their a person from an emotional hell as from a literal hell. The new counseling literature made little mention of salvation in the sense that a nineteenth-century Protestant minister might have understood it and instead, in terms familiar to anyone who had taken a quarter of clinical pastoral education, focused on relieving emotional suffering and restoring counselees to mental health.

Counseling Methods

Early pastoral counseling theories resulted in a directive style of counsel that ranged from gentle prodding to more aggressive confrontation akin, in style if not in content, to the confrontation of the reluctant Mrs. E by Ichabod Spencer described in the Introduction. Among those with a more aggressive style, it appears that no one took control of the counseling session more efficiently than John Sutherland Bonnell. Whenever Bonnell thought he had identified his counselee's problem, he leapt in with some help. In the same case example with which he illustrated the ill effects of refusing to confess sin—the long-ill woman who eventually confessed an adulterous affair with her brother-in-law—Bonnell's style of counseling is well illustrated.

To bring her to the point of confession, Bonnell confronted her and told her that people who were obsessed with the truth were usually hiding something. He said to her, "Come now . . . be frank and tell me about that lie that you have been living." When she denied any such lie, Bonnell pressed on. He said, "What is there that your sister knows about you which your husband does not?" Still she declined to confess. Bonnell responded by asking her if she had not felt the urge to confess and gain peace of mind when her husband had confessed his wrongdoing. When she acknowledged that she had, Bonnell played his hand: "How many years ago was it, six or seven, when the improper relationship between you and your brother-in-law commenced?" "Between six and seven," she said.[39] By Bonnell's account, a confession pressed from the reluctant counselee resulted in healing.

Rollo May was only slightly less confrontational and claimed that the pastor ought to direct the course of the conversation so as to "pierce to the heart of the problems."[40] May did not hesitate to interpret his counselees' behavior for them. For instance, he gave the account of a man, "Mr. Bronson," who came for counsel because he could not work productively. After listening to the man, May interpreted his behavior for him. Because of his Adlerian training, which stressed the importance of the inferiority complex, May's interpretation followed familiar lines. He began by suggesting to Mr. Bronson that he was tremendously ambitious and explained that ambition usually came from an inferiority complex. May explained that Bronson's sense of inferiority came from his position as the second child, a situation that was exacerbated because the first child was a girl. May concluded that Mr. Bronson's fear of failure and "distrust of life" illustrated his fundamental feelings of inferiority.[41]

Almost before they had begun, however, pastoral counselors found themselves questioning the efficacy of their methods. Bonnell included an example that seems, upon first examination, to be out of character. A young woman came to Bonnell and told him that a man she knew had offered to support her if she would be his mistress. She asked Bonnell what she should do. Bonnell declined to give her advice and instead asked her what she thought was the right course. She expressed anger at his refusal to advise her but then concluded her session with a clear and unequivocal statement of her own values. "If I went with this man I should feel I had turned my back upon God and broken his commandments. I don't feel they are just orders imposed from without. For years I have felt there is something within me that responds to the moral standards of the Bible. . . . I don't want a relationship with any man upon which I cannot ask God's blessing."[42] Bonnell believed that in this case, by refusing to give advice, he had strengthened her in her conviction to do right.

In retrospect, Bonnell's method with this young woman seems to fore-shadow the direction of postwar pastoral counseling. In the wake of tremendous social and cultural change that came with the war, pastoral counselors began to embrace the ideas of psychologist Carl Rogers and changed their counseling methods. While the prewar style had suited very well the Progressive ideal of transforming society through strenuous moral effort, the postwar liberal ideal, which celebrated autonomous individuals and people's ability to transform themselves, required a new method and a new professional context for pastoral counseling.

CHAPTER FOUR

From Adjustment to Autonomy

> There are many new developments in the field of clinical psychol-
> ogy, particularly in the area of counseling and psychotherapy,
> which are of interest to ministers. . . . For their part psychologists
> and psychiatrists need to do more profound thinking about the
> problem of values which is so deeply involved in all of their work.
> Here the thinking of minister and theologian should be of help.
>
> —CARL ROGERS, QUOTED IN *PASTORAL PSYCHOLOGY*

W ORLD WAR II changed pastoral counseling theory and practice
substantively. The war served to make the study and practice of
psychology more visible, more accessible, and more desirable to Americans, and this societal change benefited pastoral counselors immensely.
Clinical education and Boisen's psychology of religion continued to be
important, but they were, in some ways, overshadowed temporarily by
the counseling boom.[1] Faced with the immediacy of wartime problems,
clergy interested in counseling sought easily accessible, practical methods of counseling and found them in the work of psychologist Carl
Rogers, who advocated a kind of therapy that he called "non-directive"
and "client-centered" and that stressed client "autonomy" and minimized
counselor authority. Rogers proved to be an important ally for pastoral
counselors, along with Rollo May and Gordon Allport. All three were
psychologists with religious backgrounds or sympathies who subsequently played a critical role in establishing a "third force" in American
psychology called humanistic psychology. As the fledgling pastoral counseling movement grew, its proponents sought to foster additional professional alliances (in a strategy reminiscent of the CPE founders) with key
figures among the neo-Freudians, including Karen Horney, Erich Fromm,
and Harry Stack Sullivan. Drawing on work of both Freud and Rogers,
then, clergy began, in the context of wartime exigencies, to define more

clearly and carefully the boundaries of their theory and practice. In doing so, they found themselves redefining the liberal ideal.

Wartime Counseling

As it was for so many Americans, World War II was a pivotal moment for pastoral counselors. A wartime alliance with the federal government gave pastoral counselors a higher public profile. The psychological disciplines gained unprecedented visibility as the U.S. military used psychology in a multitude of ways, from screening draftees for "military fitness" to writing propaganda meant to convince its enemies to surrender.[2] More than that, however, the war created a demand for counselors, because Americans—both those in the military and those on the home front—encountered a host of situations unfamiliar to them and went looking for guidance. There seemed to be not nearly enough psychiatrists, psychoanalysts, and newly minted clinical psychologists to meet the demand. Clergy who had been interested in counseling prior to the war were convinced that the social dislocation created by World War II offered them a tremendous opportunity to establish the legitimacy of their new endeavor and were quick to recognize a possible niche for themselves.[3]

Some CPE supervisors, in contrast, hesitated to answer the call to counseling quickly. They held on to prewar notions about the obligations of clinically trained ministers—that they served best when they referred their parishioners to another professional, applied their religious insights effectively, and listened patiently and kindly to their parishioners' troubles. As a result of this restraint, war prompted no significant changes to the content and training methods in most CPE programs.[4] Even so, clinical educators, in order to recruit students for the program, tapped into ministers' concerns about whether they would be able to meet these wartime needs, and promised that CPE training would make them better prepared to do so. The Council for Clinical Training (CCT) pamphlet advertising clinical programs available for the summer of 1942 offered a challenge to its readers, asking them if they were ready to "calm the disabling anxieties of those whose husbands and fathers have gone to war" and "to resolve the fears and confusion of your people in the face of a world gone mad?"[5] The same pamphlet carried a testimonial from an army chaplain who claimed that clinical training had helped him both personally and professionally, underlining the utility of clinical education for both parish ministers and potential army chaplains without any claim to teaching counseling skills.[6]

Clinical educators, usually so savvy about advancing their interests, may have made a strategic error in not altering their curricula, since the greatest wartime opportunities seem to have been for ministers who knew how to offer effective counsel to their parishioners, could teach others the rudiments of counseling, and were willing to cooperate with the federal government in its wartime efforts. Pastoral counselors were welcomed on two fronts, the Office of the Surgeon General, and as part of a USO project jointly sponsored by the YMCA and Federal Council of Churches' Commission on Religion and Health. The wartime consultant for the Neuropsychiatric Branch of the Office of the Surgeon General was William Menninger. Menninger, his brother Karl, and their father, Charles, had established the Menninger Foundation in Topeka, Kansas, in the early 1920s to provide psychiatric care to the mentally ill and offer psychoanalytic and psychiatric training for health care professionals. All three Menningers supported the authority of psychiatrists, especially with regard to the practice of psychotherapy, so they were not sympathetic to the movement afoot among some clinical psychologists to offer psychotherapy. And, at least initially, during William Menninger's tenure with the Office of the Surgeon General, clinical psychologists were limited to conducting diagnostic tests.[7] But William Menninger, who saw pastoral counseling as something that was qualitatively different from psychotherapy, did support pastoral counselors' efforts to promote their work.

Pastoral counseling also received considerable impetus as a result of a joint venture launched in June of 1943 under the auspices of the USO by the Commission on Religion and Health and the Army and Navy Department of the YMCA. Together they organized counseling seminars for parish ministers and YMCA and USO staff around the country in a fascinating, and seldom acknowledged, experimental union of church and state. In some ways it was a natural alliance. The USO (United Service Organizations) had incorporated early in 1941 at the instigation of President Franklin Roosevelt to meet the recreational needs of on-leave servicemen. And while the organization had an ostensibly secular purpose, its member organizations—the YMCA, the YWCA, the National Catholic Community Service, the Jewish Welfare Board, Travelers' Aid, and the Salvation Army—were religious groups or historically sympathetic to religious endeavors.

Seward Hiltner, then executive secretary of the Commission on Religion and Health, played a key role in arranging the sessions. Hiltner, of course, had gotten his start in clinical education, serving as executive secretary of the CCT in the mid-1930s. By the time war began, however, he had managed, with his ambitious nature and sharp-edged personality, to alienate most of his former friends in that quarter and had begun to turn his attention and ambitions to counseling, exercising his considerable influence this time through the commission. Although his peers frequently found him overbearing (and his enemies were not above comparing him to Hitler), the programs he participated in seemed almost invariably to thrive. In the first year of the joint counseling training program, 2,150 people enrolled in the seminars. Those enrolled included parish clergy, USO professional personnel, armed forces chaplains, and social workers. Invitations to the seminars were also extended to Red Cross workers, civilian YMCA and YWCA secretaries, doctors, and nurses, although it is not clear how many from each of these groups actually attended. In addition, special sessions were offered to USO volunteers.

The seminars were intended to provide participants with a rudimentary understanding of "the art of counseling and listening" and were led by some key figures in the clinical pastoral education movement who had gained some experience in pastoral counseling during the prior decade.[8] Carroll Wise, who had taken over the clinical training program at Worcester State Hospital when Boisen went to Elgin State Hospital in the mid-1930s, and Russell Dicks, who had helped Richard Cabot establish the CPE program at Massachusetts General Hospital at about the same time, participated as seminar leaders. Charles Holman, who had begun to write extensively about pastoral counseling before the war, and Roy Burkhart, a parish minister who went on after the war to establish a comprehensive counseling program at the community church he pastored in Ohio, offered additional sessions. The seminars were held at USO centers all over the United States, from Baton Rouge, Louisiana, to Battle Creek, Michigan, with Holman, Dicks, and David Eitzen, a General

Conference Mennonite and a professor at the University of Southern California School of Religion, doing the largest share of the work. In addition to conducting the seminars, these leaders also "spoke to community groups, gave radio addresses, newspaper interviews, met with volunteers, visited military camps and Naval Stations and conferred with USO staff about their particular problems."[9]

The seminars addressed many issues, ranging from the importance of understanding human personality to the familiar theme of interprofessional cooperation. At first glance, the notes from presentations by Holman and Eitzen seem to suggest that the content of the seminars was still firmly rooted in prewar pastoral counseling practice. The kind of advice given to ministers and USO workers about how to approach counseling echoed prewar concerns about "adjustment," the necessity of facing problems realistically, the importance of highlighting the possibility of forgiveness for "moral failures," and the centrality of properly exercising the human will for the social good.

Carl Rogers and Non-Directive Counseling

At the same time, however, some of what seminar leaders recommended, especially when considered in conjunction with other pastoral counseling publications from the period, suggests that a critical shift—one tied to changing wartime circumstances and the influence of the USO's director of counseling services, Carl Rogers—had begun. Rogers was one of three figures who substantially influenced pastoral counseling and then went on after the war to be identified as pivotal thinkers in the humanistic psychology movement. Rogers, Harvard social psychologist Gordon Allport, and Rollo May, the Congregationalist minister whose 1938 book *The Art of Counseling* had set the early standard for pastoral counseling, all shared small town, midwestern, Protestant origins. Like May, Rogers had started out studying for the Master of Divinity degree at Union Theological Seminary. He eventually abandoned his divinity degree to pursue studies in psychology at Columbia University and then accepted a position at the Society for the Prevention of Cruelty to Children in Rochester, New York, in the society's Child Study Department. There he began to work on a new method of counseling, in part because of his dissatisfaction with the practice of the time, which he deemed "directive." Dissatisfied as he may have been with counseling practice, Rogers certainly fitted more clearly into that tradition, along with psychiatric social workers, ministers, and vocational guidance counselors, than into the tradition of experimental psychology. By his own account, while the rest of his profession busied itself studying the "learning processes of rats," he developed his ideas about the nature of effective therapy with people.[10]

At the beginning of the war, Rogers, with his religious background and interest in counseling, appeared to be an ideal choice for USO director of counseling services. The intent of USO leaders in sponsoring the seminars and cooperating with the Commission on Religion and Health had been to make sure that the men and women who visited the USO clubs received the kind of guidance they needed, particularly on religious matters. According to the final report for the project, YMCA leaders, at least, were well-satisfied with the extent to which the seminars "brought the religious nature of USO into clear perspective for community leaders, the staff of the Clubs, and the chaplains."

Rogers, however, was by this point less interested in religion than in advancing his ideas about counseling, or, as he had begun to call it, "psychotherapy"; and clergy—his former cohort—seemed the perfect allies for the project. Rogers's using the terms "counseling" and "psychotherapy" interchangeably was intentional and signaled a challenge to psychiatrists and psychoanalysts who had in previous decades claimed sovereignty in that realm. Wartime promised increasing opportunities for a wide variety of professionals to counsel returning veterans, and Rogers positioned himself to take full advantage of the boom. Three of his works, *Counseling and Psychotherapy* (1942), *Counseling with Returned Servicemen* (1946), coauthored with John Wallen, and *Client-Centered Therapy* (1951) provided the cornerstone for both wartime and postwar pastoral counseling. A handful of other works, publicized through the efforts of the Commission on Religion and Health, formed the core of advice literature for wartime ministerial counseling and included basic instruction on method and theory.

Rogers's theory contained implicit assumptions about the sanctity of personal choice, the dangers of excessive authority, and the importance of personal expression, and it represented one of the earliest articulations in religious circles of what would become the postwar liberal moral sensibility. In his work, Rogers dismissed any counseling method that relied upon advising, exhorting, reassuring, or interpreting problems in ways that intellectualized them, arguing that these approaches either drove strong-willed counselees away or made dependent people more so.[11] The best counseling, according to Rogers, created a situation in which counselees could gain insight into themselves, take "positive steps" in light of that understanding, and move toward "growth, health, and adjustment."[12] While growth, health, and adjustment were familiar terms from the prewar discussions about counseling goals, they took on new meaning in the context of Rogerian therapy. In contrast to prewar pastoral counselors, who had routinely offered advice, guidance, or direction to their counselees and worked consciously to strengthen the counselee's will to make wise or good choices, Rogers argued that the best way to encourage growth, health, and adjustment required exactly the opposite approach, something he called "non-directive" therapy.

In this kind of counseling, the counselor allowed counselees to choose the topic of discussion, raise the questions they felt were important, interpret their own behavior, and express themselves in any way they wished. Rogers advocated a counseling relationship characterized by warmth, responsiveness, and rapport between the counselor and the counselee, or "client," as opposed to one that highlighted the authority of the counselor. In fact, the most crucial element in the Rogerian counseling relationship was "permissiveness," especially with regard to the expression of emotion. Ideally, counselees in such a relationship could freely express the most hostile feelings without fear of a negative reaction from the counselor. This would free them, Rogers argued, from pressure or coercion—free them from the counselor's aims. In Rogers's judgment this was entirely appropriate, because clients had a right to select their own "life goals, even though these may be at variance with the goals that the counselor might choose for [them]."[13] More to the point, Rogers suggested, such a method encouraged self-understanding, and from self-understanding or "insight" came the right kind of growth.

Echoes of the Rogerian ideal appeared in much of the wartime advice literature for pastoral counselors but perhaps most notably in a 1945 pamphlet by Charles Holman in which he outlined procedures for conducting workshops for "clergy, chaplains, USO workers, and workers in industrial and student personnel" interested in learning to counsel.[14]

Holman was one of those counselors who had most thoroughly exhibited the Progressive moral sensibility so characteristic of prewar counselors. He had resisted the biological determinism of Freud and had insisted on the freedom of the will, the human ability to make moral choices, the efficacy of strenuous moral effort, and the minister's obligation to encourage and facilitate that effort. But by the war years, Holman had softened his view on Freud and had allowed Rogerian theories to reshape his view of counseling methods.

Evidence of Rogers's influence, or that Holman and Rogers were at the least reading the same books, talking to some of the same people, and encountering some of the same counseling dilemmas, can be found in Holman's 1943 seminar talks. Even as he expressed some sentiments that sounded compatible with his prewar views, Holman simultaneously recommended counseling strategies more obviously in line with Rogers's approach. He suggested, for instance, that the counselor maintain a "noncondemnatory attitude," not try to "force help" on people, and seek to cultivate "rapport" and "a relationship of confidence and trust."[15] Holman's pamphlet "A Workshop in Pastoral Counseling" showed an even more marked Rogerian influence. For one thing, the foreword was written by Rogers, in his capacity as USO director of counseling services. For another, Holman used Rogers's *Counseling and Psychotherapy* (1942) as one of the five texts for the workshop. In overall structure, the workshop design demonstrated the Rogerian resistance to authority. First, Holman recommended organizing the workshops without an instructor to "give authoritative answers."[16] Instead, he suggested selecting a facilitator, who would not participate but would serve to keep the group on task and making good progress. He suggested, further, that a secretary record the narrative of the group discussions and synthesize the material into a final report, under the assumption that discussion would yield a body of knowledge with practical significance. In addition, while Holman recommended specific discussion topics and included guide questions for discussion, he also allowed for the possibility that the group might generate its own questions, which he called "marginal" topics, and encouraged group members to add more sessions if necessary to address these topics.

Holman's recommended approach resembled the approach of clinical pastoral educators in that it was based on discussion of case studies and a written narrative, but it was less authoritarian in that no theological supervisor or medical doctor served as final authority and it worked on the assumption that each member of the workshop could make a viable contribution by thinking critically. In fact, commenting on the bibliography for the workshop, in which he had included books with "conflicting views," Holman said, "Uncritical acceptance of any particular point of view is not advised. Rather one's reading should stimulate him to think through the problems involved, in order that he may reach conclusions of his own."[17] The learning process Holman deemed appropriate for the workshops mirrored the process Rogers advocated for counseling.

Holman proposed that the first session of the workshop be devoted to defining counseling, and in his own definition of counseling he made the Rogerian framework apparent. He held to the prewar notion that counseling was essentially problem solving, but he stated quite firmly that any decision about a solution to the problem "must, at the last, be the counselee's own."[18] Further, he divided counseling into two types, "directive" and "non-directive," and used "therapeutic" as a synonym for "non-directive." These distinctions clearly came from Rogers, and Holman had not embraced them a decade earlier. Under the umbrella of directive counseling, Holman placed educational and vocational guidance, where he thought advice based on intelligence or aptitude tests might be offered appropriately. In contrast, Holman argued, therapeutic counseling aided the individual in achieving insight and self-understanding, and advice was inappropriate.[19]

If Holman's understanding of counseling technique had been shaped substantially by Rogers, his understanding of human nature owed more to Freudian theory or to the field he referred to as "depth psychology." In the books he wrote prior to the war, Holman had distanced himself from Freud's ideas about drives and the unconscious, observing that some psychologists questioned the existence of the unconscious and that Freud's theories regarding human instinct were reductionist. In the workshop pamphlet, he held to some of those earlier notions and built his bibliography for the section about human nature on two older works, his own *Cure of Souls* (1932) and J. A. Hadfield's *Psychology and Morals* (1925). And yet, he also began to introduce Freudian terms, using, for example, "drives" and "instincts" interchangeably with "passions" and "impulses," the terms he had once preferred, and acknowledging more fully the power of "the unconscious level of the psychic life."[20] More to the point, in the YMCA-USO seminars he had presented, he advised looking to the " 'depth' psychologists" to understand human motivation. He poked gentle fun at people who were afraid to acknowledge that the "highest and noblest experiences of life are built" on "organic hungers and appetites" and "the wild, impulsive passions," by telling the story of a little girl who brought a note from home to her physiology teacher that read " 'I don't want my Mary to learn no more about her insides.' "[21]

Freudian Theories, Rogerian Methods

It makes sense that Rogers and Freud moved to the forefront simultaneously in pastoral counseling theory, especially if Freud's theories are understood in the context of the history of science and the advancement of rational thought. World War II, and especially Hitler's Germany, had raised the specter of irrational behavior on a global scale. Some religious liberals looked to Reinhold Niebuhr's theological realism and neo-orthodox Christianity, which reaffirmed the sinfulness of human nature as an explanation for what appeared to be unexplainable. Other liberals looked to Freud, whose theory of the unconscious likewise provided an explanation for "a world gone mad" but did not consign the whole world to the asylum. To understand Freud's contribution in these terms, however, required interpreting his theory of the unconscious in a particular way. It meant seeing Freud as part of the larger Enlightenment and the humanistic project in which pastoral counselors saw themselves engaged. In this view, Freud's theory of the unconscious did not propose that human beings were irrational (even though what happened in the unconscious realm was beyond the control of the conscious or rational) but precisely the opposite. In this understanding of Freud's theory, the unconscious had a structure, one that could be—if the scientific method were applied judiciously—mapped, documented, comprehended, and even healed when it had gone awry.

Of course, alternative readings of Freud suggested exactly the opposite, that human life was deeply rooted in biological drives or instincts that were neither rational nor comprehensible by reasonable adults, drives that either found proper expression or were repressed very early in childhood only to reappear at the most inopportune moment in adulthood.

Worse, Freud's theory seemed to say that not just some but most of the human race lived at the mercy of these wild, unruly, and little understood unconscious drives. At best, in this interpretation, everybody was a little bit neurotic and no one ever fully escaped the consequences of his or her unconscious conflicts. It was this interpretation of Freud's ideas about human nature that troubled clergy, and had done so ever since they first experimented with counseling methods in the 1930s. On one level, Freud's ideas about the unconscious were acceptable, especially if they were not examined too closely. They seemed to echo the apostle Paul's sentiments when he lamented, "I do not understand my own actions. For I do not do what I want, but I do the very thing I hate."[22] At the same time, to grant the unconscious too much power suggested that human beings had no control over the choices they made; and if this were true, then what was to become of sin? What had been bedrock to pastoral counselors before the war, however, remained so after: human beings had a choice about how they lived their lives. Orthodox Freudianism implied (even if it was not what Freud had intended) a sort of relentless biological determinism that pastoral counselors resisted.

A new generation of Freudian analysts, the neo-Freudians, who included Karen Horney, Erich Fromm, and Harry Stack Sullivan, softened Freud's biological determinism and challenged the orthodox Freudianism that continued to predominate in many circles in postwar America. In contrast to orthodox Freudians, the neo-Freudians believed that social, cultural, and environmental factors contributed to the construction of human personality as much as did biology. Most neo-Freudians incorporated into their perspective a much more optimistic view of human nature and argued for the possibility of shaping personality even after the individual had reached adulthood. The earliest expression of these views came from Karen Horney, who challenged Freud's biological determinism first in a popular work entitled *The Neurotic Personality of Our Time* in 1937 and then in 1939 in the more scholarly *New Ways in Psychoanalysis*. Horney had come from Berlin to Chicago in the early 1930s and there had encountered and begun to incorporate into her psychoanalytic theory sociological and anthropological insights that would receive fuller treatment in the two later books.[23] Her work was greeted as an affront by orthodox Freudians for its challenge to the "instinctivistic roots" of psychoanalysis.[24] Pastoral counselors did not fully engage

Horney's ideas until after the war, but they had begun to read her work and include it in their bibliographies and reading lists in some CPE programs. Those same bibliographies, however, also included books by Karl Menninger, who was an orthodox Freudian and another of Horney's outspoken opponents in this period.[25]

Pastoral counselors seemed little concerned with these arguments about the legitimacy of the neo-Freudian view within Freudian circles. The problem for pastoral counselors was that, while neo-Freudian explanations of human nature made sense, their therapeutic methods were difficult to apply and fraught with danger, even for analysts who were extensively trained. Moreover, psychoanalytic methods were not particularly useful in the kind of counseling in which most clergy engaged. Although some ministers did seek psychoanalytic training, few could afford to expend either the time or the money necessary to pursue the kind of training they would have needed to apply Freud's theories effectively. In subsequent years the notion that psychoanalytic therapy was long and arduous work that sometimes took a lifetime moved from conventional wisdom to cliché in American culture and art. Certainly in the context of wartime America, securing psychoanalytic training seemed problematic to ministers, especially in the face of the pressing problems of returning soldiers and their families. While pastoral counselors recognized the importance of Freudian theory for understanding human behavior generally—sometimes a soldier said one thing when he really meant something else—they did not see themselves as engaged in psychotherapy for the purpose of healing mental illness. Instead, ministers saw themselves as offering counsel to people who were fundamentally well but who needed help solving specific problems that had arisen from their circumstances. The wartime accounts of clergy are filled with examples of specific problems. As these ministers saw it, the young "woman war worker" who found herself alone, far from home, and romanced by and attracted to a married man wanted to figure out a solution to her problem not to plumb the depths of her psyche. Similarly, the soldier disfigured by his war injuries and afraid to go home needed comfort and support, not therapy.[26]

Rogerian methods, in contrast to those of Freud or the neo-Freudians, were more easily accessible and more quickly applied to problem solving. Rogers's approach was, quite simply, more familiar. It is true that Rogers resisted the notion that counseling or psychotherapy should be about solving specific problems, arguing: "The individual and not the problem is the focus. The aim is not to solve one particular problem but to assist the individual to *grow* [Rogers's emphasis] so that he can cope with the present problem and with later problems in a better integrated fashion."[27] At the same time, Rogers assumed that anyone who had undergone Rogerian therapy would be better able to solve problems, and his method appealed to pastoral counselors on that level. Then too, the method Rogers outlined was more immediately usable by ministers, because it did not require delving into the counselee's past as did psychoanalysis. Instead, Rogerian therapy revolved around the relationship between counselor and counselee and relied upon practices that paralleled the patient, friendly listening that many pastoral counselors were accustomed to. Rogers's method was intended, of course, to be more sophisticated, and he thoroughly examined the nature of the counseling relationship and the practices associated with counseling, reproducing transcripts from electronically recorded interviews to illustrate his points. This was another aspect of Rogers's method that was familiar to some pastoral counselors, who may not have used electronic recordings but who had written either extensive case studies or verbatim reports while enrolled in CPE training.

Putting Rogerian therapy and psychoanalytic theories together resulted in an expanded notion of autonomy in which the individual was encouraged to free him- or herself, not only from the undue influence of the counselor, but also from previously unrecognized or unacknowledged motives or attitudes. Two pastoral counselors in particular explored the confluence of Rogerian therapy and psychoanalytic principles in their wartime publications.[28] The first, Congregationalist minister Rollo May, had already made a contribution to the counseling literature with the 1939 publication of the *Art of Counseling*. May's work had always been more psychoanalytically inclined than that of many of his fellow counselors. He had, after all, studied with Adler. *The Art of Counseling* had demonstrated clearly not only Adler's influence but also that of other European analysts, including Freud, Carl Jung, Otto Rank, and Fritz Kunkel. May had not, however, demonstrated any particular concern for his counselees' autonomy or any enthusiasm for anything that looked like Rogerian therapy. This suggests that there was not a causal relationship between psychoanalytic theory and non-directive therapy. At the same time, the two were by no means mutually exclusive and could be mutually constructive, something Rogers acknowledged in *Counseling and Psychotherapy* and which was clearly illustrated in May's 1943 pamphlet "The Ministry of Counseling."[29]

In the same year May published his pamphlet on counseling, Presbyterian minister Seward Hiltner published *Religion and Health*, a general exploration that began with the mental hygiene movement of the early twentieth century and included a chapter specifically on pastoral counseling. While this was probably not the very first use of the term "pastoral counseling," it did mark the point from which the term came into common use. Six years later, Hiltner published a book entitled *Pastoral Counseling* (1949), in which he explored in greater detail many of the themes that he had first raised in 1943. In 1943 he was still executive secretary at the Commission on Religion and Health, but he was also working toward completion of his doctorate at the University of Chicago. From 1950 through 1961 he was a professor of pastoral theology at the university during the years of the Federated Theological Faculty, and then, from 1961 until his retirement in 1980, professor of theology and personality at Princeton Theological Seminary.[30] Although Hiltner was ordained as a Presbyterian minister, he spent relatively little time in the parish. Two years as a student pastor and two summers in clinical training while he was in divinity school were his only practical experience. Nevertheless, he wrote prolifically and passionately on the subject.

Both Hiltner and May wrote from a Christian context, addressing particularly the concerns of the Christian minister. Both expected, however, that other counseling professionals could make use of the principles they described. At the time he wrote "The Ministry of Counseling," May had left his position as a pastor and begun work on a Ph.D. in clinical psychology. At the end of the pamphlet, however, while he cited Rogers's *Counseling and Psychotherapy*, he directed his thanks to Donald Beatty, Seward Hiltner, Russell Dicks, and Otis Rice—all CPE veterans—and Harry Bone, a clinical psychologist who taught classes at Union Theological Seminary.

Hiltner and May argued that, for the minister, counseling should not be limited to the formal interview, but should be a part of all aspects of the minister's work, from pastoral visiting to preaching, an idea that echoed Harry Emerson Fosdick's prewar stance regarding therapeutic preaching. They also agreed on three areas that were potentially problematic for ministers: knowing oneself and not allowing one's own "personality problems" to impede successful counseling, knowing the limitations of one's training and when to refer a counselee to someone else, and knowing when to introduce religion, whether in the form of talking about God, reading the Bible, or praying. Both Hiltner and May concluded that religious elements should be introduced only by the counselee, which was entirely consistent with what they also came to believe about the importance of counselee autonomy.

For Hiltner and May, protecting the counselee's autonomy was essential. Both men, in the context of describing the dangers of offering advice, underlined the extent to which offering advice or guidance undermined counselee autonomy. May insisted that "to take responsibility for another person's decisions is to remove his autonomy."[31] As Hiltner phrased it, "the decisions which people make must be autonomous decisions, that is, they must be made without coercion of any kind."[32] For May, taking away someone's autonomy challenged a fundamental Christian principle, that "each person is responsible for himself—to himself, to his fellow men, and to God."[33] For Hiltner, giving advice and violating counselee autonomy almost certainly led to counseling failure. Either the advice did not work and the counselee was angry or the advice did work and the counselee became more dependent and still could not solve his or her own problems.[34] In *Counseling and Psychotherapy*, Rogers had described a similar phenomenon but referred to the "psychologically independent" person rather than talking in terms of autonomy. Rogers's particular concern lay in the tendency of counselors to impose their own "socially approved" goals on the counselee.[35]

For May and Hiltner, the scope of autonomy went beyond freedom from coercion by other individuals to encompass freedom from unconscious restraints. Both acknowledged the power of those restraints. May encouraged counselors to ask themselves (although not to ask their counselees), "What meaning underlies the problem which the counselee brings?"[36] Hiltner, similarly, instructed that the pastor should be careful not to conclude that the first statement of the problem was the "real problem."[37] To get at the real problem and find the underlying meaning required establishing "rapport" with the counselee or parishioner and allowing him or her "talk it out," while avoiding the temptation to explain or interpret even if the counselor believed he or she recognized the "real" problem. May even suggested a kind of active listening that could advance through a series of "eloquent and encouraging grunts," in the words of May's mentor, psychologist Harry Bone, terms that echo historian Crane Brinton's disparaging caricature of non-directive therapy. Theoretically, such an approach led the counselee to "*know* himself and to *help* himself" (May's emphasis) or, in the term both Hiltner and Rogers used, to gain "insight."[38] As Hiltner noted, "Insight cannot be given; what the counselor does is to set up the conditions so that there is a chance that it may come." And with insight came growth, both spiritual and emotional, development "as an autonomous person," and the ability to make good decisions and wise choices.[39] Rogers concluded, "If the individual has a modicum of insight into himself and his problems, he will be likely to [choose his life goals] wisely."[40] For pastoral counselors, at least, this marked a shift away from the prewar counseling strategies in which the counselor worked to strengthen the counselee's will and in which "wise" choices were clearly defined by the counselor and by social or cultural norms. In Rogerian influenced counseling, the counselor worked to free the counselee's will, and the counselee defined the wise choice for him- or herself.

The necessities of war opened up possibilities for pastoral counseling practice and led pastoral counselors to think more systematically about their theory and practice. When pastoral counselors adopted the methods of Carl Rogers, their goals changed; unlike before the war, when they had viewed giving advice as a key aspect of their ministerial obligation, they saw the dangers of too much advice and began to stress the importance of preserving the counselee's autonomy. The embrace of Rogerian methods was definitive for postwar pastoral counseling and signaled the beginning of a shift from a kind of religious liberalism in which moral instruction created a better society to a stance in which moral instruction undermined the possibility of a good society, since the freely choosing individual was the necessary ingredient to a good society and a good life.

CHAPTER FIVE

Democracy and the Psychologically Autonomous Individual

And as for the "non-directive" therapy, in which the counselor
merely grunts from time to time to prove to the counseled that he
is still awake, one feels that even the philosophic anarchists of the
Enlightenment were not *that* thoroughly convinced of the natural
goodness of man.

—CRANE BRINTON, *A HISTORY OF WESTERN*

MORALS, 1958

I N RETROSPECT, PASTORAL COUNSELORS seem to have embraced a
view of human nature that was impossibly optimistic given the world-
wide war that raged around them. It would be easy to accuse them of
being naïve and foolish, but it would not be fair. Pastoral counselors
adopted their views about the possibility of human autonomy and its
centrality to human existence not in spite of what they saw around them
but *because* of it. Displaying a liberal moral sensibility, they believed that
human beings could choose freedom and that it was imperative that they
did so. As they saw it, to conclude otherwise imperiled both democracy
and Christianity and opened the door to fascism. For many pastoral
counselors and their allies, the war underscored the dangers of highly
authoritarian societies such as fascist Germany. In response to their fear
of totalitarian forms of government, they articulated one of the foundational ideas of the postwar liberal moral sensibility—that the psychological autonomy of the individual and the freedom to pursue self-realization
and personal gratification were key characteristics of the morally mature, emotionally healthy individual and were also central to a successful
democracy. In the decade after the war, and in response to their
middle-class constituency, postwar pastoral counselors increasingly

conceptualized autonomy or freedom in such a way that it was both generalized—that is, understood in terms other than the narrowly political—and also personalized—understood in terms of personal relationships and personal gratification.

Personal Autonomy and the Challenge to Fascism

Postwar pastoral counselors were undoubtedly influenced in their views by the extent to which they were engaged in ongoing conversation with German émigrés, both figuratively and literally. For instance, during the war years, Hiltner, May, and Rogers participated in a study group called the New York Psychology Group that also included theologian Paul Tillich and psychoanalyst Erich Fromm, both émigrés from Germany.[1] Fromm laid the theoretical groundwork for the importance of the autonomous, self-realizing individual, detailing the political implications of psychological autonomy, its historical framework, and its value as a weapon against fascism, in a 1941 book entitled *Escape From Freedom*. Many of his contemporaries, and historians subsequently, considered Fromm a neo-Freudian because of his sharp criticism and revision of many of Freud's core ideas. Fromm resisted the designation and throughout his career expressed a deep ambivalence about Freud's ideas.[2] Fromm, a philosopher, social psychologist, and cultural critic, settled permanently in the United States in the early 1930s. He began a romance with Karen Horney, which lasted a little over a decade and in which the exchange of ideas was such that it is impossible to say who influenced whom. The relationship ended badly. Fromm ultimately allied professionally with Clara Thompson, Harry Stack Sullivan, Janet Rioch, and Frieda Fromm-Reichmann to establish the William Alanson White Institute of Psychiatry.[3]

Fromm's antireligious sentiments complicated his relationship with pastoral counselors, but the ideas he expressed in *Escape From Freedom* nevertheless became central to pastoral counseling theory and practice in the 1950s.[4] Despite his reluctance to be considered a neo-Freudian, Fromm began his book by laying out the principles upon which he opposed Freud; he noted that his views held much in common with those of Karen Horney and Harry Stack Sullivan, the other two figures most frequently associated with neo-Freudianism.[5] Fromm's purpose was to counter Freud's biological determinism by explaining both how human beings made choices and why they made the choices they did make. To that end, Fromm presented a complex picture of human nature that took into account both biology and a diverse mix of social, cultural, and historical factors. He opposed the orthodox Freudian notion that human "inclinations" were "fixed and biologically given," asserting instead that they were the result of "the social process which creates man."[6] At the same time, Fromm was careful to note, lest he be grouped with the behaviorists, that human beings were not simply a product of their environment; they shaped their environment too: "But man is not only made by history—history is made by man."[7] Specifically, as Fromm saw it, "man's energies," such as the drive for fame and success or the drive to work, became the *productive forces molding the social process*[8] (Fromm's emphasis). Still, even as he recognized the power of social psychology, Fromm acknowledged that certain fundamental needs like hunger, thirst, sleep, and the need to belong—needs that could be understood collectively as the drive for self-preservation and that were rooted in physiological needs—"formed the primary motive of human behavior."[9] It was the drive to belong and the fear of being alone that complicated the modern conception of freedom.

Fromm maintained that freedom could leave individuals feeling isolated and alone and that, in their drive to meet the need to belong, they sometimes willingly relinquished their freedom. To illustrate the way in which psychological factors had political implications, Fromm pointed to modern fascism. He argued that "economic liberalism," increased political democracy, greater religious autonomy, and more personal freedom had created a situation in which fascism could flourish. Having freed themselves from traditional authority and become "individuals," modern human beings had found that freedom left them feeling alone and powerless.[10] Seeking to overcome the feeling of aloneness, they elected to submit their will to an authoritarian figure they believed would make them feel a part of something powerful. In Fromm's view, there was no better example of this dynamic than Hitler's Germany.[11]

Fromm was not implying that greater freedom caused fascism. He was suggesting, however, that there was more than one response to freedom. He argued that human beings could choose love and productive work as one way of meeting their need for meaning and belonging, instead of seeking security in ties that would "destroy [their] freedom and the integrity of [the] individual self."[12] In the final section of the book, titled "Freedom and Democracy," Fromm concluded that if freedom were understood in a positive sense as the freedom to realize the self "fully and uncompromisingly" and "to achieve full realization of the individual's potentialities," rather than as something alienating, then democracy would flourish. In fact, Fromm claimed, real freedom was possible only if society took as its "aim and purpose" the "growth and happiness of the individual."[13] He even went so far as to say that government had a specific obligation in this realm, noting, "Democracy is a system that creates the economic, political, and cultural conditions for the full development of the individual."[14]

Social psychologist Gordon Allport followed a similar line, further exploring the connections between democracy and the psychologically healthy or "mature" personality (who had much in common with Fromm's fully realized individual). For Allport, too, the individual's ability to make wise choices free from social pressures and authoritarian control was crucial. Well respected by his peers, Allport had studied in Germany in the early 1920s and made his name in the fields of social psychology and personality theory prior to World War II, serving as president of the American Psychological Association in 1939. Allport was the third figure who would later be considered a founder of humanistic psychology, and the one most closely allied with pastoral counseling. Like Carl Rogers and Rollo May, Allport was the son of a midwestern Protestant family. Unlike Rogers and May, however, and somewhat ironically, he never pursued a divinity degree yet was the most conventionally religious of the three, remaining steadfast in his religious commitment, which eventually led him to Boston's Church of the Advent and Anglocatholicism. Allport published both scholarly and devotional works relevant to religion.[15] He spent most of his academic career at Harvard and so did not have the same kinds of connections to the New York German émigré community that May and Rogers did, but he had strong ties to Germany from the years he had spent studying there, and he played an important role on a committee the APA created to help German psychologists escape Hitler's Germany. So, it is no surprise that he devoted some of his writing to explaining the phenomenon of fascism.

In his wartime and postwar writing, Allport explored various aspects of the mature personality, deeming such individuals crucial to the steady advance of democracy, Christianity, and science.[16] Allport's initial articulation of these ideas came, while the war still raged, in a 1944 article in *Commonweal*, a journal of religion, politics, and culture published for and by Catholic laypeople. He later wrote an entire book devoted to the subject, *The Nature of Prejudice* (1954), which was, and continues to be, widely influential among civil rights advocates. In the 1944 article, titled "The Bigot in Our Midst," Allport decried the rise of bigotry, which was to him the single greatest evidence of an immature personality. Allport repeatedly made two important associations. The first was that bigotry was a kind of emotional immaturity in which the individual fixated at an adolescent stage of development. At this stage, he argued, individuals needed to have "their backbone on the outside," by which he meant that they needed a strong authority telling them what to do. At this stage, too, they were easily led by authority, and because they felt a need to be part of an "in-group," they tended to scapegoat anyone who was different. Second, Allport identified bigotry, with its tendency to scapegoat, as fascism, and he cited Hitler's Germany as the best example of a society in which this sort of personality thrived.

In contrast, in the mature personality, said Allport, the backbone was "on the inside."[17] Mature individuals were able to make good choices on their own without a clearly defined authority structure and were not given to exclusivity. They were tolerant of diversity and not threatened by it. These characteristics, he believed, were the essence of democracy. To Allport's way of thinking, excellent exemplars of both tolerance and democracy were his own cohort of Christians and scientists. In "The Bigot in Our Midst," Allport was very clear that bigoted Christians should not be considered Christians at all, and in his postwar publications he argued that Christians who went to church and called themselves religious but who were really going to church for the security of fitting in tended to be more prejudiced. In Allport's view, they were, at best, immature Christians.[18] In line with what Fromm had argued earlier, Allport contended that the purpose of democratic society was to allow the potential of all people in a diverse society regardless of "class or kind" to "reach fruition."

The arguments of Fromm and Allport were compelling for pastoral counselors in that they tied politics to a concept that pastoral counselors held as foundational—that human beings and their society would only be transformed one individual at a time and from the inside out. Moreover, Fromm and Allport articulated a connection between autonomy and the success of both Christianity and democracy that pastoral counselors found appealing. Freedom, and more of it, would be the salvation of the postwar world.

Postwar Professional Growth

The boom in pastoral counseling, and in psychological counseling generally, continued after the war. In the immediate postwar era, the demand for professionals trained to counsel skyrocketed as Americans returned from war much more willing than in the past to believe that psychological counseling could provide solutions to their problems, relieve their emotional suffering, and even improve the quality of their lives. Pastoral counselors shared in the postwar psychology boom, because when Americans went looking for psychological help after the war, they were as likely to seek the help of their minister as they were to seek that of a psychologist or psychiatrist. Early Gallup polls indicate that among Americans who desired psychological counseling, 42 percent turned to their minister first. In particular, middle-class white Americans sought the help of pastoral counselors.[19] William Whyte, in his classic sociological study of the American suburb, *The Organization Man* (1956), detailed the struggles of suburban ministers exhausted by the demands placed on them by their parishioners who wanted psychological counseling.[20]

The postwar counseling boom resulted in a realignment between pastoral counseling and clinical pastoral education, as the momentum shifted, for the time being, to counselors. Clinical educators' continued ambivalence about pastoral counseling was particularly ironic given how much CPE teaching methods in the 1920s and 1930s had inclined trainees toward the practice of pastoral counseling and how many of the new leaders of the pastoral counseling movement had gotten their start in CPE. Granted, most CPE programs continued after the war to devote at least some portion of each quarter to counseling methods, but that did not mean that CPE leaders shared the enthusiasm for the subject displayed by some of their students.[21] To their way of thinking, too many young ministers fresh out of seminary and with only a few hours of clinical training under their belts were setting up office hours and offering counsel to their parishioners. At the first National Conference on Clinical Training in 1944, parish minister Henry Lewis, a CPE supporter, expressed his dismay over the comment from one clinical education graduate and newly minted parish minister who told Lewis that as a result of his CPE training, "he now had four one-hour interviews each week with four different parishioners on their personality problems and hoped to have more."[22] Lewis was not the only one to bemoan the trend, but in the face of wartime experiences, pleas for a return to the original intentions of CPE fell on deaf ears.

Anton Boisen's continuing call for a scientific study of religious experience received even less attention and clearly deviated from the primary objectives of both clinical pastoral educators and pastoral counselors after the war. He continued to publish throughout the 1940s and remained active in clinical education. Fred Kuether, then executive director of the Council for Clinical Training, maneuvered Boisen into quitting the chaplaincy and directorship of the CPE program at Elgin State Hospital and accepting a position as "educational consultant" for the council. Boisen took his new job seriously and delivered a scathing report at the end of his first year, criticizing CPE programs for moving away from his original vision and becoming overly enamored of counseling and the personal interview. Boisen complained that one supervisor "was quite frank in saying that he was not interested in the case-write-up, but only in the technique of interviewing." Boisen saw too much emphasis on Freudian theories—trying to "explain George Fox in terms of toilet training"—and not enough "co-operative inquiry," by which he meant the development of a research agenda and significant reading list and reference library for each of the programs. Perhaps most distressing to Boisen was the number of trainees undergoing psychoanalysis or some form of Reichian analysis.[23] But Boisen's ideas sounded quaint to his peers—a holdover from the nineteenth- and early-twentieth-century Progressive reform era—illustrating the ways in which the liberal moral sensibility had begun to shift. Boisen's ongoing interest in the psychology of religion seemed ill fitted and irrelevant to the newly discovered interest in the autonomous individual. The winds would have to change again before Boisen's ideas would enjoy a renaissance.[24]

Leaders of the emerging pastoral counseling movement took a view that differed from Boisen's and from that of the majority of their peers in CPE. In their view, the heart of the pastor's job was to be neither a scientist, as Boisen understood it, nor a member of the health care team, as CPE supervisors would have it, but a counselor, whether in the private interview or in the application of counseling principles to all ministerial duties. Clergy who self-identified as pastoral counselors still engaged in a conversation with scientists and in scientific research, but they did so to develop more effective counseling and a better understanding of their counselees and of themselves. It was this view that predominated in post-war debates about the parish minister's professional duties, particularly among those ministers who were attempting to move counseling to the center of the parish minister's professional identity.

Pastoral counseling advocates elaborated their conception of pastoral counseling in a 1954 interprofessional conference on psychotherapy and counseling held under the auspices of the New York Academy of Sciences. Representatives from the fields of medicine, psychology, social work, counseling and guidance, and the ministry gathered to explore areas of mutual interest. Reports from each of the five professional groups were published in the *Annals of the New York Academy of Sciences*, and excerpts of the clergy group's report were also published in *Pastoral Psychology*. The clergy's report, written by Wayne Oates in consultation with other members of the Commission in the Ministry, highlighted the unique contribution of the minister as counselor and stressed the value scientific insights could have for pastoral counseling and the importance of "scientific criteria of evaluation" in judging the effectiveness of pastoral counseling.[25] The authors of the report also addressed the distinction between counseling and psychotherapy, called for more research in the area of the psychology of religion, encouraged mutual cooperation among the counseling professions which would involve secular professionals referring clients to ministers as often as ministers referred parishioners to a psychologist or psychiatrist, and pointed out the need for more training opportunities even as they resisted the idea of a specialized field in pastoral counseling, noting, "The creation of a specialty of counseling among ministers, a subprofession, so to speak, is highly undesirable." Training as a counselor was intended to make a minister not less "but more a man of God to those who come to him for counsel and guidance."[26] Pastoral counselor Paul Johnson, in the published discussion of the findings, quibbled a bit with Oates's strong opposition to specialization and compared the parish minister to the general practitioner, arguing that clergy needed as much counseling training as possible for use in their parish, although not as much as would be needed by someone who wanted to be "the full-time pastoral counselor, the institutional chaplain, or the teacher of other pastors."[27]

While the commission's report made some attempt to define pastoral counseling and delineate its boundaries, in reality, pastoral counseling continued to resist easy definition. In the twenty years after World War II, ministers who self-identified as pastoral counselors continued to practice as they had before the war, without formal licensing procedures, standardized training, a professional organization, or even a clear definition of counseling. They practiced their craft in a variety of settings, serving as parish ministers, hospital chaplains, seminary faculty, and staff members at a growing number of independent counseling centers. They hailed from a variety of Protestant denominations, but the majority held membership in one or another of six denominations: Presbyterian Church in the U.S.A., the Methodist Church, the Protestant Episcopal Church, the Congregationalist Christian Church, the Baptist church (both Southern and American), or the Lutheran church (Evangelical, United, and Missouri Synod). Other denominations, including General Conference Mennonites, the Church of the Brethren, and Unitarian-Universalists, were represented in smaller numbers.[28]

Ecumenical and only loosely organized until 1965, pastoral counselors were, more than anything else, a community of discourse tied together by two professional journals—*The Journal of Pastoral Care*, which began publication in the mid-1940s, and *Pastoral Psychology*, which began publication in 1950—and an eclectic mix of educational opportunities and how-to books published in ever-increasing numbers by the leaders in the field. As a consequence, and not surprisingly, levels of expertise varied widely. Almost any minister who had read a few articles in the professional journals or taken an evening class in psychology could, and sometimes did, call him- or herself a pastoral counselor, while, at the same time, some of the leading figures in the movement had pursued extensive psychoanalytic training.

In an ongoing irony, even as chaplain supervisors persisted in discounting the role of CPE in training pastoral counselors, many ministers continued to get their start in counseling in clinical pastoral education programs where they read the counseling literature. A 1962 study, *The Churches and Mental Health*, indicated that of the 235,000 active Protestant parish ministers in the United States, between 8,000 and 10,000 had pursued clinical training and had, as a consequence, been exposed to the basic principles of counseling. In addition to CPE, ministers who wanted to learn about counseling could choose from a widening array of seminary programs and independent seminars. In 1954 alone, there were thirty-five seminars, institutes, and lecture series offered on pastoral counseling. Seventy theological schools, located from Philadelphia to Sioux Falls, South Dakota, provided courses in pastoral psychology and counseling. Forty seminaries listed clinical experience and courses in psychology in their catalogues. Seven seminaries awarded graduate degrees in pastoral theology, pastoral counseling, clinical psychology, or "guidance."[29] In 1965, the American Association of Pastoral Counselors (AAPC) was founded. That year, the annual directory, "Opportunities for Study, Training, and Experience in Pastoral Psychology" in the journal *Pastoral Psychology* listed more than double the 1954 offerings. Seminaries offering course work leading to degrees in pastoral theology, pastoral care, or pastoral counseling had more than quadrupled.[30]

Despite the growth of opportunities, little standardization of training occurred in the first two decades after World War II. The seminars, lectures, and workshops available through institutes, hospitals, councils of churches, and seminaries varied in content and length, ranging from one day to two semesters. The majority employed readings, discussions of case studies, and lectures. Some workshops, such as those administered by the Hudson River Counseling Service, covered interviewing and counseling technique. A very small number of programs included supervised experience; the Greater Newark Council of Churches, through its Department of Social Welfare, advertised "special supervised clinical experience for clergy in family and marriage counseling."[31] Among seminaries and theological schools, only a handful provided supervised fieldwork. As late as 1965 many pastoral counselors still gained much of their knowledge about counseling from reading about it. *Pastoral Psychology*'s editors, clearly assuming that clergy would gain a significant portion of the information they needed from reading, included extensive bibliographies in each annual directory. In addition, much of what they published had a practical bent; two regular features of the journal, "Readers'

Forum" and "The Consultation Clinic," allowed readers to raise questions and receive answers from specialists. For instance, the March 1956 "Consultation Clinic" raised the question of how to keep records in counseling situations. The three respondents, Rollin Fairbanks, Samuel Southard, and Aaron Rutledge had all served at one time or another as directors of counseling centers. All three gave detailed, practical advice on everything from the length of patient interviews to the appropriate size of index card for recording counselee information.[32]

Some of the training available was quite extensive, although many ministers lacked the time and resources to take advantage of that training. The Merrill-Palmer School in Detroit provided counseling services to the community, collected data for ongoing research, and offered counselor training to "graduate and postdoctoral students from such fields as psychology, social work, sociology, medicine, theology, and religious education." The school was affiliated with more than forty colleges and universities and credit earned at the school could be applied to a master's or doctoral degree at those universities. The training consisted of a minimum of ten months of full-time study over three terms and included both graduate seminars and supervised counseling experience. The counseling sessions were electronically recorded with the permission of the client so that the "counselor-in-training" could use the recordings to improve his or her counseling skills. In the interest of "self-understanding," counselors-in-training were also expected to participate in weekly counseling sessions as counselees. The program followed a format with which many CPE graduates would have been familiar. The school's director, Aaron Rutledge, prior to his employment by Merrill-Palmer, had, according to the school's promotional literature, served as "pastor, army chaplain, chaplain . . . of general and mental hospitals, supervisor of clinical training, Director of Guidance in a University, and . . . at Merrill-Palmer . . . as marriage counselor and leader of the counseling service and the training programs." Rutledge's employment history and Merrill-Palmer's curriculum illustrate the state of the field at the time. The school's program, designed to attract trainees from across disciplines, implies that counseling training had not standardized in any of the related disciplines.[33]

In the immediate postwar era pastoral counselors continued to cultivate their alliance with the neo-Freudians, reading widely from their works and maintaining good working relationships with them. For instance, several key figures in the pastoral counseling movement supplemented their divinity school training and clinical pastoral education with psychoanalytic training at the William Alanson White Institute for Psychiatry. Among these were James Ashbrook, a Baptist minister and seminary professor, and Howard Clinebell, a Methodist minister and seminary professor.[34] Institute member Clara Thompson contributed occasionally to *Pastoral Psychology,* and both she and Erich Fromm were honored as the journal's "Man of the Month," or, in Thompson's case, "Woman of the Month." Fromm's commendation came in September of 1955 after publication of *The Sane Society,* which was named the *Pastoral Psychology* Book Club selection of the month. Harry Stack Sullivan had enjoyed the honor a year earlier when he published *The Psychiatric Interview.* Despite her break with fellow neo-Freudians at the White Institute, Karen Horney continued to be much admired by pastoral counselors, served on the editorial board of *Pastoral Psychology,* and was honored posthumously in the May 1953 issue of the journal. Still others integrated neo-Freudian theories into pastoral counseling textbooks they wrote. In one extended discussion of human nature in his book *Pastoral Counseling* (1949), Seward Hiltner returned repeatedly to Horney and Rank to illustrate the interplay between biological drives and cultural imperatives in the making of human personality. Hiltner also noted that his understanding and explanation of human nature had benefited greatly from discussions with Erich Fromm.[35] In defining human nature as it related to counseling, Hiltner ranged widely through the works of cultural anthropologists Ruth Benedict and Margaret Mead and social psychologists George Herbert Mead, John Dewey, Gordon Allport, and Gardiner Murphy, as well as the Freudians, both orthodox and revisionist.[36]

In the postwar years, Rogers's method likewise retained its popularity. Despite frequent criticism from his peers in the field of psychology that he was not scientific enough, Rogers had risen in the ranks of his profession to be elected president of the American Psychological Association in 1946.[37] Pastoral counselors embraced his ideas to an even greater degree in the years immediately after World War II. After 1945 any minister who read the professional journals regularly or who had some minimal level of training in counseling had been exposed to the work of Carl

Rogers. While an outspoken minority resisted Rogerian ideas, one sympathizer declared in 1950 that Rogerian therapy had become "the touchstone of counseling perfection."[38] Four pivotal works written by pastoral counselors in the late 1940s and early 1950s addressed Rogers's ideas extensively: Seward Hiltner in *Pastoral Counseling* (1949), Carroll Wise in *Pastoral Counseling* (1951), Wayne Oates in *The Christian Pastor* (1951), and Paul Johnson in *Psychology of Pastoral Care* (1953). Although all four declared reservations about Rogerian therapy, they all included Rogers's ideas about non-directive therapy in their books, which then became the primary textbooks for most pastoral counseling programs. For his part, Rogers contributed some original pieces to the journal, *Pastoral Psychology*, and its editors regularly reprinted his most important works. During his years at the University of Chicago and the university's counseling center, Rogers influenced the research and training of clergy affiliated with the center. H. Walter Yoder went on to establish a highly regarded counseling program at his Congregational church in Michigan. Rogers and Russell Becker cowrote an article on the clergy and client-centered therapy for the inaugural issue (1950) of *Pastoral Psychology*. And Rogers's work provided the theoretical and research design framework for the study conducted by Colston and Hiltner about the context of pastoral counseling.

The Liberal Moral Sensibility: Human Potential and the Personalization of Freedom

The embrace of Rogerian theory and methods had specific consequences. Postwar pastoral counselors who looked to Rogers as their guide abandoned the prewar stance of encouraging counselees to make realistic adjustments to their situations and to lead morally conventional lives. Instead, they embraced a broad notion of limitless freedom—an abundance theory of personality—in which they assumed that autonomous individuals, freed from restraints and without obstacles in their path, would move toward more fully realizing all of their "potentialities." In this context, pastoral counselors reconceptualized the moral ideal and sought to encourage the development of "mature" or "self-realizing" individuals who possessed insight into their own behavior, cultivated emotionally intimate relationships with family and friends, "integrated" many activities without being too single-minded about any particular task, and made decisions without being unduly influenced either by unconscious factors or the persuasion of other people.[39] In practice, Rogerian pastoral counselors focused on freeing counselees to make their own choices and solve their own problems, theoretically moving them toward self-realization. Rogerian pastoral counseling was characterized by its Protestant framework and by an increasingly personalized idea of freedom.

To say that in the context of personal counseling freedom became more personalized sounds like a redundancy. Counseling had always been personal, its focus on "work with individuals" and their problems, rather than on systems or social structure. But counseling prior to the war clearly had a social end. The Deweyan idea of self-realization, for instance, assumed that the individual recognized his or her social obligations. Holman's proposals for strengthening the will were for the purpose of creating a better Christian. While freedom and democracy were considered admirable principles, none of the prewar counselors, pastoral or otherwise, imagined that freedom applied to every aspect of the individual's personal life, any more than they imagined that economic freedom meant that business could proceed unrestrained. In the 1930s they were Social Gospel Progressives living in the midst of an economic depression. Theirs was a culture of limits and they were the heirs of a Progressive ideal that had sought to relieve suffering and inspire social responsibility.

In the context of World War II, pastoral counselors had interpreted psychological freedom or autonomy in political terms, as a necessary response to fascism; but as concerns about fascism waned, pastoral counselors became less explicitly political. At war's end they were not clearly anticommunist and tended to frame their politics in terms of a general and diffuse commitment to democracy. What is very clear, however, is that in a postwar culture of abundance in which the problems of a suburban middle class seemed to dominate, they interpreted freedom in the widest possible sense. Perhaps the best metaphor for their theory of psychological autonomy comes from classical nineteenth-century liberalism: postwar counselors applied what amounted to a free market theory to the emotional and personal lives of their counselees, in the belief that the emotional market, given the right circumstances, would self-regulate.

Allowing counselees to come to their own conclusions and make their own mistakes was central to this theory. In his 1949 *Pastoral Counseling*, Hiltner demonstrated how *not* to proceed, describing the difficulties of a certain "Mrs. Godwin." While her husband was away at war, Mrs. Godwin had gone to a party, gotten drunk, and slept with another man. When her husband returned home from war, she told him the truth, and he left her. Distraught, Mrs. Godwin sought the counsel of her minister. She explained to him that she had repented and confessed and that she believed there were extenuating circumstances, among them that she had been lonely, did not love the man she had slept with, and would not have been unfaithful had her husband not volunteered to go to war in the first place. She insisted that she had done the best she could under the circumstances and that her husband was wrong to leave her.[40]

Hiltner's analysis pointed to the futility of violating the counselee's autonomy. According to Hiltner, the minister responded to Mrs. Godwin by saying: "I agree with you. You did a wrong thing, but so far as it's humanly possible, you did your part to make it right. And I can see you're truly sorry. I think I'd better go around and talk to that young man. Don't you think I should?" The minister did talk to the husband; Hiltner reported that in response to the pastor's lecture, Mr. Godwin asserted his "legalistic" stance with even greater determination. In Hiltner's opinion, the minister had failed in his dealings with the Godwins because he had "no real faith in the young woman, [and] no respect for her capacity to handle the situation if given some help and understanding." Hiltner concluded that the minister's actions not only implied disrespect for Mrs. Godwin but that no one gained anything from them: Mrs. Godwin's marriage was not restored to her, she gained no insight into herself, and Mr. Godwin remained set in his opinion.[41]

Carroll Wise described how a non-directive approach freed the counselee to make the right choice by telling the story of a young man who came to see him after having been to a series of counselors all of whom had recommended the same course of action. The young man lived with his parents, and each of his previous counselors believed that the only solution was for the young man to move out. After a series of interviews in which Wise applied a non-directive method, the young man concluded for himself that he did, indeed, need to move out. The young man decided, as a result of the counseling, that he would quit his job, move out of the house, and cease trying to change his father. In Wise's view, for this young man, the decision to take action came as a natural consequence of his gaining a greater sense of control in his life.[42] Making the choice for himself made it possible for him to act.

In matters of where to live, how to get along with one's family, whether to marry, what career to choose, or whether to accept or decline health care, the counselee's choices were sacrosanct in the non-directive approach. Even when the counselee demanded advice, guidance, or moral judgment, the good counselor was supposed to decline. The young man who came to his minister and demanded a book that he and his wife could read together that would explain to her "how a wife ought to look after her husband," the young woman considering going against doctors' advice and checking herself out of the hospital, and the unwed mother who prefaced her confession with a statement of her own worthlessness all were to be offered the same respect, the same warm relationship, and the same opportunity to work out their own salvation. And what if the parishioner chose something other than what the minister viewed as best? Theoretically, the Rogerian pastoral counselor defended the "counselee's right to go to hell if he wants to" and rejected "the right of one person or a few people to order and control the lives of others."[43]

Part of what made this approach possible for pastoral counselors was the religious context in which they were working at the time. At least some of them believed that they did not need to fear the consequences of such radical freedom because God was at work in the world and in human beings. When pastoral counselors talked about allowing individuals to tap into their inner resources, they did so believing in the power of the Holy Spirit. As Southern Baptist pastoral counselor Wayne Oates expressed it:

This is the genius of the client-centered principle of counseling: it leaves the responsibility for the solution of the problem with the person who brings it, and provides a permissive and warmly personal atmosphere in which he can objectively work through to a satisfactory solution. Religiously stated, it is the careful observance of the principle of autonomy of the individual personality before God, and a confident trust in the lawful working of the Holy Spirit "both to will and to work for his good pleasure" in the life of the person.[44]

Carroll Wise framed it in terms of "resources" available for "healing" of the personality and somehow connected that to the life and work of Christ, although he did not explain precisely what he meant.[45]

In any case, the relationship between pastoral counselor and counselee was embedded in another relationship, that of pastor and parishioner. Rogers, of course, argued that it was impossible to sustain a counseling relationship if the counselor exercised any kind of authority over the counselee. And Rogerian pastoral counselors were not claiming any kind of moral authority over their counselees. They did, however, see the relationship as powerful. As Wise argued, the Protestant minister did not grant absolution or forgiveness in the same sense as did the Roman Catholic priest, but in a counseling relationship, as a model of God's love, acted as a "mediator of the grace of God through a living relationship."[46] Russell Dicks claimed that participating in a loving relationship with the minister turned the parishioner or counselee toward God and taught the individual to "believe and trust the universe" again even in the face of suffering.[47] Equally important, counseling, as these early pastoral counselors envisioned it, was a part of the life of the church as a whole. Formal counseling, pastoral calls on persons at home, preaching, and even church administration could be conducted using non-directive principles. Under these circumstances, freedom did not look like an abyss.

Rogerian pastoral counselors likewise located self-realization in a matrix of Christian relationships and faith, arguing that Christian love and marriage provided ideal settings for self-realization. As one contributor to the journals described it, marriage gave men and women the "chance to flower [and] to achieve . . . their most noble potentialities." Foster Williams, a Methodist minister from Buffalo, New York, noted that marriage was one of the best avenues for individuals to "develop" their "unique and best potentialities." Later in the same article he asserted that, "self-realization is found only by entering into a real relationship with others."[48] Pastoral counselors and their allies were not necessarily naïve about the difficulties marriage engendered. Frequently, in the same breath in which they celebrated marriage, they acknowledged its potential pitfalls. For instance, psychiatrist Volta Hall, the same contributor who had described marriage as an opportunity "to flower," stressed that, for any marriage to succeed, the individuals had to bring a certain level of maturity to the relationship in the first place. She observed trenchantly, "Marriage . . . is not for the weak, the stupid, or the immature."[49]

Pastoral counselors offered a similar rationale for viewing sex as a means for self-realization. They argued that the sexual relations of a married couple not only gratified their physical needs but acted as a "bond of understanding between them," a "visible sign of an invisible commitment," "an outward and visible symbol of communion," and a means to expand "personal relatedness between them."[50] Pastoral counselors then took their argument one step further. They asserted that the sexual relations between married Christians cemented the relationship of those two people not only to each other, but also to God. In fact, theologian Reuel Howe argued that sex between a Christian husband and wife became an instrument of salvation. It became, in Howe's words, "an instrument for the realization of the fullness of being."[51]

Pastoral counselors linked the personal to the political, arguing that marriage and family were essential to the success of democracy. Specifically, they argued that the right kind of marriage provided a practice field for democracy. For instance, Roy Burkhart, a minister, argued that it was in the home that Americans developed the character and the "inner voice" they needed to be wise citizens of a republic. Anthropologist Margaret Mead, another occasional contributor to *Pastoral Psychology*, maintained that Americans learned democratic practices by watching the relationship between their parents. Marriage counselor Leland Foster Wood insisted that Americans could facilitate world peace if they learned "brotherhood" at home. Gordon Allport argued that marriage provided the ideal venue for achieving the maturity one needed to be a good citizen of a democracy.[52]

Pastoral counselors' views on autonomy, self-realization, and democracy, as well as marriage and family, were undoubtedly shaped by their increasingly middle-class constituency. Postwar pastoral counseling case studies suggest that most of the people they counseled were white, middle class, and, of course, Protestant—businessmen, housewives, and professionals, and members of an upwardly mobile, prosperous, blue-collar population that counted itself among the new middle class. Counseling had been the privilege of this group, as evidenced most clearly in the work of prewar pastoral counselors such as May, Holman, and Bonnell.

In clinical programs, however, where many ministers prior to the war had gotten their first taste of counseling, they had encountered a much more religiously, ethnically, socially, and racially diverse population, because the programs were in state hospitals, general hospitals, prisons, and child guidance institutions.

After the war, as the number of pastoral counselors grew, as counseling moved more fully into the parish, and as Americans became more psychologically sophisticated in general, the middle-class bias became more pronounced. Ministers continued to seek clinical training and to be exposed to a more diverse population. Pastoral counseling professional literature, however, increasingly focused on the parish and parish practice, with its much more homogeneous population. Some evidence suggests that there was simply more demand for counseling from middle-class church members than from other quarters of the population. Sociologist William Whyte in *The Organization Man* (1956) documented an "unusually heavy demand among suburbanites for personal counseling" from their ministers.[53] Whyte characterized the suburban population as primarily young, and he implied that the stresses associated with rearing a family and establishing a career created the demand for personal counsel. Whyte noted the cases of one minister who was especially popular as a counselor and broke under the strain, and another who had to take on an assistant to help with his counseling load. Logic supports Whyte's claims. Middle-class parishioners could afford, financially and in other ways, the luxury of counseling and the pursuit of self-fulfillment. While few of the leading pastoral counselors acknowledged it, the pursuit of personal autonomy required that one's fundamental needs had already been met—enough to eat, shelter, and a bed to sleep in.

Although the evidence is slippery here, it is possible to argue that there is a causative connection between the shift from a social adjustment theory to a theory of personal freedom and the middle class becoming more important to pastoral counselors. A social adjustment theory, with its implications for social control and its stress on the counselee's social obligations, had made sense in the prewar Progressive mind-set that focused on moral uplift, not only for the middle class, but also, and chiefly, for the poorer and working classes. While no postwar pastoral counselor articulated this view explicitly, the assumptions were implicit: a healthy, well-educated, white, Protestant, middle class could be trusted to make the best use of freedom.

The problem was that sometimes those middle-class parishioners made choices that their ministers did not like. It was one thing to talk about sex within marriage as a means to self-realization and another thing to look the other way when marriages in their parish broke apart as a result of adultery. For the small group of pastoral counselors who had resisted Rogers's non-directive therapy from the outset—because they thought it usurped ministers' traditional moral authority—accepting divorce without comment was not an option. They understood the regulation of marriage, divorce, love, and sex as part of the church's historic role and reminded one another frequently of that role. By the mid-1950s, Rogerian pastoral counselors were starting to feel pressure, not only from their peers but also from their parishioners, to reexamine the implications of their theory. As a result, Rogerian pastoral counselors were forced to rethink the ways in which the autonomous self was located in the matrix of relationship.

CHAPTER SIX

An Ethic of Relationships

One brief way of describing the change which has taken place in
me is to say that in my early professional years I was asking the
question: How can I treat, or cure, or change this person? Now I
would phrase the question in this way: How can I provide a
relationship which this person may use for his own personal
growth?

—CARL ROGERS, "BECOMING A PERSON," 1956

D ISCUSSION OF THE RELATIVE MERITS of Rogerian methods dominated the postwar pastoral counseling literature and was driven
mostly by the worrisome nature of Rogerian theories. Even though the
earliest advocates of Rogerian therapy and the ethic of self-realization
had tried to frame them in Christian terms, tying them to familiar themes
such as marriage and democracy and the action of the Holy Spirit, talking so much about self-realization and autonomy made some pastoral
counselors uncomfortable. It sounded selfish and it put them in an awk-
ward position—non-directive therapy undermined their moral authority
and, not surprisingly, they did not necessarily want to let go of that authority. The argument about the legitimacy of Rogerian therapy played
out most prominently in the context of a discussion about marriage, divorce, and sex. It was a logical beginning point for the discussion, since
marriage had been claimed by Rogerians as the ideal context for self-
realization and was also historically a subject on which which ministerial authority had been undisputed. Champions of the non-directive
method painted the consequences of directive therapy in baleful terms,
while more directive counselors complained that non-directive therapy
did not work. The majority of pastoral counselors struggled to find some
middle ground that more often than not led them to a style of counseling
that bordered on the manipulative.

To combat the sense that too much autonomy was dangerous and to remodel their relationship to their parishioners without returning to prewar moralism, pastoral counselors began to explore in greater detail the significance of the therapeutic relationship and then to articulate an "ethic of relationships." They relied particularly on the theology of Martin Buber and Paul Tillich. Both placed authentic relationships at the center of their thinking. In the evolving liberal moral sensibility, the individual's needs continued to be paramount and the individual's freedom to make choices remained sacrosanct; but in this newly developing ethic of relationships, the individual was also responsible for how those choices would affect other people.

Marriage and Ministerial Authority

Discussion of the role of ministerial authority in counseling centered on marriage, divorce, and sex for a number of reasons. Perhaps most obviously, everyone was talking about marriage in the 1950s. Academic and public discourse in general buzzed with talk about the soundness of marriage in the United States and the social utility of marriage. Given their ongoing concern about professional status, pastoral counselors could hardly ignore the discussion. The drive to promote marriage originated, among both pastoral counselors and their secular colleagues, in part because the institution seemed to be under assault. Two facets of 1950s life led pastoral counselors to believe that the institution of heterosexual, monogamous marriage needed to be defended. First, they pointed to Alfred Kinsey's two works on human sexuality. Almost every article that pastoral counselors wrote about sex in the 1950s, especially early in the decade, began with a reference to the Kinsey Report. One pastoral counselor devoted an entire book to the subject.[1] Kinsey suggested that married Americans were much more sexually active in illicit and adulterous relationships than anyone had ever imagined. Pastoral counselors did not dispute Kinsey's findings, but they did fear that his data would be used by the average American as a rationale for sexual license and that adulterous relationships would undermine the very foundations of American marriage.[2] Second, ministers perceived, as did many social analysts of the period, a rise in the number and social acceptability of divorce.[3]

Even if their professional colleagues had not been worried about marriage, divorce, and sex practices, however, the topic would have been important to pastoral counselors because they saw the oversight of these areas as one of their traditional responsibilities. And here it becomes apparent why a discussion of marriage might engender a discussion of ministerial authority. An assortment of articles reminding ministers of the church's historic role in regulating marriage, divorce, love, and sex appeared regularly in the journal *Pastoral Psychology,* and most of the how-to books published for pastoral counselors took a similar stance.[4] Not incidentally, most pastoral counselors took the Bible as their starting point and believed that it provided ample evidence that the church (and by extension the minister) had a mandate to foster and preserve marriage. Thus, when theologian Carl Michalson argued for the importance of marriage because it was "the continuous analogy for the deepest relation in life, the relation between God and man," he pointed to the Old Testament, with its metaphor of Israel as the bride of God, and to the New Testament, with its similar image of the church as the bride of Christ.[5] Given these assumptions, pastoral counselors thought it was logical to claim what they perceived as their historic right to offer their parishioners guidance and direction on these matters.

The Promise of Non-Directive Therapy

When pastoral tradition encountered the self-realization ethic, a host of troubling questions arose: What was to be done when the parishioner, in search of self-fulfillment or personal gratification, exercised the very autonomy Rogerian pastoral counselors celebrated and chose to divorce or to pursue an illicit affair? If happy marriage provided the ideal avenue to self-realization, how could divorce—the antithesis of marriage—also provide a means to self-realization? And where did the pastoral counselor's primary obligation lie? Was it to promote marriage or to promote autonomy? What direction or advice was the pastoral counselor permitted to offer in the context of non-directive therapy? The answer to that last question, of course, was "None." Pastoral counselors found themselves in a situation in which their authority was being challenged in an area where it had once seemed unassailable.

Almost every pastoral counselor experienced some degree of ambivalence with regard to the new theory and method. Attitudes toward non-directive counseling among pastor counselors generally fell along a spectrum. At one end were those with the least ambivalence, chief among them Seward Hiltner and Carroll Wise, who championed the counselee's autonomy. They launched an aggressive campaign to convince other ministers that the counselee's autonomy was paramount and that the non-directive method was the ideal approach to counseling. They couched their argument for a non-directive method in terms of professional survival, a familiar strategy for those who had come to counseling through CPE. When it came to questions of marriage and sex, this group tended to be more tolerant of counselees who chose to divorce.

While non-directive ministers were willing to renounce their own authority on moral matters, they were not suggesting that their parishioners seek advice elsewhere. They clearly opposed advice of all sorts and resisted the idea that consulting the right "expert" (whether minister or psychiatrist) would solve a counselee's problems. As a corollary, they argued against both a specific standard of Christian behavior that could be enforced by the minister and a specific standard of "normal" behavior that might be enforced by a psychiatrist or psychologist. This made sense, given their conviction that the "inner resources" of the counselee were more reliable than the advice of the best expert. Any sort of judgment or evaluation made by the minister or the psychiatrist was rendered useless in this view.[6]

In order to persuade their colleagues to adopt the method they believed would most effectively protect counselee autonomy and respect the counselees' inner resources, Rogerian-influenced pastoral counselors focused on the problems associated with offering advice or direction. As the centerpiece to their argument, they argued that World War II had changed Americans' moral standards and that American clergy had to respond effectively or lose their constituency. They pointed specifically to young men who were far from home and young women whose husbands were gone from home for long periods of time, both of whom found themselves sometimes in situations that caused them to rethink their moral and ethical standards.[7] Non-directive counselors insisted that, in the wake of such changes, American churchgoers would resist old-fashioned moralizing and avoid pastoral counseling if they thought they were going to get a lecture—no matter how desperate they might be for help.[8] They believed that, in order to entice parishioners to seek ministerial counsel, ministers would have to avoid the kind of counseling that one minister described as a combination of "ordering, forbidding, exhortation and exposition, cheering up and reassurance [and the] use of moral and religious authority."[9] Otherwise, as parish minister Samuel Miller predicted in a 1948 article in the *Journal of Pastoral Care*, they would find themselves perceived by their parishioners as "dominating," possessed of little insight into themselves, and "conventional" in their views.[10] Non-directive counselors were convinced that, in a postwar climate of moral contingency, a directive approach would result in dwindling numbers of parishioners.

Proponents of non-directive counseling framed their argument against directive counseling not only in terms of its professional consequences for ministers but also in terms of its consequences for counselees. They asserted that directive counseling almost always sent the intimidated parishioner scampering from the room and could be a roadblock to spiritual and emotional growth and even, in some cases, a threat to the physical well-being of the counselee. Most non-directive counselors opposed directive counseling because they believed that its methods prevented the counselee from achieving insight, personal growth, and self-realization specifically by undermining the possibility for full self-expression. Counselees unable to express themselves fully would never be able to tap into their inner resources and, hence, resolve their difficulties, or so the argument went. Non-directive counselors insisted that even if the counselor happened to stumble onto the "right" interpretation of the counselee's behavior or the "right" advice, the result would be a counselee who was overly dependent upon the counselor, again blocking self-realization. Encouraging dependence on the counselor violated counselee autonomy and constituted yet another failure in the eyes of non-directive therapists.[11]

Some counselors argued that, at its worst, the directive methodology was dangerous and could have irrevocable consequences for a counselee's life, especially when the counselor attempted to force a particular standard of behavior on a distraught human being. To impress upon his readership the dangers of a directive method, Earl H. Furgeson, parish minister at Harvard-Epworth United Methodist Church and later faculty member at Wesley Theological Seminary in Washington, D.C., described in somewhat melodramatic terms the case of a man who sought counsel from a minister regarding a divorce. He received the proper lecture from his minister about the evils of divorce and the position of the church on the matter. The man then went home, killed his wife, his two children, and himself.[12]

Those pastoral counselors who were least ambivalent about the non-directive method refused to allow the specter of divorce to undermine the principle of counselee autonomy or the importance of self-realization as a counseling goal. While they decried the necessity of divorce, they acknowledged that occasionally it represented the best option. The work of Seward Hiltner illustrates the ideas of those pastoral counselors who persisted in seeing the goal of self-realization as crucial. In a 1952 article titled "The Protestant Approach to the Family" (as elsewhere in his work), Hiltner stated unequivocally that the "personal fulfillment" of the individuals in a family was paramount. As an example, Hiltner pointed to the alcoholic father who provided financially for his family but not emotionally and hinted that divorce might be the only way to protect the members of the family.[13] Hiltner, and those who shared his beliefs, argued that each marriage had to be considered individually, that some of those marriages were redeemable and others were not, and that sometimes divorce was necessary for the parties' emotional growth and at other times divorce had just the opposite effect. The context of the individual situation needed to guide the counselee's decision. This approach suggests the moral flexibility that resulted from placing the emphasis on the individual's needs. In a framework in which individual autonomy, the counselee's inner resources, and self-realization were primary, ministerial authority and the minister's obligation to regulate marriage were deemed less important. The more committed a pastoral counselor was to these Rogerian goals, the less likely he or she would be concerned about ministerial authority. Carroll Wise was another outspoken advocate of the non-directive method. When he described marriage counseling, he insisted that successful pastoral counselors gave their counselees "complete freedom" to arrive at their own solutions even if that meant they chose divorce.[14] Wise seemed little troubled by questions about a ministerial obligation to regulate marriage and discourage divorce.

The Problems of Non-Directive Therapy

The spectrum of views among pastoral counselors regarding non-directive counseling ranged only from those who embraced Rogerian ideals eagerly to those who acknowledged their value but were less enthusiastic. Very few pastoral counselors in the 1950s opposed non-directive counseling completely. The majority of them struggled to find a middle ground on the subject. These counselors argued that the non-directive method was not the only legitimate approach to counseling, and they resisted indiscriminate application of the new method while refusing to dismiss it completely. These doubters were clearly on the defensive—responding to the promoters of the new method rather than drawing the boundaries of the debate.

One difficulty for those who were ambivalent about the new method was the all-or-nothing approach taken by its advocates, the more zealous of whom proposed carrying the "counseling attitude" (by which they meant the principles of the non-directive method) into every aspect of the minister's work. Many ministers believed that applying non-directive theories to every situation would prevent them from offering moral instruction even outside the counseling setting. Even strong supporters of the non-directive approach, like Earl Furgeson, wondered how average parish ministers could reconcile their role as preachers, in which they sought to bring "sinners to conviction and repentance," with their role as counselors, in which they were expected to accept their counselees without judgment.[15] More troubling still were purists among the non-directive pastoral counselors who discouraged introducing religious resources, such as prayer, during the counseling session except at the instigation of the counselee. Protestant ministers saw prayer as their field of expertise and wondered at the legitimacy of a counseling approach that limited its use.

Many doubters of the approach resisted the ban on offering advice in the interest of counselee autonomy. They insisted that directive counselors also respected their counselees' autonomy, that sometimes parishioners came to their ministers seeking advice, and offering advice was not necessarily wrong. Unlike their non-directive counterparts, who feared that counselees would flee if they were given too much advice, these pastoral counselors feared that their parishioners would go elsewhere if their ministers refused to give advice. Moreover, they worried that if those parishioners did go elsewhere, they would get poor-quality advice. They believed that some social science professionals were equating statistically normal behavior with morally acceptable behavior. In a 1948 editorial, *Journal of Pastoral Care* editor Rollin Fairbanks listed works he considered guilty of such an attitude. Among them were Kinsey's report on male sexuality and Robert Frank's book *Personal Counsel*.[16] The concern was that people would look to these secular sources to guide their moral decision making. Specifically, some pastoral counselors worried that non-directive counseling failed to give counselees a distinctively religious perspective on moral issues. Fairbanks, who feared that pastoral counselors had allowed themselves to be influenced too much by secular thinking, wondered, "What, then, is our pastoral canon: happiness or 'adjustment,' or obedience to a revealed theocratic norm of behavior?"[17] Fairbanks's call to adhere to a divinely ordained standard of moral behavior went largely unheeded by advocates of the non-directive approach.

Those ministers who sought to preserve what they saw as their vocational obligation to promote a "theocratic norm of behavior" and simultaneously to meet their new obligation to promote parishioner autonomy recommended a new role for the counseling minister. In a 1947 article in which he explored the relationship between minister and psychiatrist, Fairbanks suggested that the pastoral counselor might serve legitimately and effectively as a "moral expert" rather than a moral authority. For those who echoed this idea, the distinction between moral expert and moral authority was crucial. Fairbanks viewed the moral expert as someone who knew a great deal about what constituted moral behavior and about what the church considered acceptable but did not necessarily give advice in the manner of more directive counselors. In his 1951 book, *The Christian Pastor*, Wayne Oates, a leader in the Southern Baptist pastoral care movement, made a distinction between the two approaches when he suggested that there was a difference between pastoral counselors who "spoke with authority," which meant their opinion was respected because they knew what they were talking about, and the kind of counselor who told people how they ought to live.[18]

In his article, Fairbanks offered an example of what he envisioned as the role of the moral expert. He described the case of a woman who was referred by her psychiatrist to her minister because she insisted that she wanted a divorce but could not obtain one because her church opposed such action. The psychiatrist believed that her therapy could not progress unless she talked to a minister. In the course of two interviews, her minister informed her that in some cases her church did permit divorce. According to Fairbanks, once she understood her church's position, she "discovered" that she was using her church laws to disguise her own ambivalence about seeking a divorce.[19] In Fairbanks's view, the minister had not exercised his moral authority, because he did not tell the woman whether she should divorce. Instead, he acted, in essence, as an interpreter of the church's standards of Christian behavior.

Unlike their non-directive counterparts, these pastoral counselors did not think their parishioners were deserting traditional moral standards as a result of World War II. Rather, they saw parishioners wanting to maintain what they viewed as Christian standards and desiring the aid of their ministers in that task. In another illustration Fairbanks offered, a recently married couple had gone to a psychiatrist because they were unable to consummate their marriage. The psychiatrist told them that the wife was hostile toward men and recommended that the husband seek sexual satisfaction outside of the marriage. Because of their religious beliefs, the young couple deemed such an action unacceptable, and so they approached a minister, assuming that he would provide counsel that would not violate their moral standards. The minister met their expectations and agreed with them that the psychiatrist had erred.[20]

Many of the ministers who took the middle ground to which Fairbanks and Oates gave voice were practicing parish clergy who understood the complexities of everyday existence but who were also fundamentally orthodox in their theology and their understanding of ministerial obligations. They saw divorce as a challenge to God's law and to the historic teachings of the church, but they realized that the realities of life sometimes required a more forgiving and flexible stance. These pastoral counselors relied upon an eclectic mix of counseling methods, and they preferred avoiding the divorce question entirely whenever possible. To that end, they combined the non-directive approach with guidance and advice and advocated a kind of counseling intended to guide and educate so that counselees could then make wise choices for themselves.[21] They assumed that individuals who were thoroughly prepared for marriage would be less likely to divorce—a view shared, not incidentally, by some of their parishioners. In a 1959 issue of *Pastoral Psychology*, the editors published a letter from a disgruntled parishioner who complained bitterly of his pastor's failure to offer premarital counseling and who found himself, as a result, trapped in a marriage that was, he declared, "a tragically poor match."[22]

In their attempt to walk a fine line between ministerial authority and counselees' autonomy, these occupants of the middle ground sometimes resorted to a style of counseling that can only be described as manipulative. In their least subtle approach, pastoral counselors cheerfully maneuvered their counselees into choosing the "correct" course or maintaining the "right" attitude. Lutheran minister Luther Woodward, in a 1950 *Pastoral Psychology* article, suggested that the counselor make "seemingly casual suggestions" or offer "diagnostic" information to the counselee. The aim, of course, was to avoid an openly directive stance even while encouraging the counselee to abide by the standards of the minister or to accept the minister's interpretation of the situation.[23]

Premarital counseling provides an example of a more nuanced approach to the same end. The work of Roy Burkhart, pastor of the First Community Church in Columbus, Ohio, illustrates the technique of pastoral counselors who appreciated the virtues of the non-directive method but were reluctant to abdicate their role as moral arbiter. Burkhart's strategy involved designing a program for his church that helped him to follow members of his congregation in every aspect of their lives.[24] The couple who married at First Community entered a "Mr. and Mrs. Club" immediately. Upon expecting their first child, they enrolled in a Tuesday night fellowship group of expectant parents and participated in group therapy that gave them access to a wide variety of community professionals, including doctors, psychiatrists, and social workers. In addition to classes offered especially for couples, Burkhart's church provided prayer circles, house churches, and personal counseling upon request. All these activities, including Burkhart's Sunday morning sermons, focused on fostering marriage and family life.[25] In this way, Burkhart could support, in principle, the idea that counselees should be free to make their own choices; but because his parishioners were so thoroughly educated to his way of thinking, he could rely on them, in times of marital crisis, to make choices of which he would approve.

Several of the major figures in the pastoral counseling movement shared Burkhart's ideas about the importance of a thorough premarital education for marriage. Paul Johnson, a Methodist seminary professor at Boston University School of Theology, played a prominent role in the growth of clinical pastoral education in the Northeast and helped to found one of the first independent pastoral counseling centers. Johnson advocated "lifelong" preparation for marriage and stressed the important role that parents and the church community played in teaching children how to love, which, in Johnson's view, was the best preparation for marriage.[26] Johnson, like Burkhart, believed that the most effective premarital counseling was preceded by comprehensive premarital education conducted by family, minister, and church community. He insisted that a few hours of premarital counseling just prior to the wedding were insufficient.[27]

Embracing a comprehensive plan of premarital education did not require a wholesale desertion of the non-directive method. In fact, precisely the opposite was true. To consider their premarital counseling a success, most pastoral counselors believed they had to devote some time to allowing the couple to just talk. Most ministers assumed that the gentle and permissive atmosphere created by non-directive methods was most likely to elicit a discussion that would lead a couple to a greater understanding of their own expectations and behavior. Pastoral counselors assumed that this kind of open discussion allowed their counselees to learn some of the skills they would need for a successful marriage. For instance, when Foster Williams described the ideal premarital counseling program, he argued that good premarital counseling (i.e., non-directive) should teach the couple how to talk "freely, without strain" to each other, to face their relationship "realistically," and to develop problem-solving techniques.[28]

Because of the way they framed their discussion of premarital counseling, however, pastoral counselors perhaps hid from themselves the extent to which they were still acting as moral arbiters in the lives of their parishioners. For one thing, they used the terms "premarital counseling" and "premarital education" interchangeably and acted as if the information they provided to prospective couples was entirely neutral. The information that they believed could legitimately be supplied in a premarital interview included everything from instruction with regard to the church's understanding of marriage to sex education.[29] Most pastoral counselors agreed, too, that the minister should at least mention topics such as finances, in-laws, and children.[30]

The clergy hoped that premarital counseling would resolve the apparent contradictions between the demands of a non-directive approach and the more traditional demands of the minister's role. Instead, the same dichotomy that appeared elsewhere occurred in premarital counseling. Pastoral counselors who were more directive in their approach tended to give greater prominence to the minister's role as premarital instructor, and ministers who were more non-directive tended to stress the importance of allowing the couple to "just talk." We see the persistence of this dichotomy especially well illustrated in a 1952 issue of *Pastoral Psychology* in a monthly feature called "The Consultation Clinic," in which subscribers submitted questions for publication in the column and specialists in the field of pastoral counseling attempted to provide answers. The May 1952 issue addressed a letter from a parish minister who was clearly bewildered by the implications of the non-directive method. Congregationalist minister Richard Zoppel of Bridgeport, Connecticut, wrote, "It would be interesting to me to know how your readers or Advisory Board use non-directive counseling in pre-marital talks with young people. . . . So often I find myself 'telling' them what they should do. I am wondering if others find this a problem."[31]

Two of the respondents represent opposite ends of the spectrum. At the time, David Mace was a professor of human relations at Drew University. Mace was British-born and spent his early professional life as a Methodist minister in England before coming to the United States. A substantial portion of Mace's career was devoted to the study of marriage, sex, and family and to counseling in that field. From 1960 to 1967, he was executive director of the American Association of Marriage and Family Therapists, before going on to a position at Wake Forest College as professor of family sociology. He published both academic and popular pieces including contributions to *Women's Home Companion, McCall's Magazine,* and *Reader's Digest.*[32] Russell Becker, ordained in the United Church of Christ and, at the time, a member of the Federated Theological Faculty at University of Chicago, offered contrasting advice. Becker had completed a Ph.D. in theology at University of Chicago in the late 1940s and worked at Carl Rogers's counseling center while completing a dissertation on the implications of Rogerian theory for a "Christian Doctrine of Man." Becker moved from University of Chicago to a position as professor of psychology at Kalamazoo College, in Michigan, and later became minister of pastoral care at Glenview Community Church before going, in the early 1960s, to Yale Divinity School as as associate professor of theology.[33]

Both authors rejected a strictly authoritarian approach to counseling, but Mace stressed the importance of the minister's "knowledge, experience, and conviction," while Becker promoted the importance of the minister's attitude, calling for one of "acceptance, understanding, and warm personal interest." Mace responded to Zoppel's question by suggesting that Rogerian therapy was not always appropriate. Ideal conditions for non-directive counseling were when the counselee approached the therapist with a problem he or she wished to solve. Premarital counseling, in Mace's judgment, did not meet these basic characteristics. For one thing, the minister initiated counseling, and, for another, premarital counseling did not address a specific problem. According to Mace, this freed the counselor to use an entirely different approach—one that stressed instruction and guidance and the minister's role as representative of the church. Mace thought that the minister should begin by making certain that the couple understood the demands of marriage and the nature of Christian marriage. He argued that counselors could offer advice and instruction, if they did so in a manner that was "sweetly reasonable and persuasive" and did not press the minister's views upon a resistant couple.[34] Mace shared with many pastoral counselors a concern that if the minister did not give guidance and instruction, the message of the church would be lost. Worse, non-directive therapy raised the specter of a constantly shifting standard for moral behavior. To ministers like Mace, respecting the parishioner's opinion in a non-directive approach seemed to imply that if the parishioner chose to challenge the church's standards, the minister had no recourse but to agree.[35]

Russell Becker, on the other hand, in answer to the question raised by Zoppel, suggested that the principles of non-directive therapy were sound and useful even when the minister gave guidance or instruction.[36] The central principles of non-directive therapy, according to Becker, required that the counselor maintain a "deep and reverent confidence in the resources for self-responsible living which are providentially available to all" and that the minister view each parishioner as "a person in his own right, [who] has a frame of reference or perspective on things which is uniquely his own."[37] Describing the implications of this perspective for the counseling session, Becker indicated that when he counseled couples who were about to marry, he began by expressing his own belief in the importance of marriage and in the importance of talking about potential trouble spots. He then raised a specific issue such as housing or money handling. Once he had raised the issue, however, he allowed the "locus of responsibility" to shift to the couple. That is, he allowed the counselees to take the discussion in the direction they deemed necessary. Becker did not ignore the importance of the minister's role as guide and advisor. He encouraged counselors to raise questions about "the wife working, money-handling, children, contraceptive information, variation in sexual expectations of the male and female, difference in temperaments, relationships to the in-laws, church relationship, and so on." He saw a greater danger in ministers' attempting to force their view on counselees than in failing to adequately defend the interests of the church or to enforce standards for moral behavior. As a result, he emphasized respect for the counselee's opinion to a greater degree than did counselors such as Mace.[38]

The Pervasiveness of Non-Directive Therapy

While it is perhaps too strong to say that advocates of the non-directive method won the debate, it is not too much to say that the principles they promoted had become firmly embedded in the pastoral counseling theory and practice by the end of the 1950s. Pastoral counseling literature about divorce counseling reveals the nature and extent of the trend. Early in the 1950s, pastoral counselors rarely considered divorce except in the context of discussions about premarital counseling, and then almost always in terms of prevention. By the end of the decade, however, pastoral counselors were devoting more time to discussing divorce counseling than premarital counseling. In those discussions, pastoral counselors seemed to have accepted divorce as a reality and to focus on addressing strategies for meeting the needs of divorced Christians. The entire September 1958 issue of *Pastoral Psychology* explored how to provide effective counseling and a welcoming church environment for those Christians for whom divorce had become an inescapable reality.

More to the point, however, pastoral counselors in their discussion of divorce tended to highlight the importance of that warm and accepting environment upon which non-directive therapists placed such a premium. After nearly a decade in which non-directive therapy had played a role in their thinking, pastoral counselors were little tempted to resort to admonishment or calls for repentance from their counselees, as had John Sutherland Bonnell in the prewar years. Bonnell himself had made a remarkable shift that further underlines the extent to which non-directive principles had made inroads, even among the ministers most likely to cling to what they saw as their historic obligation to be moral arbiters. Bonnell, the pastor at Fifth Avenue Presbyterian Church in New York, who had in his 1938 book *Pastoral Psychiatry* described his enthusiastically directive approach to counseling, wrote an article printed in the September 1958 issue of *Pastoral Psychology* about counseling divorced and divorcing parishioners. The tone was considerably more subdued than his earlier work, perhaps the result of two decades of facing the realities and practicalities of parish life. In any case, Bonnell began by pointing out that saving a marriage was not the only or even the primary objective of the counseling pastor. He then listed what he viewed as the priorities of the counseling pastor, starting with providing the counselee with the opportunity for insight and self-understanding and moving toward reintegrating the parishioner into the life of the church.[39]

The Ethic of Relationships

Parallel to and simultaneously with their ongoing discussion of the limits of autonomy and the minister's role, pastoral counselors had been engaged in another discussion—about ways to mitigate the effects of unlimited autonomy without returning to the moralism of an earlier day. The conversation resulted in a rethinking of the meaning of Christian community. It began, however, as a discussion about the importance of the therapeutic relationship. Initially, Rogerian pastoral counselors had argued that it was the free expression of feelings and emotions that healed counselees. Consequently, they stressed the necessity of using proper technique to elicit the counselee's real feelings. This concentration on method in turn led to the criticism that non-directive counselors cared more about proper technique than about the counselee. In response to their critics, non-directive counselors acknowledged that good technique did not necessarily yield the best results, and they insisted that the counselee could experience healing only when a loving relationship had been established between counselor and counselee.[40] In a 1952 book devoted almost exclusively to a discussion of flaws in technique, Seward Hiltner stated that technique was not enough. The counselor was not, as Hiltner phrased it, a "mere bit of machinery," nor was the counselee. Indeed, Hiltner claimed that counseling was not a process at all but an "interpersonal relationship" in which two people concentrated on "clarifying the feelings and problems of one."[41]

Perhaps the most thorough articulation of the centrality of the therapeutic relationship came from another of the central figures in the growth of pastoral counseling, Carroll Wise.[42] Wise described the relationship between counselor and counselee as the "essential therapeutic element." He explained that, because "faulty" relationships injured people emotionally in the first place, healing could only occur within a healthy relationship to a third person. Wise argued the traditional Rogerian position that counselees had to feel accepted and that once they felt accepted they had to feel free to express their thoughts and feelings without fear of censure. He reasoned further, however, that counselees who had expressed themselves openly could then believe that their counselor viewed them as equals.[43] In Wise's opinion, that experience of the relationship, rather than the simple expression of feelings or even the sense of self-acceptance, served as a "potent curative force in [the counselee's] personality." Wise described the love he believed ought to develop between counselor and counselee as a "profound intangible Christian resource."[44]

Wise saw that love between the counselor and counselee as a Christian resource because counselees who experienced the curative powers of a therapeutic relationship would evaluate themselves in positive terms, and individuals who could see themselves in a positive light would feel a concurrent sense of wholeness between themselves and God. The necessary foundation for experiencing wholeness in a relationship with God, he maintained, was first to experience wholeness in a relationship with a human being.[45] In Wise's opinion, the two experiences were inextricably bound.

According to pastoral counselors, such a construction of the therapeutic relationship had important implications for the parishioner's relationships to other people. Pastoral counselors turned to the ideas of scholar and cultural critic Martin Buber about the "I-Thou" relationship to bolster their argument for the importance of a pastoral therapeutic relationship. Buber believed that troubled relationships resulted when people treated one another as objects rather than as individuals who had their own experiences and needs, that treating people as a means rather than as an end caused broken relationships. Buber called for authentic relationships between individuals and God as a means to authentic relationships between human beings.[46] Pastoral counselors expected that when counselees experienced the I-Thou relationship (being treated as a "subject" or person, not an object or "thing") in counseling, they would be able to apply it to other relationships. They theorized that people who had experienced God's love in a counseling relationship and felt a resultant sense of security could risk loving others and could afford to treat each friend and family member as a person rather than an object, as a "Thou" rather than an "It."

Carroll Wise articulated a similar sentiment. He believed that experiencing love in counseling freed the counselee from those forces that inhibited the "natural" human capacity for love and affection. Once freed, counselees could love not only themselves but others.[47] In a 1952 *Pastoral Psychology* article, Wise clarified what he meant by "love." He did not see love as some vague, "mushy" feeling toward others but as a willingness to take responsibility for the welfare of others. He believed that if parishioners knew what it felt like to be loved, they would, in turn, know how to love. He was convinced that pastoral counselors played a crucial role in teaching counselees what it felt like to be loved.

In this perception, the therapeutic relationship provided a starting point for moving the focus away from the counselee's obligation to behave according to certain standards of behavior and toward the counselee's obligation to other human beings. Albert Outler, a theologian who spent the majority of his career at Southern Methodist University's Perkins School of Theology, coined the term "ethic of relationships" to describe the moral philosophy in which relationships were the standard for behavior.[48] Pastoral counselors used the phrases "ethic of relationships," also called the "ethic of responsibility," and "responsible freedom" interchangeably. "Responsible freedom," the term Seward Hiltner preferred to use, kept the counselee's freedom central while restoring the concept of individual responsibility. Whatever the term, the guiding assumption in the ethic of relationships was that personal freedom had to be circumscribed by the needs of others. For instance, Hiltner, in the context of discussing Christians and sexuality, suggested that freedom was good only to the extent that individuals used their freedom to "expand personal relatedness."[49]

In theory, ministers who subscribed to a theory of responsible freedom were supposed to worry not so much about their parishioners' behavior as about how that behavior affected relationships. The most avid supporters of a non-directive approach feared that espousing the ethic of relationships might be interpreted as an attempt to undermine counselee autonomy and to return to moralism. As a result, they devoted a fair amount of discussion to explaining how the ethic of responsible freedom differed from conventional Christian morality, and they went to great lengths to show that the ethic of relationships was the "true" morality. Proponents of responsible freedom argued that such an ethic could be distinguished from conventional morality because it derived from inside the individual rather than being imposed by society or the church. Seward Hiltner used Paul Tillich's term "theonomy," in which ethics originated from the individual's relationship with God rather than from a law or code that was imposed from the outside. In his 1953 *Sex Ethics and the Kinsey Report*, Hiltner argued that theonomy was the fulfillment of autonomy.[50] Theonomy, according to Hiltner, was the radical doctrine of Christian freedom. Christ freed the individual from the "desires of the flesh" and from the law. And, in an Augustinian twist, Hiltner insisted that people who truly loved God could do as they pleased, because for these people true pleasure came from doing the will of God.[51] Albert Outler, in *Psychotherapy and the Christian Message* (1954), expressed a similar idea in slightly different terms. He argued that when individuals responded "from the heart" to their relationship to God, "justice" became not "an abstract calculation of rights" but a "constant and personal concern for the neighbor's well-doing and well-being."[52]

Episcopal Theological School theologian Joseph Fletcher expressed a similar sentiment when he suggested that the ethic of responsibility differed significantly from the "contractual" nature of conventional morality. Contractual morality assumed the attitude of, as Fletcher phrased it, "If you do something for me, I'll do something for you." In contrast, biblical virtues—faith, hope, and love—required nothing in return and assumed that human beings were an "end" not a "means." True biblical virtues, Fletcher observed, grew as the fruits of a self-determining person capable of I-Thou relationships.[53] Fletcher is probably best known for his writing on bioethics, beginning with *Morals and Medicine* (1954), and for his book on situation ethics published in the 1960s. The ideas for those books took shape in the context of pastoral counselors' discussion of the ethic of relationships. However, Fletcher took those ideas in a direction most pastoral counselors could not and would not go.

Buber's I-Thou construction proved useful also for protecting the autonomy of the counselee. If they viewed their counselees as subjects rather than objects, pastoral counselors would have to insist, as did Fletcher, that every individual should be viewed as a person of integrity with "a moral quality of his own." Hence, counselees had rights: "the right to say 'yes' or 'no' . . . the right to self-determination, the right to be themselves, to choose . . . to be a Thou and not an It, a subject and not an object."[54] Moral decisions, Buberians insisted, should be based upon "self-decision" and "self-choice." This was the familiar language of autonomy. Buber's theology, however, assumed that the reference point for ethical decisions was the needs of others rather than the rights of the individual. In the ethic of relationships, people had a responsibility to care for one another, and love for others was the natural consequence of having learned to love and care for oneself.

In the framework of Buber's ideas, treating other people as objects or as "Its" constituted moral failure or "sin." Seward Hiltner described the nature of sin in Buber's terms by using the example of illicit sexual relations. He suggested that the sin in a man's lusting after a woman was in his failing to view the object of his lust as a whole person. Lust, observed Hiltner, was the sin of "rejection of personal relationship." It involved the "use" of a person as though she were not a child of God.[55] The theory of the ethic of relationships as developed by pastoral counselors restored the possibility of community among autonomous individuals.

In articulating an ethic of relationships, pastoral counselors addressed the heart of the postwar liberal dilemma: How was it possible to maintain a sense of community, obligation, and personal integrity in a society where individual freedom was so important? It is a question that has become more pressing in recent years as American culture has increasingly fragmented. In the early 1950s, however, when pastoral counselors took up this question, they were unlikely to find secular sources echoing their concerns. Most popular discussions of community were framed in terms of fears of homogeneity, which was seen as a threat to individuality, rather than in terms of creating a richer or better community experience. Of course, one of the problems with community was that it was potentially regressive, threatening to limit the free choice of the individual. The ethic of relationships offered a refurbished ideal of relatedness.

Theology, then, rescued pastoral counselors from the worst implications of psychological autonomy. In the trenches of the parish, however, where theology had to be worked out, pastoral counselors had to deal with what their parishioners wanted and needed. Many of those parishioners were women, and issues concerning gender, as much as psychology or theology, shaped the direction of pastoral care and counseling.

CHAPTER SEVEN

Gendered Moral Discourse

We have our individuality in relationship. Let us swallow this
important and prickly fact. Apart from our connexions with other
people, we are barely individuals, we amount, all of us, to next to
nothing. . . . And so with men and women. It is in relationship to
one another that they have their distinct being.

D. H. LAWRENCE, "WE NEED ONE ANOTHER"

O N MAY 5, 1946, A TWENTY-EIGHT-YEAR-OLD woman who suffered
from tuberculosis was hospitalized so that part of her diseased lung
could be removed. At the suggestion of a nurse, a young hospital chaplain went to visit the patient that very day. In one extended interview, the
patient revealed to him details of her past that were too painful and too
intimate to tell anyone else. She told him that from the time she was nine
until she was sixteen, her stepfather had attempted to molest her sexually, that her mother refused to believe her reports of this, and that, as a
result, the relationship between mother and daughter had been damaged permanently. When she was sixteen years old, her stepfather died a
hero's death in a mining accident. She confided that his death had left her
with a heavy and persistent burden of guilt: "I can't say that I'm not glad
he is dead. I think that a person can't feel the way I felt about his death
and still be saved. The Bible says that no murderer can get into the kingdom. And it is as though I killed him myself, because I am glad that he
is dead."[1]

In the same interview, she told the chaplain about her life after she had
left home: that she had divorced her alcoholic husband and then remarried, that despite her newfound happiness she still felt guilty, because she
believed that people who remarried after a divorce committed adultery.
Turning to the chaplain, she asked, "Now what is right? Is it a sin to be
remarried? If I am to be right with God, does that mean I would have to

tear down all that is good and right in my relation to D [her husband]?"[2] Over a period of five days, the young chaplain listened to the woman as she retold her story. Although she compared him to a priest listening to her confession, he did not believe her guilty or in need of absolution. Instead, he suggested that restoring her relationship with her mother might ease some of the distress she felt. He reaffirmed the redemptive value of her new marriage, suggested that God accepted people at their point of need, and reinforced her belief that she had done all she could to redeem her first marriage. On the 9th of May, she died, but she had gained some measure of peace. As did many of his peers in that era, the young chaplain had listened to his counselee without offering advice or moral platitudes and instead respected her ability to come to terms with her situation through her own inner resources and through the redemptive power of healthy relationships.

Stories like this one, which Wayne Oates included in his 1955 book *Anxiety in Christian Experience*, formed the core of much of the writing about pastoral counseling. Many of the first pastoral counselors had acquired their counseling skills and knowledge in clinical pastoral education programs that used case studies as their primary teaching tool, so these counselors were accustomed to describing and analyzing the experiences of their counselees. As a result, when pastoral counselors constructed their ethic of relationships, they based their thinking not only on theological concepts and psychological principles but also on what they were learning in the counseling relationship. They did not necessarily recognize or acknowledge the powerful influence their parishioners' experience had on their counseling theory and practice, but that influence nonetheless helped shape their thinking. The stories also tell those who read them something that pastoral counselors probably never intended to reveal; they illuminate the liberal moral sensibility, including how pastoral counselors' assumptions about gender differences shaped their understanding of men's and women's moral reasoning. When they reported counseling sessions, they tended to emphasize different behavior for women than for men, but, for the most part, without being aware that they were doing so. What emerged, as a result, was a clear (and probably unintentional) impression that women resolved moral dilemmas differently than men did. Revealed was a deeply gendered view of moral discourse in which they portrayed women's moral decisions and reasoning as embedded in a web of relationships and men's moral decisions and reasoning as acted out in the context of principles and standards meant to enhance their own freedom. Many pastoral counselors viewed both the autonomy that they associated with men and the responsibility to relationships that they associated with women as critical to mature moral reasoning.[3]

Placing pastoral counselors' assumptions about gendered moral reasoning in the larger context of the history of liberal moral discourse reveals two important characteristics of the liberal moral sensibility. First, it highlights the extent to which virtue and communitarian values had been feminized and consequently minimized in nineteenth- and twentieth-century liberal moral discourse. Second, it shows the *similarities* between feminine and masculine moral reasoning as well as the differences. In this chapter, I explore pastoral counselors' assumptions about gendered moral discourse, their embrace of a gender-balanced ethic, and how historians have addressed the place of gender in liberal moral discourse. Then I analyze the work of psychologists Lawrence Kohlberg and Carol Gilligan, whose research on adolescent moral development in the 1970s demonstrated much of what pastoral counselors had claimed earlier about men's and women's moral discourse.

Constructing a Gendered Moral Discourse

Several themes and issues occurred repeatedly in the counseling transcripts and case studies in which pastoral counselors depicted women confronting moral dilemmas. First, in almost every case the women were presented as if they worried more about who might be hurt by their decision than about breaking rules or violating principles. Second, they were portrayed as placing the needs of others ahead of their own. Third, women were described as primarily concerned about emotional intimacy and relatedness. Multiple cases were reported of women who chose to protect others even when it meant violating their principles. In most of these cases, women first admitted the validity of their principles and then offered a rationale for violating them. Oates's patient with tuburculosis acknowledged this tension between principles and relationships when she wondered whether, because remarriage after a divorce was a "sin," she needed to sacrifice her good relationship with her second husband in order to be in right relationship with God. In a similar case, Southern Baptist pastoral counselor Samuel Southard described a woman who chose to divorce her husband, even though she believed that divorce was wrong, because he abused their son. She observed, "I took it myself, but couldn't bear to see him hit the boy."[4]

In his 1949 classic on pastoral counseling method, Seward Hiltner included the case of "Sheila," who consulted "Pastor Bendix" after hearing him speak. Visible in Hiltner's recounting of the case is a clear picture of Sheila's moral reasoning. Sheila revealed to Pastor Bendix that she was pregnant and unmarried. She acknowledged that, by the standards of the church, she was guilty, and she expected the minister to be shocked. In her explanation, Sheila indicated that she loved the father of her baby very much and that he had wanted to marry her all along. In her judgment, this mitigated her guilt somewhat. A real problem would arise, she thought, if the pregnancy forced her to drop out of secretarial school. She did not care much about school, but her mother did. Because Sheila's younger brother had tangled with the law, their mother had invested all her hopes in Sheila, who worried that her mother would be upset if she quit school. According to Hiltner's understanding of Sheila, the correct alternative had to be one in which no one else would be hurt.[5]

A decade later, Southern Baptist pastoral counselor James Lyn Elder told the story of "Helen Jacks," for many of the same reasons Hiltner had told Sheila's story. Miss Jacks demonstrated the same sort of moral reasoning as had Sheila. Upon arriving at her pastor's office, Miss Jacks confessed immediately that she had become involved with a married man. She had come to see her pastor because she felt a growing conviction that the affair was wrong. Like Sheila, Miss Jacks gave a nod in the direction of what she perceived as traditional Christian morality and social convention. She admitted a sense of wrongdoing that she attributed to a fear that her family would discover her improprieties and censure her. Most of all, she worried that her relationship with the man might damage his children, that the time her lover spent with her took away from his relationship with them.[6] Both Hiltner and Elder highlighted their counselees' willingness to disregard conventional mores as long as no one was being hurt by their behavior.

These women's stories also illustrate the second recurring theme in pastoral counseling accounts of female moral dilemmas, women placing the needs of others ahead of their own. In fact, Sheila had so completely subordinated her own needs that we never hear her express her own true desires. She indicated that her fiancé wanted her to marry him and that her mother wanted her to finish school, but we never find out what Sheila wanted. It is not clear whether Sheila never said what she really wanted or Hiltner never bothered to mention her desires in his account, but the resulting impression is that everybody's desires but her own mattered to Sheila. In Elder's account of Miss Jacks, on the other hand, Miss Jacks admitted that the thought of ending the relationship frightened her because the affair had given her the first "real happiness" she had experienced in a long time. Ultimately, however, Elder depicted Miss Jacks as subordinating her own needs to what she saw as the more important demands of the relationship between a father and his children.

The stories of Sheila and Miss Jacks represent a familiar scenario in pastoral counseling transcripts—women portrayed in terms of their obligations to other people. They were described as part of an ever-widening circle of responsibility that included husbands, children, mothers, fathers, mothers-in-law and fathers-in-law, friends, fellow parishioners, and professional colleagues. Several transcripts report cases of a female parishioner who went to her minister for counsel about an elderly parent who seemed to be making unreasonable demands. Other stories told of distraught daughters who sought the help of ministers because of "demanding" mothers who would not allow them to do as they wished.[7] There is a multitude of stories in which women sought the aid of a counselor when sons or daughters had problems. In many pastoral counseling accounts, women's sense of obligation extended beyond the immediate family. Included are tales of women who took on the troubles of coworkers as if they were their own. Paul Johnson described a case in which a counselee admitted that she took other people's problems "too seriously." "Mrs. N" was so concerned about a woman that she worked with that her husband said, "Why do you carry everybody's troubles on your shoulders like that? You don't have to do it!" According to Johnson, Mrs. N perceived herself as having no other choice.[8]

Pastoral counseling accounts suggest that, for many women, the guiding principle in the process of choosing right from wrong was what would sustain the relationships involved. The exception to that rule came in the arena of marriage, where the quality of the relationship clearly mattered. Pastoral counselors portrayed emotional intimacy as a central concern of women, the third recurring theme in their depiction of women's moral reasoning. The way pastoral counselors described it, women's desire for emotional intimacy frequently overrode other concerns. Women who opposed divorce in principle frequently reconsidered that position when they found themselves married to men who failed to meet their emotional needs. "Mrs. Keating" told her counselor, "It would be so much easier to make a decision one way or the other if John ran around with women, or got drunk, or did anything except what he does do—just withdraw himself." Even though her husband had committed no traditionally egregious acts, it appeared that Mrs. Keating was on the verge of leaving him, because he did not connect emotionally with her. She seemed to be saying that she wished he would behave in a manner that the church deemed "sinful," then others might agree that she was justified in leaving him. She clearly doubted her own judgment that a man's inability to love was sufficient cause to end a marriage, and yet she stood ready to do precisely that.[9]

The inverse was also true. "Mrs. Reede" had suffered considerably because of her husband's infidelities, and yet she expressed reluctance to end the relationship. In her judgment, the emotional benefits of being in the relationship exceeded the distress caused by his unfaithfulness. Financial security was not her concern; as a professional social worker who earned a good income, she could have afforded to leave him. It appeared, however, that she stayed in the marriage because she believed that her husband was capable of emotional intimacy.[10] For both Mrs. Reede and Mrs. Keating conventional moral standards were subordinated to the need for emotional intimacy. Pastoral counseling case studies and transcripts suggest that, for women, emotional intimacy was the most important feature of marriage, and the partner who failed to sustain emotional intimacy forfeited his or her right to that relationship. Returning to the story of Miss Jacks, who was involved in an affair with a married man, we see the point well illustrated. Miss Jacks indicated to her counselor that she would have been unwilling to engage in an illicit affair if the relationship between her lover and his wife had been good. Because she believed that the relationship between her lover and his wife was poor, she felt justified engaging in what the church viewed as adultery.[11] In essence, Miss Jacks implied that the wife who failed to sustain a relationship forfeited her claim to it.

When pastoral counselors reported on counseling sessions in which the counselee was a man, a whole different emphasis emerged. First, pastoral counselors' accounts of male counselees show them talking more frequently in terms of standards and principles than did their female counterparts. At the same time, the men openly challenged the authority of the minister more frequently than did women. Secondly, pastoral counseling transcripts and case studies focusing on men show them interpreting moral dilemmas in an abstract sense rather than in terms of the specific needs of others. Finally, pastoral counseling depictions of men show them embracing freedom and autonomy as their moral imperative and viewing family and friends as obstacles to good behavior.

Pastoral counseling accounts of men portrayed them as expressing their moral dilemmas in terms of the pressure on themselves to uphold standards in the face of a temptation to engage in immoral behavior, yet they were resistant to ministerial and church authority and inclined to assert their ability to define moral behavior for themselves. Unlike women, who in pastoral counseling reports seemed to simultaneously acknowledge and ignore the demands of the church, the men seemed to think that they had to either accept and adhere to or reject the church's standards. For instance, one young man came to see his minister after cheating on an exam. Even as he wondered aloud what purpose would be served by confessing, he used the counseling session to work up enough nerve to take what he perceived as the right action.[12]

Accounts of male behavior suggested that men did not frame their moral dilemmas in terms of who would be hurt, as women did, but rather in terms of whether they themselves had met their obligations and duties to the principles they believed in. In the case of the unmarried and pregnant Sheila, we see the differences clearly illustrated. Hiltner portrayed Sheila as indifferent to standards of behavior or even whether she had done her duty or met her obligations. Rather, she worried whether her boyfriend loved her and whether her mother would be hurt if she did not finish school. When we compare that to Hiltner's account of the case of "Mr. Bolton," a married man caught in an extramarital affair with his secretary, we see some important differences. Mr. Bolton excused his behavior on the grounds that he did not "love" the woman with whom he was involved nor did she love him and that he had sought sex outside of marriage because his relationship with his wife was poor. In other words, Mr. Bolton believed that he had not promised his lover anything he could not deliver and that his contract to his wife was no longer binding because of the poor quality of the relationship.[13] As Hiltner told the story, Mr. Bolton was convinced that he had met all his obligations and, hence, did not need to feel guilty. He never asked himself whether Mrs. Bolton had been hurt by his behavior—at least Hiltner never indicated that he did. Instead, Hiltner's report showed a man whose obligations, rather than the needs of others, provided the reference point for self-evaluation of his behavior.

While pastoral counselors did not attribute to men the same concern for others *needs* that they found in women, neither did they suggest that men were oblivious to the *opinions* of other people. Specifically, they repeatedly returned to the male concern about what other people thought of them and about the extent to which they measured up to some unspoken standard. But the men's concept of "other people" was always expressed in the abstract, never as specific people, such as their wife, their minister, or coworkers but rather the community in an abstract sense. For instance, "George Thomas" told his minister that he wanted people to admire and respect him, but he worried that they neither liked him nor accepted him. He wanted to be a "leader" but feared he was not. Mr. Thomas cared about what other people thought of him, but he did not describe his difficulties in terms of specific people.[14]

Similarly, pastoral counselors rarely described their male counselees as expressing the same sense of responsibility for other people that they saw women displaying. By contrast with the records about female counselees, there are almost no accounts of men approaching their ministers about refractory sons or daughters or domineering parents. An occasional minister mentioned a male parishioner who came for marital counseling, but almost all of these cases involved men who hoped the minister would correct a difficult wife who was not fulfilling her duty. The case of "Mr. Hay" is a good example. According to Mr. Hay, the trouble would begin at breakfast when his wife would announce that she wanted to eat out that night because she would be too tired to cook after returning home from work. Inevitably, an argument would ensue between them. Mr. Hay had already approached another minister for advice, and by the time he consulted the second, he and his wife were barely speaking. The then-desperate Mr. Hay asked the minister for a book that he and his wife could read together that would explain to her how "a wife ought to look after her husband."[15]

Unlike the records for female counselees, in which women are portrayed as considering emotional intimacy to be crucial to marriage, transcripts for male counselees rarely describe a man as desirous of greater emotional closeness with his wife. In fact, in many accounts, the men seem to have viewed relationships as secondary or unavoidable difficulties. Their language implies that they wanted their personal problems solved not as a road to greater intimacy with other people, but as a road to freedom. If we take pastoral counseling case reports at face value, we would have to conclude that a significant number of white, male Protestants in the mid-twentieth century shared the assumption that if they could only fix or solve their relationship problems, they would be free.

The case of young "Tom Jarrett," who came to see his minister regarding a career problem, illustrates this phenomenon.[16] Tom's father wanted him to graduate from high school and join the family insurance business. Tom, however, wanted to go to college to become a journalist. He was certain his father would be angry if he told him about this desire. In the end, Tom decided that, while he disliked upsetting his father, he really had to do whatever he thought was best for himself. He drew an analogy between his own life and the life of Christ, "You know, I just thought of it—isn't this something of the same problem Christ faced when he started preaching? His family wasn't too sold on the idea, were they?" Tom noted that Christ did what he thought was best, and ultimately his family acknowledged the validity of his choice. Like many other male parishioners portrayed in pastoral counseling accounts, Tom based his choices on what he perceived as "right" and believed it was his duty to take the consequences of living by principle—even if that meant the destruction of a relationship.[17]

While male counselees seemed to present their problems as vocational or religious, that did not mean that they did not talk about relationships. In fact, sometimes going to their minister about a religious problem or career question allowed them to admit that what they really needed to talk about was their relationships. For instance, Mr. Awkright told his minister that a passage from the Psalms that he had been reading had left him feeling "depressed." His wife had recently died, but when he sought counsel it was not about feelings of grief, at least not explicitly. By the end of the session, however, based on their discussion of the scripture passage, Mr. Awkright had realized that, although he had been praying for God to help him with his grief over his wife, he had refused to turn to his friends for emotional support. He admitted that he had isolated himself from his friends and needed to restore those relationships if he expected to recover.[18] Carroll Wise recounted the story of a young man whose story has interesting parallels to that of Mr. Awkright. This man approached his minister for counseling because the sermon of the previous Sunday had "disturbed" him. He decided shortly after counseling had commenced that the sermon had distressed him so much because it unconsciously reminded him of his father, with whom he had a difficult and unresolved relationship. While this man came to his pastor with an ostensibly religious problem, he then turned his attention to a damaged relationship.[19]

The ethic of relationships that pastoral counselors articulated in the mid-1950s mirrored the concerns that they regularly attributed to their female counselees. Concern about the needs and feelings of others when making decisions and about fostering emotional intimacy fit perfectly with pastoral counselors' talk about the "I-Thou" relationship and "true" Christian morality. In contrast, the approach to moral reasoning that they attributed to their male counselees is more compatible with pastoral counselors' ideas about autonomy and self-realization.

The Consequences for Counseling Practice

By 1965, the words associated with the concept of responsible freedom had become thoroughly embedded in the language used by pastoral counselors to analyze cases. The assumptions that accompanied an ethic of relationships had surprising consequences for the practice of pastoral counseling. Pastoral counselors clearly wanted their parishioners to find a balance between personal autonomy and their obligations to relationships, between taking care of themselves and taking care of others. The gendered subtext persisted. To their male counselees they emphasized learning the skills of relationships and taking responsibility for those relationships. To their female counselees they stressed the importance of self-fulfillment and caring for themselves.

In 1959 Wayne Oates published a collection of articles intended for the novice pastoral counselor. The collection included an account by Samuel Southard of a divorced business woman who had gone to see her minister about a problem. A man had proposed to her, and she wondered if it would be right to marry him, citing concern about her son from the previous marriage. Probing a bit further, the minister discovered that the woman felt guilty about the way her marriage had ended, because she had been forced to commit her husband to a psychiatric hospital. He had abused both her and her son; fearing that her husband was damaging their son emotionally, she had divorced him. She commented, "I've often thought that love would have cured him. But I *did* love him." She added, "Also, I was near the breaking point. I wasn't any help to my boy or to myself."[20] She believed that, in light of the advice of doctors, she had done the best she could. Nevertheless, she felt guilty because she had been taught that divorce was wrong.

The minister responded by validating her choice to do what was best for her son and herself. He acknowledged that she had an obligation as a wife to her husband but indicated that she also had an obligation as a mother to her son and as a person to herself. He reaffirmed that she had done all she could to make the situation right. The pastor suggested that her moral choices needed to be made with reference both to her own needs and to those of others. Further, he suggested that the son had needs that outweighed those of the husband. She had to make her moral choices based on a hierarchy of personal needs that included her own.[21]

Pastoral counselors who took a less directive stance than did the Southern Baptist minister just described shared the same commitment to helping their counselees balance the claims of relationships with self-interest. The Mrs. Reede mentioned above, concerned about her marriage to an unfaithful husband, was a participant in a 1961 study by Seward Hiltner and Lowell Colston. Early in counseling she expressed fear that the emotional distress caused by her cheating husband made her unproductive in her professional life. As counseling progressed, she reported that the emotions precipitated by her unfaithful husband were no longer undermining her productivity. She commented that she felt "creative and alive" at work. As to her husband, Mrs. Reede concluded that she could leave him or stay with him, but she no longer felt compelled in her choices by emotions over which she had no control.[22] She decided to stay.

Hiltner and Colston saw Mrs. Reede's counseling as a thoroughgoing success, but not because she stayed with her husband. They acknowledged that some might take issue with her choice. They posited two imaginary critics, one who thought that she should leave her husband because he was "systematically unfaithful" and the other that she should stay with him because marriage was undertaken "for better or worse." Hiltner and Colston rejected both perspectives as forms of "coercion." When they made that comment, they were, in classic non-directive form, reaffirming Mrs. Reede's right to make her own choices.[23] At the same time, they suggested that Mrs. Reede's love for her husband and reluctance to leave him were legitimate guiding principles in the decision-making process. They believed that she should not have to sacrifice her relationship with her husband in order to consider herself free. Rather, they believed that as a result of counseling in which Mrs. Reede learned about herself and her husband, she could return to the marriage fully cognizant of the difficulties awaiting her. She could as legitimately leave him, fully aware of the consequences of her choice both for him and for herself. Hiltner observed, "Personal freedom of this responsible kind is, we believe, the essence of personal morality."[24] By responsible freedom, Hiltner and Colston meant that nothing could coerce or compel Mrs. Reede because she understood both her own and her husband's actions. More importantly, Hiltner and Colston believed that if she truly understood her own motives, Mrs. Reede could legitimately choose to stay with her husband. Clearly, Hiltner and Colston were still deeply committed to protecting the autonomy of counselees, especially women, but they had restructured the way they talked about decisions to accommodate their counselees' concern about relationships.[25]

When pastoral counselors encouraged their female counselees to explore freedom, autonomy, and self-fulfillment and, at the same time, affirmed their choice to maintain any ties they viewed as legitimate, they provided both a context for women to rethink their relationships to others and a tool for women to extend the control they exercised over their lives. One example illustrates the way in which counseling provided a context in which women could resolve the tension between independence and dependence. "Sharon Troy," a counselee in the Hiltner/Colston study, went to see a counselor because she could not decide whether to marry her fiancé. While Miss Troy did not want to sacrifice herself on the altar of others, she was reluctant to end a relationship even if it was a threat to her independence. She perceived herself as rigid, inflexible, and unimaginative. She perceived her boyfriend as possessing the opposite qualities and feared that if she married him, she would become too dependent on him. In her second interview, she explained to the counselor: "For a long time I've disliked the idea of getting married because I don't like the role of a housewife and a mother. I thought of it as very dull, boring, and routine. And I thought that not having enough ambition or stimulation within myself—once I got married and was further handicapped by the responsibilities of a wife and a mother—I would just fall into this shapeless mass that knew no more than to hang up the wash and cook supper."[26] Her boyfriend agreed that she should not be dependent on him. In the course of counseling, Miss Troy focused on being less passive, not on whether to marry. As she felt more confident and less passive, she felt less frightened of the marriage role. After counseling, her worries no longer gave her a "terrified feeling—you know, that everything is just rolling in on me and if I make the step in the wrong direction about something the bottom's going to fall out." Ultimately, Miss Troy married, but she did so having reconciled her doubts. In one of her last interviews, she described herself this way: "I'm still riding along feeling very good, very capable and confident. . . . I can't feel that I'm cured. I don't even know what I would be cured of. But it's just that I have a different feeling than I had when I first started."[27] She entered the marriage only when she no longer saw it as a risk to her self and her independence.

Coming at gendered moral behavior from both sides, pastoral counselors nodded approvingly when women made choices that promoted their own independence, and they made a concerted effort to convince men to take on responsibility for emotional intimacy in relationships. In the early literature, pastoral counselors who were concerned about protecting the autonomy of the counselee sometimes recommended that the pastor approach erring male parishioners gingerly. For instance, in his 1949 book *Pastoral Counseling*, Seward Hiltner, when he recounted the story of Mr. Bolton (the man involved in an affair with his secretary), suggested a number of strategies for approaching men such as Bolton without scaring them away.[28] But Hiltner grew increasingly intolerant of men who abdicated their emotional responsibilities to wives and family. And he was not alone.

In May of 1955, the editor of *Pastoral Psychology* published portions of an encounter between a minister and an erring parishioner. A married man named Mr. Van was caught by his minister, Pastor Mix, in the church gymnasium in a compromising position with the church secretary. Mr. Van apparently felt no remorse for his behavior and became very defensive when confronted by Pastor Mix. All of the pastoral counseling specialists who commented on the case criticized Pastor Mix severely for adopting an attitude toward Mr. Van that they considered condemning and judgmental. They insisted that Mr. Van should not be browbeaten for his sin, even though each of the commentators stressed that Mr. Van had clearly erred. The responding howl from rank-and-file ministers was deafening. In subsequent letters to the editor, subscribers wrote to express their dismay over Mr. Van's behavior and lack of remorse. They criticized Mr. Van because they feared he had caused his wife and children great damage and emotional pain, and they criticized Pastor Mix because they believed he had failed to meet his responsibilities to Mr. Van's family.[29] This story illustrates the growing resistance among pastoral counselors to a kind of counseling that allowed the celebration of human freedom and autonomy to be interpreted as license to abrogate responsibilities to spouse and children.

Liberal Moral Discourse, Gender, and History

Placing pastoral counselors' gendering of moral discourse in historical context helps to explain the history of liberal moral discourse and the liberal moral sensibility. In some ways it would appear that pastoral counselors were doing something new and different by incorporating the feminine perspective into their moral theory, but they were also simply part of a larger trend in liberal moral discourse in which virtue, community, and relationships were considered the purview of women. Historians of liberalism have largely ignored this reality and instead have wondered plaintively whatever happened to virtue ethics and communitarian values in liberal thought.

Historian James Kloppenberg, in a series of essays collected in a single volume entitled *The Virtues of Liberalism* (1998), argues that the concept of civic virtue associated with early republican values all but disappeared in the nineteenth century as a result of the liberal emphasis on free market and individual rights. He documents various attempts to restore virtue or a sense of obligation to community to liberal discourse. Kloppenberg contends, for instance, that early in the twentieth century both Max Weber and John Dewey had called for something akin to an ethic of responsibility. Weber actually used the phrase "ethic of responsibility," arguing that individuals should choose values based on "accumulated social experience" and should commit to accepting "responsibility for consequences of [their] actions."[30] Similarly, Dewey talked in terms of the "moral democracy" that proceeds upon "free and open communication," "reciprocal relationships and the sort of interaction that contributes to mutual benefit."[31] Both of these social scientists clearly believed that individual freedom had to be worked out in a social context. For the most part, however, liberal thinkers worried that too much emphasis on obligation to community risked association with socialism or communism rather than democracy. Most historians have been unable to account sufficiently for the failure of liberal thinkers to articulate an adequate theory of community and virtue ethics. ("Virtue ethics" refers to the practice of defining ethical behavior in terms of virtuous acts, as did Aristotle and Thomas Aquinas.)[32]

Many historians of liberalism have failed to recognize the extent to which, by the time Dewey and Weber were writing, virtue had become feminized as a result of the rise of industrial capitalism. This lack of recognition has resulted, in large part, from a failure to address sufficiently the scholarship of women's history. In contrast, most women's historians are thoroughly familiar with the narrative in which virtue was channeled into the domestic sphere, privatized, and sexualized, so that women could be granted the responsibility of rearing children who would then become virtuous citizens.[33] The feminization of virtue, however, meant that virtue was also devalued. When women brought virtue to the public sphere in the middle to late nineteenth century, under the guise of social housekeeping, they had to defend its worth. Men who joined them in settlement house work or in the spreading of the Social Gospel had to defend their masculinity—the call for a "muscular" Christianity in this period was not an accident. Women's social activism in the Progressive era was driven to a large extent by the assumptions that women were more virtuous sexually than men and more caring, particularly for other women and for children.[34] At no point did liberal theorists attempt to reintroduce or redefine virtue or commitment to community as masculine characteristics. That was, however, precisely what pastoral counselors were doing. Or rather, it was the practical implication of implementing a theory of responsible freedom that balanced the demands of autonomy and relationships. In this approach, morally mature men were expected to accept their responsibility to relationships, and women were expected to face the abyss of freedom and claim the privileges of autonomy.

Gilligan, Kohlberg, and the Persistence of Gendered Moral Reasoning

To fully understand what happened to the liberal moral discourse in the twentieth century, it is necessary to jump over the 1950s, when theologians wrote most extensively about the ethic of relationships, to examine the study of liberal moral reasoning in the 1960s and 1970s. Two preeminent educational psychologists explored moral reasoning among children and adolescents in order to understand the principles that guided moral decision making. Their research ended up highlighting the same kind of gendered moral discourse so evident in the pastoral counseling literature. Lawrence Kohlberg and Carol Gilligan made groundbreaking contributions to psychological research on moral development. Gilligan's work in the early 1980s brought attention to the issue of gender in a way that no one had before.[35] Kohlberg, writing in the 1960s and 1970s, argued, based on studies of male populations only, that human beings progress through stages in their moral development, and in the highest stage manifest a kind of moral autonomy in which they make moral decisions guided entirely by "the universal principles of justice, of the reciprocity and equality of human rights, and of respect for the dignity of human beings as individuals."[36] In the 1970s and early 1980s, Gilligan, a colleague of Kohlberg's at Harvard, conducted a series of studies based entirely on female populations and concluded that women tended to make moral choices based not on abstract principles of justice (what Gilligan called a "justice ethic") but on an "ethic of care," in which women asked not what was right but who would get hurt.[37]

Gilligan criticized Kolhberg's moral development scale, arguing that it was gender-biased and that, measured on Kohlberg's scale, women never reached moral maturity. In fact, on Kohlberg's scale, many women never moved beyond stage three. This was the heart of the argument between Kohlberg and Gilligan. As Gilligan saw it, because women used a different set of moral principles to guide their moral reasoning, they scored lower on Kohlberg's scale. Kohlberg insisted that the justice principle was the best and most universal way to approach moral dilemmas. In other words, his theory was prescriptive as well as descriptive. Gilligan was not interested in prescribing a universal ethic. In her view, however, Kohlberg had set up an essentially male model of moral reasoning, claimed it to be universal, and then judged women as wanting.

Gilligan and Kohlberg emphasized the differences in their theories, but the two theories actually had much in common. Both assumed that the morally mature individual was guided by principles rather than rules. Kohlberg highlighted the principles of justice, fairness, and human rights, while Gilligan highlighted the principles of compassion and responsibility to relationships. Both saw the best principles as being "self-chosen" (Kohlberg's word) rather than imposed by some authority, whether social or religious. Hence, both assumed that their subjects engaged in a kind of moral reasoning that was more sophisticated than just following the rules out of a fear of punishment. Finally, both recognized that most individuals felt some sort of obligation to other people. For Kohlberg that obligation was met by pursuing justice and equal rights for all people. For the women in Gilligan's study, that obligation was met by taking care of others and by maintaining a network of relationships. In both cases, the morally mature individual cared about others, the one in more abstract terms (justice), the other in more personal and specific terms (compassion or care).

In the Kohlberg and Gilligan studies, we hear the same language that had permeated pastoral counselors' discussions of moral decision making a decade earlier. While both Kohlberg and Gilligan acknowledged that individuals, whether male or female, frequently moved back and forth between the two moral perspectives, neither saw an integration of the two perspectives as necessary or valuable. Neither Kohlberg nor Gilligan embraced a gender-balanced ethic in quite the way pastoral counselors did. It is difficult, moreover, to draw a straight historical line from pastoral counselors to Kohlberg and Gilligan. There is no evidence that either psychologist considered works of pastoral theology as part of their research, and neither saw religion as critical to moral reasoning, even though for many Americans religion had historically played an integral role in their understanding of right and wrong.[38] Neither psychologist documented the religious affiliation of their subjects. Gilligan simply did not include religion as part of her research, and for Kohlberg, those whose moral reasoning was based on the authority of religious tradition or religious revelation scored lower on his scale of moral development. Both might have discovered a significant connection between religion and moral reasoning had they explored that question. This may be especially true of Gilligan, for her subjects included young women who attended the elite women's undergraduate institutions of the northeast and had a high likelihood of having been exposed to mainline or liberal Protestant thinking.

Even though no evidentiary line runs from the work of pastoral counselors in the 1950s to the work of Kohlberg in the 1960s and 1970s and Gilligan in the 1980s, there is still a connecting thread: they share a common language in which ethics are based on principles rather than on rules and in which we find the very heart of the postwar liberal moral sensibility. The story of "Mrs. Wright" from the Colston and Hiltner study of the late 1950s is an example of the kind of moral reasoning pastoral counselors celebrated—that of an autonomous individual in relationship with others who made choices based on general principles of justice and caring. Mrs. Wright initially presented her problem as a difficulty between herself and a seventeen-year-old niece who had come to live with her recently. When she started to talk, however, she spent a significant portion of the session describing a legalistic Christian upbringing that had led her to believe in the superiority of a Christian way of life and its principles. As a result of her upbringing, she believed she had a duty to uphold and enforce certain values such as the "family structure in our society."[39] As counseling progressed, Mrs. Wright abandoned her narrowly construed code of behavior, and she came to recognize the possibility of more than one correct way to behave. At one point, she commented that the Bible confused her, because "to be a Christian I'm supposed to believe that this is divine, that this comes straight from God. And it bothers me that I seem to see that there is a life that can be just as good without it, provided we would know how to structure it. . . . as a child I was taught—that this [the Bible] is the absolute, this is it. There is no deviation. And then to discover that this is not true, that there are other ways that are equally as good and could be better . . . ."[40]

Mrs. Wright found the possibility of relative truth to be "shattering." At a crucial moment in the counseling, however, she decided to find out why she felt the need to define things "as black and white."[41] She began by discarding the need for absolutes in her dealings with her niece and resolved "genuinely to listen." She entered her niece's "frame of reference" and concluded that she did not need to stand in judgment. Mrs. Wright commented that she was able to refrain from judging her niece because she had come to understand that "many of us do things at a certain time [because we have been] influenced by our life experience."[42] Near the close of her counseling experience, Mrs. Wright indicated that she believed she had reached a new level in her relationship to God— something akin to a conversion experience, despite the fact that she had previously doubted the reality of others' conversion experiences. Her restored relationship to God did not lead her back to a legalistic religion. In fact, in a follow-up interview, she told her counselor that she wanted "to understand the process of being related to God, without demanding that some authority line this out for her."[43] Mrs. Wright was able to envision a relationship to God and to other people that allowed both herself and the people she loved to be free.

Pastoral counselors came closer than anyone to a moral language that was gender-balanced. In their writing they brought together the two sides of the liberal moral tradition, the feminine ethic of community and relatedness and the masculine ethic of autonomy and self-realization, but without returning to the kind of moralism they so distrusted. Neither the liberal thinkers who preceded them nor those since have come as close to envisioning such an ethic. But the moment was fleeting. The history of liberal moral discourse demonstrates the power of individual autonomy as icon and symbol. So it was, perhaps, to be expected that when pastoral counselors took up the banner of women's equality, they did so almost entirely in the traditional masculine language of rights, challenging the domestic ideal and arguing for the rights of women to autonomy and self-realization.

CHAPTER EIGHT

The Language of Rights and the Challenge to the Domestic Ideal

If I were permitted to express a bold suggestion, I would say that
psychotherapy and the experiences of pastoral counseling have
helped to reintroduce the female element, so conspicuously lacking
in most Protestantism, into the idea of God.

—PAUL TILLICH, "THE IMPACT OF PASTORAL

PSYCHOLOGY ON THEOLOGICAL THOUGHT," 1960

IT WAS A CURIOUS TURN to the story of pastoral counseling and the
liberal moral sensibility. After working very hard to articulate an ethic
of responsibility that would be responsive to the interests and desires of
their female parishioners, pastoral counselors failed to see the implications of that ethic for their politics. Very early in the 1950s they took up
the banner of women's causes—much earlier than one might expect given
the common historical narrative of women's experience in the 1950s. But
when they took up that banner and made their case for women's equality,
they did so almost exclusively in the language of autonomy and freedom,
which was, of course, the masculine language of rights. How did it happen that pastoral counselors ended up making their argument in classical
liberal terms rather than by taking ideas about an ethic of relationships
into the political arena? Once again pastoral counselors' discussion of
love, marriage, sex, and divorce provides a fruitful beginning point for
examining their views. The discussion in pastoral counseling literature
suggests that certain familiar presuppositions underlay the rejection of
the domestic ideal and the negative assumptions about women that typically accompanied it. Specifically, an examination of the postwar discussions in pastoral counseling suggests that ideas about autonomy and self-
realization, about the significance of the female perspective, and about

the part of culture and society in shaping human personality worked together to broaden pastoral counselors' understanding of women's role and their nature and to lay the groundwork for an argument for women's rights.

Rethinking Gender

Pastoral counselors' views on Rogerian therapy and on autonomy and self-realization seemed to correlate with they way they viewed gender roles. Apparently, ministers who could entertain the possibility that authority vested in the individual rather than in themselves as clergy or in the church as institution could also accept with greater equanimity their parishioners' choice to live outside the parameters of socially prescribed roles. For instance, Seward Hiltner, who by the early 1950s was on the faculty at Princeton's Presbyterian seminary and serving as editorial consultant for *Pastoral Psychology*, was one of the most outspoken advocates of both Rogers's non-directive therapy and women's equality. Hiltner opened the May 1953 issue of the journal, which happened to be devoted entirely to the "women's role," with a scathing editorial in which he complained bitterly about the circumstances that prevented women from making a "contribution" to the field of pastoral psychology. Hiltner condemned the "club" or fraternity mentality among ministers that made them reluctant to welcome female clergy; he criticized denominations that refused to place women in the parish as ministers; he objected to the assumption that a woman who married would voluntarily end her professional career; and he urged women to take matters into their own hands by pursuing advanced degrees.[1]

The work of Ralph Eckert, a marriage counselor from Riverside, California, and an occasional contributor to *Pastoral Psychology*, illustrates the connection between counselors' methods and their views on gender roles, but from the other end of the spectrum. Eckert claimed he had tried non-directive marriage counseling but found it did not work, by which he meant that sometimes his counselees chose to divorce. Eckert assumed that divorce was always wrong and that the counselor knew what was best for the counselee. As a result, he had turned to something he called "action-oriented counseling." His example of one case where he succeeded in preserving a marriage by this method reinforces the impression that ministers who were most rigid about their own authority were most rigid in their understanding of gender roles. In a June 1961 article, Eckert reported with satisfaction the case of a "brilliant professional woman" who, given a "clue" from Eckert that it was her own "dominating" nature that was destroying her marriage, decided to give up her job, become pregnant, and take on the duties of a minister's wife in order to bolster her husband's sagging ego and thereby save her marriage. Not only did Eckert intervene, but he did so in a way intended to make certain that the woman accepted her wifely duties.

The pastoral counselors who were most ambivalent about their own authority and about parishioner autonomy tended to be the most ambivalent about gender roles. Roy Burkhart, pastor of the First Community Church in Columbus, Ohio, whose comprehensive counseling and premarital education program illustrated so well the doubts some pastoral counselors had regarding non-directive counseling, showed evidence of similar ambivalence about gender roles. A first reading of Burkhart's interpretation of the Bernreuter Personality Inventory, which he recommended as a tool for marriage counseling, suggests that he had very clear ideas about what constituted acceptable behavior for men and women.[2] For instance, he argued that if the "boy" were self-sufficient, dominant, and extroverted, problems in the marriage would be minimal. Conversely, he suggested that if the "girl" were dominant and self-sufficient, she would have to change if she wished to help her husband fulfill his role in the marriage. Burkhart argued that the minister should assist the girl "to adapt herself creatively to the boy's recessive nature."[3] He apparently assumed a world in which the man played the role of breadwinner and leader and the woman the role of homemaker and follower. He even remarked at one point, "When a girl marries a boy, she marries his life work and all that goes with it," implying, of course, that she had no life work of her own.[4]

The evidence seems to suggest that Burkhart promoted a particular domestic ideal that subordinated women's needs to men's, but a second interpretation is possible. He seemed to be very clear about his beliefs: "If either one is dependent it is better that it be the wife."[5] The wording of this sentence is crucial, however. It implies the possibility of a marriage in which neither party is dependent. Later in the same article, Burkhart indicated that it was not only possible, but preferable. He observed,

"Some men like a dependent wife, a 'clinging vine,' but the man who is most secure prefers a woman who is an individual in her own right, who can stand on her own two feet and take her place by his side."[6] Burkhart's disdain for any man who preferred a dependent wife is evident. He implied that a mature man would choose a wife he could treat as an equal. Of course, he failed to explore what it would mean for church and society if women truly were treated as equals. His ideas are significant because they are representative of much of the literature of the late 1940s and very early 1950s. On the one hand, Burkhart clearly spoke in stereotypical terms about men's and women's roles. On the other hand, he harbored suspicions that those stereotypes were inadequate, damaging, and at odds with what he believed about the importance of self-realization and personal autonomy.

Some evidence, then, suggests that ministers who thought individual autonomy was important were less given to gender stereotyping. It was not true of all; believing in freedom and autonomy did not have to yield a change in attitudes toward women. After all, two centuries earlier, Enlightenment thinkers had, for the most part, excluded women from their vision of political and economic freedom (as had the founders of the United States) by arguing that women were different from men and hence not entitled to the same rights. Two other ingredients were necessary before general talk about autonomy by pastoral counselors could be transformed into specific talk about autonomy for women. First, these counselors had to be convinced that women's opinions and perspective deserved respect and attention. Second, they had to believe that women had a right to autonomy in the same way that men did. And, indeed, both of these phenomena did occur.

As noted earlier, most pastoral counselors did take the concerns of their female parishioners seriously and moved those concerns to the center of pastoral counseling theory and practice. It took the addition of the third and final element, however, to transform the narrative and change the way some pastoral counselors thought and talked about women. Postwar pastoral counselors became convinced that social, cultural, and environmental factors shaped human personality more than biology did. This view was consistent with much that they encountered in the work of the neo-Freudians like Horney and Fromm who challenged the biological determinism of Freud. Having first rejected the assumption that biology was destiny, pastoral counselors were more willing to accept as a corollary that gender roles were culturally rather than biologically derived. When pastoral counselors accepted the idea that women's nature was shaped by more than their ability to bear children, they found themselves less able to justify the practice of gender stereotyping.

These three factors—an ongoing commitment to individual autonomy, a respect for the power of their female constituency, and a growing conviction that culture rather than biology determined human personality—provided the ground for some pastoral counselors to dismantle their narrow understanding of women. As a result, early in the 1950s, a subtext started to appear in pastoral counseling literature, in which some pastoral counselors and their secular colleagues began to reject the practice of limiting women to a domestic life, to view their female parishioners in broader and more positive terms—so much so that women became heroines of the counseling narrative—and, eventually, to make explicit arguments for women's social, political, and economic equality. Throughout the 1950s, those pastoral counselors who supported a broader understanding of women's role and nature did so almost always by voicing some combination of the three elements—the right to autonomy, the importance of the female perspective, and the influence of cultural forces on human personality—in defense of their position. To the extent that they stressed these concepts, they subverted the older domestic ideal and moved beyond negative and rigid depictions of women.

A Critique of the Domestic Ideal

Plenty of evidence suggests that the domestic ideal of male breadwinner and stay-at-home wife and mother persisted in pastoral counseling literature. Of course, pastoral counselors did not use the term "domestic ideal," but, in the early days of both *Pastoral Psychology* and the *Journal of Pastoral Care*, more than one contributor stressed a woman's accepting her wifely role as crucial to marital success. For instance, in 1950 the editor of *Pastoral Psychology* published a fictional account in which the female characters represented all of men's worst nightmares. In this scenario, lovable Jim was seduced by working woman Patsy. The story implied that Jim never would have succumbed to temptation if his wife, Mimi, had not been so caught up in her "club work" or, for that matter, if Patsy had not been there in the workplace to tempt him. The subtext suggested that when women accepted and performed their domestic role they saved themselves and their husbands from the scourge of adultery. Around the same time, psychiatrist Erich Lindemann published his analysis of marital discord in the *Journal of Pastoral Care*. Lindemann assumed that a successful marriage required that the wife give up career and education to follow her husband wherever he went. Lindemann confessed sympathy for the plight of the married woman. Although he acknowledged that sex roles were culturally rather than biologically derived, he accepted those roles and reinforced them, even going so far as to suggest that children were essential to any "real" marriage.[7]

Among pastoral counselors, however, the sort of one-dimensional understanding of women's nature that we see in the story of Jim and Patsy and in Lindemann's understanding of marriage roles was actually relatively rare. The counternarrative, with its challenge to domesticity, emerged early in the decade and gained strength as it progressed. In its inaugural year, 1950, *Pastoral Psychology* raised the issue of women's domestic duties by publishing a reprint of Margaret Mead's article "What Is Happening to the American Family?" Not surprisingly, Mead's work did not challenge explicitly the division of labor into spheres in which women were homemakers and men were breadwinners. She did, however, suggest that conditions of modern life made homemaking less rewarding than it had ever been before and that it was unfair to expect women to take on that role without asking them whether they wanted to. Mead appealed to her reader's sense of justice by pointing out that the United States was a country that prided itself on freedom of choice in matters of vocation. To underline her point, she asked the reader to imagine a man answering the question, "What are you going to do?" by saying he wanted to be a lawyer unless he got married, in which case he would have to live on a farm for the good of the children. Mead argued that most married women would choose to stay home if they had a choice, but that they did not want society to take their choice for granted. She suggested a two-fold solution. First, married women should not be expected to devote themselves wholly to homemaking, nor should they be stigmatized for choosing to work outside the home. Second, fathers should be more involved in parenting. In one sense, neither suggestion appears especially radical, but both challenged the very heart of capitalist culture—the father as breadwinner. The vision of mother as wage earner, with her own money, her own interests, and her own life, and father willingly active in the domestic sphere countered the dominant paradigm.[8]

Three years later, in the same 1953 issue in which Seward Hiltner condemned attempts to prevent women's entry into the professions, psychoanalyst Clara Thompson challenged the domestic ideal in much more systematic and explicit terms. She understood, as would Betty Friedan a decade later, that Freud's biological determinism provided the essential framework for the domestic ideal.[9] Thompson challenged Freud's idea that "a woman is a castrated man, and [that] most of her troubles arise from resentment of this," arguing that the theory of penis envy left the therapist with nothing to do but "to make the woman reconciled to her fate and to make her willing to accept certain compensations for her lack of manly assets," eventually accepting "a child as a compensation for the lack of a penis."[10] In reality, Thompson argued, women's sense of inferiority resulted not from their lack of penises (i.e., from their biological make-up) but from living in a society that denied them equality of opportunity socially, politically, and economically while simultaneously devaluing the only work open to them—that of mother and homemaker. Thompson suggested that "a feeling of futility," common among middle-class and formerly professional women who were confined exclusively to the home, resulted from limitation of their choices, and she insisted that assumptions about women's biological nature drove them to assume a role that society valued little. The solution, in Thompson's view, was to reject the idea that biology was destiny and offer women real choices with regard to family and career. She posited that American women should not have to sacrifice either one.

Mead, Hiltner, and Thompson all drew upon the same pool of assumptions when they argued that women should not be limited to a domestic life. For one thing, all three assumed that women should have autonomy, especially with regard to their choice of career. Hiltner, more than Mead or Thompson, advanced the idea that women had a special contribution to make and that society was diminished when it limited women's contribution to the domestic sphere. Thompson, to a greater extent than Hiltner or Mead, assumed that gender roles were shaped by culture and openly challenged the assumption that a woman's ability to bear children destined her for life at home.

Obviously, none of these authors offered a clear, coherent, and systematic challenge to the domestic ideal. All saw the home as uniquely feminine and assumed that women did not want to lose their right to stay home if they so chose. And yet their work did have a subversive effect on that ideal. The subversive nature of the counternarrative can only be understood if the work of individuals is located in the context of the larger conversation about human personality that was going on at the time. Margaret Mead's work is a good example of this. Mead has never been the darling of American feminism, in part because of the thorough drubbing she took at the hands of Betty Friedan in a chapter of *The Feminine Mystique* entitled "The Functional Freeze and Margaret Mead." Friedan argued convincingly that Mead's work, specifically her book *Male and Female*, served to reinforce the part of the feminine mystique that assumed that biology was destiny. But Friedan also conceded that Mead's work could be read with quite a different interpretation: "She might have passed on to the popular culture a truly revolutionary vision of women finally free to realize their full capabilities. . . . She had such a vision more than once."[11] Friedan concluded that Mead's challenge to the domestic ideal was less important than her contribution to the feminine mystique. Friedan was right on one level: every time Mead slipped toward biological determinism, she encouraged a very narrow understanding of women's nature. But Mead's work and life, taken as a whole and located within the context of a larger discussion with other social scientists about personal autonomy, come to mean something else. This was true, too, of pastoral counselors and their colleagues in sociology, psychology, and anthropology. No matter what their intention or the detours they might have taken, wherever they maintained a commitment to personal autonomy, a respect for individual women, and an allegiance to the idea that human personality was culturally derived, they moved—albeit erratically, tortuously, and frequently oblivious of the destination—toward a vision of women's equality and away from a vision of female domestic bliss.

Heroines of the Narrative

The middle of the decade saw not only a challenge to the domestic ideal but an increasing reluctance to portray women in negative or stereotypical terms. The earliest contributors to pastoral counseling journals tended to describe women in terms of pathology or weakness. In one 1950 fictional drama (similar to the story of Jim and Patsy), husband Allan accused wife Ginny of being "neurotic," "childlike," and "illogical." The play was printed with commentary by two well-known pastoral counselors and a psychiatrist, none of whom came to Ginny's defense, of course.[12] In fact, the tone of some the literature in those early years bordered occasionally on hostility toward women. Perhaps the most obvious examples of this can be found in the work of Russell Dicks, who in 1936 had coauthored *The Art of Ministering to the Sick* with Richard Cabot. Dicks also wrote a book about pastoral care and counseling in 1944 that remained popular in clinical pastoral education programs throughout the 1940s. The latter book went through several editions, but the earliest gives a good indication of Dicks's mind-set. At one point or another, Dicks trotted out almost every stereotype associated with women at the time. He peopled his works with clinging, neurotic, obsessive women who manipulated their environment through their physical appearance and unplanned pregnancies. Dicks even attributed the "thousands" of problems experienced by "psychoneurotics" discharged from military service to emotionally immature mothers, an attitude consistent, by the way, with much of the popular secular literature.[13]

Dicks's work also provides one of the best examples of the way in which images of women were eventually transformed. Because *Pastoral Work and Personal Counseling* went through several revisions, we can see very clearly the change in Dicks's language and in his attitudes toward women. For instance, in the first edition of his book, Dicks described his encounter with a young woman who had decided to divorce her husband in order to pursue a career as a writer. Exploring the nature of the woman's relationship to her husband, Dicks asked her about the couple's sexual relations. He came close to accusing her of being sexually manipulative. When she indicated that the sexual relationship in her marriage had never been satisfactory, Dicks charged her with being frigid intentionally in an attempt to force her husband to divorce her. In the

1949 revised edition, Dicks modified his analysis and admitted that he had been "too judgmental." This assessment of his own behavior implies that he was beginning to question his authority to judge the woman. His analysis of her decision to leave her husband shows the same significant shift. In the first edition, Dicks declared that the young woman had made a mistake in leaving her husband before her children were grown, implying that her obligations as a mother should have taken precedence over her desire for a career. In the 1949 version, he repeated his opinion but added the comment "or maybe it wasn't a mistake. Who can say!" So, as early as 1949, some pastoral counselors were challenging the assumption that a woman's responsibilities as a mother should determine all her choices.[14] By the 1963 revised edition, Dicks had removed the example from the book and, in addition, had edited from his book almost all of the language that described women in terms of pathology.[15]

Dicks's transformation was the most thoroughgoing among leaders in the movement, but others underwent similar changes. Even Seward Hiltner began to revise his views. For example, in his 1950 book *The Counselor in Counseling*, Hiltner tended to see domineering, controlling mothers as the culprit in a remarkable number of the case studies he described. By the 1959 publication of his book *The Christian Shepherd*, however, Hiltner was celebrating women's special talents for psychology and urging ministers to tap the hidden resources of the "wise," middle-aged women of their congregations.[16]

While no one called explicitly for an end to gender stereotyping, evidence suggests that there was at least a growing awareness that women were being portrayed in narrow and unfair terms. *Journal of Pastoral Care* editor Rollin Fairbanks wrote most of the book reviews for the journal in the 1950s, and his concerns emerge clearly in his reviews. In a 1956 review of Kinsey's report on female sexuality, Fairbanks lamented the fact that Kinsey's report on male sexuality had been given so much more attention and publicity than the report on female sexuality. Even though he wished that most Americans had paid more attention to Kinsey's findings about women, he believed that the report would have been even more valuable if women themselves had done the research and writing. In a departure from much of the literature, Fairbanks recognized the urgent need for women to have the right to speak for themselves: "Only when more women speak and write for their own sex will we have a balanced and accurate body of knowledge about one of the most important of human relationships."[17] In a 1958 review of Frank Caprio's *The Sexually Adequate Female*, Fairbanks was sharply critical of the book because of its "regrettable masculine bias which infers that woman's primary raison d'etre is to gratify the sexual needs of her man."[18] Fairbanks's reviews suggested not only that he respected women and their point of view but that he believed they had a right to an autonomous existence. Once again, familiar themes repeated themselves: the importance of personal autonomy, the value of women's perspective, and the conviction that a woman's biology should not control her destiny.

Simultaneously, two remarkable changes occurred that probably were linked to pastoral counselors' willingness to see women in a more positive and less narrowly defined role. Most obviously, women began to appear as heroines in counseling narratives rather than as villains. Most surprisingly, male pastoral counselors began to talk about embracing for themselves characteristics they defined as "feminine." At the very least, pastoral counseling literature evidenced, by the late 1950s and early 1960s, considerably more sympathy for women's concerns than it had immediately after World War II.

In the 1930s and 1940s, narratives of counseling encounters portrayed women as the source of family, marital, and social troubles and suggested that in order for those troubles to be resolved, the woman would have to change. In the early 1940s, in his book *Getting Down to Cases*, Charles Holman described intervening on behalf of his male counselee "John," who was willing to do anything to save his marriage except cook and clean. Holman saw this as a reasonable position and encouraged "Maybelle," a woman with a master of fine arts degree, to rescue the marriage by accepting the domestic responsibilities of cooking and housekeeping.[19] In his book *Religion and Health* around the same time, Seward Hiltner attributed the problems of his client "Mary" to a domineering and overprotective mother and discounted the effect that a frequently absent and emotionally distant father might have had on her emotional development.[20] In general, not only did men fare better in prewar counseling narratives than did women, they also, apparently, fared better in the counseling session. Initially, pastoral counselors seemed to approach their male parishioners with greater deference and a greater desire to avoid offending them. For instance, both Seward Hiltner and Wayne Oates included in their early works about counseling accounts of philandering husbands and accompanied those accounts with guidance for approaching these men in a way that would not intimidate them or scare them away.[21]

By the late 1950s and early 1960s, however, the counseling narratives that pastoral counselors constructed more often depicted men either as problems or as peripheral figures, while women were portrayed as central characters, more highly skilled at solving emotional problems than were their male counterparts. For instance, Seward Hiltner characterized "Mr. Coe" as a drug-addicted, mother-dependent, unreliable person who had so little insight into himself and his behavior "as to be frightening."[22] "Mrs. Coe," on the other hand, who had faced her inner demons and taken control of her life by leaving her abusive husband, appeared as the heroine. Elsewhere, Hiltner stated explicitly that women were just better at understanding themselves psychologically than were men.[23] Knox Kreutzer's 1959 account of "Marion Farad's" psychological and spiritual transformation treated Farad's husband as a peripheral figure—weak, ineffectual, and almost irrelevant.[24] And in 1961 when Lowell Colston and Seward Hiltner published the results of their research comparing counseling in a religious setting with that in a secular venue, they drew a group portrait of strong women taking steps to change their own lives by ending abusive relationships, confronting philandering husbands, and acknowledging their own autonomy.[25]

Much of the work that saw women as heroines and men as problems did not necessarily challenge the domestic ideal, but it did avoid the pitfall of portraying women as pathological and as a problem to be solved. Instead, men became the problem. Irving Sands, a medical doctor and occasional contributor to the *Journal of Pastoral Care*, illustrated this point in his discussion of men's and women's roles. Sands deplored the male practice of escaping to the golf course on Saturday mornings while the female was forced to stay home and care for the children. He objected, likewise, to the "weekend automobile culture" and encouraged, instead, family activities centered in the home. Sands saw the home as symbolically female and the car as symbolically male, and he wanted the feminine to triumph.[26] Similarly, when the editors of *Pastoral Psychology* in 1955 published the account of a man who had committed adultery and suggested that the minister should not be too judgmental of this man, a general howl arose from rank-and-file pastoral counselors, who believed that the adulterous man needed to be held accountable for behavior that had probably damaged his wife and family emotionally. None of the objectors suggested that he needed to be handled gingerly or with undue respect in order to retain him as a member of the church. The claim of wife and family to justice seemed to be a higher priority.[27]

More telling than pastoral counselors' willingness to portray women sympathetically was their interest in embracing the feminine for themselves. Some went so far as to acknowledge that the new model of ministry that pastoral counselors had promoted was based on a feminine model of being. In one of his books on pastoral care, *The Christian Shepherd* (1959), Seward Hiltner pointed out the importance of feminine characteristics for ministers, especially pastoral counselors. He began by explaining that masculinity and femininity were culturally constructed. The feminine, according to Hiltner, was linked in American culture to introspection, tenderness, humility, and "subjective knowledge."[28] He defined subjective knowledge as the "process by which we attempt to [enter] understandingly [into] the frame of reference of another person." The masculine, on the other hand, was linked in American culture to a life of action rather than introspection and to objective or scientific knowledge rather than intuitive knowledge. In Hiltner's judgment, feminine subjectivity was essential as a counterbalance to masculine objectivity, especially for the Christian minister engaged in pastoral counseling. Objective knowledge alone was inadequate, because it could not provide the "tender and solicitous concern that is always the essence of Christian shepherding."[29] Possessing objective or masculine knowledge only constituted a real danger for counselors. According to Hiltner, ministers who concentrated only on the objective circumstances of their parishioners' lives and not on how people felt about their own lives risked misusing the knowledge they had gained. The result, Hiltner believed, would be an attempt by the minister at social control—an effort to remake the counselee in the image of the counselor. Essentially, Hiltner was arguing that the so-called feminine characteristics were necessary to a noncoercive ministry that would respect the inner resources of the counselee. James Ashbrook, a Baptist minister and seminary professor, in a 1963 *Pastoral Psychology* article, went even further. Drawing on the work of Margaret Mead and Carl Jung, he argued that people could not be fully human unless they recognized and accepted both the masculine and the feminine within themselves. The implications were clear: the man who was afraid to face and cultivate the "feminine" qualities within himself risked failing to live up to his full potential.[30]

The Argument for Women's Equality

Ashbrook was part of a new generation of scholars who had begun to address the question of women's equality more systematically. These young men (and they were still mostly men, despite all the talk about women), who came to study with Wayne Oates in Louisville or Seward Hiltner in Chicago or Paul Johnson in Boston, understood more completely than did their teachers the implications of the psychological, sociological, and anthropological theories they encountered in the classroom. In particular, as they confronted the assumption that gender characteristics were culturally rather than biologically derived, one question became unavoidable: if biology was not destiny, how could American society justify the limitations it placed upon women? In response, this generation of pastoral counselors argued, in classic liberal terms, for the expansion of women's roles. That is, they argued for the right of the individual female to equality of opportunity.

In a series of *Pastoral Psychology* articles edited by Southern Baptist minister and pastoral counselor, Samuel Southard, pastoral counselors examined the implications for both men and women of changing sex roles. (It is important to note that all of the contributors used the term "sex roles" in a manner very much akin to current use of the term "gender roles.") Three of the articles in that series articulated, in unequivocal terms, something that looked very much like the liberal feminist position. William Douglas, an assistant professor at Boston University School of Theology, Lester Kirkendall, a family life professor at Oregon State University, and James Ashbrook all addressed questions about women's equality in very similar terms.[31] Douglas's article, published in June of 1961, illustrates the basic arguments very well. Douglas launched his attack against sex discrimination at the same point as Betty Friedan would when she wrote *The Feminine Mystique*. He attacked the domestic ideal that limited women to domestic pursuits, subordinated them to men's authority, and left them feeling bored, frustrated, and stymied at every turn. He accused Protestant denominations of participating in the construction of that ideal and of sending the message that "woman as wife and mother deserves respect and protection, but woman as leader, authority, and spokesman defies both Nature and Scripture."[32]

Douglas recognized that the domestic ideal was grounded in assumptions about women's biological nature. Hence, to the argument that women's biology suited them for nothing but childbearing, Douglas responded by arguing that sex differences were "more a matter of culture than biology."[33] Citing the work of Margaret Mead and Carl Jung, Douglas argued that masculinity and femininity were culturally defined points on a continuum rather than rigid, biologically determined categories, observing that "even if we *could* [his emphasis] distinguish the 'feminine temperament,' we would find some who were biologically male with 'more' of it than some who were biologically female."[34]

Because his audience was largely Christian, Douglas offered a fascinating parallel argument about the Bible. Douglas seemed to be arguing that in the same way that sex characteristics were cultural artifacts, the apparently clear biblical mandate for silencing and subordinating women was also a cultural artifact that should be discarded. Douglas suggested that the mandate was less clear if the text were read with more careful attention paid to "the intention of Scripture as a whole," as well as to the cultural and practical context of specific passages. For instance, he argued that the Bible, as a whole, encouraged equality of the sexes and the "*mutual*" (his emphasis) submission of men and women. He pointed to specific scripture that seemed to support this, such as Genesis 1:27, in which the creation story is told in a way that suggests that "God's image" included both male and female. Douglas concluded his argument by recalling the practice of the early church, in which women exercised considerable control before the authority of men became institutionalized in the Roman Catholic Church. Douglas challenged his readers to consider this evidence and with it the possibility that the church, when it called for the subordination of women, might have misinterpreted scripture and "falsely deified the patriarchal perspective of Middle Eastern culture."[35]

Implicit in Douglas's argument was the assumption that if women were not biologically different (other than the ability to bear children), then no argument could be made for their inherent inferiority. By impli-

cation, he seemed to be arguing that if women were not inherently inferior and the Bible did not specifically limit their sphere of contribution,
then they ought to be offered the same opportunities as were men. Based
on these assumptions, Douglas argued that the "proper goal" for women
should be "equality of *opportunity*" (his emphasis) granted upon the
basis of individual merit. Hence, the basic challenge facing the church, as
he saw it, was, "Can we see women as individuals with talents and dedication, rather than as members of a class automatically assumed to be
inferior and defective?"[36]

As the capstone of his argument, Douglas offered the possibility of a
sort of communal self-realization, maintaining that only if the church
gave women equal standing would it realize "the potential inherent in
the body of Christ."[37] In fact, he contended that "God's purposes" could
not be completely accomplished without granting women equal status.
Douglas implied that if the church expected to succeed and to do the
work of God in the twentieth century, it would have to stop limiting
women to a domestic life and offer its female constituency access to
power and authority.[38] Like those who had preceded him, Douglas
appealed to the importance of individual autonomy, the power of culture in shaping human personality, and value of incorporating a female
perspective.

Not all pastoral counselors embraced the argument for women's
equality or attempted to abandon gender stereotyping. In a 1957 *Pastoral Psychology* article on Christian love in the home, Vere Loper articulated the middle-class, domestic ideal with a vengeance.[39] Loper spent
his entire career in the parish ministry, primarily serving as minister of
the First Congregational Church in Berkeley, California. His discussion
of gender roles and the wife's obligation to her husband illustrates the
potentially regressive nature of an ethic of relationships and hints at why
pastoral counselors interested in women's equality made their argument
in terms of women's rights rather than in terms of human obligation to
relationships. In his article, Loper began by recommending that the wife
be "careful of her appearance knowing that her husband takes joy in her
attractiveness," reminding his readers that "Bibles keep homes together,
but red dresses have their importance." He urged the wife not to save the
disciplining of children for her husband in the evening but instead to

make the "homecoming a source of joy to her husband." Loper instructed the husband, for his part, to express his love with material gifts—a new dress or a "jewel" on the occasion of the wife giving birth, for instance. Loper also reminded the husband to be aware that his wife sometimes needed relief from home and children. He did not, of course, propose that the husband should dry dishes, run the vacuum, or bathe the children. Instead, he encouraged the husband to be "sensitive and responsive" to his wife's "social needs, [and] her desire for friends," by which he apparently meant that husbands should take their wives out to dinner occasionally. In Loper's understanding of the relationship between the sexes, women were primarily wives, mothers, and ornaments to their husbands. Men were breadwinners and providers. More important, Loper explicitly rejected the primacy of individual rights. He argued that Christian partners should not think about their relationship in terms of "rights and privileges" but in terms of making their "loved one happy."[40] In this we see the problems with an ethic of relationships illustrated. If a woman's moral decisions were to be made with regard to the needs of her husband, and he expected the house to be vacuumed, the children well disciplined, dinner ready, and his wife attractively dressed each day when he arrived home from work, maintaining autonomy and pursuing self-realization became difficult for women.

It is important not to overstate the feminist quality of pastoral counseling literature. Clara Thompson, William Douglas, and James Ashbrook, who led the way among pastoral counselors in thinking about women's equality, all felt they had to make excuses for early feminists, whom they portrayed as strident, hostile, and too eager to be like men. Psychologist Ruth Hartley, in her 1961 contribution to the series on masculinity and femininity, went even further, devoting most of her article to reassuring men that women did not really want equality or power. Presumably because she believed that many men felt threatened by the impending changes, Hartley concluded by suggesting that changes in sex roles could best be facilitated by strengthening the egos of male children.[41] Another contributor to the series, psychologist Aaron Rutledge, insisted that the fewer the distinctions between male and female, the greater the possibility of healthy relationships. At the same time, however, he peopled his discussion of sex roles with references to nagging, possessive, overbearing women.[42] It must also be noted that pastoral counselors did little in the real world to advance the cause of women's equality. It is one thing to articulate an argument for women's equality on paper and another to take up political action or even to welcome women as equals into professional ranks. Women did enter seminaries and theology and divinity schools in ever increasing numbers beginning in the mid-1960s. In disproportionate numbers, women who entered seminary chose to study pastoral care and counseling, but they continued to find themselves blocked from the pulpit and from professional advancement.

Despite their best intentions to envision equality for women, pastoral counselors found themselves falling prey to many of the stereotypes of the day. And while they flirted with a truly original theory of women's equality, they were never able to fully articulate that theory. As with liberal thinkers before them, pastoral counselors clung to a highly individualistic understanding of freedom and equality, one that celebrated feminine characteristics but took shape around the notion that those characteristics were culturally constructed and that the best argument for women's equality had to be based on an argument for women's *right* to that equality, as well as on the fundamental sameness of women and men. In a liberal political framework, that was the only argument that made sense. Arguing for difference repeatedly opened the door to treating women differently and as less than men. And yet, the expanded notion of what it meant to be human that came from pastoral counselors' discussion of gender roles continued to percolate through the literature as they began to rethink their own role in the parish in the early to middle 1960s.

CHAPTER NINE

Resurrection of the Shepherd

Psychotherapy is definitely antimoralistic. It avoids commandments because it knows that neurotics cannot be healed by moral
judgments and moral demands. The only help is to accept him
who is unacceptable, to create a communion with him, a sphere of
participation in a new reality. Psychotherapy must be a therapy of
grace or it cannot be therapy at all. There are striking analogies
between the recent methods of mental healing and the traditional
ways of personal salvation. But there is also one basic difference.
Psychotherapy can liberate from a special difficulty, religion shows
to him who is liberated and has to decide about the meaning and
aim of his existence a final way. This difference is decisive for the
independence as well as the cooperation of religion and
psychotherapy.

—PAUL TILLICH, *MINISTRY AND MEDICINE*

IN HUMAN RELATIONS (1955)

GENDER PERSISTED AS an important and formative theme in pastoral
counseling. In the early 1960s, pastoral counselors began to rethink
their theological heritage and reclaim theological language after nearly
two decades of relying more heavily on psychological language. The role
they chose for themselves was caregivers, a choice that owed much to
what they saw as the feminine perspective and led them to talk more
often of pastoral care than pastoral counseling. In one sense they had
never abandoned their theological roots, and so talking about returning
to or revisiting their theological origins is perhaps not entirely accurate.
But a concern for reframing their psychological discoveries in theological
terms certainly moved to the forefront in the late 1950s. Their renewed
interest in the theological framework derived in part from the explicitly
religious concerns expressed by a constituency that was made up primar-

ily of people who saw themselves as parishioners rather than counselees. The religious concerns of their parishioners prompted pastoral counselors to reexamine the meaning of redemption, the importance of Christian community (*koinonia*), and their own role as ministers, most of them still stubbornly refusing to return to their prewar understanding of ministerial authority. Their choice to emphasize the importance of relationships and caregiving helped them to avoid some of the pitfalls secular counselors encountered in the early and middle 1970s, when the latter came under fire from cultural critics such as Christopher Lasch and Robert Bellah for promoting a fundamentally selfish world view. It also moved clergy who self-identified first as pastoral counselors toward greater specialization and professionalization, and this shift made counseling less a task of every parish minister and more a task of specialists who practiced in a context other than the parish.

The Importance of the Parishioner

Part of the impulse to reconsider the role of the minister came from parishioners. While ministers' worries about counselee autonomy, questions about the efficacy of non-directive therapy, and the articulation of an ethic of relationships dominated the professional discussion, parishioners' worries about explicitly religious issues ran as a subtext through that discussion. Parishioners viewed their ministers as mediators of their relationship with God, and they wanted pastors who served as representatives of a transcendent God. While many counselees accepted the idea that they ought to make their own moral choices without the intervention of a minister, sometimes—when they had broken their own ideal of themselves and somehow violated their relationship with others or with God—they wanted absolution. In other words, even though most of the parishioners whom pastoral counselors described in their case studies seemed not to believe that absolute standards for right and wrong existed, they still sometimes did things about which they felt guilty. Then they counted on the relationship between minister and God. For instance, one young woman called her minister because she felt desperate and suicidal. When she met with the minister, she told him that she was pregnant and did not know whether the baby's father was her husband or her neighbor. She said to the minister, "My sister keeps telling me that it wasn't adultery, but it is, it is!" According to pastoral counselor Samuel Southard, when she had confessed and felt accepted by her minister, she felt free to examine the disappointments in marriage that had led her to have an affair with her neighbor.[1] For parishioners who had violated their own principles or ideals, the minister could serve as a mediator of forgiveness. So, for example, in response to one parishioner's doubts about herself, the pastoral counselor emphasized the idea that God offered forgiveness. She responded, "I feel so much better talking to you about this. I never saw it in that light. I mean, that I didn't have all the responsibility and that God does forgive people when they are divorced."[2]

Parishioners seemed also to value their minister's ability to perform the common religious rituals. Many came to their minister wanting and expecting the special rituals, beliefs, and traditions of the church to be applied to their situation. One woman requested communion from her pastor because she was about to travel many miles to undergo surgery from which she feared she would not recover.[3] Others came to talk about becoming church members or about having their children baptized. Sometimes those decisions were accompanied by considerable anxiety, and the person hoped the minister would offer some comfort, as in the case of the young woman who wanted to change her membership from the Roman Catholic Church to a Protestant denomination.[4]

Many parishioners responded positively when they received comfort and support. "Pastor Sellers" made a routine visit to the "Olsen" family, who had joined his church the previous Sunday. During his visit, he discovered that, because of layoffs at the company where he worked, Mr. Olsen was working night shift after years of having a day shift job. He also discovered that Mr. Olsen's elderly mother lived with them and that her presence created great tension for Mrs. Olsen. Although Pastor Sellers visited without telephoning first and caught Mrs. Olsen in the middle of baking and with her house in disarray, she expressed what appeared to be genuine gratitude for his visit and the prayer he offered at the end of the visit. The transcript of the visit indicated that when the minister finished praying, Mrs. Olsen was "wiping tears from her eyes." She then said to him, "Thank you so much for coming today, Brother Sellers. I can't tell you how much it has helped to talk with you." Mrs. Olsen welcomed both the visit and the prayer and considered herself much helped by these traditional functions of the minister.[5]

Most importantly and most frequently, parishioners looked to ministers to help them understand their problems and to reaffirm the validity of the religious experience. One pastor went to visit a hospitalized parishioner who was trying to decide whether to undergo surgery. The patient told the pastor that her faith had sustained her through many difficulties. He replied, "It is wonderful to hear this. It has not been easy for you to achieve it." In response she smiled and said, "You preachers really do know what we are up against, don't you?" She then went on to tell him of her doubts and fears and how ultimately her relationship to both God and family had been strengthened through her illness. She clearly valued the pastor because he was a minister. With him, she expected to be able to frame the discussion of her suffering in religious terms, and she appreciated his understanding.[6]

Counselees were especially grateful for the ministrations of clergy when they confronted grief, suffering, or death. Religion provided the framework for interpreting these situations. Parishioners tolerated considerable ineptitude on the part of their minister if he at least fulfilled his traditional functions. "Pastor Barton" rolled into his visit to the newly widowed "Mrs. Henshaw" like a runaway train.[7] He warned her immediately of the dangers of "self-pity," suggested that her feelings of grief were wrong, and finished by urging her to live her own life and to avoid lavishing too much motherly love on her newly fatherless son. Mrs. Henshaw was patient with Pastor Barton, despite his lack of ministerial finesse. She teased Pastor Barton a bit and suggested that in his honesty with her he operated with a "sharp knife." He replied that truth was a "two-edged sword." She admitted that she saw the dangers of self-pity, did not want to run her son's life, and had no doubts about her ability to live her own life or to support herself financially. But then she very gently corrected Mr. Barton's assumption that grief was something that could simply be laid aside. She said, "But it is going to take awhile to get over the feeling of emptiness." Mr. Barton's bulldozer style did not deter Mrs. Henshaw from attempting to interpret her grief to him. She expected him to offer her some framework in which she could understand what had happened to her. She said, "Tell me Mr. Barton, why do I sometimes get confused about the meaning of life? The day seems complete—the year—so much of nature seems complete. A caterpillar completes one cycle and becomes a butterfly. But we never seem to complete anything. . . . Why isn't the cycle of our lives ever complete?"

Mrs. Henshaw assumed that God placed people on earth to complete a task, and she could not understand why God would take them from earth before they had completed their task. She assumed that religion could provide her with answers and that Pastor Barton, no matter how he went about it, was the most likely person to interpret her situation for her. Before he left, Mrs. Henshaw thanked him for the "dignity" with which he had conducted the funeral service for her husband. She also told him, "You have given me new purpose and courage." She again teased him a little and said that should she find herself "weakening," she would call him and he could return with his "sword." Again, the minister served as a representative of traditional religious values: Mrs. Henshaw expected Pastor Barton to reaffirm the traditional Christian promise that death had meaning.[8]

Pastoral Identity

The persistence of their parishioners' desire that their ministers fulfill a traditional role prompted pastoral counselors to think about pastoral identity. Particularly in the late 1950s and early 1960s, some pastoral counselors began to wonder if, in their zeal to identify with the therapeutic culture, they had sold their birthright for psychological pottage.[9] Some wondered, in fact, whether their enthusiasm for Rogerian and Freudian principles had resulted in a pastoral counseling theory that was not especially Christian. There had always been dissenters from the Rogerian model, as well as dire warnings about the dangers of appropriating Freudian theory.[10] Increasingly, however, doubts had crept into the minds of even the most ardently Rogerian and the most loyally Freudian pastoral counselors. Critics continued their attack on secular theories at two familiar points—Freud's theory of the unconscious and Rogers's theory of human nature. The most vitriolic of the criticisms of Freudian theory in this period came not from a pastoral counselor but from a psychologist. O. Hobart Mowrer's book on the "crisis" in psychiatry and religion provoked widespread discussion among pastoral counselors.

Mowrer's work was part of a larger antipsychiatry movement that involved an intraprofessional critique of psychiatric theory and practice and that focused particularly on another familiar point of contention—the etiology of mental illness.

Psychologists and psychiatrists in the movement, among them, in addition to Mowrer, Thomas Szasz and William Glasser, were critical of the medical model of psychiatric diagnosis. Szasz called it the "myth of mental illness" in his 1960 book of the same title. Those who took this view rejected the notion that mental illness was an illness in the first place and argued instead that emotional distress resulted from irresponsible or immoral behavior, an unwillingness to "face reality," in William Glasser's terms, and the failure to make restitution. In his book, *The Crisis in Psychiatry and Religion* (1961), Mowrer argued that, especially in the case of neurosis, thinking in terms of sin rather than sickness was the "lesser of two evils."[11] Mowrer was especially critical of pastoral counselors for having embraced not just the medical model but specifically Freudian psychoanalysis. This combination, in Mowrer's view, was deadly, because it relieved the counselee of any responsibility for his or her behavior. According to Mowrer, sometimes the counselee really was guilty of something and needed to confess and make restitution in order to regain emotional equilibrium. These counselees, in Mowrer's view, would get no relief from the kind of counseling offered by either pastoral counselors or psychoanalysts.[12]

Mowrer argued that Freud's theory of unconscious drives allowed individuals to avoid taking responsibility for their behavior. He insisted that sin caused mental illness, and he called for a return to a style of counseling that looked remarkably like that of John Sutherland Bonnell in the prewar years. While most of Mowrer's ideas were met with skepticism and viewed by many pastoral counselors as too extreme, the questions Mowrer raised were taken seriously and debated thoroughly.[13] Most pastoral counselors expressed reluctance to join Mowrer in saying that the unconscious life was irrelevant and that all mental illness resulted from poor moral choices. Many pastoral counselors thought that in some cases, at least, Freud was right: the behavior of some people resulted from something other than conscious choice.[14] Mowrer included Rogerian therapy under the umbrella of Freudian psychoanalysis, even though Rogers clearly did not consider himself or his method Freudian.[15]

In some ways this was a convenient way to paint all of contemporary psychotherapy with the same Freudian brush. In reality, American psychiatry and psychology, while heavily dominated by Freudian psychoanalysis, had never been entirely psychoanalytic in its approach and had always been more diverse than Mowrer was willing to acknowledge.

While pastoral counselors in the early 1960s did not couch their critique of Rogers in Freudian terms, doubts about Rogerian therapeutic technique continued to multiply and earlier concerns were reiterated. Early in the 1950s, non-directive pastoral counselors had outnumbered the doubters; but by the early 1960s, increasing numbers of pastoral counselors had doubts about one of the fundamental Rogerian assumptions—that, given the right climate, the individual would always make the best choice. Pastoral counselors were fully aware that such a view required extreme optimism about human nature. They had never reconciled themselves to the Rogerian prohibition of any exercise of authority in the counseling relationship. In 1958 in the "Consultation Clinic" section of *Pastoral Psychology*, Eugene Kreves, minister of the Lisle Congregational Church, in Lisle, Illinois, raised a familiar concern when he wrote to suggest that, "too much stress had been put upon Rogerian technique" and, in a scriptural allusion, that refusing to give guidance was similar to sending a hungry man away with a stone instead of bread.[16] Invited to respond, Rogers simply disagreed with Kreves and declared that he would rather send the counselee away with "the nourishing bread of self-direction."[17] And yet, even as more pastoral counselors began to suggest that Rogerian therapeutic techniques might not be universally applicable, most pastoral counselors demurred from judging Rogers's theory entirely wrong nor did anyone seriously consider a full-scale desertion of Rogerian method. All of the respondents to Kreves's challenge were generally supportive of Rogers and stressed the importance of an accurate understanding of his theories.[18] Robert Elliott, an assistant professor of pastoral theology at Southern Methodist University, maintained that Rogerian principles had "powerful Christian implications." As an example, he pointed to the "terrible freedom" God gave to human beings "to choose for or against him." Elliott argued that in light of this freedom, given by God to everyone, Christians should respect the "freedom and responsibility" of other people.[19] Rogers's principles of counseling, according to Elliott, affirmed each person's "right and responsibility . . . to choose in and for his own life." He also reaffirmed Kreves's right to reject Rogerian methods: "If somebody is pressuring Mr. Kreves to use a counseling technique which forbids the pressuring of the counselee, then something is certainly haywire."[20]

In any case, many pastoral counselors still feared being overly authoritarian more than being permissive and still perceived the training they had received in seminary as authoritarian. Lutheran pastoral counselor William Hulme told the story of listening to his fellow ministers complain about the dangers of Rogerian therapy until one man stood up and observed, "I am not a bit afraid that we will go off the deep end on nondirective counseling—not with the seminary training we received."[21] He did not fear that ministers would ever become too permissive. Nevertheless, more than one pastoral counselor would have agreed with the editorial in the summer 1958 issue of the *Journal of Pastoral Care* which called for its constituency to reexamine the traditional Christian basis for pastoral care and contended that ministers ought to consider at least the possibility of a legitimate, non-neurotic, nonabusive clerical authority.[22]

A Return to the Language of Theology

In his book on counseling and theology, Hulme argued that Rogerians had to formulate a response to these criticisms. He believed that when the earliest pastoral counselors had "rejected" their own theological heritage in favor of psychological principles, they had "confused" the average parish minister, who tended, in Hulme's view, to be a "traditionalist."[23] As a solution, Hulme called for a return to using theological ideas rather than psychological concepts as the reference point for pastoral counseling theory. Hulme warned that if pastoral counselors did not address the place of theology in pastoral counseling, the counseling movement would become a "point of dissension within the church.[24] Although pastoral counselors disagreed about the relative merits of Freudian and Rogerian theory, few would have dissented from Hulme's assessment and prescription.

Dogged by criticism within their own ranks and facing a constituency that consistently expressed itself in religious terminology, Rogerian pastoral counselors did indeed return to the language of theology. They argued, however, that their identity crisis had occurred because of the way they had used words.[25] Knox Kreutzer, a pastoral counselor who worked at an independent counseling center in Washington D.C., concluded that theology and psychotherapy had necessarily separate languages. He believed that when pastoral counselors had attempted to unite the two terminologies by defining terms that could be used interchangeably, theology had been "defined away."[26] Kreutzer urged his colleagues to remember that psychotherapy dealt with questions that were immediate, specific, and practical, while theology addressed questions of "ultimate meaning" and was expressed in abstract language.[27] Pastor Douglass Lewis, describing something similar, stated that psychology and theology might each have unique aspects that could not be expressed in the language of the other; and he argued that it was wrong to ask which was "true," because each might speak the truth in the context of its own language. Lewis called for a "marriage" of the two disciplines in which each would maintain its own identity.[28]

Rogerian pastoral counselors resisted those who wished to restore ministerial authority or a commonly held standard of moral behavior, but they agreed that Christianity had a valuable tradition that ought to be preserved. They referred to that tradition as "classical" Christianity or as their "theological heritage." Classical Christianity encompassed traditional beliefs in the transcendence of God, the authority of revelation, and the divinity and historicity of a Christ who played a redemptive role in society.[29] Classical Christianity claimed to offer insight into human nature and into the way the world worked. Even the most loyal Rogerians worried that both Freud's and Rogers's theories relegated such a religion to the realm of illusion. They framed their new answers to secular psychotherapies in familiar Christian terms.

In answer to Freudian determinism, pastoral counselors claimed a traditional Christian position that humanity was both free *and* determined.[30] The most frequently cited scriptures on this account were the Pauline Epistles, especially Romans 7. David Roberts was among the first to discuss this topic, which he did in his *Psychotherapy and a Christian View of Man* (1950). Pastoral counselors continued to struggle with the implications of Freudian theory as they had from the outset, arguing that, while Freud's theory of the workings of the human unconscious might be accurate, it should not be interpreted to mean that humans were completely at the mercy of unconscious forces. At the same time, they insisted, no one was completely free from unconscious or deterministic influences either. Pastoral counselors argued that human beings could be held morally responsible only to the extent that they were free, but only God could judge the extent of the individual's freedom and, hence, the extent to which that individual could be held responsible for his or her behavior.[31] If, indeed, only God could judge the extent of human freedom, then any attempts by community or minister to enforce certain standards of behavior were wrong, or so the argument went. In a 1956 contribution to the *Journal of Pastoral Care*, pastoral counselor Howard Clinebell observed that forcing someone to obey the "ethical code of a particular subculture" made that individual less self-determining and so less moral.[32] Truly moral behavior required self-determination.

Likewise, in answer to the elements in Rogerian humanism that seemed to disregard evil in human nature, pastoral theologians attempted to articulate a theory of sin that did not pull them into the murky waters of moralism. In order to achieve this end, pastoral counselors defined sin as estrangement or alienation from God, rather than as specific deeds or even as the violation of someone else's rights.[33] Baptist minister James Ashbrook, a frequent contributor to both *Pastoral Psychology* and *Journal of Pastoral Care*, insisted that sin was not a specific act but a state of "brokenness" in which the individual was separated from self, others, and God.[34] Grace was the restoration to a relationship with God that, in turn, restored the sinner to a relationship with other members of the Christian community.

It was logical that at this point, finally, pastoral counselors began to address the work of theologian Reinhold Niebuhr. One of the most prominent American theologians of the twentieth century, Niebuhr had skirted questions about psychology for most of his career. In contrast, Paul Tillich had addressed such questions specifically and had enjoyed a friendly and mutually constructive relationship with pastoral psychologists. Then, in 1955, Niebuhr published his book *The Self and the Dramas of History,* and Perry LeFevre, who edited the Chicago Theological Seminary *Register,* invited Carl Rogers to review the book. Seward Hiltner, long-time pastoral consultant to *Pastoral Psychology,* and editor Simon Doniger decided that Rogers's review would provide an ideal opportunity for a dialogue between Niebuhr and Rogers. In June of 1958, Hiltner and Doniger published a chapter of *Dramas of History* and a reprint of Rogers's "provocative" review from the *Register*. They invited three scholars to comment on the review and Niebuhr's chapter and invited Rogers and Niebuhr to respond. Niebuhr, because of other commitments, declined to participate. The three respondents—Hans Hofmann, director of the Program in Religion and Mental Health at the Harvard Divinity School, Walter M. Horton from Oberlin College, and Bernard M. Loomer, professor of religion in the Federate Theological Faculty of the University of Chicago—all focused almost exclusively on Niebuhr's ideas.[35] Hiltner was exasperated by their decision to do so and promised future articles in *Pastoral Psychology* that would address Rogers's position.

Pastoral psychologists' problem with *Dramas of History* was Niebuhr's understanding of human nature or, more precisely, of "the self." The portion of the book published in *Pastoral Psychology* was the chapter in which Niebuhr made the case that a Freudian understanding of human nature did not sufficiently explain human sinfulness. In that chapter, Niebuhr addressed the interrelationship of conscience, will, and "the self," arguing that human beings always put themselves and their own interests first, even when they appeared to be putting someone else's interests first. This tendency for "the self" to place its own concerns first—Niebuhr described it as "the bondage of the self to its self"—was, in Niebuhr's view, "original sin." He concluded that "emancipation" could be achieved "only by 'grace' and not by the strength of one's willing."[36] Niebuhr argued, further, that Freudian theory was inadequate because it explained human selfishness in terms of a vestigial "infant ego-centricity" instead of recognizing its centrality to human character, nature, and condition.[37]

Niebuhr's ideas were useful to pastoral counselors as they revisited questions about the sinfulness of human nature, but they were not necessarily central or formative. Rogers's response illuminates the persistent divide between pastoral counselors and Niebuhr. Rogers's difficulties with Niebuhr were partly intellectual and partly personal. For one thing, Rogers took exception to Niebuhr's tendency to dismiss his opponents' views with terms such as "absurd," "erroneous," "blind," "naive," "inane," and "inadequate."[38] Rogers observed wryly, "It seems to me that the only individuals who come off well in the book are the Hebrew prophets, Jesus (as seen by Niebuhr), Winston Churchill, and Dr. Niebuhr himself."[39]

But the differences were more than personal. Rogers faulted Niebuhr in two areas that Rogers considered essential—his view of science and his view of human nature. With regard to science, Rogers observed that after reading Niebuhr's book he found himself "offended by Niebuhr's dogmatic statements and . . . ready to turn back with fresh respect to the writings of science, in which at least the *endeavor* [Rogers's emphasis] is made to keep an open mind."[40] According to Rogers, Niebuhr had rejected the determinism that he perceived in attempts by scientists to understand and explain human nature. Determinism was, in many ways, a code word for both Freudian theories and behaviorism. Rogers, of course, had trouble with both of these theories too, but he thought that Niebuhr was calling for "scientists" to abandon entirely attempts to find "orderliness in man's inner nature or in his outer behavior." That is, Niebuhr appeared to be arguing that study of human nature fell outside "the realm which can be understood by empirical science."[41] Rogers was particularly aggravated by Niebuhr's claim that human beings were both determined and free and by his assumption that any kind of systematic, scientific examination of human experience led to determinism.

The nub of the problem for Rogers, however, came in Niebuhr's view of human nature and consequently his view of sin, both of which stood in direct contrast to Rogers's views. Rogers objected especially to Niebuhr's "conception of the basic deficiency of the individual self," which in turn shaped Niebuhr's understanding of sin. Niebuhr, according to Rogers, was "quite clear" in defining original sin as "self-love, pretension, claiming too much, grasping after self-realization."[42] In response, Rogers pointed to his own experience of "more than a quarter of a century" as a psychotherapist, claiming that he had found precisely the opposite to be true: "In the great majority of cases, they [clients] despise themselves, regard themselves as worthless and unlovable."[43] Rogers stated unequivocally, "I could not differ more deeply from the notion that self-love is the fundamental and pervasive 'sin.' Actually it is only in the experience of a relationship in which he is loved (something very close, I believe, to the theologians' *agape*) that the individual can begin to feel a dawning of respect for, acceptance of, and finally, even a fondness for himself."[44]

Niebuhr saw human beings as possessed of a free will. They were not "determined," either by their toilet training or by their environment in a behaviorist sense. Human beings could, as a result, be held responsible for their actions. What limited human freedom, according to Niebuhr, was the "universal inclination" of human beings to selfishness and self-love. He argued that their selfishness was the "original sin" and that only "grace" could free them from their selfishness.[45] Rogers, likewise, believed that human beings had a free will, but he also believed that it was possible to scientifically examine, analyze, and generalize about human behavior. He did not believe that talking about the "structures of nature" obviated human freedom. He also did not believe that the natural condition of human beings was selfishness and self-love. Most people, he had concluded, did not love themselves enough, and he argued that only loving relationships—the kind of love Rogers thought resembled *agape* love—could help people love themselves. For Niebuhr, the path to redemption came with recognition of one's sinfulness and subsequent repentance. For Rogers, redemption came through loving, tender relationships.

Pastoral counselors' refurbished definition of sin, in which sin meant broken relationships and redemption meant restoration of those relationships, had more in common with Rogers's definitions than with Niebuhr's. Restoration of a relationship with God resulted in the restoration of relationships in general and provided the basis for a theory of Christian community. In late 1950s and early 1960s pastoral counseling literature, terms used to describe the Christian community proliferated: "a fellowship of the forgiven," "*koinonia*," "community of faith," "community of reconciliation," "covenanted community."[46] For pastoral counselors, Christian community was unique because it promised a restored relationship with God. The new understanding of community differed from, but did not preclude, the understanding of community that had derived from the ethic of relationships. When pastoral counselors thought about themselves and their parishioners as sinners, however, it changed their understanding of relationships between people. The community of the redeemed that pastoral counselors had begun to describe by the early 1960s differed theoretically from a community of individuals who simply cared for one another.

All the talk about sin raised the specter of old-fashioned moralism, but Rogerian pastoral counselors resisted such conclusions. They argued that the moral imperatives to which Christians gave their assent should derive from their relationship to God, not from the demands made by the community. Hence, even when pastoral counselors used traditional Christian terms like "revelation" or "truth," they insisted that those words needed to be understood not as a code of behavior (like the Ten Commandments) demanding obedience, but as a "confrontation of God and men in a living relationship."[47] Wayne Clymer, a professor of practical theology and a regular contributor to the *Journal of Pastoral Care*, argued explicitly that revelation was not a "truth," a "philosophy," or a "creed," but a relationship with God.[48]

Rogerian pastoral counselors who objected to the anti-Freudian sentiments of O. Hobart Mowrer did so because his ideas threatened a return to just the sort of moralism they dreaded. For instance, Chaplain Douglass Lewis insisted that Mowrer was only interested in a return to an objective standard of moral behavior. As a result, Lewis contended, Mowrer could "find no place for the concepts of justifying grace, Christ's atonement, or the Holy Spirit." In contrast, Lewis argued, pastoral counselors, as a group, were loyal to the presupposition that Christ's death and resurrection meant something, and they saw their parishioners simultaneously as sinful human beings and as people living under grace.[49] While the language of theology presented certain difficulties in that it could quickly become dead orthodoxy or result in traditional moralism, it also provided the language of Christian community: the "symbols of solidarity" and the "security of belonging."[50] Pastoral counselors increasingly argued that "personhood" achieved by right relation to God could only be acted out in the context of the Christian community.[51]

The Counselor as Minister

Because pastoral counselors had reintroduced the concept of sin and hence placed the counselee "under both judgment and grace," theoretically, the role of the counselor as minister (rather than as therapist) expanded.[52] The counselee needed someone who had the authority to represent simultaneously God's judgment and God's mercy, or so the argument went. Pastoral theologian Homer Jernigan, a professor of pastoral psychology at Boston University, asserted, "The authority of judgment and the authority of mercy are inseparably related in the redemptive role of the pastor."[53] It was important that the new authority of the minister not be mistaken for the old ministerial authority. Pastoral counselors remained committed, at least in theory, to the protection of the parishioner's autonomy and to the "phenomenological principle" in which the counselor attempted to enter the counselee's frame of reference. Such a minister needed a special kind of authority. Charles Stewart, professor of preaching and pastoral care at a Denver seminary, argued that the authority of the pastoral counselor did not come from his ordination, the Bible, or from the "apostolic succession" but from his competence in relating to God and man and in his ability to be a channel of God's healing power.[54]

If the minister was God's channel and representative, counseling turned inevitably to what one counselor called "ultimate questions," by which pastoral counselors meant spiritual matters.[55] In fact, Seward Hiltner argued that the aim of the counselor should be, in the end, nothing less than "salvation or redemption in the religious sense."[56] Most pastoral counselors were quick to point out that addressing ultimate questions and attempting to restore the counselee to a relationship with God did not mean subordinating the counselee's emotional needs to "evangelistic ends."[57] Nevertheless, the new wisdom held that as God's representatives, parish ministers served as mediators who possessed expertise in the field of "ultimate questions."

Pastoral counselors continued to stress the importance of a loving, accepting counseling relationship as the central curative element. As Seward Hiltner noted, people who came to their minister expecting a rigid authority figure and found acceptance benefited the most from counseling.[58] Pastoral counselors who stressed the healing power of the counseling relationship stressed its ability to make a "face-to-face" encounter with God possible. Earlier arguments had highlighted the importance of learning how to love from an encounter with God, while later arguments in addition emphasized the significance of recognizing and taking responsibility for one's own sinful behavior.[59] Pastoral counseling theorists seemed to believe that healing came both from being loved and from the self-knowledge that resulted from God's judgment. Their arguments implied that the counselee could escape the pastor's judgment but not God's judgment nor the judgment of their own hearts.

Robert Bonthius gave the example of a female college student who had come to see him because she found herself overly disturbed by some comments that had been made to her in three separate incidents. A former high school classmate had taunted her for failing to accomplish anything that, in his estimation, justified the title voted her in high school—"most likely to succeed." Her religion professor had challenged a statement she had made in class, and she had felt humiliated by his challenge. A fundamentalist minister had questioned her faith because she could not point to a specific conversion experience, and he had then gone on to rail about higher education in general. According to Bonthius, the loving, accepting counseling relationship the young woman experienced allowed her to look honestly at herself and to decide that she had perceived herself as worth something because she was pursuing her education at an elite academic institution. When anyone challenged that perception of herself, she reacted strongly. She concluded that she would be less threatened by those who criticized her if she discarded the idea that she was better than others because of her education.

Bonthius argued that, in the counseling relationship, this young woman could encounter the "truth." Like his counterparts, he defined "truth" as a "face-to-face" encounter with God. But since God did not have a physical manifestation, God's presence had to be mediated through human fellowship. Bonthius believed that in a loving counseling relationship individuals were enabled to recognize the "evil" or "sin" in their lives. He defined sin as "living against reality." While he acknowledged the difficulties that the term "sin" raised in the minds of some pastoral counselors, he insisted that people had to be able to identify the part of the problem they had created themselves and that could be rectified by themselves. According to Bonthius, only a loving, accepting relationship between counselor and counselee provided an adequate avenue to the self-knowledge necessary to recognize one's own sins.[60]

Changing Counseling Goals

In the early 1960s, then, pastoral counseling theory was characterized by a commitment to four principles or goals. First, the pastoral counselor sought to help the individual to recognize his or her own responsibility or "sin." Self-awareness or a sense of "failure" or "sin" was the starting point on the road to health.[61] Second, once self-awareness and the end of estrangement from self had been achieved, the counselor sought to end the estrangement or alienation of the individual from others and from God.[62] Third, pastoral counseling sought the restoration of the individual to participation in the life of the church. And finally, pastoral counselors sought to help the counselee make connections between the counseling experience and religious experience. One extended example illustrates the application of these goals. In the fall of 1958, Knox Kreutzer presented a paper in which he detailed the events of a case he considered successful. Using the elements of his counseling relationship with the woman mentioned earlier named Marion Farad, he attempted to illustrate what he called the "theology of psychotherapeutic experience." Marion Farad and her husband Donald approached Kreutzer for help after hearing him speak at their church. The Farads were having trouble with their fifteen-year-old daughter, Evie, and the relationship between Mrs. Farad and Evie was deteriorating rapidly. The Farads insisted that the problems were between Marion and Evie. As a result, Kreutzer elected to continue counseling with only Mrs. Farad. The thirty-three-year-old Mrs. Farad described herself as "depressed" and "guilty" because of her "failure as a mother." Kreutzer described her manner as one of "meekness," characterized by "sheepishness" and a "great deal of hesitancy in her conversation."[63]

Despite her initial reticence, Mrs. Farad detailed the events of her early life in an account that culminated in the confession that she had been pregnant when she married. Kreutzer indicated that Mrs. Farad reported that her husband had been only "mildly disturbed" at the discovery that his fiancée was pregnant, had declared his love for her, and had married her "gladly." On the other hand, Mrs. Farad described herself as having been "humiliated" and "mortified." She admitted that she hated being pregnant and felt her pregnancy had "ruined everything," because it prevented her from going to college as she had planned. Two later pregnancies had not provoked the same reaction. As she examined her feelings about her first pregnancy, Mrs. Farad realized that some of her anger and resentment at Evie originated in those events. Kreutzer discovered after his counselee had confessed her premarital pregnancy that Mrs. Farad was very troubled that Evie was "boy crazy." He suggested that Mrs. Farad's attempts to control her daughter's life were a reaction to what had happened to her fifteen years earlier.

As counseling continued, Mrs. Farad discovered that she had what Kreutzer described as "hedonistic" impulses that she wished to repress. She told Kreutzer about a neighbor whom she described as male, unemployed, a Sunday school teacher at a local church, and very "attentive" to her. She wondered what Kreutzer thought of this situation, and he replied "this was the way Sunday School teachers tried to seduce wives across the street." She expressed shock at Kreutzer's interpretation, but it led to a further confession on her part. She admitted another incident with a neighbor who had come to remodel the basement of the Farad home. Mr. Farad, who traveled frequently with his business, was out of town. She admitted that on one occasion the neighbor had kissed her. As counseling progressed, she elaborated on the story. She indicated that she had gone into the basement to "watch him work." When she turned on the Victrola for him, he asked her to dance and then kissed her. The same scenario occurred on several occasions, although Mrs. Farad indicated that the encounters had never gone beyond "light necking."[64]

Kreutzer argued that as Mrs. Farad became more aware of and more comfortable with her "hedonistic" impulses, her relationship with her daughter and with her husband improved. She could, according to Kreutzer, "see her ambivalence toward her daughter as a function of her own problem." That is, Mrs. Farad's repressive relationship with Evie was a product of identifying with her flamboyant and hedonistic daughter and an attempt to repress those hedonistic impulses in both of them. According to Kreutzer, Mrs. Farad's insight into her impulses reduced the power they had over her, and her relationship with Evie improved. But there was another unforeseen consequence. As she became more comfortable with herself, she became less meek and more assertive. The change in her personality necessitated a change in her relationship with her husband. Mr. Farad was a man of "ordered" and mild temperament, and Mrs. Farad had "used" him, by Kreutzer's account, as an "external conscience" in the control of her repressed impulses. Mr. Farad had taken his relationship with his wife for granted. According to Kreutzer, as a result of Mrs. Farad's counseling, Mr. Farad "rediscovered" his wife, and a new relationship gradually evolved.

Kreutzer indicated that Mrs. Farad had used her church membership in a similar manner, relying upon the church to help her control impulses she deemed unacceptable. As she proceeded in counseling, however, and found what Kreutzer called "her freedom and her power of being," the church supported and encouraged her in her growth. Kreutzer used the example of Farad's involvement in a study group at her church that was examining the ideas of Tillich. When she first joined the group, she felt frustrated and inadequate. As counseling freed her from investing her energy in repression and gave her the freedom to assert herself, she gradually lost her feelings of inadequacy in the context of the church.

The account of Mrs. Farad followed a basic progression, advocated by increasing numbers of pastoral counselors in the period between 1955 and 1965, that began with the counselees' identifying the factors in their lives that contributed to poor interpersonal relationships. In Mrs. Farad's case, her relationship to her own mother, unresolved hostility over her unplanned pregnancy, and an inability to accept certain of her own feelings had led to unhappiness in her relationships with her daughter and her husband. Once she identified her hidden impulses and was no longer effectively dissociated or estranged from herself, she could reestablish good relationships with her family members. In time, a better relationship with her Christian community also developed, and they supported her in her newfound freedom.

For Kreutzer, pastoral counseling went further than its secular counterpart. The goal of theologically defined pastoral counseling was not only to address the parishioners' concrete and specific problems but to help parishioners determine the ultimate meaning of their experience. Kreutzer argued that analogy provided the method for relating psychotherapeutic language to theological language. Kreutzer believed that because the psychotherapeutic experience had occurred in the language of the "immediate," it was his job as a pastoral counselor to "build appropriate analogical bridges" to the language of the ultimate, that of theology. Kreutzer demonstrated the analogical method in relation to three concepts: freedom of the will, salvation, and faith. Kreutzer and Mrs. Farad discussed the analogy between what Paul described in Romans 7:15, 24 ("I do not understand my own actions. For I do not what I want, but I do the very thing I hate . . . Wretched man that I am! Who will deliver me from this body of death?") and her inability to love Evie as she wanted to because of her own repressed hedonism. Kreutzer was not saying that they were the same experience but that the two experiences were like one another.

Kreutzer conducted a similar conversation with Mrs. Farad about salvation, based on Tillich's three-fold definition of salvation—regeneration, justification, and sanctification. The process began on Mrs. Farad's part with the sense that something was wrong that sent her in search of help. Kreutzer argued that this was analogous to the "judgment of the Gospel" that challenged people to change their lives.[65] Regeneration, as defined by Tillich, meant being "grasped in a relationship through which the saving, accepting power of the New Being" operated. Mrs. Farad indicated that she had been "grasped" in her relationship with Kreutzer and that this had been a saving, accepting experience for her because of the acceptance she had received from Kreutzer when she confessed her most intimate experiences. The counseling relationship, as Kreutzer pointed out to her, was analogous to the experience of regeneration.

Justification meant accepting that one had been accepted. In Tillichian terms, Farad needed to understand that a being greater than herself had accepted those very feelings within her that she deemed unacceptable. Regeneration and justification restored the relationship and ended the estrangement of the individual from God. Kreutzer, using Tillich's ideas, defined sanctification as the process in which the personality was transformed, particularly in relation to the church. Kreutzer indicated that Mrs. Farad was aware of the transformation that had occurred both in her family relationships and in her relationship to her community of believers and that she quickly grasped the analogy between that and sanctification.

At Mrs. Farad's instigation, she and Kreutzer discussed the meaning of faith. Again, Kreutzer relied on Tillichian models and defined faith as the state of being concerned ultimately about the "New Being in Jesus as the Christ."[66] He further described faith as the ability to accept oneself despite feeling unacceptable and as a state in which one has the courage through the power of the New Being to be oneself despite the threat of non-being. Kreutzer suggested that for Mrs. Farad admitting and recognizing her hedonistic impulses was threatening in a way that was analogous to the threat of non-being and that her choice to reveal her inner self was an "act of courage." Kreutzer argued that the loving relationships that Mrs. Farad experienced as a result of counseling were analogous to a state of faith.[67]

What did an analogous relationship between the psychological and the theological mean? Pastoral counselors never clearly articulated the connection. Kreutzer simply treated Marion Farad's psychological and religious difficulties as separate entities. He used her experience in relationships to help her understand her spiritual experience. The effect, however, was to split the work of counselor and minister. Treating the religious experience as analogous to, but different from, the psychological experience raised the possibility that the person who did the psychological counseling did not have to do the pastoral counseling and that pastoral counseling, in order to be called "pastoral," did not have to address psychological problems but did have to address "ultimate questions."

Pastor as Caregiver

In essence, the triumph of theological language reconfigured the meaning of pastoral counseling. In the first decade after World War II, anyone who believed that counseling skills were central to pastoral practice could legitimately be called a pastoral counselor. By the early 1960s, although many clergy still viewed counseling skills as an important set of tools for the minister, those who had once argued that the counseling role was central to the parish minister's role began to suggest alternative models. As a result, the professional literature began to focus less on "counseling" and "psychotherapy" and more on "pastoral care."[68] At this point the role of the "pastoral care specialist" moved to the center of the discussion. Pastoral care specialists carefully distinguished between the work of pastoral psychotherapy, pastoral counseling, and pastoral care. Psychotherapy involved addressing the parishioner's unconscious difficulties in an extended number of private interviews between pastor and parishioner. Pastoral counseling, likewise, involved formally scheduled interviews but was both less intensive and less extensive than psychotherapy. Pastoral care encompassed all of the minister's obligations for tending to the relationships within the Christian community. Most pastoral care specialists argued that, while it was helpful to understand the workings of the unconscious, there was almost no place in the parish for the practice of psychotherapy. The new pastoral counseling theory had contributed to this shift by its emphasis on ultimate questions and religious experience.[69]

A series of practical difficulties further cooled the parish minister's enthusiasm for pastoral psychotherapy in particular. First, more than one minister complained in letters or articles to the journals that intensive therapy took extraordinary amounts of time. If parish ministers had even a few parishioners with whom they conducted psychotherapy, they did not have time to fulfill their other duties as minister. Part of the problem with methods described by pastoral counselors such as Knox Kreutzer was that they required the investment of large amounts of time in psychotherapy before they could be applied. Kreutzer worked at an independent counseling center and could afford to take as much time with a counselee as was required. Most parish clergy did not have enough time to invest in individual psychotherapy and still meet the other requirements of their office. The question of what constituted adequate training for ministers who wished to offer psychotherapy persisted. As other counseling and psychotherapeutic professionals sought training, licensure, and certification, the lack of such standards for ministerial counselors became more problematic.

Even among pastoral care specialists who still believed that the parish minister needed some counseling skills, the role of counselor diminished in importance. Pastoral care specialists viewed counseling as one effective tool to be used by the parish minister in a limited way to achieve limited goals. They argued that counseling ought to focus on specific problems or crises and address conscious rather than unconscious difficulties. Pastoral care specialists argued that if after several interviews counseling pastors felt no progress was being made, they should refer the parishioner in question to a psychotherapist, because there was a significant possibility that unresolved unconscious conflict was getting in the way of resolution of the present difficulties.[70] In the 1960s, fewer parish ministers and pastoral care specialists than in the previous two decades saw counseling as the point of reference for the rest of their professional activities or as the activity that defined the rest of their professional life.

Gradually, the professional reference point for ministers returned to one much more recognizable to the traditional seminary graduate than to someone in a secular counseling program. The "new" professional model was of caregivers and professional bearers of burdens. Sheilah James Hawes, a senior at Colgate Rochester Divinity School, contributed an article to the *Journal of Pastoral Care* in which she described how she believed the pastor ought to work when dealing with an unwed mother. Hawes urged pastors to discard any stereotypes they might hold regarding unwed mothers as "oversexed" or "morally inferior," to familiarize themselves with applicable community resources, to offer emotional support, "genuine warmth," and "honest respect" for the young woman, and to involve themselves in agencies designed to protect unwed mothers and their children. In other words, in her view, pastors had to rid themselves of their prejudices, know when to refer, maintain an accepting and forgiving relationship, and become involved in changing community structures, not just personal lives. In Hawes's estimation, counseling skills were important, but the minister's primary job was to be a representative of the Christian community. The minister extended acceptance "based on this theological assumption—that every human being is a brother deemed so loved by God that his son died on his behalf."[71] In the context of the accepting relationship, the minister mediated reconciliation to God, to family members, and to the larger Christian community. Ultimately, pastoral care specialists saw themselves as people who ministered to a congregation that was not sick, sinful, or even self-realizing, but rather a congregation of the redeemed.

By contrast, in the late 1950s and early 1960s, clergy who still self-identified as pastoral counselors had increasingly seen themselves as specialists and had begun to talk about the possibility of a professional organization to oversee standardization of training for pastoral counselors and certification of the growing number of pastoral counseling centers. In the 1961 annual directory published by *Pastoral Psychology*, Seward Hiltner submitted an extended and contentious letter to the editor opposing the call for "credentials" for pastoral counselors and "a national association of specialists in pastoral counseling."[72] Hiltner objected on a number of grounds, but, articulating his generation's vision of pastoral counseling, he objected most strenuously to the notion that counseling was a specialty ("All ministers do counseling whether they call it that or not") and that pastors might potentially have to answer to a governing body other than the church that ordained them ("The clergyman's credentials as clergyman come from his ordination"). Three years later he had lost the battle, as the fledgling American Association of Pastoral Counselors (AAPC) took shape, but he continued to resist. In an article published in *Pastoral Psychology* in the spring of 1964, Seward Hiltner grumbled again, this time with a revised set of objections. He objected partly because the newly organized AAPC did not devote enough of its attention to establishing training standards but instead spent its time delineating a hierarchy of membership. He objected particularly because the new association implied that the pastoral counselor could exist without ties to the denomination or congregation and that the counselor would be paid by the counselee rather than by the church. It implied, in other words, that one could be a pastoral counselor without being a pastor; pastoral counseling, he declared, was "an activity called 'counseling' carried on by a person called 'pastor.'" Initially, Hiltner, the dean of pastoral counseling, refused to join the new organization.[73]

Despite his objections to a specialization in pastoral counseling, Hiltner probably did as much as anyone to end the era in which pastoral counseling was central to pastoral identity. In the 1950s he had published *Preface to Pastoral Theology* (1958) and *The Christian Shepherd* (1959). In both books, Hiltner drew heavily on the same principles that had informed his counseling theory, but in neither book did he portray counseling as a point of reference for the pastor's professional life. Both works depicted the pastor as a caregiver—a mediator of loving interpersonal relationships, a symbol of God's love, and a person who never judged or condemned. The characteristics Hiltner had once recommended for a good pastoral counselor he now encouraged in the good pastor.[74]

The leadership of the new generation of pastoral counseling specialists, however, fell to others. Howard Clinebell, an associate professor of pastoral counseling at Southern California School of Theology, played a crucial role in articulating the direction the movement would take. In the same issue of *Pastoral Psychology* in which Seward Hiltner had declined to join the new association, Clinebell, in a careful, reasoned manner (but with an occasional jab at Hiltner), laid out the origins, purpose, and direction of the new organization. He explained that the American Association of Pastoral Counselors had grown out of a conference of invited pastoral counseling center directors organized by the American Foundation of Religion and Psychiatry. At the conference in the spring of 1963, representatives from 100 pastoral counseling centers agreed, nearly unanimously, that there was an "urgent and inescapable need for some form of effective self-regulation for church-related counseling programs and of persons engaged in specialized ministries of counseling." According to Clinebell, the newly formed organization named among its purposes establishing communication among members, setting standards for adequate training, providing certification for counseling centers, encouraging interfaith cooperation, and fostering research "into the relationship between the behavioral sciences and religion and especially in the area of therapy and counseling." The AAPC call for more research picked up on a concern that had been percolating through the professional literature throughout the previous decade. The new AAPC intended to situate itself in this tradition of scientific research. Clinebell noted, too, the importance for the AAPC of demonstrating the "unique contribution of the minister-counselor" and certification as a means to "protect the public from incompetence."[75]

These pastoral counselors sought to professionalize their practice. While they did not immediately seek licensure, they did adopt much of the structure associated with other professionals in the behavioral sciences and began to think and talk about themselves as therapists. In some ways, the move to professionalize shifted them away from the center of the discussion about pastoral theology and ministerial identity. But it likewise helped to sustain their professional identity over the next forty years and into the twenty-first century.

In February 1970, the editors of *Pastoral Psychology* offered an extended reflection on the future of the field. The editors invited prominent theologians, psychologists, doctors, and social scientists to comment on the topic "Pastoral Psychology: The Next Twenty Years." The contributors were united in their assessment that the pastoral or religious aspect of the clergy's work in psychology would dominate in subsequent years. For instance, the journal's pastoral consultant, James Lapsley, in the opening editorial, said that the time had come to rename the field "pastoral theology."[76] Margaret Mead, who wrote the opening essay, ". . . As Seen by a Social Scientist," predicted an end to the trend of the previous several decades in which the secular sciences had dominated and pastors had focused on accumulating knowledge from the sciences to better understand themselves and their parishioners. Mead anticipated an expanding social agenda for ministers and a greater role for religion on more equal footing with the sciences.[77] Wayne Oates looked for a more complete integration of counseling and clinical training into theological education and for, simultaneously, a stronger research agenda among clinically and psychologically trained ministers.[78] Howard Clinebell reframed the argument for the uniqueness of pastoral counselors' contribution (in contrast to secular therapists) and projected a growing demand for specialists in pastoral counseling and for pastoral counseling centers.[79] The return to theological language and an emphasis on "ultimate" or religious concerns was seen as strengthening the relationship between theology and the sciences. The direction pastoral counselors took did not satisfy everyone, however, and even as pastoral counselors were struggling to define and expand the parameters of their professional practice, another group of Christian therapists offered an alternative.

CHAPTER TEN

Christian Counseling and the Conservative Moral Sensibility

The fact is this. Among the men who are pushing back the
frontiers of human knowledge, there are devoted men of God who
know and honor God's Word. There are those in psychology,
psychiatry and other professions who consistently use the Bible in
their counseling. They attest that the Bible advances itself ahead of
every generation and continues to be the most effective tool and
remedy in the hands of any counselor.

—CLYDE NARRAMORE, *THE PSYCHOLOGY OF
COUNSELING* (1960)

IN THE EARLY 1960S, as pastoral counselors moved toward a model of
caregiving for the pastor and specialization for the pastoral counselor,
a new kind of counseling began to take shape. Its proponents self-identified
as evangelical, fundamentalist, or conservative Christians and referred
to the counseling and psychotherapy they offered as Christian, in contrast to pastoral or secular counseling. In his important inaugural essay
for the *Journal of Psychology and Theology*, editor Bruce Narramore
explained the distinctive characteristics of "Christian psychology" and
"Christian counselors," challenging Christians who wished to counsel to
approach the practice with the right attitude: "a respect for the complete
inspiration and authority of the Scriptures," "a commitment to the scientific method and rigorous academic study," "a personal commitment
to Jesus Christ," and "respect for both the Christian and the secular
community." The terms Narramore chose to use were problematic, since
other kinds of counseling, such as pastoral counseling, were also Christian. Narramore did not say that pastoral counselors were not Christian,
but he did say that the liberal church had been too much influenced by

psychoanalysis, Carl Rogers, and existentialism, and he noted, "They have no hope of developing a biblically sound perspective of psychology since they have forsaken the authoritative teachings of the Scriptures."[1]

Throughout this chapter I use the terms "Christian counselors" or "evangelical counselors" and "Christian counseling" because those were the words these counselors used to describe themselves and the work they were doing. I have elected to use their terms, but by doing so I do not mean to imply that I agree with Narramore's assessment of pastoral counselors and liberal churches.

These Christian counselors were concerned about what they saw as increasing secularization of American society and especially the secular and, in some cases antireligious, nature of psychological theories. They were particularly critical of the pastoral counseling movement, arguing that pastoral counselors were too much in debt to secular psychology, particularly Rogers and Freud, and so were failing to meet their pastoral obligations to their counselees.[2] There was clearly some overlap of traditional pastoral counselors and the new evangelical counselors, since critiques of Rogers and Freud had appeared regularly in the pastoral counseling literature for nearly two decades. But, for the most part, the evangelical critique of psychiatry and pastoral counseling came from a different social and cultural location. Christian counseling was dominated by psychologists and psychiatrists rather than clergy. Because they already had established professional credentials, they did not worry much about the distinction between psychotherapy and counseling that had bothered pastoral counselors, who had been engaged in carving out a professional niche. But they did struggle to define a distinctively Christian therapy, and during this process the outlines of a shared conservative moral sensibility emerged. The liberal moral sensibility is illuminated in contrast to it.

The Professional Context of Christian Counseling

At least one part of the professional context in which Christian counseling emerged was the antipsychiatry movement that was provoking so much discussion among pastoral counselors in the early 1960s. Unlike their pastoral counseling colleagues, however, a significant number of evangelical counselors found the antipsychiatry movement appealing.

This resulted in part from their perception that most non-Christian psychiatrists ignored, discounted, or were openly hostile to religion and religious values. Psychologist O. Hobart Mowrer and psychiatrist William Glasser were not clergy, but they raised questions that Christian counselors found compelling. Mowrer's critique of Freud's ideas regarding the etiology of mental illness and William Glasser's specific instructions about how to apply that critique in therapeutic settings combined in a particularly attractive package.

Glasser's *Reality Therapy,* published in 1965 with a preface written by Mowrer, gave detailed guidance about how to challenge "the myth of mental illness" in the therapeutic setting. In the first half of the book, Glasser laid out the basic concepts of reality therapy and explained how it differed from conventional therapy. The second half of the book was devoted to illustrating the practice of reality therapy in a variety of mental health settings. One of the most important things about reality therapy was that it offered an alternative to psychoanalysis, in much the same way that Rogers's non-directive counseling offered an accessible alternative for pastoral counselors. Reality therapy was not really systematic but instead was idiosyncratic and based on the needs of the client or patient. It was in some ways characterized by what one did not talk about—the past or the origin of one's problems. The patient was encouraged to talk about *what* he or she was doing rather than *why* he or she was doing something—to focus on behavior rather than on the feelings associated with that behavior or insight into the origin of that behavior. This meant, according to Glasser, that almost any topic was open to discussion, from sports to philosophy, so that the relationship or "involvement" between the therapist and the patient deepened. In the context of a warm and loving relationship in which the patient was respected, he or she could devise a plan for his or her life: face reality, take responsibility, and engage in "right or moral behavior." Glasser defined right or moral behavior as "when a man acts in such a way that he gives and receives love, and feels worthwhile to himself and others."[3] Glasser acknowledged that this kind of therapy did not always make people "happy," but he declared that it would give them a certain amount of peace and, although he did not use the word specifically, success. In the case studies Glasser included in his book, he described individuals achieving success in their work and in fostering stable relationships. One young man went to medical school, while another completed multiple projects and was promoted even in the midst of recurring bouts of depression; one young woman lost fifty pounds, and another gave up sexual promiscuity.[4]

Some evangelical counselors also turned to the work of Anton Boisen for their understanding of the etiology of mental illness. Mowrer played an important role in giving Boisen a higher profile among these counselors than one might expect, given his social location within liberal Protestantism. In his discussion of church, clergy, and psychology, Mowrer cited Boisen's works frequently, including references to personal correspondence with Boisen. In his chapter in *The Crisis in Psychiatry and Religion* (1960), entitled "Guilt, Confession, and Expiation," Mowrer quoted Boisen extensively. In his collection *Morality and Mental Health* (1967) he included an excerpt from Boisen's *Exploration of the Inner World* (1936). References to Boisen subsequently appeared in the works of evangelical counselors. For instance, Gary Collins, in his book *Search for Reality* (1969), used Boisen's definition of mental illness when he defined abnormality, noting the possibility, as Boisen had argued, that emotional illness could be caused by an individual's failure to live up to his or her own expectations or standards.[5] In some ways, the embrace of Boisen by the antipsychiatry movement and Christian counselors made sense. More than thirty years earlier, Boisen had also launched a critique of the psychiatric establishment that included a rejection of Freud's ideas. At the same time, there were significant differences between Boisen and his new champions which they failed to recognize. Boisen, in contrast to many in the antipsychiatry movement, saw a more complicated psychological process in which the struggle toward God and the perception of failure in that struggle caused the personality to disintegrate before reintegrating. In Boisen's model, simple confession did not necessarily lead to healing.

In some ways, the antipsychiatric movement had more in common with the kind of counseling advocated by John Sutherland Bonnell and Charles Holman, who in the 1930s had promoted pastoral counsel that drew a straight line from sin (especially unconfessed sin) to emotional distress and who advocated a strenuous moral effort as part of one's mental hygiene. The language Glasser used in describing the counseling process, in which the counselee had to "face reality" in order to succeed, echoes that of Holman in *Cure of Souls*, in which he too talked about the importance of facing reality in the interest of making adjustment, or that of Cabot and Dicks, who argued in *The Art of Ministering to the Sick* that growth required "not turning away from reality." Most Christian counselors did not cite the cure of souls literature, perhaps because it was so firmly embedded in the liberal tradition.

Boisen's work was probably more attractive because it also focused on the scientific study of religious experience and the integration of psychology and theology rather than on pastoral practice—an emphasis that appealed to the psychologists and psychiatrists who dominated in Christian counseling. Almost all of its leaders had psychology backgrounds, even if they, for one reason or another, subsequently took positions at seminaries, divinity schools, and schools of theology. For instance, Donald Tweedie was a professor of psychology who started out at Gordon College and later moved to a position as director of the Pasadena Community Counseling Center, which was associated with the School of Psychology at Fuller Theological Seminary. Fuller's School of Psychology was founded with the specific purpose of providing a Ph.D. in clinical psychology that integrated a theological perspective rather than offering training in pastoral counseling or pastoral psychology.[6] Clyde Narramore, one of the seminal figures in evangelical counseling, had a doctorate in education and came out of the guidance tradition. His nephew, Bruce, with whom he founded the Narramore Foundation, held a Ph.D. in psychology from the University of Kentucky. Paul Tournier, another influential figure, was a Swiss medical doctor. Gary Collins, who held a Ph.D. in clinical psychology from Purdue University and exercised a long-term and wide-ranging influence on the movement, was on the faculty at Trinity Evangelical Divinity School for twenty years beginning in the mid-1960s.

The dominance of counselors with doctoral degrees in psychology in the movement helps explain a number of of its characteristcs. First, there was almost no debate about the relative merits of counseling versus psychotherapy. In the 1940s the question of turf and which professions could legitimately offer counsel and psychotherapy was still highly contested. In the intervening years, clinical psychologists had made a strong move to claim that territory for themselves. By the 1960s, ministers were viewed increasingly as inadequately trained trespassers encroaching upon territory that rightfully belonged to psychologists. Among evangelical psychologists the question was not *whether* they should offer counseling or psychotherapy but *how* they would integrate the principles and practices of their faith with the principles and practices of their profession. The dominance of psychology Ph.D.s did not mean that evangelical and fundamentalist ministers without that degree were not engaged in counseling. The result was sharp and occasionally bitter disagreements between the two groups, disputes that escalated in the 1980s over the issue of whether ministers ought to offer either counseling or psychotherapy.

In the late 1960s and early 1970s, the disagreements were still relatively minor. In fact, two parish ministers exercised significant influence on Christian counseling and, probably not incidentally, represented the most conservative end of the spectrum. Tim LaHaye had no background or expertise in counseling or psychology and later moved on to other interests, but he claimed expertise in counseling on the basis of eighteen years in the parish ministry, and he based his book, *The Spirit-Controlled Temperament* (1966), on a handful of books and the lectures of leading Christian psychologists, especially Henry Brandt. Jay Adams, on the other hand, who also had significant parish experience, had a fair amount of postgraduate seminary education, including exposure to clinical pastoral education and a period of training with O. Hobart Mowrer. Both LaHaye and Adams eventually came under fire from their colleagues, LaHaye because he was not scholarly enough and Adams both for his methods, something he called "nouthetic counseling," and for his combative style.

Historian David Powlison details the criticisms leveled at Adams by other evangelical counselors in what Powlison terms a "jurisdictional" dispute. He records evangelical counselors' dislike for what they saw as Adams's misinterpretation of both the Bible and secular psychologies (and his misunderstanding of the relationship between the two), his heavy-handed moral judgments and directive style, and, most importantly, his insistence that counseling was the special province of ministers and lay people, while psychologists were specifically excluded. Powlison argues that evangelical psychotherapists won the jurisdictional war in the 1980s, while the independent organizations for nouthetic counseling that Adams established languished.[7] In the late 1960s and early 1970s, however, the battle had only just begun, and Adams was still very much a part of the conversation. In spite of their differences, Adams and the evangelical psychotherapists shared a common moral sensibility.[8]

One other prominent figure in the evangelical counseling movement is important, because of the way his work illustrates two significant trends in Christian counseling. John Drakeford, professor of psychology and counseling at Southwestern Baptist Theological Seminary, established a thriving pastoral counseling training program based on the theories and methods of "integrity therapy." Like Adams, Drakeford was familiar with both traditional pastoral counseling and clinical pastoral education, was not a psychologist, and had studied with Mowrer, at which point he was exposed to the basic concepts of integrity therapy, a term he credited Mowrer with coining.[9] Although Drakeford's primary commitment was to training ministers, his integrity therapy was built on group therapy and made extensive use of lay counseling. Both Adams and Drakeford emphasized the role of lay involvement in the counseling process. Drakeford specifically credited Mowrer's approach with restoring the minister to the counseling process and opening the position of counselor to any "perceptive and interested" person who wished to help.[10] In the jurisdictional battles within evangelical counseling, the issue of lay counseling remained a contentious one; ministers tended to embrace it and the degreed psychologists viewed it with suspicion.

Drakeford's association with the Southern Baptist denomination is also important. Historically, Southern Baptists had thrown their lot with clinical pastoral education and pastoral counseling. Both were part of a larger trend among Southern Baptists, who had managed for decades to maintain a quirky mix of southern progressivism and old-fashioned evangelical fervor.[11] In the 1970s, conservatives launched the historic "takeover" of the Southern Baptist Convention, which was firmly established by the 1990s.[12] The new leadership steered the denomination toward alliances with other evangelicals rather than with the mainline denominations. In his affiliation with the antipsychiatry movement and his embrace of lay therapy, Drakeford represented the leading edge of the conservative groundswell within the Southern Baptist Convention.

Southern Baptists were important to the emerging Christian counseling movement, but they did not predominate. Instead, neoevangelicals controlled much of the discourse of "Christian counseling." Those conservative Christians who self-identified as neoevangelicals were heirs to the Calvinist fundamentalist tradition that had developed since the 1920s and was characterized by a commitment to biblical inerrancy, dispensational premillenialism, and political and religious separatism. That movement had led to the founding of numerous new seminaries, colleges, churches, and parachurch organizations. Neoevangelicals tended to be more willing than their predecessors had been to make alliances with other evangelicals, including Pentecostal, Holiness, and Anabaptist Christians. And, as George Marsden has argued in *Reforming Fundamentalism*, by the middle to late 1960s, neoevangelicals controlled Fuller Theological Seminary, which was also the site of one of the earliest doctoral programs in Christian psychology.[13] Fuller, along with Trinity Evangelical Divinity School in Illinois and Gordon Conwell Theological Seminary in Boston, represented the heart of fundamentalist and neoevangelical theological education, while Wheaton, Westmont, and Gordon Colleges played a similar role at the undergraduate level.[14]

As religious outsiders in their secular profession, evangelical psychologists, counselors, and psychotherapists were intensely aware of the issues of professional credentialing and scholarly legitimacy. They entered the fray at about the same time that traditional pastoral counselors began to distance themselves from the parish and establish an independent professional existence (the American Association of Pastoral Counselors incorporated in 1964) and at about the same time that the lines between the various vocational groups—clinical psychologists, psychiatric social workers, and guidance personnel—were beginning to reify, fashioning carefully delimited standards for accreditation or certification.[15] The context of professionalization helps to explain the uneasy relationship between the Christian psychologists and counseling clergy, whether mainline or evangelical. It meant, too, that evangelical Christians who wished to counsel needed secular professional credentials as well as their own professional organizations that were recognized by secular institutions such as the American Psychological Association (APA). They sought both.

For instance, Bruce Narramore, who had earned a Ph.D. in psychology from the University of Kentucky, was instrumental in founding Christian doctoral education that became APA accredited. He was founding dean of Rosemead Graduate School of Psychology, which later merged with Biola University and oversaw the establishment of the premier academic journal for evangelical psychologists, the *Journal of Psychology and Theology*. The administration at Fuller Theological Seminary followed suit, establishing a School of Psychology in 1965 and the Pasadena Community Counseling Center, which served the school's research agenda, and hiring Donald Tweedie and Paul Barkman, both with Ph.D.s in clinical psychology.[16] Wheaton College, the flagship of neoevangelical undergraduate education, and George Fox University had established clinical psychology doctoral programs by the turn of the twenty-first century. To underline the possibility of combining high professional standards and committed faith, evangelical psychologists were quick to point out past presidents of the APA who were outspokenly Christian, such as Paul Meehl and Gordon Allport.

Evangelicals also launched a number of professional associations and related journals for counselors and psychotherapists, although they did not rely on those associations for accreditation or certification, instead looking to the APA for validation. Rosemead's *Journal of Psychology and Theology* focused on attracting both academic and professional readers. The Christian Association for Psychological Studies (CAPS), established in the mid-1950s, published the *Journal of Psychology and Christianity* with an eye on a similar market. The American Association of Christian Counselors (AACC), which, under the leadership of Gary Collins, in the 1990s grew phenomenally, published the more practically oriented *Journal of Christian Counseling*.

The Conservative Moral Sensibility

The individuals who came together, then, to establish "Christian counseling" included a diverse group of theologically conservative Protestants—fundamentalists, neoevangelicals, the new evangelical alliance—and counted among their ranks Christian psychologists, psychiatrists, psychotherapists, and ministers as well as a number of old-style pastoral counselors hailing primarily from Southern Baptist and Evangelical Lutheran backgrounds. The outlines of this approach to counseling were first articulated in a handful of seminal works published between 1960 and 1975 that illuminate the contours of the conservative moral sensibility.[17] In general, the central recurring issues in the evangelical counseling literature revolved around questions about the proper "integration" of

psychology and theology. More specifically, early members of this movement devoted a significant amount of print to exploring the apparent
lack of interest in values and moral standards among secular psychologists, the authority of scripture in effective counseling, the power of God,
the depth of human sinfulness, and the importance of all these concepts
for the theory and practice of Christian counseling. In their discussions
the conservative moral sensibility predominated and stood in stark contrast to the liberal moral sensibility.

Psychiatry and Values

Early practitioners of Christian counseling argued that secular therapists, psychiatrists in particular, did not pay enough attention to matters
of values. What these Christian counselors meant by "values" ranged
widely. It seemed to encompass not only questions of right and wrong but
questions about human nature and specifically about whether human
beings had a spiritual dimension that should be addressed as part of
therapy. Donald Tweedie's *Logotherapy and the Christian Faith* (1961)
is a good example of this critique. The book resulted from Tweedie's
interest in identifying psychological theories that were compatible with
Christian values. Tweedie had been a professor of psychology at Gordon
College before moving to Fuller Theological Seminary and the directorship of the counseling center there. Earlier, on a sabbatical from Gordon,
Tweedie had spent some time at the Vienna Polyclinic, where Viktor
Frankl was the director of the neurological and psychotherapeutic department of the clinic, engaging Frankl in conversation, observing
Frankl's clinical activities, and reading his published works.[18]
  Tweedie was looking for a psychological theory in which the spiritual
dimension of human existence was accepted and valued, and he argued
that Frankl's logotherapy and existential analysis offered a viable alternative to what the rest of psychology was offering. In Tweedie's judgment, most modern psychology had been too much influenced by behaviorism, psychoanalysis, and a relentless empiricism that had resulted in a
rejection of anything that even hinted at religion or metaphysics. Tweedie
argued that one's philosophy of human nature and whether one believed
that human beings possessed a spiritual dimension were critical. In his
view, behaviorism was notoriously mechanistic. Psychoanalysis was

equally problematic given that Freud had written an entire book in which he had described religion as an illusion.[19] From Tweedie's perspective, scientific psychology refused to consider as valid anything that could not be measured in a laboratory, and this attitude had bred a generation of psychologists who at best saw the religious impulse as immaturity and at worst as mental illness. Psychology had, as Tweedie expressed it, "traded its birthright of philosophical self-consciousness for the pottage of positivistic verification."[20]

Equally damning in Tweedie's view was that psychology was not truly scientific in the first place. Many of its presuppositions, he argued, were just as much acts of faith as any religious belief, even as it claimed superiority by virtue of being more scientific.[21] As Tweedie saw it, secular psychiatrists—who were the particular object of evangelical distrust and disdain—had first devalued values, then imposed their own values, either implicitly or explicitly, on their patients.[22]

The Authority of Scripture

The values that members of the Christian counseling movement claimed as important they found in the Bible. In fact, the authority of the scripture was one of the most important guiding principles for these counselors; it shaped their theory and practice fundamentally, and it is pivotal to understanding the conservative moral sensibility. Without exception, Christian counselors called for a biblically based psychology and a therapeutic method guided by the authority of the scripture. While they all agreed on the centrality of the scripture, they disagreed about what that meant for the relationship between religion and science. The scientific method and biblical revelation sometimes were pitted against each other. Jay Adams, for instance, stated very clearly at the beginning of his 1970 work, *Competent to Counsel*, that his book was not based on "scientific findings." His book, he claimed, was "presuppositional." That is, he worked from the presupposition that "the inerrant Bible is the Standard of all faith and practice. The Scriptures, therefore, are the basis, and contain the criteria by which I have sought to make every judgment."[23] Adams did not deny the importance of science. In fact, he claimed it as a "useful adjunct for the purposes of illustrating, filling in generalizations with specifics, and challenging wrong human interpretations of

Scripture."[24] Adams seemed to be arguing that it was acceptable to illustrate biblical principles with scientific examples, but it was not acceptable to illustrate scientific principles with biblical examples, because the latter would imply that science had a greater authority than the Bible, a view Adams rejected. To maintain that authority, Adams insisted that everything human beings needed to know about human nature and psychology could be found in the Bible, and science served only to corroborate biblical principles.

Gary Collins, who was also representative of the conservative moral sensibility and placed a high value on the authority of the scripture, drew somewhat different conclusions about the relationship between science and religion. For a significant portion of his career, Collins was a professor and chair of the Division of Psychology and Counseling at Trinity Evangelical Divinity School. While Adams wanted to subordinate science to religion, Collins wanted to put religion and science on an equal footing. More accurately, making an argument that was narrower and more easily defensible, Collins attempted to place Christian and secular psychotherapy on an equal footing. He argued that this could be achieved only by establishing a sound scientific and intellectual base for Christian counseling and by making a logical and rational case for the Christian view. He also argued, however, that to make the case for the legitimacy of Christian counseling it was necessary to recognize that both Christian and secular therapy began at the same point—with a series of assumptions that were "unstated, unrecognized, and uncritically accepted by faith."[25] He pointed out that Christians had an obligation to "clarify [their presuppositions], to state them explicitly, to test them against the revealed words of scripture, to support them philosophically, and to postulate them as convincingly as we know how."[26]

The difference in these two men's social locations shaped their views regarding the scientific method. Adams, a Reformed clergyman, set the world of scholarship aside in a sphere separate from the world of faith. Collins, with a Ph.D. in psychology, called for the use of the academic apparatus, including "journals, books, lectures, and classroom discussions," to demonstrate the viability of a Christian framework.[27] Collins was not saying that Christian psychologists ought to allow the Christian world view to be subordinated to the scientific world view. Instead, he was arguing that each Christian psychologist had an obligation to be an "intellectual witness to non-Christian psychologists" and to defend a biblically based psychology using terms and methods that secular psychologists would understand. This, Collins argued, required using "carefully designed research techniques" and "solid data" to demonstrate the greater logic of theism compared to naturalism, the superiority of revelation to empiricism, the desirability of a biblically based ethics, and the practicality of a life based on a relationship with a "loving and forgiving God."[28]

The difference between Collins and Adams is well illustrated in their approach to the Bible and what they thought the Bible contributed to psychological knowledge and counseling methodology. Adams saw the Bible as definitive and the sole authority in all matters. Collins, while equally enamored of scripture and unwilling to limit the "power of the Word of God" in any way, was reluctant to say that Christians who had a Bible need never consult a psychologist. Instead, Collins argued that the Bible contained good examples of counseling as well as words of encouragement and comfort but was not the only source of psychological help.[29]

For those of a conservative moral sensibility, their beliefs about the authority of the scripture also had consequences for what they believed about moral standards. Regardless of where he or she fell on the spectrum of the conservative moral sensibility, each author seemed to see it as a duty to mention that moral standards were objective. By "objective standards" they meant that there were rules that had to be followed, rules that transcended time and place, rules that existed outside of subjective experience. In his critique of the kind of psychology that focused on "adjustment," for instance, Gary Collins argued that the Bible taught that God has "standards of right and wrong which go beyond culture" in contrast to a "culturalistic" view in which there was no "external standard of behavior."[30]

Most simply, following objective moral standards meant that when the counselee faced moral choices, the Christian counselor was supposed to use the Bible as the starting point for guiding and instructing the counselee. Clyde Narramore, who, along with Paul Tournier, led the way in defining the basic character of evangelical counseling in the early 1960s, devoted an entire chapter of his book, *The Psychology of Coun-*

seling (1960), to "The Use of Scripture in Counseling." Applying the scripture in this way was predicated on certain assumptions about the nature of the Bible which in turn led Christian counselors to assume that the Bible provided a clear and objective standard of behavior. For these counselors, affirming the revealed and authoritative nature of scripture was essential.[31] To claim the Bible as a guide for living, it was necessary, in their view, to establish the absolute authority and reliability of the Bible.

Narramore began his chapter on using scripture in counseling with an extended discussion of the power and nature of the Bible. He began by describing the transformative effect of scripture in the lives of two men, one a hydraulic engineer and the other a "top man of science" who while vacationing in the country "strolled into a nearby Bible conference . . . and invited Christ into his life." In telling these stories Narramore made a number of assumptions that were revealing of the conservative moral sensibility. When he claimed that the men were "transformed by God's Word," he also claimed that God's Word was "the same as the Living Word who had come from heaven [Jesus Christ]" to die for the sins of human beings. It was Jesus who transformed lives, and the Bible was powerful only to the extent that it was identified with Jesus. Narramore went on to celebrate the Bible, claiming, "No sound technique or valuable discovery of science will ever be contrary to or complete without, the revelation of God's Word" and that, no matter what human beings might say, the Bible remained "the objective and eternal Word of God."[32] The Bible was also, according to Narramore, a "glorious authority for life itself," a "manual and guide book for our daily lives," and, quoting Paul's Second Epistle to Timothy, "God-breathed—given by His Inspiration— and profitable for instruction."[33] Narramore included an appendix of Bible verses that could be used in counseling, grouping the verses under headings such as "anxiety and worry," "comfort," "sin," and "temptation." About half of the verses were intended for giving comfort and encouragement. The other half were to be used to direct, guide, and advise the counselee. Narramore included a separate listing of Bible verses intended to be used in "soul winning."[34]

Probably no work so clearly illustrates the diverging paths of the liberal and conservative moral sensibilities than Joseph Fletcher's *Situation*

Ethics, published in 1966 just as the American cultural revolution was escalating. Fletcher was a senior member of the clinical pastoral education movement and had participated in the founding of the Graduate School of Applied Religion in the 1930s. In the 1950s, when pastoral counselors were struggling to define the "ethic of relationships" and the nature of "responsible freedom," Fletcher had contributed significantly to the debate. His publications in the 1960s represented the logical conclusion of work begun decades earlier. Fear of and discomfort with situation ethics, a term Fletcher coined, was palpable in both popular and professional journals of conservative Christians. At the time he wrote *Situation Ethics,* Fletcher considered himself a Christian and believed that situation ethics were not simply compatible with a Christian ethic but were, in fact, the way Jesus himself made ethical decisions. Fletcher deviated from the conservative moral sensibility in two critical and fundamental ways. First, he insisted that the only absolute in human existence was love: "Love is a predicate . . . the one and only *regulative* principle of Christian ethics."[35] Everything else, including the definition of good and evil and right and wrong, depended on the situation or the circumstances. There was, in other words, no objective standard for moral behavior. He dismissed rules and codes as legalism and moralism and a violation of love.

The second problem with Fletcher's thinking, for conservative Christians, was his attitude toward biblical authority. While he quoted frequently from the Bible, he did not consider himself a biblicist and certainly did not see the Bible as offering an objective standard for moral behavior. In Fletcher's view, the final authority in every moral decision had to be love, not the Bible. For Fletcher, moral decision making was grounded in something he called neo-casuistry. Classical casuistry moved from individual cases to principles and rules. Fletcher embraced the old case method—it echoed his own experience in the case study method used in CPE—but rather than moving from cases to larger principles or rules, Fletcher considered each case independently and made decisions about right and wrong depending on the situation. He was not above taking a shot or two at the legalists, moralists, and biblicists, accusing them of a kind of cowardice. He disparaged their need for rules and their unwillingness to take moral risks—to risk being wrong or mistaken or to "sin bravely," a phrase he borrowed from Martin Luther. Fletcher by no means represented all liberal theologians of the era. What he did represent was the ethic of responsibility taken its furthest and perhaps logical conclusion—the polar opposite of the conservative moral sensibility.

Christian counselors' commitment to the authority of scripture also shaped their beliefs about gender. It was here that the doctrine of biblical inerrancy and more specifically biblical literalism became pivotal. Margaret Bendroth in *Fundamentalism and Gender* argued that late-nineteenth and early-twentieth-century arguments among evangelicals for women's equality in the life of the church were based on a "non-literal and thematic reading" of scripture that was rooted in "Wesleyan and perfectionist" Christianity.[36] The problem for evangelical counselors in the latter half of the twentieth century was that neoevangelical dominance in "Christian counseling" meant that a quite different approach to scripture prevailed.

In general, Christian counselors tended not to mention gender explicitly except where forced to. Their writing reveals the sort of gender stereotyping that was common and generally accepted in those years, including the use of the inclusive "he" to talk about human nature and a tendency to use examples from women's experience to illustrate pathology. Even among those whose thought fell on the more liberal end of the spectrum, the tendency was to assume that women's problems revolved around home and household and men's problems revolved around work and achievement. And while none among them would have claimed to support the double standard in sexual behavior, examples of sexual dysfunction or misconduct tended to be drawn, again, from women's experience. The image of Eve, the temptress, persisted.

When specific discussions of gender equality arose, Christian counselors turned to the Bible—to a certain way of reading the Bible. This approach is best illustrated in an article printed in the *Journal of Psychology and Theology* in the mid-1970s. While the author's views did not reflect those of all Christian counselors, they did represent the views of some, particularly those who favored a literal reading of scripture and emphasized biblical inerrancy. The author was George W. Knight III, an assistant professor of New Testament at Covenant Theological Seminary, who offered an interpretation from the perspective of reformed theology. Knight started by reaffirming the "inspiration, inerrancy, and absolute authority" of the Bible. On this basis Knight argued that the

New Testament gave clear instruction regarding God's order and the roles established by God, including the roles of men and women in the marriage relationship and the roles of men and women in church leadership. Knight argued that, while the Bible clearly affirmed the "spiritual equality" of men and women, it equally clearly affirmed a hierarchical relationship between men and women in which women were to submit to men as part of a larger hierarchy in which men submitted to Christ and Christ to God.[37]

Knight was careful to argue not only for a particular view of scripture but also for a particular approach to exegesis. He insisted that only those "didactic passages" that specifically addressed the relationship of husbands and wives and the place of women in the church could be used to understand the roles of men and women. The subtext here was that using the scripture to extract general principles regarding men's and women's roles was an improper and unacceptable approach to exegesis.[38]

Other views both of the scripture and of women's roles percolated through the constituency. One disgruntled reader canceled his subscription to the journal after the Knight article was published. The letter writer, Richard Nielson, described Knight's work as an "offensive piece of twaddle" and his scholarship as "sophomoric." Nielson was also quick to point out the inconsistency of treating the biblical discussion of women's roles as normative and the discussion of slavery as situational. The editors responded in carefully neutral language that they had "attempted to publish articles on the role of women from various evangelical perspectives" and then gave the references for the other articles.[39] One of the reasons Knight had written the article in the first place was because the argument that there was a biblical basis for women's equality had been gaining currency in evangelical circles. Knight pointed particularly to recent articles in *Christianity Today*, to a book by the journal's editor, Harold Lindsell, called *The World, the Flesh, and the Devil* (1973), and to a book by two women, Leeza Scanzoni and Nancy Hardesty, entitled *All We're Meant to Be: A Biblical Approach to Women's Liberation* (1974). Knight was most troubled by what he saw as a tendency among these Christians to argue that the scripture regarding women's subordination was culturally relative and not "normative" for the present. Instead, Knight argued that the only portion of the New Testament that was culturally relative and meant to regulate existing conditions was the teaching on the relationship of servants and masters. He apparently meant this as a preemptive strike against those who might accuse him of suggesting that the Bible supported slavery. Knight did not explain why this one particular case was culturally relative and others were not. In any case, his argument was framed to engage evangelicals who interpreted scripture differently than he did and who drew very different conclusions, even as they took a "high" view of scripture.

The *Journal of Psychology and Theology* had earlier given equal time to Virginia Ramey Mollenkott. Mollenkott was a psychologist widely read in evangelical circles in the 1970s who spoke strongly in favor of gender equality. She and those who shared her views drew on scripture but with a broader and more contextual reading—just the sort of reading to which Knight objected. Both kinds of evangelicals placed a high value on scripture, but they disagreed about how scripture should be interpreted. Those with the most literal interpretation of scripture represented one end of the spectrum of the conservative moral sensibility and had the most specific understanding of gender roles. In their view, the Bible was very clear about what women should and should not be allowed to do. It was, moreover, a moral issue for them; allowing or encouraging women to teach in defiance of the Bible violated God's law.

Evangelicals on the other end of the spectrum also placed a high value on scriptural authority, but they argued that scripture should be interpreted in its cultural context and read in terms of the larger principles it was conveying. This was no less a high view of scripture, and these evangelicals were every bit as orthodox in their theology and in their view of the transcendence of God, every bit as convinced that the Bible was the inspired word of God, but were also convinced that human beings were required to read and interpret the Bible with the aid of God's Spirit. For evangelicals of this bent, to be evangelical meant to believe in the miraculous and supernatural presence of the God in the world but not necessarily to subscribe to a position of biblical literalism and inerrancy, which they regarded as the legacy of fundamentalism.

A Transcendent, Sovereign God

Christian counselors did tend to place a greater emphasis on the power, transcendence, and sovereignty of God than had their counterparts in pastoral counseling. By the mid-1960s pastoral counselors were certainly talking more explicitly about God's power to change lives, but not in the same language that their evangelical counterparts did and certainly not with the same emphasis on the miraculous and supernatural. Christian counselors' beliefs about the nature of God, like their beliefs regarding the authority of scripture, had consequences for their theory and practice. Almost without exception, psychologists who self-identified as evangelical claimed belief in a transcendent, sovereign God who intervened in human affairs and made change possible. Consequently, they also reaffirmed the sinfulness of human nature and the absolute impossibility of change apart from God. That is, they juxtaposed human helplessness with the power of God. These beliefs had important consequences for counseling theory—especially given what they believed about the etiology of mental illness—and for counseling practice.

In particular, the affirmation of human sinfulness led to their criticizing the work of Sigmund Freud and Carl Rogers. In the view of Christian counselors, both men had advanced theories that undermined the concepts of human sinfulness and personal responsibility. Mowrer had argued that Freudian and Rogerian approaches thus hindered healing and were ineffective. To evangelicals it seemed that the views of Freud and Rogers also undermined God's sovereignty, by challenging a biblically ordained hierarchy. Freud's theory of the unconscious, in which mental illness resulted from unresolved instinctual conflicts, seemed to suggest that human beings were sick not sinful and so could not be held responsible for their behavior. This argument got much of its energy from Mowrer's critique and was expressed most vociferously by Jay Adams. Adams argued that Freud sent individuals digging in their past in order to find someone to blame for their inadequacies instead of squarely facing their sin, repenting, and attempting to conform to biblical standards.[40] Adams complained, "The idea of sickness as the cause of personal problems"—an idea Adams attributed to Freud—"vitiates all notions of human responsibility."[41] Evangelicals' objections to Freud and psychoanalysis were strengthened by the fear that psychoanalytically oriented psychiatrists would, in the name of mental health, actively work to free individuals from their inhibitions, which would, in turn, transform them into "impulsive, irresponsible sinners."[42]

Much of Rogerian theory was considered equally problematic. Rogers's assumptions about the fundamental goodness of human beings were deemed overly optimistic and seemed to stand in direct opposition to what the Bible said about human nature. Both Freud and Rogers were thus seen as circumventing, in different ways, what was for Christian counselors a fact—human sinfulness. Freudian theory excused the individual from responsibility for sin while Rogerian theory ignored or downplayed the presence of sin in the life of the individual.

For Christian counselors, this was as much a theological issue as a psychological one. Not all of them assumed that *all* mental illness was caused by sin. Nor did they assume that because they rejected much of Freud's theory that they need necessarily reject the idea that some guilt was false and unnecessary. They struggled with how to distinguish between real, or true, guilt caused by breaking God's laws and false guilt accompanied by a vague sense of discomfort and worry about having failed to meet one's own or others' expectations. Paul Tournier, the Swiss medical doctor who widely influenced early evangelical counseling, elaborated the terms of this debate in his book *Guilt and Grace*. Tournier aimed at a popular audience, and the book consisted of a collection of anecdotes drawn from his medical practice and personal experience. Bruce Narramore and Bill Counts took up the same themes in their book, *Freedom from Guilt*, also aiming for a popular audience but taking a more systematic approach to addressing the issue. In their book, Narramore and Counts argued that some of the difficulties could be resolved by defining guilt more carefully. They divided guilt into four categories: "civil" or "legal" guilt, in which individuals broke the civil law and were guilty whether they felt guilty or not; "theological" guilt, which was caused by Adam's fall and the sinfulness of human nature and caused separation from God, but which could be remedied by salvation; "psychological" guilt, the *feeling* of guilt, regardless of whether the individual was truly guilty; and "constructive sorrow," the term that Narramore and Counts preferred to "true guilt," and which led to permanent change in the life of an individual.[43] The distinction between true and false guilt was an important one because, from the perspective of Christian counselors, the only kind of guilt that most psychiatrists acknowledged or addressed was psychological guilt, and they failed to ask whether that guilt was legitimate. Evangelical psychologists, as well as many in the antipsychiatry movement, argued that true guilt needed to be addressed because, for some individuals at least, recognizing their own sinfulness, repenting, and making restitution led to emotional healing.

Similarly, although they rejected Rogers's optimism about human nature, they did not assume that there was nothing good about human beings, and they struggled to find a balance between acknowledging human sinfulness and encouraging self-esteem in their counselees. Narramore and Counts took up the question specifically: How was it possible to acknowledge one's fallenness and maintain a good sense of self-esteem? Returning to their fourfold definition of guilt, Narramore and Counts argued that while individuals needed to recognize that they were indeed fallen, they also needed to recognize that they were special, created in the image of God, and loved unconditionally by God. They argued, further, that salvation removed the theological guilt of individuals so that even if they sinned after they became Christians, that sin did not separate them from God or mean that God loved them any less. According to Narramore and Counts, this understanding of human nature explained all the evil in the world—something Rogers's theory failed to do—while avoiding "worm theology" which they saw as psychologically unhealthy.[44]

Some Christian counselors did agree with the secular antipsychiatry movement about the etiology of mental illness and, like Glasser and Mowrer, drew a direct line from sin to mental illness. Adams made this argument most forcefully, drawing examples from the time he spent working with Mowrer at Illinois. In chapter 3 of *Competent to Counsel*, Adams argued that, with the exception of "organically generated difficulties," there was no mental illness, only sin and an unwillingness to face and confess that sin.[45] To illustrate his point, he recounted the apparently remarkable effect of confronting mentally ill people and requiring them to tell the truth about what was bothering them. Adams gave the example of "Mary," who would begin to scream and cry in therapy sessions when progress appeared imminent and who had been diagnosed as manic-depressive. When her counselors ignored her tantrums and confronted her, telling her that they knew she was hiding something, she immediately quieted; and eventually she revealed her secret—an adulterous affair with a neighbor. "Steve" was a young man from a local college

whose diagnosis was catatonic schizophrenia and who was uncommuni-
cative and unresponsive. His counselors treated him as if he understood
every word they were saying to him, and he very shortly began to respond. In time, he admitted that he had feigned illness in order to avoid
taking responsibility for having failed all of his university classes because
he had spent too much time working on the school play.[46] In his stories,
Adams portrayed mentally ill people as impostors, not suffering emotional distress caused by unconfessed sin but fabricating emotional distress to cover up sin. He generally agreed with Mowrer's claims about the
importance of facing, confessing, and making restitution for sin, but he
disassociated himself from Mowrer because of Mowrer's refusal to acknowledge the existence of a transcendent God and of biblically based
standards for moral behavior. Mowrer argued that moral standards derived from doing what was best for the most people, which Adams condemned as "subjectivism."[47]

For Christian counselors who saw a direct causal link between sin
and mental illness, counseling could not proceed without first securing
the salvation of the counselee. LaHaye, Adams, and Clyde Narramore
made this point explicitly, arguing that counselors who began by addressing the salvation of the counselee would see miraculous results.[48]
They understood the link between sin and healing in a manner roughly
similar to Mowrer's and Glasser's. Unlike Mowrer and Glasser, however,
the Christian counselors believed that healing came from God, not from
the acts of confession and restitution.

Tim LaHaye described a successful counseling encounter with a young
man who came to him angry and disgusted with his wife, who was under
psychiatric care and was, in the husband's description, "psychotic" and
nearly impossible to live with. LaHaye, working from the principle that
no real help could be offered to the young man unless he had accepted
Christ, began by outlining the plan of salvation using a Campus Crusade
for Christ tract called the Four Spiritual Laws that LaHaye's sixteen-
year-old daughter had been given at a training conference for that organization. The results, according to LaHaye, were nothing short of miraculous. The young man, after first claiming that he did not believe in
Jesus, agreed to invite Jesus Christ into his life. Having done so, he wept.
Then, although he had earlier spent an hour detailing all of his wife's
weaknesses, he told LaHaye that he now realized it was not, after all, his

wife's fault, but that the problem was him. According to LaHaye, two months later the young man's wife became a Christian and no longer needed psychiatric care.

The kinds of assumptions LaHaye and Adams made were also implicit in the work of Tweedie, Collins, and even Clyde Narramore's nephew Bruce, but these latter counselors were unwilling to argue that the starting point for all counseling was salvation. They were no less convinced of the power of God and the necessity of the Holy Spirit to change lives, but they did not as a consequence believe that all mental illness was caused by sin. For instance, Gary Collins took a significantly different view of the etiology of mental illness in his book, *Search for Reality* (1969). Vernon Grounds, in the foreword to the book, praised Collins, in what sounded like a tacit rebuke of LaHaye and Adams, for his refusal "to endorse the uncritical, streamlined explanations which are prevalent in some Biblically-oriented circles—e.g., all emotional disturbance is attributable to an individual's sin; psychology and Christianity are irreconcilable enemies; every valid answer to personality needs and problems is found only in the Word of God."[49]

Collins was every bit as biblical in his approach as was Adams, even laying out his commitment to biblical inerrancy early in the book.[50] He began his chapter titled "Why Do Christians Crack Up?" by acknowledging that the cause of mental illness (or "abnormality") could be in some counselees "strictly spiritual."[51] He also asserted that mental illness could be a problem, temptation, or trial "permitted" by God to build virtues such as patience or humility. In a turn of argument that sounded very much like Anton Boisen's arguments about the morally sensitive individual (and Collins cited Boisen when defining abnormality), Collins pointed out that many Christians might appear abnormal by the standards of society or secular psychology. He cited sexual behavior in particular, saying, "A sex-obsessed and pleasure loving society has no place for a philosophy which says we should not make provision for the flesh to fulfill the lust thereof."[52] Drawing on Erich Fromm's work, Collins argued that in a sick society people could potentially share the same pathology.[53] Finally, Collins suggested two other possible causes of mental illness, ones that were more familiar to the secular psychologist. First, something might have happened in the individual's childhood to cause mental illness later in life, and, second, the illness might be the result of a "physical malfunctioning."[54]

Because of what he believed about the etiology of mental illness—that some mental illness did not have a spiritual cause—Collins did not assume that an individual had to be "saved" first before he or she could receive any effective psychological help. At the same time, he wanted to be clear that Christianity did offer the possibility of a life of "peace and power" that was "superior to every alternative." And while, unlike Adams and LaHaye, he did not claim that Christian belief was the only path to emotional health and stability, he did insist that individuals who wanted a particular kind of help—that superhuman wisdom and divine strength that came from God—did need to be saved before they could receive it.[55]

For the most conservative of the Christian counselors, like LaHaye, Adams, and Clyde Narramore, the counselor's obligation did not stop with salvation. An ongoing transformation of the counselee's life was necessary. In fact, this was what they regarded as the real work of Christian counseling—helping the counselee to identify and confess sin and then develop spiritual practices meant to allow the Holy Spirit to work. LaHaye called this the Spirit-filled temperament, and Adams referred to the process as sanctification, describing it as a "growth away from sin and toward righteousness" in which individuals were "transformed into the likeness of Christ."[56] LaHaye delineated the characteristics of the Spirit-filled temperament and then the steps to be taken to achieve it, which included self-examination, confession of all known sin, complete submission to God, a specific request to be filled with the Spirit, and an affirmation of belief by the individual that he or she had become filled with the Spirit. LaHaye cautioned against expecting a feeling or an ecstatic experience, and he distinguished between being filled by the Spirit and walking or "abiding" in the Spirit. The latter involved guarding against grieving the Spirit, repeating the five steps to being filled—multiple times daily if necessary—and pursuing a plan of regular Bible reading, daily prayer, and yielding to the Spirit, witnessing, as well as making walking in the Spirit a "habit."[57]

Jay Adams identified a similar process when he described sanctification, contending that the Holy Spirit transformed lives through "the ministry of the Word, the sacraments, prayer, and the fellowship of God's people." Given the power of the Holy Spirit, Adams wondered, "How can counseling that is removed from the means of grace expect to effect the permanent changes that come only by growth in grace?"[58] In any case, in the same way that salvation was only possible through the power of God, so was the transformed life accomplished only through the power of the Holy Spirit. In this way of thinking, spiritual health and mental health were intimately linked and were sustained by daily confessing of sin and living a life in the Spirit.

Clyde Narramore also advocated a plan of spiritual growth and formation for Christians as a shield against mental illness and as a support of mental health. Narramore argued that, for a "great majority" of Christians, their problems were spiritual and stemmed from "not letting Christ control their actions." As an example, he pointed to the case of a woman who was grieving so severely over the loss of her only son that she considered suicide. Narramore observed that the woman had allowed her life to be centered on her son rather than on Christ. Her counselor, Narramore explained, focused on the woman's spiritual state, and shortly after she rededicated her life to Christ "completely," she began to recover her "mental and emotional well-being."[59] Narramore's plan for keeping Christ at the center of the individual's life and thus encouraging mental health involved steps similar to those advocated by LaHaye and Adams; they included daily prayer, daily Bible reading, regular church attendance, witnessing and personal testimony, and reading devotional "Christ-centered" books.[60]

In this approach to the attainment and sustenance of mental health, confession was the centerpiece, both at the point of salvation and as part of the ongoing transformation. Confession was important both for its palliative effect and for its redemptive effect. It required, however, more than speaking aloud one's sin. It also required repentance. Adams turned to the Bible for his thesis on confession, using a verse from Proverbs: "He who conceals his transgressions will not prosper: but he who confesses and forsakes them will obtain mercy."[61] Adams elaborated, highlighting the importance of both confessing and forsaking sin in order to enjoy relief and pardon. He pointed to the Epistle of James to make the case that physical suffering could be caused by unconfessed sin and that for this reason the church had a particular role in healing. But Adams was careful to also point out that one did not confess just to be healed. Later in the same chapter he described "true confession" as "repentance before God," declaring, "It can never be but a technique by which one may obtain relief from his misery or 'makeup' with another." That is, the ultimate goal was not the relief of suffering or even the restoration of relationships; it was the individual's being right with God and admitting to God that he or she had violated God's principles.[62]

In this we hear echoes of the prewar liberal moral sensibility. On one level, some of the Christian counselors' assumptions did not differ that much from those of Charles Holman, who had recommended daily devotional practices as an aid to good mental hygiene, or John Sutherland Bonnell, who had described in vivid detail the power of confession. On another level, it was a whole new animal, or rather, an animal revived from the nineteenth century and refurbished for the twentieth century. Earlier liberal ideas about the connection between sin and emotional distress were based on an assumption of fundamental human goodness and a belief that earnest moral striving would pay dividends. While repentance and redemption may have been implicitly accepted in the liberal moral sensibility, they were rarely taken up as central issues. They were assumed, rather than made explicit.

In the conservative moral sensibility, moral striving and outward manifestations of good or moral behavior were meaningless unless one also assumed God's power to transform and the individual's helplessness to change him- or herself. LaHaye specifically asserted that one of the causes of depression was "hypocrisy," one example of which was attempting to change oneself without the help of the Holy Spirit.[63] Jay Adams went a step further, arguing that attempting to achieve change without the Spirit was a "rebellion against God," because it assumed human autonomy and undercut the need for grace by assuming that human beings were fundamentally good, and it resulted in "a legalistic works-righteousness that will lead ultimately to despair since it divests itself of the life and power of the spirit."[64] Works by evangelical counselors conveyed a sense of the overmastering power of God that pastoral counselors did not have or did not express.

Not all Christian counselors placed such an emphasis on the absolute power of God in contrast to the absolute helplessness of human beings. Many of the same themes persisted but were espoused less rigidly. Again, Gary Collins's work is a good example. Collins invoked the Holy Spirit almost as often as Adams or LaHaye but not with the same detail and specificity. He did not prescribe exactly how to be filled with the Holy Spirit. Instead, as part of his discussion of how religious belief, and especially Christian beliefs, offered a healthy way to deal with problems, he quoted extensively from scripture, highlighting passages that illustrated the role of the Holy Spirit in encouraging, comforting, and teaching the believer. Collins framed the Christian life as one that involved a personal relationship with Jesus, the necessity of growth in that relationship, and the likelihood of both hardship and "supernatural power" to meet that hardship. Collins did not use the word "sanctification," but he was describing a process similar to the one outlined by LaHaye and Adams and was claiming that this was the road taken by the psychologically sound and emotionally healthy individual.[65] At the very end of his book *Search for Reality*, Collins again reaffirmed his commitment to a biblical and spiritual approach to psychology, commenting, "It must always be remembered that psychology is a *tool* of the church. It is the Holy Spirit who convicts men of sin. The Holy Spirit and the Bible teach men and enable them to grow spiritually. In His work the Holy Spirit can and does use tools. Modern psychology might be one of these tools. If evangelicals carefully avoid over dependence on psychology, this exciting science of behavior can be a valuable aid both in our understanding of each other and in the work to which we have been called by God."[66] So, while the level of detail varied, the fundamental principles were consistent throughout the evangelical counseling literature of the period.

The conservative moral sensibility, with its ideas about the depth of human sinfulness and the power of God, also had a much more clearly defined sense of sin and a clearer sense of what needed to be done in order for a person to be delivered from that sin than did the liberal moral sensibility. Sin came from refusing to yield control of one's life to Jesus—the insistence upon keeping self on the throne. In Bible tracts, Christian psychology, revival meetings, Youth for Christ, and C. S. Lewis's writings, as well as a host of evangelical para organizations, this message was repeated. Only the death of self, only the yielding up of control to a greater power would result in change.

The moral sensibility associated with the "Christian counseling" movement that emerged in the late 1950s and early 1960s incorporated a handful of principles that stand in stark contrast to the principles associated with pastoral counseling, a contrast that deepened in the years between 1965 and the turn of the twenty-first century. For Christian counselors' beliefs about the authority of scripture, the transcendent power of God, and the sinfulness of human nature shaped their theory and practice in fundamental ways, leading them to stress the importance of adherence to objective moral standards drawn from the Bible and of recognizing the helplessness of human beings to change themselves without the intervention of God. In contrast, pastoral counselors' emphasis on the importance of cultural context, human relatedness, and personal autonomy sound areligious. From the perspective of pastoral counselors, the views of these Christian counselors sound narrow, disrespectful of human need, and moralistic—a return to the very approach they had worked so hard to escape. Placed side by side, the two perspectives seem to having nothing to say to each other. And yet, both sets of assumptions were deeply moral and deeply Christian. It is their proponents' inability to recognize and respect the historical legitimacy of the others' views that has made civil discourse between them nearly impossible in recent years.

Epilogue

HOWARD CLINEBELL WAS the quintessential post–World War II pastoral counselor. Tracing his intellectual development and the changes in his life over four decades allows one to simultaneously trace both the history of pastoral counseling and the evolution of the liberal moral sensibility. In 1999, in response to a request from the editors of the *American Journal of Pastoral Counseling*, Clinebell recalled the greatest influences on his own understanding and practice of pastoral counseling, and the outlines of the liberal moral sensibility are illuminated in that account. Clinebell entered Union Theological Seminary in 1947, on the eve of the publication of some of pastoral counseling's seminal works. Books by Dicks, Hiltner, Wise, Johnson, and Oates followed one another in quick succession during the late 1940s and early 1950s. Clinical pastoral education broadened and strengthened its base. A multitude of training possibilities in seminaries, institutes, and seminars became available simultaneously to clergy and other professionals interested in pastoral counseling. Clinebell rode that wave of professional development and, following founders of the pastoral counseling movement like Hiltner and Oates, helped shape the movement's parameters in subsequent years.

Like so many other pastoral counselors, Clinebell had come of age in a midwestern, small town environment and was the grandchild of farmers. In the account of his life, he made explicit the connection between his early years on the farm and his later interest in "growth and process theory."[1] While the rest of his colleagues did not consciously make the same connection, it is remarkable the number of them who shared a midwestern, rural, or small town childhood. Clinebell saw a causal relationship between his rural past and the psychological theories he embraced, and it was probably true that a rural past contributed an impetus for many young ministers to "make good" and achieve professional status. The early concern of clinical educators to protect the status of parish ministers makes even more sense when one realizes that the majority of these ministers were small town or farm boys in a rapidly urbanizing environment.

A tragic event early in his life shaped the rest of Clinebell's career, and he read the event in an appropriately psychodynamic framework. When he was four years old, his younger sister died on her first birthday. In retrospect, Clinebell recalled a period of "inappropriate guilt" that lasted into his adulthood and prompted him to pursue a career in the ministry.[2] The psychodynamic framework that informed Clinebell's interpretation of this early tragedy was particularly fashionable among counseling ministers at the time Clinebell took up the postgraduate study of pastoral psychology and counseling at seminary in New York City. His education, as Clinebell recalled, "began to challenge and expand the horizons of my Mid-Western provincialism."[3] While at Union Seminary, he studied with theologians David Roberts and Paul Tillich and with the neo-Freudians associated with the William A. White Institute. Clinebell took seminars at the institute in a certificate program in applied psychiatry for the ministry that was administered jointly by Columbia University and Union. He participated in seminars with Erich Fromm, Frieda Fromm-Reichmann, and Harry Stack Sullivan.[4] Rollo May was also participating in the seminars, although at that point not teaching at the institute.[5]

As with many pastoral counselors, neo-Freudian theories profoundly shaped Clinebell's thought but parish experience had an equally powerful influence. Clinebell worked his way through Union serving as pastor in a Long Island church and there discovered, as he phrased it, that the "long-term, uncovering, reconstructive, neo-Freudian approach, was not what most of my counselees wanted or needed." Again like many fellow pastoral counselors, Clinebell continued to find the psychodynamic approach useful for understanding some behavior that was otherwise unexplainable but he began to look for alternative counseling methods. Influenced by Wise, Oates, Hiltner, and Johnson, he developed his own methods. By the late 1950s, having migrated west to California and spent some time as a minister of counseling for a large church and director of a pastoral counseling center, he accepted a full-time position on the faculty at the School of Theology at Claremont. From his position there, he reinterpreted and synthesized the work of the founders in his book, *Basic Types of Pastoral Counseling* (1966).

Clinebell's career illustrates the ambivalent relationship between clinical pastoral education and pastoral counseling. Before going to New York for postgraduate studies, Clinebell studied at Garrett Biblical Institute, the Methodist seminary in Evanston, Illinois. Russell Dicks was working in the Chicago area at the time and teaching two courses in pastoral care and counseling at Garrett. Taking Dicks's classes made Clinebell aware that he needed more training. Around the same time, he met Anton Boisen, who likewise much influenced his thinking, but Clinebell apparently did not enroll in CPE that year. So, while he acknowledged the importance of CPE in shaping some of his ideas and he later enrolled in clinical training while in New York (1947-48 and again in 1956-57), most of his practical training in counseling occurred in a much different milieu, one that was deeply embedded in the conversation pastoral counselors were having with major proponents of the humanistic psychology movement.

That observation brings us to a noticeable omission from Clinebell's professional genealogy. In describing his intellectual roots, Clinebell did not even mention Carl Rogers, who figured so prominently in the thinking of many pastoral counselors and who is identified so absolutely with humanistic psychology. But this makes sense, too, if the basic narrative of the history of pastoral counseling and CPE is kept in mind. By the time Clinebell had accepted a position at Claremont and had turned to scholarly publication, pastoral counselors' fascination with Rogers had faded. In fact, Clinebell's *Basic Types of Pastoral Counseling* challenged Rogers's method explicitly. Given Clinebell's appreciation of psychodynamics, it is ironic that he did not recognize the extent to which his own ideas served as point and counterpoint to Rogers's. Early in the book, Clinebell offered a "revised model for pastoral counseling," one that he viewed as more suited to the parish ministry than was the older model, which he described aptly as "Rogers with a dash of Freud." He claimed that he had no desire to dispense with the Rogerian method and intended to keep and incorporate its best attributes into the revised model, but he also intended to "recover the strengths of the pre-Rogerian period."

Clinebell was just a bit younger than the founders of CPE or the very earliest pastoral counselors, and it was perhaps a combination of that age difference and his personal psychology that made him much more willing to acknowledge the influence of women on his professional life. As a young adult, Clinebell had studied philosophy at DePauw University and then earned a bachelor of divinity degree at Garrett, where he was greatly influenced by Georgia Harkness.[6] His decision to pursue graduate studies in pastoral psychology and counseling resulted not so much from studying CPE but from the influence of Regina Westcott Wieman, who had written an important book with her then-husband, Henry Nelson Wieman, called *Normative Psychology of Religion* as well as a book of her own called *Family and Church*. Clinebell mentioned, too, the importance of the work of Dorothy Walters Baruch, author of children's books and popular books on childrearing for their parents, and Peggy Way's influence on his thinking about psychotherapy, particularly the influence of "social context and justice issues on health and illness."[7]

In the tradition of his Progressive forebears, Clinebell saw the implications of counseling for social change. As he described it, he became "increasingly aware of the hyper-individualism of Western thought, including pastoral counseling" and moved toward a model of counseling that was more "holistic and more empowering of clients so that they could become agents who worked with others to lessen the social pathologies that were breeding sickness in themselves and others."[8] By his account, his counseling method moved from an individualistic, intrapsychic focus to a focus on relationships: couples, families, and healing social systems. Continuing, as did many of his colleagues in pastoral counseling, to both counsel and teach, his shift toward a focus on social systems moved him toward a focus on healing the environment. He expressed himself most passionately about this in his book *Ecotherapy, Healing Ourselves, Healing the Earth* (1996). His focus on environmental awareness moved Clinebell toward greater global awareness. He saw and participated in an increasingly international pastoral care and counseling movement, including conventions of the International Congress on Pastoral Care and Counseling, which, he remarked, went beyond the "Western, male, white, and middle-class origins" of the American pastoral care and counseling movement. He also joined the International Pastoral Care Network for Social Responsibility, which originated in the mid-1980s out of the American Association of Pastoral Counselors. Clinebell described the Pastoral Care Network as made up of individuals committed to "using our dual training (in theology and psychology) to help make a healthy, just and peaceful society, and a healthy natural environment the heritage of all the children of the human family."[9]

Clinebell's progression from intrapsychic to international concerns reflects the expanding vision of religious liberals generally and pastoral counselors specifically and helps us to see why conversation between those of liberal and conservative moral sensibilities is so difficult. When we ask the fundamental questions, it appears at first as if liberals and conservatives live worlds apart: How do we know how to live? In the liberal moral sensibility, we know how to live by studying human experience and the experience of other Christians; in the conservative moral sensibility, we know how to live by studying the Bible. What are the most important values? In the liberal moral sensibility, the primary values are relieving suffering and achieving human potential, autonomy, relatedness, and community; in the conservative moral sensibility, the primary value is saving souls, in the belief that the best possible service to any individual is to secure his or her salvation. How are we to live a "good" life and achieve high moral standards? In the liberal moral sensibility, we achieve high moral standards through a kind of Christian pragmatism, testing each decision against a variety of standards, including scripture, community, and individual conscience; in the conservative moral sensibility, we achieve high moral standards by conforming to the image of God and through the working of the Holy Spirit. How do we decide the roles of men and women in society? In the liberal moral sensibility, gender roles are defined by human beings and through a pragmatic evaluation of human experience; in the conservative moral sensibility, gender roles are defined by the Bible and by the structure of authority articulated there. It appears to be a divide that cannot be crossed.

On the one hand, a study of moral sensibility seems to indicate that liberals and conservatives have nothing to say to one another—at least not anything civil. And yet, the historical record also suggests other possibilities. While this irreconcilability seems the case for the arguments of the likes of Joseph Fletcher and Jay Adams, who represented the far ends of the moral sensibility spectrum, in reality, most people live somewhere in the middle rather than on either end. When historian David Powlison tried to describe the response to Jay Adams's nouthetic counseling and found himself creating an elaborate genealogy of "conservative conservatives," "liberal conservatives," "conservative liberals," and "liberal liberals," he was illustrating this very phenomenon. Pastoral counselors and evangelical counselors, if they listen carefully when the other talks, hear the echoes of familiar ideas grounded not only in a shared religious heritage but also in a shared intellectual heritage. Both are trying to map the territory between faith and science. That common ground is the starting point for civil discourse, not only for counselors, but perhaps also for anyone trying to talk across a great divide of moral sensibility.

NOTES

Introduction

Epigraph. Robert H. Felix, "The Hard Core of Counseling," *Pastoral Psychology* 1 (April 1950): 34.

1. Ichabod S. Spencer, *A Pastor's Sketches: Or Conversations with Anxious Inquirers Respecting the Way of Salvation*, second series (New York: M. W. Dodd, 1855), 61. See also Seward Hiltner, *Preface to Pastoral Theology* (Nashville: Abingdon Press, 1958), 72–73.

2. Spencer, *A Pastor's Sketches*, 66.

3. Ibid., 63.

4. Ibid.

5. Ibid., 67.

6. Seward Hiltner and Lowell G. Colston, *The Context of Pastoral Counseling* (New York: Abingdon Press, 1961), 91–92.

7. Ibid., 91–107.

8. Ibid., 104.

9. Howard Kirschenbaum, "Carl Rogers's Life and Work: An Assessment on the 100th Anniversary of His Birth," *Journal of Counseling and Development* 82, no. 1 (2004): 119.

10. Kirschenbaum, "Carl Rogers's Life and Work," 116–117.

11. Three of Rogers's works in particular figured prominently in the development of pastoral counseling theory and method. Carl R. Rogers, *Counseling and Psychotherapy: Newer Concepts in Practice* (Cambridge, MA: Houghton Mifflin, 1942); Carl R. Rogers and John L. Wallen, *Counseling with Returned Servicemen* (New York: McGraw-Hill, 1946); and Carl R. Rogers, *Client-Centered Therapy: Its Current Practice, Implications, and Theory* (Boston: Houghton Mifflin, 1951).

12. Hiltner and Colston, *Context of Pastoral Counseling*, 43.

13. Ibid., 65–66. Colston and Hiltner pointed out that, while they did not turn away anyone who requested counseling, they also did not include in the research everyone who received counseling.

14. Ibid., 64.

15. Ibid., 172–173.

16. Ibid., 170.

17. In an article first published in *Cross Currents: A Quarterly Review* in 1953, entitled "Persons or Science? A Philosophical Question," Rogers ruminated on the tension he felt between maintaining the kind of objectivity required as a "scientific investigator" trying to "ferret out some of the truth about therapy" and achieving the subjectivity required to be a good therapist. In other words, while Rogers discouraged giving direction, advice, or guidance, he did not do so in the interest of maintaining objectivity. Carl R. Rogers, "Persons or Science? A Philosophical Question," *American Psychologist* 10, no. 7 (1955): 267.

18. A number of historians in the latter half of the twentieth century examined the relationship between religion and psychology. One of the most important for my purposes is E. Brooks Holifield, in his book that places both pastoral counseling and clinical pastoral education in the larger context of pastoral care (see n. 21). For an account of the interaction of religion and science in the nineteenth and early twentieth centuries, see Ann Taves, *Fits, Trances, and Visions: Experiencing Religion and Explaining Experience from Wesley to James* (Princeton, NJ: Princeton University Press, 1999). For other important works examining the history of the clergy's use of psychology, especially clinical pastoral education, see Charles E. Hall, *Head and Heart: The Story of the Clinical Pastoral Education Movement* (n.p.: Journal of Pastoral Care Publications, 1992); Edward Thornton, *Professional Education for Ministry: A History of Clinical Pastoral Education* (Nashville: Abingdon Press, 1970); Robert Charles Powell, "Healing and Wholeness: Helen Flanders Dunbar (1902–1959) and an Extra-Medical Origin of the American Psychosomatic Movement, 1906–1936" (Ph.D. diss., Duke University, 1974); Allison Stokes, *Ministry after Freud* (New York: Pilgrim Press, 1985); Robert C. Powell, "Fifty Years of Learning through Supervised Encounter with Human Living Documents," 1975, Box 14, Folder 219, Association for Clinical Pastoral Education, Records 1930–1986, Pitts Theology Library Special Collections, Archives and Manuscripts Department, Emory University. Several historians have examined the interest in mind cure and New Thought that immediately preceded the first clinical pastoral education programs. See Raymond J. Cunningham, "The Emmanuel Movement: A Variety of American Religious Experience," *American Quarterly* 14, no. 1 (Spring 1962): 48–63; Raymond Joseph Cunningham, "Ministry of Healing: The Origins of the Psychotherapeutic Role of the American Churches" (Ph.D. diss., Johns Hopkins University, 1965); Rennie B. Schoepflin, *Christian Science on Trial: Religious Healing in America* (Baltimore: Johns Hopkins University Press, 2003); Sanford Gifford, *The Emmanuel Movement: The Origins of*

Group Treatment and the Assault on Lay Psychotherapy (Boston: Harvard University Press for The Francis Countway Library of Medicine, 1997).

19. For an extended discussion of the meaning of religious liberalism, especially theologically, see Gary Dorrien's three-volume work, *The Making of American Liberal Theology.*

20. Jane Austen, *Sense and Sensibility*, in *The Oxford Illustrated Jane Austen* (1923; reprint, New York: Oxford University Press, 1988), 6.

21. E. Brooks Holifield, *A History of Pastoral Care in America: From Salvation to Self-Realization* (Nashville: Abingdon, 1983), 144–152. See Holifield's discussion of the three-faculty psychology of the early nineteenth century—intellect, the affections, and the will.

22. The term "moral orientation" has most frequently been the province of educational and developmental psychologists. The most prominent voices in that debate have been psychologists Lawrence Kohlberg and Carol Gilligan. See Chapter 7, where I discuss their work in relation to that of pastoral counselors. At least one biologist has argued that moral orientation is biological, or to be more precise, visceral, and that the "gut" reaction people sometimes have about what is right and wrong has a biological base. Jay Schulkin, "Moral Sensibility, Visceral Representations, and Social Cohesion: A Behavioral Neuroscience Perspective," *Mind and Matter* 3, no. 1 (2005): 31–55. I do not weigh in on this particular question because I am not interested so much in the origins of moral sensibility as in its historical implications. It might be accurate to describe what I am doing as descriptive ethics, although since I am working from the perspective of a historian rather than an anthropologist, I describe ethics in their historical context in an attempt to understand how they have changed over time.

23. George Lakoff has attempted something similar in the realm of communications theory and linguistics, examining the moral conceptual systems of American liberals and conservatives in the 1990s. See George Lakoff, *Moral Politics: What Conservatives Know that Liberals Don't* (Chicago: University of Chicago Press, 1996).

24. Wendy J. Deichmann Edwards and Carolyn De Swarte Gifford, eds., *Gender and the Social Gospel* (Urbana: University of Illinois Press, 2003), 2–3.

25. Ibid., 3.

26. For an examination of the crisis in Protestant authority and influence, see William R. Hutchison, ed., *Between the Times: The Travail of the Protestant Establishment* in America, *1900–1960*, Cambridge Studies in Religion and American Public Life (1989; reprint, New York: Cambridge University Press, 1990). For more on the "decline" of liberalism, see Richard Wightman Fox, "Experience and Explanation in Twentieth-Century American Religious History,"

in *New Directions in American Religious History*, ed. Harry S. Stout and D. G. Hart (New York: Oxford University Press, 1997). For the secularization argument, see, for instance, Joan Jacobs Brumberg's description of the transformation of anorexia nervosa from a "legitimate act of personal piety into a symptom of disease" and the concurrent triumph of doctors over clergy. Joan Jacobs Brumberg, *Fasting Girls: The Emergence of Anorexia Nervosa as a Modern Disease* (Cambridge, MA: Harvard University Press, 1988): 98–100. See also T. J. Jackson Lears, *No Place of Grace: Antimodernism and the Transformation of American Culture, 1880–1920* (New York: Pantheon Books, 1981); D. H. Meyer, "American Intellectuals and the Victorian Crisis of Faith," in *Victorian America*, ed. Daniel Walker Howe (Philadelphia: University of Pennsylvania Press, 1976); Paul A. Carter, *The Spiritual Crisis of the Gilded Age* (DeKalb: Northern Illinois University Press, 1971).

The most forceful arguments about secularization theory have come from sociologists. David Martin, in particular, has defined the parameters of the debate. See David A. Martin, "Toward Eliminating the Concept of Secularization," in *Penguin Survey of the Social Sciences 1965*, ed. Julius Gould (Baltimore: Penguin Books, 1965), 169–182; David A. Martin, *A General Theory of Secularization* (New York: Harper and Row, 1978); David A. Martin, "Secularisation and the Future of Christianity," *Journal of Contemporary Religion* 20, no. 2 (2005): 145–160; and David A. Martin, *On Secularization: Towards a Revised General Theory* (Burlington, VT: Ashgate, 2005). For an assessment of the viability of secularization theory and its larger context, see Steve Bruce, ed., *Religion and Modernization: Sociologists and Historians Debate the Secularization Theory* (Oxford: Clarendon Press, 1992) and Steve Bruce, *God Is Dead: Secularization in the West* (Malden, MA: Blackwell Publishing, 2002). Susan Curtis describes the loss of Protestant authority in her book *A Consuming Faith*, but she stresses the influence of the consumer culture rather than the authority of scientific discourse. Susan Curtis, *A Consuming Faith: The Social Gospel and Modern American Culture* (Baltimore: Johns Hopkins University Press, 1991). In the 1990s, scholarship about secularization focused on the relationship between Protestant intellectuals and the university; see Julie A. Reuben, *The Making of the Modern University: Intellectual Transformation and the Marginalization of Morality* (Chicago: University of Chicago Press, 1996); George M. Marsden, *The Soul of the American University: From Protestant Establishment to Established Nonbelief* (New York: Oxford University Press, 1994); Bradley J. Longfield and George M. Marsden, eds., *The Secularization of the Academy* (New York: Oxford University Press, 1992). See also James Turner, *Without God, Without Creed: The Origins of Unbelief in America* (Baltimore: Johns Hopkins University Press, 1985).

27. Machen did not believe religious liberalism was in decline. In fact, he worried that just the opposite was true. He argued that the manner in which liberal Christians accommodated science—abandoning "fundamental" doctrines if those doctrines conflicted with science—had resulted in a kind of Christianity that was not truly Christian. This distinction between true Christians and liberal Christians persisted in much of the rhetoric throughout the twentieth century. J. Gresham Machen, *Christianity and Liberalism* (New York: Macmillan, 1923).

28. Niebuhr's place in American religious liberalism has been hotly contested. Niebuhr's views have been interpreted as neoorthodox, neoconservative, and, most recently, neoliberal. See Gary J. Dorrien, *The Making of American Liberal Theology: Idealism, Realism, and Modernity, 1900–1950* (Louisville, KY: Westminster John Knox, 2003).

29. Gary Dorrien, in his monumental work on liberal theology, argues for the vitality of liberal theology in the twentieth century but contends that it should not be understood entirely in terms of its Social Gospel heritage, which was characterized by optimism and a belief in the possibility of "building the kingdom of God" on Earth. Dorrien, *The Making of American Liberal Theology: Idealism, Realism, and Modernity, 1900–1950*, 3–4.

30. See Ann Douglas, *The Feminization of American Culture* (New York: Alfred A. Knopf, 1977); Karin E. Gedge, *Without Benefit of Clergy: Women and the Pastoral Relationship in Nineteenth-Century American Culture*, Religion in America (New York: Oxford University Press, 2006).

31. James T. Kloppenberg, *The Virtues of Liberalism* (New York: Oxford University Press, 1998), esp. chap. 9, "Why History Matters to Political Theory."

Chapter One: Anton Boisen and the Scientific Study of Religion

Epigraph. Anton T. Boisen, *Out of the Depths: An Autobiographical Study of Mental Disorder and Religious Experience* (New York: Harper and Brothers, 1960), 132.

1. Boisen, *Out of the Depths*, 112, 202. Sorting out the numbers of psychotic episodes that Boisen suffered is difficult. While in the hospital for the first time in the early 1920s, he wrote to a friend and indicated that he had suffered similar episodes at least four times previously. In retrospect, Boisen characterized his experiences as either "problem-solving experiences" or as decisions "marked by deviation from the normal." In the first category, which he also referred to as "psychotic episodes," he included all of the incidents that resulted in hospitalization. In the latter group, he included his religious conversion and his call to the ministry. I refer to any event that led to Boisen's hospitalization as "major." One

such episode occurred while he was already in the hospital convalescing from an earlier psychotic break; when he suffered the new episode, he was returned to what he called the "disturbed" ward.

2. Ibid., 151–152.

3. Ibid., 60.

4. Dorothy Ross, *The Origins of American Social Science* (New York: Cambridge University Press, 1991), 390.

5. Stuart A. Rice, ed. *Methods in Social Science: A Case Book Compiled under the Direction of the Committee on Scientific Method in the Social Sciences of the Social Science Research Council* (Chicago: University of Chicago Press, 1931).

6. Mark C. Smith, *Social Science in the Crucible: The American Debate over Objectivity and Purpose, 1918–1941* (Durham, NC: Duke University Press, 1994), 20. For example, economist A. B. Wolfe saw science as a sort of *via media* between conservatism and radicalism. He argued, "The leading social function of scientific method is thus to delimit emotional or interest conflict to the sphere of ends or purposes, and to diminish, so far as humanly possible, the rôle played by subjective illusion and emotional astigmatism in the ordering of human affairs. In a word, the moral function of the scientific method is to rationalize interest conflicts." A. B. Wolfe, *Conservatism, Radicalism, and Scientific Method: An Essay on Social Attitudes* (New York: Macmillan, 1923), 203.

7. Smith, *Social Science in the Crucible*, 21, 23.

8. Anton Boisen, "Scientific Method in the Study of Human Nature," discussion outline, Box 195, Folder 2851, Association for Clinical Pastoral Education, Records 1930–1986, Pitts Theology Library Special Collections, Archives and Manuscripts Department, Emory University (hereafter, Pitts Collections, Emory).

9. Anton T. Boisen, "Economic Distress and Religious Experience: A Study of the Holy Rollers," reprint from *Psychiatry: Journal of the Biology and Pathology of Interpersonal Relations* 2, no. 2 (May 1939), Box 195, Folder 2849, Association for Clinical Pastoral Education, Records 1930–1986, Pitts Collections, Emory. See also Boisen's account of his first interview for a pastorate, in which he was rejected because he was "not sufficiently versed in the gentle art of drilling for water, that is, of eliciting tears." Boisen, *Out of the Depths*, 66. Boisen had a healthy skepticism of overly emotional religion and a greater trust in the rational processes. This did not mean he rejected the supernatural. In his assessment of the differences between himself and his teacher George Albert Coe, he commented that for him, unlike Coe, "Faith in the reality of mystical experience was fundamental." Boisen, *Out of the Depths*, 62.

10. Glen H. Asquith, Jr., "Anton T. Boisen and the Study of 'Living Human Documents'," *Journal of Presbyterian History* 60 (1982): 244–265.

11. Boisen, *Out of the Depths*, 20.

12. Ibid., 34–35.

13. Ibid., 46.

14. Ibid., 50.

15. Ibid., 59.

16. Ibid., 67.

17. Ibid., 71.

18. It was another three years before the organization's leaders applied to the court for permission to dissolve. *Time*, 23 December 1923.

19. Boisen, *Out of the Depths*, 77.

20. Ibid., 100.

21. Ibid., 100–101.

22. Ibid., 109.

23. For an excellent explanation of theories of psychophysical parallelism and the somatic paradigm in American psychiatric medicine, see Eric Caplan, *Mind Games: American Culture and the Birth of Psychotherapy* (Berkeley: University of California Press, 1998), esp. chaps. 3, 4, and 5.

24. Anton T. Boisen, *The Exploration of the Inner World: A Study of Mental Disorder and Religious Experience* (New York: Harper and Brothers, 1936), 5.

25. Boisen's conclusion about the nature of schizophrenia goes against much recent psychiatric opinion, which associates schizophrenia with dopamine imbalances in the brain and underlying genetic causes.

26. Anton T. Boisen, "Schizophrenia and Religious Experience" (esp. pp. 55–57), reprinted for private circulation from the Collected and Contributed Papers Published on the Sixtieth Anniversary of the Elgin State Hospital, December 1932, Box 194, Folder 2845, Association for Clinical Pastoral Education, Records 1930–1986, Pitts Collections, Emory. Boisen regularly reminded his readers of the possibility that mental illness could also result from malignant character tendencies, but he never developed this idea, and it is difficult to determine its origin. Boisen's views differed from those of some of his contemporaries in the eugenics movement who perceived moral degeneracy and "feeblemindedness" as a function of genetics and heredity rather than as an accumulation of poor choices on the part of the patient. The most infamous case from the time was that of Carrie Buck, who was deemed mentally incompetent by the State of Virginia in 1924 and underwent compulsory sterilization.

27. Boisen, "Schizophrenia and Religious Experience." The analogy of mental disorder to fever recurs in Boisen's work. See also Boisen, *Exploration of the Inner World*, 29; and Anton T. Boisen, "The Problem of Sin and Salvation in the Light of Psychopathology," reprinted for private circulation from *The Journal of*

Religion 22, no. 3 (July 1942), Box 195, Folder 2851, Association for Clinical Pastoral Education, Records 1930–1986, Pitts Collections, Emory.

28. Anton T. Boisen, "The Form and Content of Schizophrenic Thinking" (n.d.), Box 195, Folder 2851, Association for Clinical Pastoral Education, Records 1930–1986, Pitts Collections, Emory.

29. Ibid., 27.

30. Ibid., 28.

31. Ibid.

32. Ibid.

33. Ibid., 29.

34. Ibid., 30.

35. Ibid.

36. Boisen, *Out of the Depths*, 109.

37. Ibid., 111.

38. There is no evidence that doctors at Bloomingdale were using psychoanalysis, and Boisen did not indicate why he thought he would be subject to analysis if he went there. Bloomingdale Asylum was established in 1821 and was the antecedent of the current Payne Whitney Clinics administered by the Weill Cornell Department of Psychiatry.

39. Boisen, *Out of the Depths*, 121–126.

40. Ibid., 134. Letter from Coe to Boisen dated September 1, 1921.

41. Caplan, *Mind Games*, 122–123. Caplan argues convincingly that the success of Worcester and McComb's Emmanuel Movement played a crucial role in moving the medical profession toward claiming psychotherapy as its exclusive territory. For a detailed description of the theories and methods of the Emmanuel Movement which places the movement in the larger context of American religious experience, see Ann Taves, *Fits, Trances, and Visions: Experiencing Religion and Explaining Experience from Wesley to James* (Princeton: Princeton University Press, 1999), 314–325.

42. Caplan, *Mind Games*, 123 and 127. Neurasthenia had been conceptualized several decades earlier by medical doctor George Miller Beard and became a popular diagnosis among the white middle class.

43. Elwood Worcester, Samuel McComb, and Isador H. Coriat, *Religion and Medicine: The Moral Control of Nervous Disorders* (New York: Moffat, Yard, and Company, 1908), 43.

44. Ibid., 272. For more about the Emmanuel Movement, see Sanford Gifford, *The Emmanuel Movement: The Origins of Group Treatment and the Assault on Lay Psychotherapy* (Boston: Harvard University Press for the Francis Countway Library of Medicine, 1997).

45. Boisen, *Out of the Depths*, 138–142.

46. Edward E. Thornton, *Professional Education for Ministry: A History of Clinical Pastoral Education* (Nashville: Abingdon Press, 1970), 50.

47. Ibid., 46.

48. Richard C. Cabot, *Adventures on the Borderlands of Ethics* (New York: Harper and Brothers, 1926).

49. Boisen, *Out of the Depths*, 150.

50. Thornton, *Professional Education for Ministry*, 77. In order to pursue three degrees simultaneously, Dunbar secured the services of two secretaries who attended classes for her and took notes for her. For a discussion of Dunbar's influence and her relationship to the others, see Robert Charles Powell, "Healing and Wholeness: Helen Flanders Dunbar (1902–1959) and an Extra-Medical Origin of the American Psychosomatic Movement, 1906–1936" (Ph.D. diss., Duke University, 1974), 197–201, 208–212, and 223. See also Allison Stokes, *Ministry After Freud* (New York: Pilgrim Press, 1985).

51. Anton Boisen, "Our Objectives," lecture at the first annual meeting of the Council for the Clinical Training of Theological Students (CCTTS), Box 1, Folder 1, Association for Clinical Pastoral Education, Records 1930–1986, Pitts Collections, Emory.

52. "Clinical Psychology for Religious Workers," from First Annual Report of the Council for Clinical Training of Theological Students, 1930, Association for Clinical Pastoral Education, Northeast Region, Records 1932–1985, Andover Harvard Theological Library, Manuscripts and Archives, Harvard Divinity School.

53. Boisen, *Out of the Depths*, 151.

54. Anton T. Boisen, "An Adventure in Theological Education and Pastoral Service, 1937: A Statement of the Aims and Accomplishments of the Council for the Clinical Training of Theological Students in the Chicago Area," Box 195, Folder 2849, Association for Clinical Pastoral Education, Records 1930–1986, Pitts Collections, Emory. Boisen did not promote training by clinical practice to the exclusion of reading. In a report on CPE in the mid-1940s, he criticized other CPE supervisors for failing to develop sufficiently their libraries and reading lists for students.

55. Boisen, *Out of the Depths*, 169. Carroll Wise, "Clinical Pastoral Training—The Early Years," unpublished manuscript, Box 3, Folder 36, Association for Clinical Pastoral Education, Records 1930–1986, Pitts Collections, Emory.

56. The origins of the split between Cabot and Boisen and a later split in the council that led to the formation of the Institute of Pastoral Care in 1932 are explored in greater detail in chapter 2. Boisen's view that the reasons for the split were both personal and ideological was probably at least partly accurate. He and

Dunbar differed sharply with Cabot and Guiles regarding the etiology of mental illness. Boisen failed to recognize, however, that maneuvering for control of the council probably also played a critical role. Guiles and Dunbar were struggling for administrative control of the fledgling organization, and Cabot simply did not like Dunbar. The concentration of extraordinarily strong-willed people had probably doomed the joint endeavor from its inception. See E. Brooks Holifield, *A History of Pastoral Care in America: From Salvation to Self-Realization* (Nashville: Abingdon, 1983), 234; Charles E. Hall, *Head and Heart* (n.p.: Journal of Pastoral Care Publications, 1992), 35–41; Thornton, *Professional Education for Ministry*, 52; Powell, "Healing and Wholeness," 216–217.

57. Boisen, *Out of the Depths*, 157.

58. Ibid., 155.

59. All of Boisen's most serious episodes occurred in late fall and resulted in hospitalization through November and December. We do not have enough information to propose an explanation, but it hardly seems like a coincidence.

60. Boisen, "Schizophrenia and Religious Experience."

61. Boisen, *Exploration of the Inner World*, 16.

62. R. G. Hoskins and M. H. Erikson, "The Grading of Patients in Mental Hospitals as a Therapeutic Measure," *American Journal of Psychiatry* 11 (1932): 103–109.

63. Boisen included a copy of ward observation notes in a 1946 unpublished manuscript in which he attempted to articulate a standardized plan for clinical training. Anton T. Boisen, "Clinical Training in the Service of the Mentally Ill: A Beginning Course," 1946, Record Group 001, Association for Clinical Pastoral Education, Records 1930–1986, Pitts Collections, Emory.

64. Boisen, *Exploration of the Inner World*, 18.

65. Ibid., 18–27.

66. Ibid., 48–57.

67. Ibid., 114.

68. Ibid., 62, 63–64, 66.

69. Ibid., 81.

70. Boisen, "An Adventure in Theological Education."

Chapter Two: The Methodology of Clinical Pastoral Education

Epigraph. Helen Flanders Dunbar, "A Few Words as to the Significance of the Newly Established Council for the Clinical Training of Theological Students," first annual report of the Council for the Clinical Training of Theological Students, Box 6, Folder 4, Association for Clinical Pastoral Education. Northeast

Region. Records, 1932–1985, Andover-Harvard Theological Library, Harvard Divinity School.

1. For more on the Judge Baker Guidance Center, see Kathleen W. Jones, *Taming the Troublesome Child: American Families, Child Guidance, and the Limits of Psychiatric Authority* (Cambridge, MA: Harvard University Press, 1999), 9–10. Founded originally to work with juvenile offenders under the direction of psychiatrist William Healy and psychologist Augusta Bronner, the center moved toward a broader constituency that included young people with "nondelinquent emotional and behavior problems." Jones traces the history of Judge Baker Guidance Center and focuses on issues of professional authority encountered by child guidance workers.

2. Dunbar's attempts to centralize control of the training programs eventually caused trouble between her and the independent-minded theological supervisors.

3. Russell L. Dicks, "Annual Report on the Training of Theological Students at the Massachusetts General Hospital in the City of Boston, Mass., 1934," Box 206, Folder 3054, Association for Clinical Pastoral Education, Records 1930–2005, Pitts Theology Library Special Collections, Archives and Manuscripts Department, Emory University (hereafter, Pitts Collections, Emory).

4. Carroll Wise, "Clinical Pastoral Training—The Early Years," unpublished manuscript, Box 3, Folder 36, Association for Clinical Pastoral Education, Records 1930–1986, Pitts Collections, Emory.

5. Mark Smith, in his history of the social sciences between the world wars, argues that, as the second generation of social scientists came of age in an academic and institutional system that penalized activist scholarship, they embraced objectivity and efficiency as their goals and avoided the moral vision of the previous generation. While CPE supervisors still believed their work had a moral purpose—the relief of suffering—they also emphasized the professional implications of clinical training for clergy much more than did Boisen, who represented that early generation of social scientist reformers and moralists. Mark Smith, *Social Science in the Crucible: The American Debate over Objectivity and Purpose, 1918–1941* (Durham, NC: Duke University Press, 1994).

6. For accounts of CPE history written by clinical pastoral educators, see Charles E. Hall, *Head and Heart* (n.p.: Journal of Pastoral Care Publications, 1992); Edward E. Thornton, *Professional Education for Ministry: A History of Clinical Pastoral Education* (Nashville: Abingdon Press, 1970). For a brief general treatment of CPE as part of the larger history of pastoral care in the United States, see E. Brooks Holifield, *A History of Pastoral Care in America: From Salvation to Self-Realization* (Nashville: Abingdon, 1983), 231–249.

7. Boisen's views on the etiology of mental illness are detailed elsewhere, but for an expression of those views in the context of clinical training, see the lecture he gave at the first annual meeting of the CCTTS. Anton Boisen, "Our Objectives," lecture at the first annual meeting of the CCTTS, Box 1, Folder 1, Association for Clinical Pastoral Education, Records 1930–1986, Pitts Collections, Emory.

8. Wise, "Clinical Pastoral Training—The Early Years."

9. Holifield, *A History of Pastoral Care*, 234. See also Hall, *Head and Heart*, 35–41; Thornton, *Professional Education for Ministry*, 52; Robert Charles Powell, "Healing and Wholeness: Helen Flanders Dunbar (1902–1959) and an Extra-Medical Origin of the American Psychosomatic Movement, 1906–1936" (Ph.D. diss. Duke University, 1974), 216–217.

10. It is a curious footnote to this story that in the early 1930s, just as the CCTTS was splitting into factions, Boisen and Dunbar were both cementing their friendship with Elwood Worcester. In addition to his ongoing correspondence with Boisen, Worcester worked regularly with Dunbar during the years when she was director of the Joint Committee on Religion and Medicine sponsored by the Federal Council of Churches and the New York Academy of Medicine to explore psychosomatic medicine (1931–1936). He mentioned neither colleague in his autobiography, despite his personal relationships with both and the importance of both to the study of religion and health in this era. More curious still is the attitude of Worcester's daughter, Dr. Blandina Worcester, who in a 1978 interview simply refused to discuss Dunbar's relationship with her father. Sanford Gifford, *The Emmanuel Movement: The Origins of Group Treatment and the Assault on Lay Psychotherapy* (Boston: Harvard University Press for The Francis Countway Library of Medicine, 1997), 107. Charles Hall, in his combination memoir-history of CPE, speculated on the reasons for the council split and offered some anecdotal evidence that gender played a critical role in the difficulties. He noted that Guiles once commented that Cabot disliked Dunbar because "she had outsmarted him on most occasions." Hall also recorded Russell Dicks's opinion that the split resulted from Dunbar's use of her "feminine wiles" to convince Guiles to take her side against Cabot. Hall, *Head and Heart*, 18, 38.

11. Thornton, *Professional Education for Ministry*, 89.

12. "Annual Catalogue 1937," published by the Council for the Clinical Training of Theological Students, Box 6, Folder 4, Association for Clinical Pastoral Education, Northeast Region Papers, 1932–1985, Andover-Harvard Theological Library, Harvard Divinity School.

13. The pamphlet describing the council for 1939 indicates that Dunbar guided the council from 1930 through 1936. After 1936, Robert Brinkman was council director, followed in the 1940s by Frederick Kuether. See "An Opportu-

nity for Theological Education," 1939, Box 1, Folder 10, Association for Clinical Pastoral Education, Records 1930–1986, Pitts Collections, Emory. Historian Robert Powell sees Dunbar's post-council years as a period of decline, but she continued to write prolifically, authoring some of her most important contributions to the field of psychosomatic medicine. See Powell, "Healing and Wholeness," 270–275.

14. Joseph F. Fletcher, "The Development of the Clinical Training Movement Through the Graduate School of Applied Religion," in *Clinical Pastoral Training*, ed. Seward Hiltner (New York: Federal Council of Churches, Commission on Religion and Health, 1945), 1.

15. Ibid., 2.

16. Ibid.

17. Joseph F. Fletcher, "Standards for a Full-Time Program in the Light of the Experience of The Graduate School of Applied Religion," in *Clinical Pastoral Training*, ed. Seward Hiltner (New York: Federal Council of Churches, Commission in Religion and Health, 1945), 31–35.

18. Glenn T. Miller, " 'Professionals and Pedagogues: A Survey of Theological Education," in *Altered Landscapes:* Christianity in America, 1935–1985, ed. David W. Lotz Jr., Donald W. Shriver, Robert T. Handy, and John F. Wilson (Grand Rapids, MI: William B. Eerdmans Publishing, 1989), 35. See also Glenn T. Miller, *Piety and Profession: American Protestant Theological Education, 1870–1970* (Grand Rapids, MI: William B. Eerdmans Publishing, 2007).

19. See, for instance, Floyd Nelson House, *The Development of Sociology*, 5th ed. (New York: McGraw-Hill, 1936); Gordon Hamilton, *Theory and Practice of Social Case Work* (New York: Columbia University Press, 1940); Stuart A. Rice, *Methods in Social Science: A Case Book Compiled Under the Direction of the Committee on Scientific Method in the Social Sciences of the Social Science Research Council* (Chicago: University of Chicago Press, 1931).

20. Carroll A. Wise, "The Development of the Training Program for Theological Students at the Worcester State Hospital," 1935, Box 158, Folder 2444, Association for Clinical Pastoral Education, Records 1930–2005, Pitts Collections, Emory.

21. Alexander D. Dodd, "The Rhode Island State Hospital, 1932," annual report from the Third Annual Conference of the Council for the Clinical Training of Theological Students, Box 194, Folder 2844, Association for Clinical Pastoral Education, Records 1930–2005, Pitts Collections, Emory. See also Elmer P. Wentz et al., "Clinical Training for Theological Students at Mayview, Pa, 1932," A report written by the summer students, Box 194, Folder 2844, Association for Clinical Pastoral Education, Records 1930–2005, Pitts Collections, Emory.

22. Leon R. Robison, "Report of the Theological Group at Franklin School, 1934, Institute of the Pennsylvania Hospital, Philadelphia, Pa," Box 206, Folder 3054, Association for Clinical Pastoral Education, Records 1930, Pitts Collections, Emory. Judge Baker Guidance Center had a mission similar to that of Franklin. Seminarians interviewed students and took family histories then served as big brothers or probation officers for the boys.

23. Ibid. See the previous year's report also: L. R. Robison, "Report of the Theological Group at Franklin, Summer—1933," annual report, Box 157, Folder 2438, Association for Clinical Pastoral Education, Records 1930–2005, Pitts Collections, Emory.

24. Seward Hiltner, "Clinical Training in Philadelphia, Summer of 1936," annual report, Box 115, Folder 1630, Association for Clinical Pastoral Education, Records 1930–2005, Pitts Collections, Emory.

25. H. M. Hildreth, "The Syracuse Psychopathic Hospital, 1932," annual report prepared for the Third Annual Conference of the Council for the Clinical Training of Theological Students, Box 194, Folder 2844, Association for Clinical Pastoral Education, Records 1930–2005, Pitts Collections, Emory.

26. Rothe Hilger, "The Work of the Council for the Clinical Training of Theological Students at the Judge Baker Guidance Center—Summer of 1933," annual report, Box 157, Folder 2438, Association for Clinical Pastoral Education, Records 1930–2005, Pitts Collections, Emory.

27. Wise, "Development of the Training Program for Theological Students."

28. Blank case study format dated 1940, Box 204, Folder 3024, Association for Clinical Pastoral Education, Records 1930–2005, Pitts Collections, Emory. The folder also includes two other blank formats, one dated 1931 and the other dated 1936. The later version of the case study format did not differ significantly from the earlier versions except that the earlier ones were intended for use in a psychiatric hospital and the later one was designed for use with delinquent boys and included specific questions relevant to their situation.

29. Anton T. Boisen and Victor V. Schuldt, "The Elgin State Hospital, 1933," annual report, Box 157, Folder 2438, Association for Clinical Pastoral Education, Records 1930–1986, Pitts Collections, Emory.

30. Ibid.

31. Wentz et al., "Clinical Training for Theological Students at Mayview, Pa., 1932."

32. Robert E. Brinkman, "First Annual Report on the Training of Theological Students at the New Jersey State Hospital at Greystone Park, N.J., 1934," Box 206, Folder 3054, Association for Clinical Pastoral Education, Records 1930, Pitts Collections, Emory. Similar case studies were used by Boisen at Elgin State. It is not clear from the historical record whether Boisen wrote the case

studies and Brinkman, the theological supervisor at Greystone, used them verbatim, or if Brinkman borrowed the idea from Boisen and wrote his own case studies. Case studies with similar names show up in a number of programs, but it is not immediately apparent whether everybody was using the same material. There was a drive for standardization going on, but most CPE supervisors had strong opinions about the content of their programs and might have resisted using material from other supervisors.

33. Donald C. Beatty, "Mayview Training Center, 1933," annual report on Pittsburgh City Home and Hospitals in Mayview, Pa., Box 157, Folder 2438, Association for Clinical Pastoral Education, Records 1930–2005, Pitts Collections, Emory; Harold M. Hildreth, "Syracuse Psychopathic Hospital, 1933," annual report, Box 157, Folder 2438, Association for Clinical Pastoral Education, Records 1930–2005, Pitts Collections, Emory.

34. Leonard S. Edmonds, "Rochester State Hospital, 1939," supervisor's report, Box 113, Folder 1576, Association for Clinical Pastoral Education, Records 1930–2005, Pitts Collections, Emory.

35. Rollin Fairbanks, "Standards for Full-Time Clinical Training in the Light of the New England Experience," in *Clinical Pastoral Training*, ed. Seward Hiltner (New York: Federal Council of Churches, Commission on Religion and Health, 1945), 38; Fletcher, "Standards for a Full-Time Program," 34; Frederick C. Kuether, *The Place of Clinical Training in the Theological Curriculum as Training Supervisors See It*, ed. Seward Hiltner (New York: Federal Council of Churches, Commission on Religion and Health, 1945), 89.

36. "Annual Report of the President, 1938," Box 1, Folder 9, Association for Clinical Pastoral Education, Records 1930–2005, Pitts Collections, Emory.

37. Council for the Clinical Training of Theological Students, Annual Catalogue, 1937, Box 1, Folder 7, Association for Clinical Pastoral Education, Records 1930–2005, Pitts Collections, Emory. Section I for a list of council members.

38. "Annual Catalogue, 1937," Box 1, Folder 7, Association for Clinical Pastoral Education, Records 1930–2005, Pitts Collections, Emory.

39. "A New Opportunity in Theological Education" (pamphlet), 1935, Box 1, Folder 3, Association for Clinical Pastoral Education, Records 1930–2005, Pitts Collections, Emory.

40. Brinkman, "First Annual Report on the Training of Theological Students at the New Jersey State Hospital at Greystone Park, N.J., 1934."

41. Russell L. Dicks and Ida M. Cannon, "Massachusetts General Hospital," annual report, 1933, Box 157, Folder 2438, Association for Clinical Pastoral Education, Records 1930–2005, Pitts Collections, Emory. Ms. Snow's role as consultant was made possible through a gift from Richard Cabot. The details

are not clear, but Cannon's wording in the report suggests that Snow was already on the social service staff at MGH and Cabot gave enough money to pay her salary half-time to serve as a consultant.

42. "Schedule of Conferences—1933 Student Group," from Mayview Training Center, Box 157, Folder 2438, Association for Clinical Pastoral Education, Records 1930–2005, Pitts Collections, Emory.

43. "Schedule of Conferences—1933 Student Group." See also the program reports for the Franklin School and Worcester State Hospital in the same year. L. R. Robison, "Report of the Theological Group at Franklin, Summer—1933"; Carroll Wise, "Report on the Clinical Training of Theological Students in the Worcester State Hospital, Summer of 1933," annual report, Box 157, Folder 2438, Association for Clinical Pastoral Education, Records 1930–2005, Pitts Collections, Emory. The seminar content for each program reflected the priorities of the sponsoring institution; at Franklin School (a school for children), the seminars highlighted children's problems and psychiatric solutions, while at Worcester State Hospital (a psychiatric hospital) the program devoted more seminar hours to topics related to a general understanding of mental illness. The concern for mastering certain basic information was ongoing. See, for instance, the description of the program at Rhode Island State Hospital under the direction of Alexander Dodd in 1932. Dodd, "The Rhode Island State Hospital, 1932." Dodd's schedule of seminars included presentations by hospital staff on "the somatic bases of mental illness," "mental hygiene and religion," and "psychiatric social work."

44. Robison, "Report of the Theological Group at Franklin, Summer—1933." We do not know whether the student's evaluation of his or her own skills was accurate, but his evaluation of the program suggests that the supervisor had, at the very least, successfully communicated the goals of the program.

45. Robert E. Brinkman, "Report of Activities at Greystone Park, New Jersey, 1935," Box 111, Folder 1535, Association for Clinical Pastoral Education, Records 1930, Pitts Collections, Emory.

46. Dicks, "Annual Report on the Training at the Massachusetts General Hospital, 1934."

47. Hiltner, "Clinical Training in Philadelphia, Summer of 1936"; Harold Hildreth, the theological supervisor at Syracuse Psychopathic Hospital, thought there was no better way for students to learn about a variety of social services than through clinical training. The student, Hildreth argued, learned about how social agencies handled the unemployed, the "aged," the sick, the "foreign population," alcoholics, and the "marital maladjusted." Hildreth, "Syracuse Psychopathic Hospital, 1933."

48. For a discussion of religion and mental health in America in the twentieth century, see Donald Meyer, *The Positive Thinkers: Religion as Pop Psychology from Mary Baker Eddy to Oral Roberts* (New York: Pantheon Books, 1980). On both Elwood Worcester and mind cure see Raymond Cunningham, "The Emmanuel Movement: A Variety of American Religious Experience," *American Quarterly* 14 (1962): 48–63; Raymond Joseph Cunningham, "Ministry of Healing: The Origins of the Psychotherapeutic Role of the American Churches" (Ph.D. diss., University of Pennsylvania, 1965). For a discussion of clinical training specifically, see Hall, *Head and Heart* (n. 6 above). See also Holifield, *A History of Pastoral Care in America*; Thornton, *Professional Education for Ministry*; Powell, "Healing and Wholeness" (n. 9 above); Allison Stokes, *Ministry after Freud* (New York: Pilgrim Press, 1985).

49. Stokes, *Ministry after Freud*, 102.

50. Their dissatisfaction with theological education was entirely consistent with criticisms coming from other, more influential, quarters. Historian Glenn T. Miller has suggested that in the 1920s and 1930s the whole concept of seminary education was undergoing revision. During this period, ministers first began to define theological education as ministerial education or education intended to prepare the parish minister. An influential study commissioned by the Conference of Theological Schools suggested that seminaries ought to reorganize themselves to train ministers. Miller, "Professionals and Pedagogues," 190–191. See also, Miller, *Piety and Profession*, esp. chap. 6.

51. For good examples of the struggle to control professional culture, especially in relation to the medical profession, see Jones, *Taming the Troublesome Child* (n. 1 above); Rennie B. Schoepflin, *Christian Science on Trial: Religious Healing in America* (Baltimore: Johns Hopkins University Press, 2003).

52. Carroll A. Wise, "The Development of the Training Program for Theological Students at the Worcester State Hospital." In this case, the doctors seemed to value Beaven for his youth and his similarities to the patient and not for his theological training; but Wise, determined to demonstrate the utility of clinically trained clergy, was reluctant to acknowledge that something other than Beaven's religious beliefs had led the doctor to choose Beaven.

53. Seward Hiltner, *Religion and Health* (New York: Macmillan, 1943), 106.

54. Dodd, "The Rhode Island State Hospital, 1932."

55. Hilger, "Council for the Clinical Training of Theological Students—Summer of 1933." Hilger's position at the center is not clear. He was not the supervisor. In the early years, however, second year students sometimes worked in settings where there was no formal program and supplemented their work with seminars at established programs. This may have been the case here. Hilger

probably had previous training at Massachusetts General. It would have made no sense to simply repeat the MGH program, but he could work at Judge Baker and sit in on seminars at MGH. The program at St. Charles had a similar arrangement in the summer of 1933. Beatty, "Mayview Training Center, 1933."

56. Dicks and Cannon, "Massachusetts General Hospital, 1933."

57. Annual report, Worcester State Hospital, 1934, Box 206, Folder 3054, Association for Clinical Pastoral Education, Records 1930, Pitts Collections, Emory.

58. Wise, "Development of the Training Program for Theological Students" (1935).

59. Hiltner, "Clinical Training in Philadelphia, Summer of 1936."

60. Brinkman, "First Annual Report on the Training of Theological Students at the New Jersey State Hospital at Greystone Park, N.J., 1934."

61. Richard C. Cabot and Russell L. Dicks, *The Art of Ministering to the Sick* (New York: Macmillan, 1936), 255.

62. "Clinical Experience for Students of New England Theological Schools Yearly Report," 1936, Box 20, Folder 7, Association for Clinical Pastoral Education, Northeast Region. Papers, 1932–1985, Andover-Harvard Theological Library, Manuscripts and Archives, Harvard Divinity School.

63. "Clinical Experience for Students of New England Theological Schools Yearly Report," 1936.

64. Ibid.

65. Verbatim report by a student in an IPC clinical training program, Box 6, Folder 3, Association for Clinical Pastoral Education, Northeast Region, Andover-Harvard Theological Library, Manuscripts and Archives, Harvard Divinity School.

Chapter Three: The Minds of Moralists

Epigraph. Rollo May, *The Art of Counseling* (1939; reprint, New York: Abingdon Press, 1967), 179.

1. Eric Caplan, *Mind Games: American Culture and the Birth of Psychotherapy* (Berkeley: University of California Press, 1998), 123.

2. Ibid., 117–148. For a detailed description of the theories and methods of the Emmanuel Movement which places the movement in the larger context of American religious experience, see Ann Taves, *Fits, Trances, and Visions: Experiencing Religion and Explaining Experience from Wesley to James* (Princeton: Princeton University Press, 1999), 314–325.

3. Sanford Gifford, *The Emmanuel Movement: The Origins of Group Treatment and the Assault on Lay Psychotherapy* (Boston: Harvard University Press

for The Francis Countway Library of Medicine, 1997). See also Frank Shorter, *A History of Psychiatry: From the Era of the Asylum to the Age of Prozac* (New York: John Wiley & Sons, 1997). Shorter documents the increasingly intimate relationship between psychiatry and psychoanalysis, as well as the expanding influence of psychiatrists.

4. Caplan, in *Mind Games*, makes a strong argument for the idea that psychiatrists used psychotherapy to establish their cultural authority. See also Roy Lubove, *The Professional Altruist: The Emergence of Social Work as a Career* (Cambridge, MA: Harvard University Press, 1965), 72. As a part of his account of the professionalization of social work, Lubove explores the alliance of psychiatrists and social workers in the mental hygiene movement. Elizabeth Lunbeck examines the expanding cultural authority of psychiatrists but focuses on gender and sexuality as the central issues. Elizabeth Lunbeck, *The Psychiatric Persuasion: Knowledge, Gender, and Power in Modern America* (Princeton: Princeton University Press, 1994).

5. Shorter, *A History of Psychiatry*, 25.

6. Mark Courtney, "Psychiatric Social Workers and Early Days of Private Practice," *Social Science* (June 1992): 199–214.

7. Donald H. Blocher, *The Evolution of Counseling Psychology* (New York: Springer, 2000), 20, 21.

8. Alice R. McCabe, "Pastoral Counseling and Case Work," reprint from *The Family*, Box 17, Folder 7, Association for Clinical Pastoral Education, Northeast Region, Papers, 1932–1985, Andover-Harvard Theological Library, Manuscripts and Archives, Harvard Divinity School.

9. Their fellow professionals likewise struggled with how to name themselves and describe their practice. Although E. G. Williamson coined the term "clinical counseling" in the late 1930s, no separate division for counseling psychology existed in the major professional organizations until after the merging of the American Association of Applied Psychology and the American Psychological Association in 1945. In a similar manner, the term "pastoral counselor" did not come into common use until after World War II.

10. Roy J. DeCarvalho, "Rollo R. May (1909–1994): A Biographical Sketch," *Journal of Humanistic Psychology* 36 (Spring 1996): 8. See also Robert H. Abzug, "Rollo May as a Friend to Man," *Journal of Humanistic Psychology* 36 (Spring 1996): 17–22.

11. May, *The Art of Counseling*, 15.

12. Ibid., 21.

13. Ibid., 24.

14. John Sutherland Bonnell, *Pastoral Psychiatry* (New York: Harper & Brothers, 1938), 24.

15. Ibid., xii.

16. Ibid., 54.

17. Ibid., 129.

18. Ibid., 130.

19. Charles Holman, *The Cure of Souls: A Socio-Psychological Approach* (Chicago: University of Chicago Press, 1932), 45.

20. Ibid., 61.

21. Ibid., 187.

22. Ibid., esp. chap. 15.

23. Ibid., 317.

24. Ibid., 183.

25. Bonnell, *Pastoral Psychiatry*, 173–179.

26. Ibid., 181.

27. Holman, *The Cure of Souls*, 56.

28. Ibid., 155. Holman also used the term "self-realization," describing it as the primary goal of the person. He cited W. C. Bowers' *Character through Creative Experience* and Thomas's *Maladjusted Girl* to define self-realization as the development of "potentialities," the unification and socialization of the personality, and the satisfaction of wishes. Few pastoral counselors talked in terms of self-realization prior to the 1940s, but the term would become, with a somewhat revised definition, a buzzword for postwar pastoral counselors.

29. Richard Cabot, "Spiritual Ministrations to the Sick," reprint from *Religion and Life*, Association for Clinical Pastoral Education, Records 1930–2005, Pitts Theology Library Special Collections, Archives and Manuscripts Department, Emory University.

30. Ibid.

31. Ibid.

32. Ibid.

33. Ibid.

34. Ibid.

35. Richard C. Cabot and Russell L. Dicks, *The Art of Ministering to the Sick* (New York: Macmillan, 1936), 378.

36. Ibid., 18.

37. Ibid.

38. Ibid., 19.

39. Bonnell, *Pastoral Psychiatry*, 175–176.

40. May, *The Art of Counseling*, 123.

41. Ibid., 136–139.

42. Bonnell, *Pastoral Psychiatry*, 117.

Chapter Four: From Adjustment to Autonomy

Epigraph. Carl R. Rogers, quoted in *Pastoral Psychology* 1, no. 1 (February 1950): 66. The editors of *Pastoral Psychology* frequently used quotations from well-known psychologists and theologians as filler in the journal.

1. This is not meant to underplay the importance of either Boisen or clinical pastoral education programs. Boisen's work enjoyed a bit of a renaissance in the 1960s, as pastoral counselors returned to grappling with questions of sin and salvation (see chapters 9 and 10). As evidenced by their annual catalogues, clinical pastoral education programs continued to enjoy growing enrollments throughout the postwar period and remained one of the primary sources of training and education for aspiring pastoral counselors.

2. Ellen Herman, *The Romance of American Psychology* (Berkeley: University of California Press, 1995), esp. chaps. 2, 3, and 4. See also James H. Capshew, *Psychologists on the March: Science, Practice, and Professional Identity in America, 1929–1969* (New York: Cambridge University Press, 1999), chap. 2.

3. For an example of pastoral counselors' view of the wartime experience and its potential, see Russell L. Dicks, *Pastoral Work and Personal Counseling* (New York: Macmillan, 1944), 113; Charles I. Carpenter, "Suggestions from the War Fronts on the Needs of Pastoral Work We Must Meet," in *Clinical Pastoral Training*, ed. Seward Hiltner (New York: Federal Council of Churches, Commission on Religion and Health, 1945), 153.

4. The 1948 Annual Catalogue for the Council for Clinical Training identified three major program goals. Those goals included helping theological students and clergy to understand people's problems, "emotional and spiritual," to develop a method for "working with people," and to know how to "work co-operatively" with other professional groups. The catalogue also included a rationale for working with an institutionalized population, even though most clergy served in parish or other noninstitutional settings. Annual Catalogue, 1948, Council for Clinical Training, Inc., Box 2, Folder 18, Records of the Association for Clinical Pastoral Education, Pitts Theology Library Special Collections, Archives and Manuscripts Department, Emory University, Atlanta, GA (hereafter, Pitts Collections, Emory).

5. Council for Clinical Training, pamphlet, 1942, Box 1, Folder 13, Records of the Association for Clinical Pastoral Education, Pitts Collections, Emory.

6. Council for Clinical Training pamphlet, 1942.

7. Capshew has argued that it was the Veterans Administration and the Public Health Service that "practically created a new mental health specialty" at the

end of the war by providing funds to train clinical psychologists to work with newly returned veterans. Capshew, *Psychologists on the March*, 132-140 and 171.

8. A Report of Seminars on Personal Counseling on Wartime Problems Conducted by the Y.M.C.A., Box 201, Folder 2959, Records of the Association for Clinical Pastoral Education, Records 1930–1986, Pitts Collections, Emory. The Army and Navy Department of the YMCA also published pamphlets on counseling, including Charles Holman's "A Workshop in Personal Counseling," Box 200, Folder 2925, and Rollo May's "The Ministry of Counseling," Box 201, Folder 2956.

9. A Report of Seminars on Personal Counseling on Wartime Problems Conducted by the Y.M.C.A.

10. Carl R. Rogers, *On Becoming a Person: A Therapist's View of Psychotherapy* (Boston: Houghton Mifflin, 1961), 9, 10. See also Brian Thorne, *Carl Rogers* (London: Sage Publications, 1992), 8–11.

11. Carl R. Rogers, *Counseling and Psychotherapy: Newer Concepts in Practice* (Cambridge, MA: Houghton Mifflin, 1942), 24, 25.

12. Ibid., 29

13. Ibid., 127.

14. Charles T. Holman, "A Workshop in Personal Counseling," Box 200, Folder 2925, Records of the Association for Clinical Pastoral Education, Records 1930–1986, Pitts Collections, Emory.

15. "Principles and Techniques of Counseling," excerpts from address by Holman at seminar on personal counseling in wartime, Box 200, Folder 2925, Records of the Association for Clinical Pastoral Education, Records 1930–1986, Pitts Collections, Emory.

16. Holman, "Workshop in Personal Counseling."

17. Ibid., 15.

18. Ibid., 17.

19. Ibid., 18.

20. Ibid., 48.

21. "What Lies Behind Behavior Problems," excerpts from address by Holman at seminar on personal counseling in wartime, Box 200, Folder 2925, Association for Clinical Pastoral Education, Records 1930–1986, Pitts Collections, Emory.

22. Romans 7:15, RSV. Pastoral counselors commonly used the Revised Standard Version. This passage in the King James Version reads, "For that which I do, I allow not: for what I would, that do I not; but what I hate, that do I."

23. Susan Quinn, *A Mind of Her Own: The Life of Karen Horney* (New York: Summit Books, 1987), 269

24. Quinn, *A Mind of Her Own*, 322, 359–361. Biographer Susan Quinn quoted orthodox analyst Otto Fenichel who was highly critical of *New Ways in Psychoanalysis*. Quinn records that the Association for the Advancement of Psychoanalysis, the group with which Horney was identified, failed to gain recognition from the more orthodox American Psychoanalytic Association, which, in turn, excluded Horney from important intradisciplinary debate. The most important psychoanalytic journals of the day refused to review her work.

25. For an example of one of the bibliographies, see Dan M. Potter, Supervisor's Report, 1943, Rochester State Hospital, Box 113, Folder 1578, Association for Clinical Pastoral Education, Records 1930–1986, Pitts Collections, Emory.

26. Holman, "Workshop in Personal Counseling," 32, 29. Holman includes the example of the young woman war worker and the disfigured soldier as sample case studies in his workshop materials.

27. Rogers, *Counseling and Psychotherapy*, 28.

28. Of course, Rogers was also influenced by Freudian theories, but he was highly resistant to admitting that influence. At most he acknowledged a debt to Karen Horney and Otto Rank. His bibliography for *Counseling and Psychotherapy*, however, was firmly grounded in the literature of child guidance, social work, and consulting psychology.

29. Rogers acknowledged that the idea that therapists ought not to allow their own values to unduly influence the patient or client originated, to some extent, in psychoanalytic therapies. Rogers, *Counseling and Psychotherapy*, 127.

30. For a brief time in the 1950s, four theology schools united under the aegis of the University of Chicago as the Federated Theological Faculty. The four schools represented the core of the midwestern religious liberal tradition and included the University of Chicago Divinity School (Baptist), the Chicago Theological Seminary (Congregationalist), the Meadville Theological School (Unitarian), and the Disciples of Christ Divinity House. See *Time* magazine April 18, 1955.

31. May, "The Ministry of Counseling," 19.

32. Seward Hiltner, *Religion and Health* (New York: Macmillan, 1943), 168.

33. May, "The Ministry of Counseling," 19.

34. Hiltner, *Religion and Health*, 168.

35. Rogers, *Counseling and Psychotherapy*, 126

36. May, "The Ministry of Counseling," 15.

37. Hiltner, *Religion and Health*, 182.

38. Historian Brooks Holifield traces the origins of "insight" to Freud and theological realism. E. Brooks Holifield, *A History of Pastoral Care in America:*

From Salvation to Self-Realization (Nashville: Abingdon, 1983), 250–251. Rogers, May, and Hiltner obviously owed an intellectual debt to Freud in their use of the term "insight" to refer to "a process of becoming sufficiently free to look at old facts in a new way, an experience of discovering relationships among familiar attitudes, a willingness to accept the implications of well-known material," especially in regard to problem solving, but they might have been equally indebted to Wolfgang Köhler's comparative psychology and the theories of gestalt psychologists.

39. Hiltner used the extended example of a young woman named Mary and her contentious relationship with her mother to illustrate his points and to point to the causal relationship between insight and autonomy. See Hiltner, *Religion and Health*, 183–195, 200.

40. Rogers, *Counseling and Psychotherapy*, 127.

Chapter Five: Democracy and the Psychologically Autonomous Individual

Epigraph. Crane Brinton, *A History of Western Morals* (New York: Harcourt, Brace, 1958), 459.

1. Allison Stokes, *Ministry after Freud* (New York: Pilgrim Press, 1985).

2. Fromm disliked the connection with the neo-Freudians, and when someone asked him about it in 1966, he replied, "I've never actually been happy about that label." Don Hausdorff, *Erich Fromm* (New York: Twayne Publishers, 1972), 26. See also Daniel Burston, "Erich Fromm: Humanistic Psychoanalysis," in *Humanistic and Transpersonal Psychology: A Historical and Biographical Sourcebook*, ed. Donald Moss (Westport, CT: Greenwood Press, 1999), 282.

3. See Susan Quinn, *A Mind of Her Own: The Life of Karen Horney* (New York: Summit Books, 1987), 363–369, for an explanation of the split and the difficulties between Horney and Fromm, about which little is known.

4. Some pastoral counselors felt that Fromm's critique of religion was legitimate. An editorial by Seward Hiltner in the September 1955 *Pastoral Psychology*, the same issue that celebrated publication of Fromm's *The Sane Society*, noted, "Fromm has no objection to a God who is, for instance, the ground of being; but this he regards as quite different from the God of the Western historic religions, whom he sees as capricious and tyrannical."

5. Erich Fromm, *Escape From Freedom* (New York: Holt, Rinehart, and Winston, 1941), 10.

6. Ibid., 13.

7. Ibid., 14.

8. Ibid.

9. Ibid., 17.

10. Ibid., 269–270.

11. Ibid., esp. chap. 6, "Psychology of Nazism."

12. Ibid., 23.

13. Ibid., 270.

14. Ibid., 274. Fromm rightly worried whether such a government might be a paradox—creating a bureaucracy to achieve ends that ultimately violated individual freedom, a theme he took up in his postwar writing.

15. For information on Allport's religious commitments, especially before the war, see Ian A. M. Nicholson, *Inventing Personality: Gordon Allport and the Science of Selfhood* (Washington, DC: American Psychological Association), 2003.

16. In many ways, Allport was elaborating themes that he had first articulated prior to the war but which became more pressing as a result of the war and the spread of fascism. See Katherine Pandora, *Rebels within the Ranks: Psychologists' Critique of Scientific Authority and Democratic Realities* (New York: Cambridge University Press, 1997).

17. Gordon W. Allport, "The Bigot in Our Midst," *Commonweal*, October 6, 1944; reprint; Box 194, Folder 2822, Association for Clinical Pastoral Education, Records 1930–1986, Pitts School of Theology Library Special Collections, Archives and Manuscripts Department, Emory University, Atlanta, GA (hereafter, Pitts Collections, Emory).

18. Gordon W. Allport, "The Mature Personality," *Pastoral Psychology* 3 (May 1952): 21. In an argument sympathetic to pastoral counselors' views, Allport suggested that marriage and the family provided the ideal venue for achieving maturity.

19. E. Brooks Holifield, *A History of Pastoral Care in America: From Salvation to Self-Realization* (Nashville: Abingdon, 1983), 274. A 1947 book by Murray Lieffer about Methodists' expectations of their clergy showed that a high percentage (87%) saw a minister who could not could counsel as undesirable. Murray Howard Leiffer, *The Layman Looks at the Minister* (Nashville: Abingdon-Cokesbury Press, 1947),155.

20. William H. Whyte, Jr., *The Organization Man* (New York: Simon and Schuster, 1956), 379–380.

21. Annual Catalogue of the Council for Clinical Training, 1948, Box 2, Folder 18, Pitts Collections, Emory.

22. Henry Lewis, "Clinical Training in Preparation for the Parish Ministry," in *Clinical Pastoral Training*, ed. Seward Hiltner (New York: Federal Council of Churches, Commission on Religion and Health, 1945), 75.

23. The interest of CPE supervisors in Reichian psychology later caused something of a scandal. At one point, Wayne Oates claimed that the council was being taken over by Reichians. Wayne Oates, "Manuscript Version of Encyclopedia Entry on Clinical Training, 1955," from the *Twentieth-Century Encyclopedia of Religious Knowledge*, Box 2, Folder 21, Pitts Collections, Emory.

24. Anton T. Boisen, *Problems in Religion and Life: A Manual for Pastors, with Outlines for the Co-operative Study of Personal Experiences in Social Situations* (New York: Abingdon-Cokesbury Press, 1946), 13. See also "Religion and Personality Adjustments," "The Problem of Sin and Salvation," "Clinical Training for Theological Students," and "The Training Program of 1945" Box 195, Folder 2851, Pitts Collections, Emory. All of these books and articles underline the extent to which Boisen persisted in his views regarding mental illness and the purpose of clinical pastoral education, and they illustrate the broad audience he enjoyed, a much broader audience than many of his peers in CPE received. "Religion and Personality Adjustments" was published originally in 1942 in *Psychiatry: Journal of the Biology and Pathology of Interpersonal Relationships*. "The Problem of Sin and Salvation," also published in 1942, appeared in the *Journal of Religion*. Boisen wrote an article on clinical training originally published in the *Chicago Theological Seminary Register* in January 1945. He submitted the report on clinical training in the summer of 1945. See also Letter from Frederick Kuether, Jr., to Charles F. Reed, 24 February 1945, Box 8, Folder 134, Pitts Collections, Emory.

25. Wayne E. Oates, "The Findings of the Commission in the Ministry," *Pastoral Psychology* 7 (March 1956): 15, 21.

26. Ibid., 20.

27. Paul E. Johnson, "The Pastor as Counselor: Discussion of the Findings of the Commission in the Ministry," *Pastoral Psychology* 7 (March 1956): 27.

28. Because the professional boundaries of pastoral counseling were so ill-defined prior to 1965, it is difficult to measure the participation of the various Protestant denominations. Despite the resistance of some CPE supervisors to the notion that they were training counselors, one of the best sources for numbers of ministers who were interested in counseling is the Association for Clinical Pastoral Education (ACPE). The association formed in 1967 as an umbrella organization for four clinical pastoral education programs that had previously operated independently. The Council for Clinical Training (CCT) and the Institute of Pastoral Care (IPC) were interdenominational organizations formed in the prewar years, while the Southern Baptist Association of Clinical Pastoral Education, and the Lutheran Advisory Council were organizations that represented the interests of their respective denominations. The CCT's 1955–56 annual catalogue indicated that of the 224 participants in 1954, 159 came from one

or another of four denominations: the Protestant Episcopal Church, the Presbyterian Church in the U.S.A., the Methodist Church, and the Congregational Christian Church. At the same time, the CCT counted among its participants that year representatives from denominations as diverse as the African Methodist Episcopal Church, the Mennonite Church, the Disciples of Christ, and the Reformed Church in America, among others. From the *Clinical Pastoral Training Annual Catalog, 1955–1956* (New York: Council for Clinical Training, 1955): 22.

29. See Department of Pastoral Services of the National Council of Churches of Christ in the U.S.A., "Opportunities for Study, Training, and Experience in Pastoral Psychology—1954," *Pastoral Psychology* 4 (January 1954): 25–43. There is no way to determine, of course, precisely how many students participated, but the variety of opportunities is telling. Pastoral counseling training was not limited to seminary students. Some seminars and workshops were aimed at ordained clergy already working in a parish. For instance, Carroll Wise taught "A Workshop in Counseling" in the summer of 1955 for ministers. The seminar topics included "causes and symptoms of pathological personalities; the process of counseling and psychotherapy; the relation of psychiatry, psychotherapy and theology." "Notes and News" *Pastoral Psychology* 6 (June 1955): 56.

30. Department of Ministry Vocation and Pastoral Services of the National Council of the Churches of Christ in the U.S.A., "Opportunities for Study, Training, and Experience in Pastoral Psychology—1965," *Pastoral Psychology* 15 (January 1965): 22–26.

31. Ibid., 18–19.

32. Rollin J. Fairbanks, Samuel Southard, and Aaron L. Rutledge, "The Consultation Clinic: Keeping Records in Counseling Situations," *Pastoral Psychology* 7 (February 1956): 43–48.

33. Aaron L. Rutledge, Counselor Training at Merrill-Palmer School, Box 202, Folder 2987, Pitts Collections, Emory.

34. See "Man of the Month," *Pastoral Psychology* 8 (October 1957): 8, 65; "Man of the Month," *Pastoral Psychology* 13 (April 1962): 4, 66.

35. Seward Hiltner, *Pastoral Counseling* (Nashville: Abingdon-Cokesbury Press, 1949), 26–33.

36. In an academic style currently out of fashion, Hiltner included extensive discursive footnotes in which he explored in greater depth theoretical debates that had influenced his thinking. See especially notes 34 through 51 of *Pastoral Counseling*, 256–263.

37. James H. Capshew, *Psychologists on the March: Science, Practice, and Professional Identity in America, 1929–1969* (New York: Cambridge University Press, 1999), 141.

38. *Editorial, "The Focus of Therapy," Journal of Pastoral Care* 4 (Spring–Summer 1950): 63. Rogerian therapy was not, however, accepted uncritically by ministers. For a more extended examination of pastoral counselors' debate regarding the relative merits of Rogerian therapy, see chapter 6.

39. For examples of how pastoral counselors described self-realizing individuals, see Roy A. Burkhart, "Church Program of Education in Marriage and the Family," *Pastoral Psychology* 2 (November 1951): 14; Gordon W. Allport, "The Mature Personality," *Pastoral Psychology* 3 (May 1952): 21; Robert Bonthius, "Christian Self-Acceptance," *Pastoral Psychology* 3 (September 1952): 71; Luther E. Woodward, "The Bearing of Sexual Behavior on Mental Health and Family Stability," *Pastoral Psychology* 4 (March 1953): 12; W. Clark Ellzey, "How to Keep Romance in Your Marriage," *Pastoral Psychology* 5 (October 1954): 47–49; Lester Kirkendall, "Premarital Sex Relations: The Problem and Its Implications," *Pastoral Psychology* 7 (April 1956): 53; Foster J. Williams, "A Community Program of Premarital Counseling," *Pastoral Psychology* 10 (December 1959): 40; Carroll Wise, "Education of the Pastor for Marriage Counseling," *Pastoral Psychology* 10 (December 1959): 45–46.

40. Hiltner, *Pastoral Counseling*, 23.

41. Ibid.

42. Carroll Wise, *Pastoral Counseling: Its Theory and Practice* (New York: Harper Brothers, 1951), 131–132.

43. Ibid., 131; H. Walter Yoder, "Moral and Psychiatric Evaluations," *Journal of Pastoral Care* 2 (Fall 1948): 4.

44. Wayne E. Oates, *The Christian Pastor* (Philadelphia: Westminster Press, 1951), 123.

45. Wise, *Pastoral Counseling*, 97.

46. Ibid., 97.

47. Russell L. Dicks, *Pastoral Work and Personal Counseling* (New York: Macmillan, 1944), 137, 141.

48. Volta Hall, "Intra-Personal Factors in Marriage," *Pastoral Psychology* 3 (May 1952): 39; Williams, "A Community Program of Premarital Counseling," 40.

49. Hall, "Intra-Personal Factors in Marriage," 39. Theologian Carl Michalson recognized the "paradox" of marriage, as did social psychologist Gordon Allport. Michalson, "Faith for the Crisis of Marriage," *Journal of Pastoral Care* 11 (Winter 1957): 195; Allport, "The Mature Personality," 19, 23.

50. William C. Menninger, Howard C. Schade, and Lloyd E. Foster, "Adultery," *Pastoral Psychology* 1 (September 1950): 29; Bonthius, "Christian Self-Acceptance," 71. Seward Hiltner, "Sex—Sin or Salvation?" *Pastoral Psychology* 3 (September 1952): 33; Michalson, "Faith for the Crisis of Marriage," 201.

51. Reuel Howe, "A Pastoral Theology of Sex and Marriage," *Pastoral Psychology* 3 (September 1952): 36, 37.

52. Burkhart, "Church Program of Education in Marriage and the Family," 14; Margaret Mead, "What Is Happening to the American Family?" *Pastoral Psychology* 1 (June 1950): 49–50. Mead joined the editorial advisory board of *Pastoral Psychology* in 1963 after a decade of contributing regularly to the journal; Allport, "The Mature Personality," 21; Leland Foster Wood, "Family: Starting Point for World Brotherhood," *Pastoral Psychology* 3 (May 1952): 8. For other examples of the assumption that marriage and family contributed to social stability (as well as to the stability of the church community) see Erich Lindemann, "The Stresses and Strains of Marriage," *Journal of Pastoral Care* 4 (Spring–Summer): 24; Thomas Bigham, "The Religious Element in Marriage Counseling," *Pastoral Psychology* 3 (May 1952): 18; Irving J. Sands, "Marriage Counseling as a Medical Responsibility," *Journal of Pastoral Care* 10 (Fall 1956): 136–137; Waller B. Wiser, "Launching a Program of Premarital Counseling," *Pastoral Psychology* 10 (December 1959): 15.

53. Whyte, *Organization Man*, 379–380.

Chapter Six: An Ethic of Relationships

Epigraph. Carl R. Rogers, "Becoming a Person: Some Hypotheses Regarding the Facilitation of Personal Growth," *Pastoral Psychology* 7, no. 61 (March 1956): 9. Rogers based the article on lectures he had presented at Oberlin College the previous year and included a version of the article in his collected essays, published under the title *On Becoming a Person*. Carl R. Rogers, *On Becoming a Person: A Therapist's View of Psychotherapy* (Boston: Houghton Mifflin, 1961).

1. See Seward Hiltner, *Sex Ethics and the Kinsey Reports* (New York: Association Press, 1953).

2. See, for instance, Luther E. Woodward, "The Bearing of Sexual Behavior on Mental Health and Family Stability," *Pastoral Psychology* 4 (March 1953): 12–14; William M. Baxter, "The Relationship of Faith to Sexual Morality," *Journal of Pastoral Care* 9 (Summer 1955): 77. In addition to countless incidental mentions of the Kinsey Reports in pastoral counseling literature, two full-length articles appeared in *Pastoral Psychology*. See esp. Karl A. Menninger, "Kinsey's Study of the Sexual Behavior in the Human Male and Female," *Pastoral Psychology* 5 (February 1954): 43–48; Sylvanus M. Duvall, "Christ, Kinsey, and Mickey Spillane," *Pastoral Psychology* 7 (October 1956): 22–25. The editor of the *Journal of Pastoral Care*, Rollin J. Fairbanks, thought the topic was so important that he published a review of Kinsey's book on female sexuality

three years after its original date of publication. Rollin J. Fairbanks, review of *Sexual Behavior in the Human Female*, by Alfred C. Kinsey et al. in *Journal of Pastoral Care* 10 (Summer 1956): 111. For more on Kinsey, see James H. Jones, *Alfred C. Kinsey: A Public/Private Life* (New York: W. W. Norton, 1997).

3. Ralph P. Bridgman, "Discord, Divorce, and Reconciliation," *Pastoral Psychology* 9 (September 1958): 17.

4. For articles describing the church's role in regulating marriage and sexuality throughout history, see Roland Bainton, "Christianity and Sex," *Pastoral Psychology* 3 (September 1952): 10–26, 82; Roland Bainton, "Christianity and Sex (Part II)" *Pastoral Psychology* 4 (February 1953): 12–29; Joseph Fletcher, "A Moral Philosophy of Sex," *Pastoral Psychology* 4 (February 1953): 31–37; William Graham Cole, "Church and Divorce: Historical Background," *Pastoral Psychology* 9 (September 1958): 39–44. For articles on the Bible and sex, see Sylvanus M. Duvall, "Sex Morals in the Context of Religion," *Pastoral Psychology* 3 (May 1952): 33–37; William E. Hulme, "A Theological Approach to Birth Control," *Pastoral Psychology* 11 (April 1960): 25–32.

5. Carl Michalson, "Faith for the Crisis of Marriage," *Journal of Pastoral Care* 11 (Winter 1957): 195. See also Thomas Bigham, "The Religious Element in Marriage Counseling," *Pastoral Psychology* 3 (May 1952): 18.

6. H. Walter Yoder, "Moral and Psychiatric Evaluations," *Journal of Pastoral Care* 2 (Fall 1948): 2–3.

7. See Seward Hiltner's account of Mrs. Godwin cited near the end of chapter 5; Russell Dicks on wartime counseling, Russell L. Dicks, *Pastoral Work and Personal Counseling* (New York: Macmillan, 1944), 114.

8. Dicks, *Pastoral Work and Personal Counseling*, 89.

9. Paul E. Johnson, "Methods of Pastoral Counseling," *Journal of Pastoral Care* 1 (September 1947): 28.

10. Samuel H. Miller, "Sources of Professional Hostility," *Journal of Pastoral Care* 2 (Summer 1948): 6.

11. These themes appeared throughout the publications of the major figures in pastoral counseling; for specific examples, see Seward Hiltner's account of Mrs. Godwin in *Pastoral Counseling* (Abingdon-Cokesbury Press, 1949), 23; Carroll Wise's discussion of the importance of expressing oneself in counseling in *Pastoral Counseling: Its Theory and Practice* (New York: Harper Brothers, 1951), 40, 45, 51, 53–54; and Russell Dicks's account of one of his earliest attempts at counseling in *Pastoral Work and Personal Counseling*, 157.

12. Earl H. Furgeson, "Preaching and Counseling Functions of the Minister," *Journal of Pastoral Care* 2 (Winter 1948): 13.

13. Seward Hiltner, "The Protestant Approach to the Family," *Pastoral Psychology* 3 (May 1952): 27. Carroll Wise, another enormously influential figure

in CPE and pastoral counseling, shared many of Hiltner's ideas. For Wise's views on marriage counseling, see Carroll Wise, "Education of the Pastor for Marriage Counseling," *Pastoral Psychology* 10 (December 1959): 45–48.

14. Wise, *Pastoral Counseling*, 96–97.

15. Furgeson, "Preaching and Counseling," 13.

16. Editorial, *Journal of Pastoral Care* 2 (Winter 1948): 36–38.

17. Ibid., 37.

18. Wayne E. Oates, *The Christian Pastor* (Philadelphia: Westminster Press, 1951), 27–32.

19. Rollin Fairbanks, "Cooperation between Clergy and Psychiatrists," *Journal of Pastoral Care* 1 (September 1947): 5. For similar examples see Henry H. Wiesbauer, "Pastoral Counseling," *Journal of Pastoral Care* 2 (Spring 1948): 23.

20. Fairbanks, "Cooperation between Clergy and Psychiatrists," 9.

21. Waller B. Wiser, "Launching a Program of Premarital Counseling," *Pastoral Psychology* 10 (December 1959): 15. Curiously, both Carl Rogers and Jay Adams, an anti-Rogerian conservative Christian counselor who later developed his own method of counseling, argued that using Rogerian methods selectively was impossible, since the approach required a particular view of the counseling relationship and human nature. See Rogers's response to the complaint of a Congregational Church minister that too much emphasis had been placed on non-directive methods. "The Consultation Clinic: Too Much Stress on Rogerian Technique?" *Pastoral Psychology* 9 (June 1958): 45. For more on Adams's critique of Rogerian therapy, see chapter 10.

22. Anonymous, "On the Importance of Premarital Counseling," *Pastoral Psychology* 10 (December 1959): 61. The editors of *Pastoral Psychology* ran a regular feature called "Readers' Forum" in which readers could submit questions and comments about the content of the journal. Typically, the editors refused to publish anonymous material, but the letter had been sent originally to *Christian Century*, which published it and also asked *Pastoral Psychology* to publish it, so they agreed to do so out respect for their "sister publication" and despite their own "deep general suspicion of unsigned letters."

23. Luther Woodward, "Contribution of the Minister to Moral Hygiene," *Pastoral Psychology* 1 (February 1950): 25.

24. Roy Burkhart was ordained in the Congregational Christian Church in 1929, earned his Ph.D. from University of Chicago, and spent the rest of his professional life serving as pastor for First Community Church. In addition to his frequent contributions to professional journals such as *Pastoral Psychology*, Burkhart published many books and pamphlets aimed at a popular audience. Burkhart was much admired by his colleagues for the comprehensive mental health program he developed at First Community Church. He further extended

his influence through lectures and a radio broadcast called "The Lighted Window." "Man of the Month," *Pastoral Psychology* 4 (June 1953): 6, 66.

25. Roy Burkhart, "Church Program of Education in Marriage and the Family," *Pastoral Psychology* 2 (November 1951): 10–14. Several of the most influential early leaders of pastoral counseling approached counseling in the same manner as did Burkhart. See, for instance, Russell Dicks, *Principles and Practices of Pastoral Care* (Englewood Cliffs, NJ: Prentice-Hall, 1963). For Dicks's views on premarital counseling see Russell Dicks, "Pre-marital Counseling: The Minister's Responsibility," *Pastoral Psychology* 1 (October 1950): 41–43; Paul E. Johnson, *The Psychology of Pastoral Care* (New York: Abingdon-Cokesbury Press, 1953). For Johnson on premarital counseling see Paul E. Johnson, "Emotional Problems in Premarital Counseling," *Pastoral Psychology* 10 (December 1959): 18–24; Oates, *The Christian Pastor*. For Oates on premarital counseling, see Wayne E. Oates, *Premarital Pastoral Care and Counseling* (Nashville: Broadman Press, 1958), chap. 3. To understand the ambivalence that some pastoral counselors felt about the non-directive method in marriage counseling, see especially "The Consultation Clinic: Non-directiveness in Marital Counseling," *Pastoral Psychology* 3 (May 1952): 52–58.

26. Johnson, "Emotional Problems in Premarital Counseling," 19. See also Andrew D. Elia, "Teamwork in Premarital Counseling," *Pastoral Psychology* 10 (December 1959): 33. Elia was a medical doctor who contributed to a special issue on premarital counseling published by *Pastoral Psychology* late in the 1950s. Elia shared the beliefs of his pastoral colleagues that premarital education fostered strong families and that the primary responsibility for that education rested with the church.

27. Johnson, "Emotional Problems in Premarital Counseling," 20. Johnson claimed the middle ground between directive and non-directive therapy. Rather than stressing either the autonomy of the parishioner or the authority of the minister, Johnson stressed ministers' responsibility to really love their parishioners; he used Martin Buber's concept of "I and Thou" as his model for the relationship between counselor and counselee.

28. Foster J. Williams, "A Community Program of Premarital Counseling," *Pastoral Psychology* 10 (December 1959): 41.

29. Earl H. Furgeson, "The Aims of Premarital Counseling," *Journal of Pastoral Care* 6 (Winter 1952): 31; Wiser, "Launching a Program of Premarital Counseling," 17.

30. Elia, "Teamwork in Premarital Counseling," 37. Roy Burkhart included a description of the premarital counseling sessions that he conducted and suggested that, in addition to finances, the minister should discuss church affiliation, sex, how to keep love growing, and the honeymoon. Roy A. Burkhart, "A

Program of Premarital Counseling," *Pastoral Psychology* 1 (October 1950): 28.

31. Richard R. Zoppel, "The Consultation Clinic: Non-directiveness in Marital Counseling," *Pastoral Psychology* 3 (May 1952): 52.

32. "Man of the Month," 9 (September 1958): 8, 66.

33. "Man of the Month," 12 (May 1961): 6, 66.

34. David R. Mace, "Non-directiveness in Marital Counseling," *Pastoral Psychology* 3 (May 1952): 56.

35. For other examples of pastoral counselors who believed that non-directive counseling was not always feasible or who advocated a more aggressive agenda for counseling see Elia, "Teamwork in Premarital Counseling," 38; Eugene Smith, "Lord's Prayer in Pre-Marital Counseling," *Pastoral Psychology* 1 (October 1950): 34; Bigham, "Religious Element in Marriage Counseling," 17–18.

36. For another example of a pastoral counselor who shared Becker's views on premarital counseling see Furgeson, "The Aims of Premarital Counseling," 37. Seward Hiltner and Carroll Wise also advocated the counseling method Becker described.

37. Russell Becker, "Non-directiveness in Marital Counseling," *Pastoral Psychology* 3 (May 1952): 56.

38. Ibid., 57.

39. John Sutherland Bonnell, "Counseling with Divorced Persons," *Pastoral Psychology* 9 (September 1958): 12, 14.

40. Carl Rogers made a similar shift about the same time. Carl Rogers, *Client-Centered Therapy* (Boston: Houghton Mifflin, 1951), 3–19.

41. Seward Hiltner, *The Counselor in Counseling* (New York: Abingdon-Cokesbury Press, 1950, 1951, 1952), 11.

42. Wise, *Pastoral Counseling*, 40, 45, 51, 53–54.

43. See also Reuel L. Howe, "The Role of Clinical Training in Theological Education," *Journal of Pastoral Care* 6 (Spring 1952): 8; William Hulme, *Counseling and Theology* (Philadelphia: Muhlenberg Press, 1956), 4.

44. Wise, *Pastoral Counseling*, 150–151.

45. Ibid., 82–83.

46. One of the earliest explications of Buber's ideas came in a 1952 article by Joseph Fletcher in *The Journal of Pastoral Care*. Fletcher cited as his sources, Buber's *I and Thou* (1937) and *Between Man and Man* (1948). Fletcher used the terms "subject" and "object" in a phenomenological sense. "Subject" did not mean subject in the sense of subjects in a scientific study but rather subject as in "subjective"—from the person's point of view or frame of reference. A subject, person, or in Buber's language a "Thou" was alive, had opinions, and could respond to the people and the surrounding world. As a result, subjects had rights

and responsibilities. Objects, on the other hand, were material things or "Its." In good relationships, people respected one another's freedom to choose what they wanted for themselves and treated the other as a Thou and not an It. Joseph Fletcher, "Concepts of Moral Responsibility," *Journal of Pastoral Care* 6 (April 1952):42–44. In contrast, an extended discussion of Buber's ideas did not appear in *Pastoral Psychology* until 1956. Contributors to *Pastoral Psychology* were more likely to turn to the work of Paul Tillich, perhaps because Tillich's work appeared regularly in the journal either as original contributions or reprints. In addition, Buber, while well-educated, was not schooled in either psychology or theology, making it perhaps less likely that pastoral counselors would turn to his work initially. One of the most famous theologians of the mid-twentieth century, Reinhold Niebuhr apparently did not hold the same appeal for pastoral counselors as he did for other Americans; with the exception of a handful of articles published late in the 1950s and early 1960s in *Pastoral Psychology*, his work almost never appeared in the journals in any form.

47. Wise, *Pastoral Counseling*, 151–152.

48. See Outler's earliest discussion of these ideas in Albert Outler, "A Christian Context for Counseling," *Journal of Pastoral Care* 2 (Spring 1948): 8–11. See also William A. Yon, "The Pastoral Approach: Detachment or Involvement?" *Journal of Pastoral Care* 8 (Spring 1954): 29. Yon used the term "mutuality."

49. Seward Hiltner, "Sex—Sin or Salvation?" *Pastoral Psychology* 3 (September 1952): 32–33.

50. Hiltner, *Sex Ethics and the Kinsey Reports*, 9–10.

51. Ibid., 14.

52. Albert Outler, *Psychotherapy and the Christian Message* (New York: Harper and Brothers, 1954), 232.

53. Fletcher, "Concepts of Moral Responsibility," 42–44.

54. Ibid.

55. Hiltner, *Sex Ethics and the Kinsey Reports*, 11. See also Reuel Howe, "A Pastoral Theology of Sex and Marriage," *Pastoral Psychology* 3 (September 1952): 36.

Chapter Seven: Gendered Moral Discourse

Epigraph. Lawrence was quoted in *Pastoral Psychology* (March 1956).

1. Wayne E. Oates, *Anxiety in Christian Experience* (Philadelphia: Westminster Press, 1955), 81.

2. Ibid., 82.

3. I use the phrase "moral reasoning" in the way it is most commonly used by psychologists—to describe the process whereby an individual addresses or

resolves a moral dilemma, distinguishes between right and wrong, and chooses how to behave. I use the phrase "moral discourse" in a straightforward way to describe both the narrative that pastoral counselors constructed about their counselees' moral reasoning and the stories that counselees told them about their moral dilemmas. In other words, I use "moral discourse" to refer to talking and writing about morality in everyday interactions.

4. Samuel Southard, "Pastoral Counseling and Christian Doctrine," in *An Introduction to Pastoral Counseling*, ed. Wayne E. Oates (Nashville: Broadman Press, 1959), 249. Seward Hiltner cited a similar case in *Preface to Pastoral Theology* (Nashville: Abingdon Press, 1958), 157–158.

5. Seward Hiltner, *Pastoral Counseling* (Nashville: Abingdon-Cokesbury Press, 1949), 213–215.

6. James Lyn Elder, "The Attitudes of the Pastoral Counselor," in *An Introduction to Pastoral Counseling*, ed. Wayne E. Oates (Nashville: Broadman Press, 1959), 55, 60.

7. For example, see Edgar Newman Jackson, *Understanding Grief: Its Roots, Dynamics, and Treatment* (New York: Abingdon-Cokesbury Press, 1957), 206.

8. Paul E. Johnson, *The Psychology of Pastoral Care* (New York: Abingdon Press, 1953), 200;. Also, in a study by Hiltner and Colston, two participants expressed similar concerns for other women; see Seward Hiltner and Lowell G. Colston, *The Context of Pastoral Counseling* (New York: Abingdon Press, 1961), 76, 141.

9. Hiltner, *Pastoral Counseling*, 82–83. Hiltner never indicated the outcome of Mrs. Keating's dilemma. Edward Thornton related a similar story about "Beth," who throughout her twenty-eight-year marriage had been involved in a number of short-lived affairs. By Beth's own account, her interest in other men diminished when she and her husband finally established emotional intimacy. Edward Thornton, *Theology and Pastoral Counseling* (Englewood Cliffs, NJ: Prentice Hall, 1964), 65.

10. Hiltner and Colston, *Context of Pastoral Counseling*, 141.

11. Elder, "Attitudes of the Pastoral Counselor," 60.

12. Hiltner, *Pastoral Counseling*, 221.

13. Ibid., 128.

14. William Hulme, *Counseling and Theology* (Philadelphia: Muhlenberg Press, 1956), 111, 124–125. See also the case of Ben, who flouted community standards consistently, creating an impression of not caring about others' opinions of him. According to Hulme, when Ben finally did something that earned the actual censure of the community, he discovered that he did care what they thought.

15. Hiltner, *Pastoral Counseling*, 49–50.

16. Although some readers may object to classifying vocational choices as moral decisions, the counselees in these cases clearly saw their choices in terms of right and wrong. In Protestant Christianity, which has traditionally viewed the Christian calling and worldly vocation as inseparable, choices about one's life work take on moral implications.

17. James Lyn Elder, "Pastoral Counseling and the Communication of the Gospel," in *An Introduction to Pastoral Counseling*, ed. Wayne E. Oates (Nashville: Broadman, 1959), 205. See also the case of "John," who feared ridicule from his family for being a Christian; Southard, "Pastoral Counseling and Christian Doctrine," 236–237.

18. Hiltner, *Pastoral Counseling*, 206.

19. Carroll Wise, *Pastoral Counseling: Its Theory and Practice* (New York: Harper Brothers, 1951), 129.

20. Southard, "Pastoral Counseling and Christian Doctrine," 248–249.

21. Ibid.

22. Hiltner and Colston, *Context of Pastoral Counseling*, 144.

23. Ibid., 205.

24. Ibid.

25. See also Seward Hiltner's description of the case of Mrs. Coe in which he praised Mrs. Coe's minister because he had so successfully fostered self-confidence in her. She left her abusive husband and ultimately learned to make decisions without the help of her minister. Hiltner also affirmed Mrs. Coe's reasoning that the needs of her child took precedence over the needs of her husband. Hiltner, *Preface to Pastoral Theology*, 157.

26. Hiltner and Colston, *Context of Pastoral Counseling*, 232.

27. Ibid., 234.

28. Hiltner, *Pastoral Counseling*, 128. Wayne Oates included similar wording in his early work, *The Christian Pastor* (Philadelphia: Westminster Press, 1951), 117–118.

29. Seward Hiltner, Robert E. Elliott, Thomas E. McDill, Ray Schultz, John T. Shaffer, Carl E. Wennerstrom, and Joseph S. Willis, "Pastoral Symposium: A Case of Adultery (Part II) *Pastoral Psychology* 6 (June 1955): 11; "Readers' Forum," *Pastoral Psychology* 6 (December 1955): 53–58.

30. James T. Kloppenberg, *The Virtues of Liberalism* (New York: Oxford University Press, 1998), 93.

31. Ibid., 95.

32. For an explanation of virtue ethics in the United States, see Kloppenberg, *Virtues of Liberalism*, 4–6.

33. Two of the classic works on this subject are Linda K. Kerber, *Women of the Republic: Intellect and Ideology in Revolutionary America* (Chapel Hill: Institute of Early American History and Culture, University of North Carolina, 1980); and Mary Beth Norton, *Liberty's Daughters: The Revolutionary Experience of American Women, 1750–1800* (Ithaca, NY: Cornell University Press, 1980). In a later work on women and intellectual history, Kerber noted the absence of women in the discussion of virtue. See Linda Kerber, *Toward an Intellectual History of Women* (Chapel Hill: University of North Carolina Press, 1997), 107. For an early attempt to sort out the gendered differences in virtue see Ruth H. Bloch, "The Gendered Meanings of Virtue in Revolutionary America," *Signs* 13, no. 1 (Autumn 1987): 37–58. For more on the privatization and sexualization of virtue, see also Mary P. Ryan, *Cradle of the Middle Class: The Family in Oneida County, New York, 1790–1865* (New York: Cambridge University Press, 1981); Nancy F. Cott, *The Bonds of Womanhood: Woman's Sphere in New England, 1780–1835*, 2nd ed. (New Haven, CT: Yale University Press, 1997); and Barbara Welter, "The Cult of True Womanhood, 1820–1860," *American Quarterly* 18, no. 2 (1966). See also John Patrick Diggins, *The Lost Soul of American Politics: Virtue, Self-Interest, and the Foundations of Liberalism* (New York: Basic Books, 1984), see esp. the chapter "Society, Religion, and the Feminization of Virtue." Diggins's work is the exception that proves the rule. In a chapter about the feminization of virtue, Diggins offers little about women and instead explicates the work of Alexis de Tocqueville and Henry Adams.

34. On social housekeeping and "female dominion," see Robin Muncy, *Creating a Female Dominion in American Reform* (New York: Oxford University Press, 1991). Seth Koven and Sonya Michel, *Mothers of a New World: Maternalist Politics and the Origins of Welfare States* (New York: Routledge, 1993). See also Eleanor Flexner and Ellen Fitzpatrick, *Century of Struggle: The Woman's Rights Movement in the United States*, enlarged ed. (Cambridge, MA: Belknap Press of Harvard University, 1996).

35. The literature on moral development has grown enormously in the last several decades. For the most recent discussions of these questions from the perspective of psychologists, see Melanie Killen and Judith G. Smetana, eds. *Handbook of Human Development* (Mahwah, NJ: Lawrence Erlbaum Associates, 2006).

36. Kohlberg initially explored these concepts in his dissertation and then elaborated on them in subsequent works. His later work focused, in particular, on the practical implications of his theories. Catherine Walsh, "The Life and Legacy of Lawrence Kohlberg," *Society* 37 (January 2000): 36. For an explanation of Kohlberg's stages of moral development, see especially, Lawrence

Kohlberg, *The Philosophy of Moral Development: Moral Stages and the Idea of Justice.* (San Francisco: Harper and Row, 1981), 19.

37. Carol Gilligan, *In a Different Voice: Psychological Theory and Women's Development* (Cambridge, MA: Harvard University Press, 1982), 2. To support her argument, Gilligan referred to three studies she had conducted, "*the college student study,*" "*the abortion decision study,*" and the "*rights and responsibilities study*" (Gilligan's emphases).

38. For Kohlberg's views on religion, see his *Philosophy of Moral Development,* 302–305. Gilligan simply did not mention religion of any sort, at least not in her groundbreaking 1982 book, *In a Different Voice.*

39. Hiltner and Colston, *Context of Pastoral Counseling,* 111.

40. Ibid.

41. Ibid., 115.

42. Ibid., 116–117.

43. Ibid., 130.

Chapter Eight: The Language of Rights and the Challenge to the Domestic Ideal

Epigraph. Tillich placed a greater emphasis on the influence of Freud than did many pastoral counselors and in this quotation was referring to Freud's attack on the "threatening father," which made room for "the image of the embracing and supporting mother." Tillich, likewise, attributed "nonjudging and nondirecting acceptance of the mentally disturbed" to psychoanalysis, a notion to which Rogers and his supporters would almost certainly have taken exception. Tillich does, nevertheless, acknowledge the extent to which pastoral counseling moved questions of gender to the center. Paul Tillich, "The Impact of Pastoral Psychology on Theological Thought," *Pastoral Psychology* 11, (February 1960): 19–20.

1. Seward Hiltner, "Ladies and Gentlemen," *Pastoral Psychology* 4 (May 1953): 9.

2. Roy A. Burkhart, "A Program of Premarital Counseling," *Pastoral Psychology* 1 (October 1950): 28–31.

3. Ibid., 30.

4. Ibid., 31.

5. Ibid., 30.

6. Ibid. 31.

7. William C. Menninger, Howard C. Schade, and Lloyd E. Foster, "Adultery," *Pastoral Psychology* 1 (September 1950): 24–29; Erich Lindemann, "The

Stresses and Strains of Marriage," *Journal of Pastoral Care* 4 (Spring–Summer 1950): 24–31.

8. Margaret Mead, "What Is Happening to the American Family?" *Pastoral Psychology* 1 (June 1950): 49–50.

9. Clara Thompson, "Towards a Psychology of Women," *Pastoral Psychology* 4 (May 1953): 29–38.

10. Ibid., 29.

11. Betty Friedan, *The Feminine Mystique* (1963; reprint, New York: Dell Publishing, 1984), 136.

12. Lloyd E. Foster, Thomas J. Bigham, and John A. P. Millet, "Marriage on the Verge of a Break Up," *Pastoral Psychology* 1 (May 1950): 48.

13. Russell L. Dicks, *Pastoral Work and Personal Counseling* (New York: Macmillan, 1944), 67.

14. Ibid., 84–85; Russell L. Dicks, *Pastoral Work and Personal Counseling: An Introduction to Pastoral Care*, rev. ed. (New York: Macmillan, 1949), 122–123.

15. Russell L. Dicks, *Principles and Practices of Pastoral Care* (Englewood Cliffs, NJ: Prentice-Hall, 1963), esp. chap. 1. Although the title and publisher are different, this is essentially the same book as *Pastoral Work and Personal Counseling*, but edited further.

16. Seward Hiltner, *The Counselor in Counseling: Case Notes in Pastoral Counseling* (New York: Abingdon-Cokesbury Press, 1950), 48–49; Seward Hiltner, *The Christian Shepherd: Some Aspects of Pastoral Care* (New York: Abingdon Press, 1959), 140.

17. Rollin Fairbanks, review of *Sexual Behavior in the Human Female*, by Alfred C. Kinsey et al., in *Journal of Pastoral Care* 10 (Summer 1956): 111–112.

18. Rollin Fairbanks, review of *The Sexually Adequate Female*, by Frank S. Caprio, in *Journal of Pastoral Care* 12 (Fall 1958): 190.

19. Charles Holman, *Getting Down to Cases* (New York: Macmillan, 1942), 97.

20. Seward Hiltner, *Religion and Health* (New York: Macmillan, 1943), 182–192, 205.

21. Seward Hiltner, *Pastoral Counseling* (Nashville: Abingdon-Cokesbury Press, 1949), 126–127; Wayne E. Oates, *The Christian Pastor* (Philadelphia: Westminster Press, 1951): 117–118.

22. Seward Hiltner, *Preface to Pastoral Theology* (Nashville: Abingdon Press, 1958), 156.

23. Hiltner, *The Christian Shepherd*, 140.

24. Knox Kreutzer, "Some Observations on Approaches to the Theology of Psychotherapeutic Experience," *Journal of Pastoral Care* 13 (Winter 1959): 198.

25. See Seward Hiltner and Lowell G. Colston, *The Context of Pastoral Counseling* (New York: Abingdon Press, 1961), 66–91, 92–106, 130–146.

26. Irving J. Sands, M.D., "Marriage Counseling as a Medical Responsibility," *Journal of Pastoral Care* 10 (Fall 1956): 135.

27. Seward Hiltner, Robert E. Elliott, Thomas E. McDill, Ray Schultz, John T. Shaffer, Carl E. Wennerstrom, and Joseph S. Willis, "Pastoral Symposium: A Case of Adultery (Part II)," *Pastoral Psychology* 6 (June 1955): 11; "Readers' Forum," *Pastoral Psychology* 6 (December 1955): 53–58.

28. Hiltner, *The Christian Shepherd*, 96.

29. Ibid.

30. James B. Ashbrook, "The Church as Matriarchy," *Pastoral Psychology* 14 (September 1963): 49.

31. William Douglas, "Women in the Church: Historical Perspectives and Contemporary Dilemmas," *Pastoral Psychology* 12 (June 1961): 13–20; Ashbrook, "Church as Matriarchy," 38–49; Lester A. Kirkendall, "Captives to the Double Standard," *Pastoral Psychology* 16 (February 1965): 23–32.

32. Douglas, "Women in the Church," 14.

33. Ibid., 17.

34. Ibid.

35. Ibid., 18.

36. Ibid., 20.

37. Ibid., 16.

38. Ibid.

39. "Man of the Month," *Pastoral Psychology* 9 (December 1957): 6, 66.

40. Vere V. Loper, "Christian Ties Hold Homes Together," *Pastoral Psychology* 8 (December 1957): 9–14.

41. Ruth E. Hartley, "Some Implications of Current Changes in Sex Role Patterns," *Pastoral Psychology* 12 (November 1961): 38, 40, and 46.

42. Aaron L. Rutledge, "Male and Female Roles in Marriage Counseling," *Pastoral Psychology* 13 (October 1962): 14.

Chapter Nine: Resurrection of the Shepherd

Epigraph. Tillich was quoted in *Pastoral Psychology* (March 1956).

1. Samuel Southard, "The Emotional Health of the Pastoral Counselor," in *An Introduction to Pastoral Counseling*, ed. Wayne E. Oates (Nashville: Broadman Press, 1959), 45.

2. Samuel Southard, "Pastoral Counseling and Christian Doctrine," in *An Introduction to Pastoral Counseling*, ed. Wayne E. Oates (Nashville: Broadman Press, 1959), 249. Southard believed that the minister had taken a risk in assuming such a directive stance, but he concluded that the risk had been worthwhile.

3. Newman S. Cryer, Jr., and John Monroe Vayhinger, eds., *A Casebook in Pastoral Counseling* (London: Pierce and Smith, 1952; New York: Abingdon Press, 1962), 21.

4. Seward Hiltner, *The Christian Shepherd: Some Aspects of Pastoral Care* (New York: Abingdon Press, 1959), 105–107.

5. Wayne E. Oates, "Making the Contact: Informal Pastoral Relationships," in *An Introduction to Pastoral Counseling*, ed. Wayne E. Oates (Nashville: Broadman Press, 1959), 82–83.

6. Southard, "Pastoral Counseling and Christian Doctrine," 245.

7. Hiltner, *The Christian Shepherd*, 43–47.

8. Ibid. For other examples of counselees' expectations, see Cryer and Vayhinger, *Casebook in Pastoral Counseling*, 21–23, 71–76.

9. E. Brooks Holifield, *A History of Pastoral Care in America: From Salvation to Self-Realization* (Nashville: Abingdon, 1983), 311–348. Holifield describes the turn to theology as a response to the limitations of the therapeutic culture and as an attempt to qualify and limit the meaning of "self-realization" and "growth."

10. Frederick R. Knubel, *Pastoral Counseling* (Philadelphia: Muhlenberg Press, 1952), 16. Knubel described Rogerian pastoral counseling as "humanism," "pantheism," and an "insidious" danger to Christianity. Samuel Miller expressed a similar distaste for psychoanalysis. Samuel H. Miller, "Exploring the Boundary Between Religion and Psychoanalysis," *Journal of Pastoral Care* 6 (Summer 1952): 1–11.

11. O. Hobart Mowrer, *The Crisis in Psychiatry and Religion* (Princeton, NJ: D. Van Nostrand, 1961), 50.

12. See especially Mowrer's discussion of pastoral counselors' inadequate understanding of sin and his discussion of the critical role played in healing by restitution. Mowrer, *Crisis in Psychiatry and Religion*, 78, 100.

13. One critic warned that, while Mowrer's ideas seemed to fit well with conservative theology, his ideas were not necessarily the only or right way for the Christian therapist to proceed. Edward Pohlman, "Psychologists Take Another Look at Sin," *Journal of Pastoral Care* 15 (Fall 1961): 144. See also Seward Hiltner's editorial in *Pastoral Psychology* entitled "A New Moralism." Given Hiltner's longstanding support for the non-directive approach, his dislike of Mowrer's ideas was to be expected. Hiltner did agree, however, to publish an

article by Donald Krill, a psychiatric social worker, that he considered even-handed in its evaluation of Mowrer's theories. See Donald F. Krill, "Psychoanalysts, Mowrer, and the Existentialists," *Pastoral Psychology* 16 (October 1965): 27–36.

14. William Hulme, *Counseling and Theology* (Philadelphia: Muhlenberg Press, 1956), 2.

15. O. Hobart Mowrer, ed., *Morality and Mental Health*, Rand McNally Psychology Series (Chicago: Rand McNally, 1967), vii.

16. Eugene Kreves, contribution to "The Consultation Clinic: Too Much Stress on Rogerian Technique?" *Pastoral Psychology* 9 (June 1958): 45.

17. Carl R. Rogers, contribution to ibid., 45.

18. In some ways, the pool of respondents was guaranteed to be sympathetic. Of the five respondents, one of whom was Rogers, two, H. Walter Yoder and Russell J. Becker, had worked with Rogers at the University of Chicago's counseling center.

19. Robert E. Elliott, contribution to "The Consultation Clinic: Too Much Stress on Rogerian Technique?" 49.

20. Ibid., 48.

21. Hulme, *Counseling and Theology*, 5.

22. "Editorials," *Journal of Pastoral Care* 12 (Summer 1958): 103.

23. Hulme, *Counseling and Theology*, 6.

24. Ibid.

25. Seward Hiltner argued, for instance, the importance of recognizing that psychological language could also be a theological language. Hiltner, *Preface to Pastoral Theology* (Nashville: Abingdon Press, 1958), 26.

26. Knox Kreutzer, "Some Observations on Approaches to the Theology of Psychotherapeutic Experience," *Journal of Pastoral Care* 13 (Winter 1959): 198.

27. Ibid.

28. Douglass Lewis, "Do Psychology and Theology Speak the Same Language?" *Journal of Pastoral Care* 18 (Fall 1964): 162–163. See also Alfred A. Cramer, "The Minister and Ethical Neutrality," *Journal of Pastoral Care* 18 (Spring 1964): 27.

29. Hiltner, *The Christian Shepherd*, 12.

30. For instance, see Shirley Page, "Some Further Observations on Sin and Sickness," *Journal of Pastoral Care* 13 (Fall 1959): 148–149; David Roberts, *Psychotherapy and a Christian View of Man* (New York: Charles Scribner's Sons, 1950), chap. 6; Carroll Wise, *Psychiatry and the Bible* (New York: Harper and Brothers, 1956), 10; James Ashbrook, "Necessity and Freedom in a Concrete Case," *Journal of Pastoral Care* 14 (Summer 1960): 115–117.

31. Howard John Clinebell, *Understanding and Counseling the Alcoholic through Religion and Psychology* (New York: Abingdon Press, 1956), 163. R. Lofton Hudson, "Sin and Sickness," *Journal of Pastoral Care* 14 (Summer 1956): 73.

32. Clinebell, *Counseling the Alcoholic*, 164; Hudson, "Sin and Sickness," 73.

33. See for instance, Hudson, "Sin and Sickness," 67; Hiltner, *The Christian Shepherd*, 12; Paul Johnson, *Person and Counselor* (Nashville: Abingdon Press, 1967), chap. 2; Edward Thornton, *Theology and Pastoral Counseling* (Englewood Cliffs, NJ: Prentice-Hall, 1964), 94; Wayne E. Oates, *Anxiety in Christian Experience* (Philadelphia: Westminster Press, 1955), 68; S. F. Nishi, "A Theological Perspective on Sexual Morality," *Journal of Pastoral Care* 15 (Winter 1961): 214–215.

34. James B. Ashbrook, "The Impact of the Hospital Situation on Our Understanding of God and Man," *Journal of Pastoral Care* 10 (Spring 1956): 4, 9. Carroll Wise defined sin as destructive forces that separate man from man and man from God. Wise, *Psychiatry and the Bible*, 21.

35. Seward Hiltner, "Rogers and Niebuhr," *Pastoral Psychology* 9 (June 1958): 7–8.

36. Reinhold Niebuhr, "The Dialogue Between the Will and Conscience of the Self," *Pastoral Psychology* 9 (June 1958): 14.

37. Niebuhr, "Dialogue," 14.

38. Carl Rogers, "Reinhold Niebuhr's *The Self and the Dramas of History*: A Criticism," *Pastoral Psychology* 9 (June 1958): 15.

39. Rogers, "A Criticism," 15.

40. Ibid.

41. Ibid., 16.

42. Ibid., 17.

43. Ibid.

44. Ibid.

45. Niebuhr, "Dialogue," 14.

46. Arnd Hollweg, "The Dialogue Between Group Dynamics and Interpersonal Theology," *Journal of Pastoral Care* 18 (Spring 1964): 20; Fred Paddock, "A Philosophical Investigation of the Relation Between Psychoanalysis and Theology," *Journal of Pastoral Care* 13 (Spring 1959): 41; Homer Jernigan, "Pastoral Counseling and the Identity of the Pastor," *Journal of Pastoral Care* 15 (Winter 1961): 198; Charles W. Stewart, "Relationship Counseling," *Journal of Pastoral Care* 13 (Winter 1959): 217; Oates, *Anxiety in Christian Experience*, 148; Thornton, *Theology and Pastoral Counseling*, 123–125.

47. Hollweg, "Dialogue," 20.

48. Wayne K. Clymer, "Can the Counselor Be a Prophet?" *Journal of Pastoral Care* 10 (Fall 1956): 155.

49. Lewis, "Do Psychology and Theology Speak the Same Language?" 164–165.

50. Hulme, *Counseling and Theology*, 7.

51. Hollweg, "Dialogue," 20–21.

52. Paddock, "A Philosophical Investigation," 41.

53. Jernigan, "Counseling and the Identity of the Pastor," 197.

54. Stewart, "Relationship Counseling," 216, 219.

55. Clymer, "Can the Counselor Be a Prophet?" 158.

56. Seward Hiltner and Lowell G. Colston, *The Context of Pastoral Counseling* (New York: Abingdon Press, 1961): 31.

57. Robert H. Bonthius, "What Is 'Christian' Counseling?" *Journal of Pastoral Care* 13 (Summer 1959): 76; Douglas Burgoyne, "Some Basic Concerns for the Clergyman as Counselor," *Journal of Pastoral Care* 15 (Summer 1961): 74–75.

58. Hiltner and Colston, *Context of Pastoral Counseling*, 22.

59. Bonthius, "What Is 'Christian' Counseling?" 74–75. For another example that pastoral counselors believed that healing came from an encounter with God that resulted in facing one's own sinfulness, see Wayne E. Oates, "Pastoral Counseling and the Experience of Prayer" in *An Introduction to Pastoral Counseling*, ed. Wayne E. Oates (Nashville: Broadman Press, 1959), 218–219. In the "Readers' Forum" feature of *Pastoral Psychology*, Methodist minister, John T. Shaffer, commenting on a hypothetical church member who had committed adultery, referred to the powerful effects of the "judgment of love." "Readers' Forum," *Pastoral Psychology* 6 (December 1955): 58. Other discussions of judgment include H. Walter Yoder, "Judgmental Attitudes in Pastoral Counseling," *Journal of Pastoral Care* 9 (Winter 1955): 221–224; editorial, "Judgment and Response in Counseling," *Journal of Pastoral Care* 9 (Winter 1955); 233; Carroll Wise, *The Meaning of Pastoral Care* (New York: Harper and Row, 1966): 80–85. Samuel Southard, a Southern Baptist, served as guest editor for the December 1965 issue of *Pastoral Psychology*, which was devoted to authority and discipline in pastoral care.

60. Bonthius, "What Is 'Christian' Counseling?" 74–75. Bonthius described the counseling session in the language of psychotherapy and then explicated it in the language of theology. See also Hiltner, *The Christian Shepherd*, 19. Hiltner argued that the ultimate goal of all pastoral work was to relate the Gospel to the individual's everyday needs.

61. Ashbrook, "The Impact of the Hospital," 10. Anton Boisen offered a theory very similar to this back in the 1930s. He referred to the "ancient theo-

logical doctrine that conviction of sin is a first step in the process of salvation." Not surprisingly, a Boisen renaissance of sorts occurred in the 1960s. Boisen differed from his colleagues, however, because as an early twentieth century Progressive he was much more comfortable with a socially imposed code of conduct. Anton Boisen, *Out of the Depths: An Autobiographical Study of Mental Disorder and Religious Experience* (New York: Harper and Brothers, 1960), 166.

62. Here the discussion began to echo some of Anton Boisen's ideas first articulated twenty-five years earlier. Boisen had remained active, if not prominent, in clinical pastoral education, continuing his research in the psychology of religion. He continued too, to contribute to the journals and published his autobiography, *Out of the Depths*, in 1960. Upon Boisen's death in 1965, Seward Hiltner assessed his contribution to the field of pastoral psychology. Hiltner identified several spheres of influence, including Boisen's study of theology through "living human documents," his theories about the spontaneous reorganization of human personality in the face of disintegration, the part Boisen played in founding clinical pastoral education, and his contribution to the psychology of religion. Hiltner acknowledged the difficulties of Boisen's personality but reaffirmed his personal debt to Boisen. Seward Hiltner, "The Heritage of Anton T. Boisen," *Pastoral Psychology* 16 (November 1965): 5–10.

63. Kreutzer, "Some Observations on Approaches," 201.

64. Ibid., 204.

65. Seward Hiltner described something similar in his definition of "judgment." Hiltner, *The Christian Shepherd*, 39.

66. Kreutzer, "Some Observations on Approaches," 208.

67. Ibid.

68. Jernigan, "Counseling and the Identity of the Pastor," 194–195. Jernigan argued that ministers needed to define a "normative" pastoral role.

69. It is important not to overstate the extent to which pastoral counseling theory in the late 1950s and early 1960s was "new." A significant number of the concerns that came to dominate discussions of pastoral counseling and professional practice had been introduced as early as the 1954 conference on counseling and psychotherapy. See, for instance, Wayne E. Oates, "The Findings of the Commission In the Ministry," *Pastoral Psychology* 7 (March 1956): 15–24; Paul E. Johnson, "The Pastor as Counselor: Discussion of the Findings of the Commission in the Ministry," *Pastoral Psychology* 7 (March 1956): 25–28; John Sutherland Bonnell et al., "Further Comments on the Report of the Commission in the Ministry," *Pastoral Psychology* 7 (March 1956): 31–35.

70. Hiltner and Colston, *Context of Pastoral Counseling*, 28.

71. Sheilah James Hawes, "Pregnancy Out of Wedlock," *Journal of Pastoral Care* 19 (Fall 1965): 160.

72. Seward Hiltner, " 'Credentials' for Pastoral Counseling?" *Pastoral Psychology* 11 (January 1961): 45.

73. Hiltner, "A Critique," 16. In a 1973 article, Carl Rogers seemed to see the same dangers lurking for psychologists, who had focused so eagerly on certification and licensure; and he called for them to "do away with professionalism," a challenge few listened to or accepted. Carl R. Rogers, "Some New Challenges," *American Psychologist* 28, no. 5 (May 1973): 382.

74. Paul E. Johnson expressed similar ideas in an article he published in the mid-1960s. Paul Johnson, "The Spirit of Counseling," *Pastoral Psychology* 14 (January 1964): 31–36.

75. Howard J. Clinebell, Jr., "The Challenge of the Specialty of Pastoral Counseling," *Pastoral Counseling* 15 (April 1964): 17–28. A detailed discussion of licensure and certification falls outside the scope of this work. In the 1980s and 1990s, several high profile cases raised the question of jurisdiction with regard to clergy malpractice. Some pastoral counselors resisted licensure because they feared it would violate separation of church and state and allow state control of ministerial practice. Refusing to license pastoral counselors, however, opened them to challenges to their competence. See for instance, "Is Bad Counseling by Clergy a Proper Issue for the Courts?" *New York Times*, April 14, 1996.

76. James N. Lapsley, "Pastoral Psychology and the Future," *Pastoral Psychology* 21 (February 1970): 7.

77. Margaret Mead, "Pastoral Psychology: The Next Twenty Years . . . As Seen by a Social Scientist," *Pastoral Psychology* 21 (February 1970): 8–15.

78. Wayne Oates, "Pastoral Psychology: The Next Twenty Years . . . In Relation to Theological Education," *Pastoral Psychology* 21 (February 1970): 49–55.

79. Howard J. Clinebell, Jr., "Pastoral Psychology: The Next Twenty Years . . . In Pastoral Counseling," *Pastoral Psychology* 21 (February 1970): 34.

Chapter Ten: Christian Counseling and the Conservative Moral Sensibility

Epigraph. Clyde Narramore, *The Psychology of Counseling: Professional Techniques for Pastors, Teachers, Youth Leaders and All Who Are Engaged in the Incomparable Art of Counseling* (Grand Rapids, MI: Zondervan, 1960), 240.

1. Bruce Narramore, "Perspectives on the Integration of Psychology and Theology," *Journal of Psychology and Theology* 1, no. 1 (January 1973): 9 and 16.

2. Jay Adams, *Competent to Counsel* (Nutley, NJ: Presbyterian and Reformed Publishing, 1970), xi, xii, and chap. 6. Gary Collins argued that too

much emphasis on counseling in the parish took the pastor away from other important tasks, such as Bible study, prayer, and sermon preparation. Collins also suggested that an "over acceptance of psychology has ruined the witness of many churches and seminaries." Gary Collins, *Search for Reality: Psychology and the Christian* (Wheaton, IL: Key Publishers, 1969), 203.

3. William Glasser, M.D., *Reality Therapy: A New Approach to Psychiatry* (New York: Harper and Row, 1965), 69.

4. Ibid., 50, 177, 179, 185.

5. Collins, *Search for Reality*, 46. Narramore mentioned the importance of Boisen's contribution. Narramore, "Perspectives on the Integration of Psychology and Theology," 8; Jay Adams also mentioned Boisen as a pivotal figure but did not embrace his views.

6. George Marsden, *Reforming Fundamentalism: Fuller Seminary and the New Evangelicalism* (Grand Rapids, MI: William B. Eerdmans Publishing, 1987), 234.

7. David Arthur Powlison, "Competent to Counsel? The History of a Conservative Anti-Psychiatry Movement" (Ph.D. diss., University of Pennsylvania, 1996), see esp. chaps. 8 and 9.

8. In the 1973 inaugural issue of the *Journal of Psychology and Theology*, Bruce Narramore counted LaHaye, along with Jay Adams, Seward Hiltner, William Hulme, Wayne Oates, and David Roberts, among the theologians and ministers who had contributed to "bringing psychology to the attention of the church." Narramore, "Perspectives on Psychology and Theology," 5.

9. J. Drakeford, *Integrity Therapy* (Nashville: Broadman Press, 1967), 9–10.

10. Ibid.

11. On southern progressivism see William Link, *The Paradox of Southern Progressivism* (Chapel Hill: University of North Carolina Press, 1992).

12. Timothy George points out that Southern Baptist Convention moderates saw the events as a "takeover," while conservatives claimed it as a "turnaround." The essay is part of a collection that examines the changes in the denomination from multiple perspectives. Timothy George, "Toward an Evangelical Future," in *Southern Baptists Observed: Multiple Perspectives on a Changing Denomination*, ed. Nancy Tatom Ammerman (Knoxville: University of Tennessee Press, 1993), 276.

13. Marsden gives a number of examples of the openness of neoevangelicals at Fuller to other evangelical groups, including the appointment of Paul Barkman to the Pasadena Community Counseling Center. Barkman considered himself "an Arminian and not a Calvinist, and an Anabaptist rather than a pietist." Marsden saw this trend as the end of neoevangelicalism and the advent of yet another kind of evangelicalism made up of a loose coalition of like-minded

conservative Christians. Marsden, *Reforming Fundamentalism*, 235. I would argue that it is precisely at this point that talking in terms of a moral sensibility is useful and makes sense.

14. Marsden, *Reforming Fundamentalism*, 260.

15. The dominance of psychologists in evangelical counseling at the very moment when psychology was establishing its dominance in the field of counseling and psychotherapy meant that the late 1970s and 1980s saw quite a bit of "minister bashing" by them and an aggressive assault on ministerial competence from both secular and religious sources. Pastoral counselors had entered the field at a time when professional lines were much more permeable and ministers were not automatically dismissed as incompetent.

16. Marsden, *Reforming Fundamentalism*, 233–235.

17. In identifying the most important early works, I draw from Bruce Narramore's 1973 essay on the integration of psychology and theology. Narramore argued that Gary Collins, Quentin Hyder, Clyde Narramore (Bruce Narramore's uncle), Marion Nelson, and Paul Tournier had written books that helped the Christian psychologist gain "respectability within the Christian community." Paul Barkman, Donald Tweedie, and John Drakeford had illuminated the connections "between biblical truth and the various schools of psychological thinking." And, according to Narramore, Jay Adams and Tim LaHaye had made a contribution from the "ministerial side." Narramore also noted the contribution of thinkers who more clearly belonged in the school of pastoral counseling, including Anton Boisen, Oskar Pfister, Seward Hiltner, Wayne Oates, William Hulme, and David Roberts. See Bruce Narramore, "Perspectives on the Integration of Psychology and Theology," 5. Evangelical counseling enjoyed dramatic growth in the late 1970s and early 1980s. Integrationists gained the upper hand and a number of key works were published that defined the field and its practice, including Collins's *The Rebuilding of Psychology* (1977) and John Carter and Bruce Narramore's *The Integration of Psychology and Theology* (1979). Another shift occurred in the 1990s when the biblicists—those who highlighted the importance of the Bible for counseling—established dominance. Adams's nouthetic counseling enjoyed a concurrent resurgence. As I indicated earlier, however, in the mid-1960s and early 1970s, evangelical counselors were just beginning to sort out some of their most important issues and had not begun the jurisdictional battles that would later ensue.

18. Donald Tweedie, *Logotherapy and the Christian Faith: An Evaluation of Frankl's Existential Approach to Psychotherapy* (Grand Rapids, MI: Baker Book House, 1961), 24.

19. Gary Collins offered a similar criticism but identified the three major negative influences as psychoanalysis, Watson's behaviorism, and a "third force,"

humanistic psychology. Gary R. Collins, "Psychology on a New Foundation," *Journal of Psychology and Theology* 1, no. 1 (January 1973): 22–23.

20. Tweedie, *Logotherapy and the Christian Faith*, 24; Tweedie's biblical allusion to Esau, who sold his birthright to his brother in exchange for a bowl of something to eat, was a familiar one among evangelical counselors and those in the antipsychiatry movement; the same kind of criticism was sometimes leveled at evangelical Christians generally. In his book *The Crisis in Psychiatry and Religion*, published the same year as Tweedie's book, O. Hobart Mowrer wondered, "Has evangelical religion sold its birthright for a mess of psychological pottage?" O. Hobart Mowrer, *The Crisis in Psychiatry and Religion* (Princeton, NJ: D. Van Nostrand, 1961), 60. See also John E. Walvoord, "Why Theology?" *Journal of Psychology and Theology* 1, no. 1 (January 1973): 28–33. Tweedie did not specifically cite Mowrer's work, but in arguing that "psychologists and psychiatrists were becoming increasingly sensitive to theological concepts," he did cite the symposium held at the 1950 American Psychological Association meeting entitled "The Role of the Concept of Sin in Psychotherapy." Mowrer participated in that symposium and published the paper he presented there under the title, "Some Constructive Features of the Concept of Sin." See Tweedie, *Logotherapy and the Christian Faith*, 22; See also Mowrer, *Crisis in Psychiatry and Religion*, 40.

21. Tweedie, *Logotherapy and the Christian Faith*, 155. Jay Adams made a similar argument in *Competent to Counsel*, arguing "In the area of psychiatry, science has given way to humanistic philosophy and gross speculation." Adams, *Competent to Counsel*, xxi. See also Collins, "Psychology on a New Foundation," 23.

22. Adams, *Competent to Counsel*, 12.

23. For his ideas on presuppositional analysis, Adams relied on the work of Cornelius Van Til of Westminster Theological Seminary. Adams, *Competent to Counsel*, xxi.

24. Ibid.

25. Collins, "Psychology on a New Foundation," 25.

26. Ibid., 26.

27. Ibid.

28. Ibid., 27, 26. Collins articulated similar views in his book *Search for Reality* (p. 11).

29. Collins, *Search for Reality*, 117.

30. Ibid., 24.

31. Narramore did not use the terms "inerrancy" or "infallibility," nor did most of his peers. These terms became more important later in the debate. Early evangelical counselors claimed the authority of the Bible (especially in relation

to science), located its origins with God, and highlighted its practicality as a guide for living, a comfort in time of trouble, and as the answer to life's problems through the plan of salvation.

32. Clyde Narramore, *Psychology of Counseling*, 238–239.

33. Ibid., 239.

34. Ibid., 258, 268–269, 271.

35. Joseph Fletcher, *Situation Ethics: The New Morality* (Philadelphia: Westminster Press, 1966), 60–61.

36. Margaret Lamberts Bendroth, *Fundamentalism and Gender, 1875 to the Present* (New Haven, CT: Yale University Press, 1993), 7. Bendroth also describes the debate about feminism in evangelical circles in the late twentieth century.

37. Knight used the notion of "headship," citing I Corinthians 11:3: "But I would have you know, that the head of every man is Christ; and the head of the woman is the man; and the head of Christ is God." George W. Knight III, "The New Testament Teaching on the Role Relationship of Male and Female with Special Reference to the Teaching/Ruling Functions in the Church," *Journal of Psychology and Theology* 3, no. 3 (Summer 1975): 220.

38. Knight, "New Testament Teaching on Role of Male and Female," 218.

39. Richard Nielson, "Letter to the Editor," *Journal of Psychology and Theology* 3, no. 4 (Fall 1975): 319.

40. Adams, *Competent to Counsel*, 5–6.

41. Ibid., 5.

42. Bruce Narramore interpreted evangelical resistance to psychoanalysis in these terms in his 1973 article on the integration of psychology and theology.

43. Bruce Narramore and Bill Counts, *Freedom from Guilt* (Santa Ana, CA: Vision House Publishers, 1974), 34–37.

44. Narramore and Counts. *Freedom from Guilt*, 41–45. "Worm theology" referred to the theological perspective that emphasized the sinfulness and depravity of human nature. This view was popularly expressed in the Isaac Watts hymn "At the Cross": "Alas! and did my Savior bleed And did my Sovereign die? Would He devote that sacred head For such a worm as I?" In contrast, Narramore and Counts advocated a theology that could explain human sinfulness and yet affirm human worth.

45. Adams, *Competent to Counsel*, 29.

46. Ibid., 29–35.

47. Ibid., xvi–xix.

48. Adams qualified this point a bit, pointing out that human beings could not presume to say who would be saved—that was up to God. In addition, draw-

ing on the Westminster Catechism, he argued that it was a good thing to attempt to get non-Christians to conform to Christian standards, even if they did not become Christians, because, while it could not earn them salvation, it grieved God less than if they were to continue sinning. Adams, *Competent to Counsel*, 70.

49. Gary Collins, *Search for Reality*, foreword.

50. Ibid., 10.

51. Ibid., 57. Later in the book, as part of his discussion of neurosis in the church, Collins cited Marion H. Nelson's book by the same title. Examples of neurosis included inferiority and insecurity, dishonesty, rigidity, difficult relationships, and guilt (76–87).

52. Collins, *Search for Reality*, 59.

53. Ibid., 60. In citing Fromm, Collins demonstrated another characteristic that set him apart from Adams. Adams dismissed without exception the work of secular psychologists and liberal theologians; Collins was more willing to engage the ideas of people with whom he disagreed, while being careful to reaffirm his own evangelical commitments.

54. Collins, *Search for Reality*, 60.

55. Ibid., 44.

56. Adams, *Competent to Counsel*, 21.

57. Tim LaHaye, *The Spirit-Controlled Temperament* (Wheaton, IL: Tyndale House Publishers, 1966), 62–67.

58. Adams, *Competent to Counsel*, 21–22.

59. Clyde Narramore, *Psychology of Counseling*, 113.

60. Ibid., 116–117.

61. Proverbs 28:13.

62. Adams, *Competent to Counsel*, 105, 121.

63. LaHaye, *The Spirit-Controlled Temperament*, 102.

64. Adams, *Competent to Counsel*, 20.

65. Collins, *Search for Reality*, 39.

66. Ibid., 204. Collins referred to the power of the Holy Spirit in overcoming the sinful nature of human beings and saw refusal to be controlled by the Holy Spirit as one potential source of psychological abnormality. In a discussion of neurosis, Collins identified the indwelling power of the Holy Spirit as "the only really effective and permanent answer to the problem of discouragement" (31, 59, 103).

Epilogue

1. Howard Clinebell, "The Greatest Influence on My Pastoral Counseling," *American Journal of Pastoral Counseling* 3, no. 1 (1999): 51.

2. Ibid., 52.

3. Ibid.

4. Ibid., 53. Clinebell noted that he was more influenced by Sullivan's books than by his lectures. Sullivan's lecture style was apparently too opaque even for most graduate students.

5. Ibid.

6. Ibid., 52.

7. Ibid., 54.

8. Ibid., 55.

9. Ibid., 57.

Frank, Robert, 129
Frankl, Viktor, 215
freedom: ethic of relationships and, 139–41; gender roles and, 163–66; men and, 150–51; personalization of, 114–21; responsible, 151–53; views on, 188–89
Freedom from Guilt (B. Narramore and Counts), 225, 226
Freud, Sigmund, 64, 73
Freudian theory: Boisen and, 26, 27; CCT and, 47; Christian counseling and, 224, 225; domestic ideal and, 168; Dunbar and, 45; Fromm and, 103–6; Holman and, 77–78, 94–95; human nature and, 76; interpretation of, 95–96, 97; Mowrer and, 185–86; problems with, 188–89; of psychoanalysis, 64–65, 97
Friedan, Betty, 169, 175
friendship, therapeutic, 57–58, 71
Fromm, Erich, 86, 96, 103–5, 113, 235
Fromm-Reichmann, Frieda, 103, 235
Fuller Theological Seminary, 210, 213, 214
functional mental illness, 17, 25–26, 36–37, 44, 78
Fundamentalism and Gender (Bendroth), 221
Furgeson, Earl H., 126–27, 128

Garrett Biblical Institute (Evanston, Illinois), 236
gender: Christian counseling and, 221–23; moral reasoning and, 12–13. *See also* gendered moral discourse; gender roles; men; women
Gender and the Social Gospel (Edwards and Gifford), 9–10
gendered moral discourse: consequences of, 151–55; constructing, 144–51; in historical context, 155–57; writings about pastoral counseling and, 142–44
gendered moral reasoning, 12–13, 157–60, 274n. 3
gender roles: domestic ideal, and critique of, 166–69; equality of

women and, 175–79; views on, 163–66
Getting Down to Cases (Holman), 172
Gifford, Carolyn, 9–10
Gilligan, Carol, 157–59, 243n. 22
Glasser, William, 185, 208–9
goals of counseling, 80–83, 98, 195–200
God, views of, and Christian counseling, 223–32
Grounds, Vernon, 228
growth, as goal of counseling, 80–83, 98
Guiles, Philip, 32, 34, 43–44, 45
guilt, 225–26. *See also* sin
Guilt and Grace (Tournier), 225

Hadfield, J. A., 94
Hall, Volta, 118–19
Handy, Robert T., 9
Hardesty, Nancy, 222
Harkness, Georgia, 237
Hartley, Ruth, 178
Hawes, Sheilah James, 202
healing, and Protestantism, 55–58
Healy, William, 67
Hilger, Rothe, 57–58
Hiltner, Seward: on Boisen, 285n. 62; career of, 89; CCT and, 46; on counselor as minister, 194; CPE and, 51, 55; on credentials in pastoral counseling, 202–3; on feminine characteristics in counselors, 174; Freudian theory and, 47; gendered moral discourse and, 145, 146; gender roles and, 168–69; on healing, 57; on the nature of sin, 140; New York Psychology Group, 103; non-directive therapy and, 125; *Pastoral Counseling*, 99–101, 113, 114, 116, 154–55; *Pastoral Psychology* and, 163, 189; on responsible freedom, 139; self-realization and, 127; study with Colston, 5–6, 114, 152–53, 154, 159–60, 173; on the therapeutic relationship, 137; views of men, 172–73; views of women, 171, 172

Hofmann, Hans, 190
Holifield, E. Brooks, xi, 242n. 18
Holman, Charles: on adjustment, 80; daily devotion and, 231; on facing reality, 209–10; Freudian theory and, 76–78; *Getting Down to Cases*, 172; pamphlet by, 92–95; and strengthening of will, 115; USO seminars and, 89, 90
Holt, Arthur, 31–32
Holy Spirit, work of, 232
Hopkins, C. Howard, 9
Horney, Karen, 86, 96–97, 103, 113
Horton, Walter M., 190
Hoskins, Roy G., 37
Howe, Reuel, 119
Hulme, William, 187
humanistic psychology, 5, 70, 86, 98–101, 102–3
human nature: Freud and, 95–96; Niebuhr and, 191–92; Rogers and, 186, 189, 192, 225; views of, 75–77, 102–3

insight, 92, 101, 264n. 38
Institute of Pastoral Care, 46, 47–48
integrity therapy, 212
Interchurch World Movement, 23
International Pastoral Care Network for Social Responsibility, 237–38
interview, the: in CPE, 43, 58–60; therapeutic, 59–61, 62, 67
"I-Thou" relationship, 138, 140

James, William, 18, 36, 75–76, 77
Jernigan, Homer, 193
Johnson, Paul, 108–10, 114, 132, 146
Journal of Christian Counseling, 214
Journal of Pastoral Care: book reviews in, 171–72; on clerical authority, 187; description of, 11, 110; on gender roles, 173; Lindemann article in, 167
Journal of Psychology and Christianity, 214

Journal of Psychology and Theology, 206, 214, 221, 223
Judge Baker Guidance Center, 40, 49, 55, 57–58, 67, 251n. 1
Jung, Carl, 73, 98

Keller, William S., 47
Kinsey, Alfred, 123–24, 129, 171
Kirkendall, Lester, 175
Kloppenberg, James, 15, 156
Knight, George W., III, 221–23
Kohlberg, Lawrence, 157–59, 243n. 22
Kreutzer, Knox, 173, 188, 196–200, 201
Kreves, Eugene, 186
Kuether, Fred, 108, 252n. 13
Kunkel, Fritz, 73, 98

LaHaye, Tim, 211, 227–28, 229, 231
Lane, Arthur Garfield, 53
Lapsley, James, 204
Lasch, Christopher, 181
lay counseling, 212
LeFevre, Perry, 189
Let's Be Normal! (Kunkel), 73
Lewis, Douglass, 188, 193
Lewis, Henry, 108
liberal moral sensibility: Boisen and, 16–17, 20–21, 36–39; characteristics of, 144; civil discourse and, 233, 238–39; counseling and, 62–63; CPE and, 43; definition of, 7–8; gendered discourse and, 143–44; history of, 13–14, 155–57; importance of studying, 8–9; non-directive approach and, 114–21; pastoral counselors and, 11–13; post-WWII, 91–92, 102–3; Rogerian theory and methods and, 114–21
Lindemann, Erich, 167
Lindsell, Harold, 222
listening to patients, 58–60, 74–75, 81, 98, 101
Logotherapy and the Christian Faith (Tweedie), 215
Loomer, Bernard M., 190
Loper, Vere, 177–78

Mace, David, 133, 134–35
Machen, J. Gresham, 10
marriage: Burkhart's views on, 164–65; divorce counseling, 135–36, 163–64; emotional intimacy and, 147–48; ministerial authority and, 123–24; premarital counseling, 131–35
Marsden, George, 213
Maslow, Abraham, 5, 70
Massachusetts General Hospital (MGH), 41–42, 49, 54, 55, 67, 80
May, Rollo: career of, 69–71; case example from, 72; Clinebell and, 235; counseling style of, 84; humanistic psychology and, 5, 86; on moral problems, 76; New York Psychology Group, 103; works of, 98–101
McCabe, Alice, 68
McComb, Samuel, 29, 30, 64
Mead, George Herbert, 27, 36, 67–68, 113
Mead, Margaret, 113, 119, 167–69, 204–5
medical social work, 67
Meehl, Paul, 214
men: abstract sense and, 149; in counseling sessions, 172–73; freedom and, 150–51; moral dilemmas and, 143–44, 148–51, 154–55, 157–59; obligations and, 148–49; relationships and, 149–51, 154–55
Menninger, Karl, 88, 97
Menninger, William, 88
mental hygiene movement, 65
mental illness: etiology of, 26, 27–28, 78–80, 185, 209, 226–29; functional, 17, 25–26, 36–37, 44, 78; organic, 17, 25, 44; religion and, 25–26, 225–26. See also under sin
Merrill-Palmer School (Detroit), 112
MGH. See Massachusetts General Hospital
Michalson, Carl, 124
middle class, bias toward, 119–21
Miller, Samuel, 126
ministerial authority: authoritarianism compared to, 187; counselor and, 193–95; marriage and, 123–24;

non-directive therapy and, 124–27; premarital counseling and, 132–33; restoration of, 188
Mollenkott, Virginia Ramey, 223
moral authority: moral expert compared to, 129–30; non-directive therapy and, 122–23. See also ministerial authority
moral discourse, 275n. 3
moral imperatives, Christianity and, 192–93
Morality and Mental Health (Mowrer), 209
moral life, and mental health, 80, 83
moral orientation, 243n. 22
moral reasoning, and gender, 12–13, 157–60, 274n. 3
Morals and Medicine (Fletcher), 140
moral sensibility, definition of, 7–8. See also conservative moral sensibility; liberal moral sensibility
moral standards, and Christian counseling, 218
Mowrer, O. Hobart: Adams and, 211, 226, 227; antipsychiatry movement and, 208, 209; integrity therapy and, 212; moralism and, 193; pastoral identity and, 184–86; sovereignty of God and, 224
Murphy, Gardiner, 113

Narramore, Bruce, 206–7, 210, 213–14, 225, 226
Narramore, Clyde, 210, 218–19, 227, 228, 229, 230
National Conference on Clinical Training, first (1944), 108
Nature of Prejudice, The (Allport), 106
neo-casuistry, 220
neoevangelicals, 212–13
neo-Freudians, 86, 96–97, 103, 112–13, 235
New York Psychology Group, 103
Niebuhr, Reinhold, 10, 95, 189–92, 274n. 46
Nielson, Richard, 222
non-directive approach: Adams on, 271n. 21; Christian counseling and,

224–26; development of, 4–5; gender roles and, 163–66; human nature and, 189; liberal moral sensibility and, 114–21; moral authority and, 122–23; Mowrer and, 185; pervasiveness of, 135–36; popularity of, 113–14; problem solving and, 97–98; problems with, 128–35, 186; promise of, 124–27; science and, 6

Normative Psychology of Religion (Wieman and Wieman), 237

note taking, 50–51

Oates, Wayne: *Anxiety in Christian Experience*, 142–43, 144–45; *The Christian Pastor*, 114, 129; on client-centered counseling, 117; on future of pastoral psychology, 205; report to interprofessional conference by, 109–10; views of men, 172–73

Organization Man, The (Whyte), 107, 120

Origins of American Social Science, The (Ross), 18

Outler, Albert, 138–39

Out of the Depths (Boisen), 21

parishioners, and counseling clergy, 181–84

Parker, Richard, 55

pastoral care, as preferred to counseling, 180, 200–204

pastoral counseling: Bonnell and, 73–75; changes during WWII, 86–90, 92–95; directive method and, 83–84; goals of, 80–83, 98, 195, 200; Holman and, 76–78; human nature and, 75–77; liberal moral sensibility and, 62–63; May and, 70–73; politics and, 106–7; popularity with ministers prior to WWII, 68–70; post-WWII boom in, 107–14; problems addressed by, 71–73; problems with, 201; Progressive context of, 63–70

Pastoral Counseling (Hiltner), 99–101, 113, 114, 116, 154–55

Pastoral Counseling (Wise), 114

pastoral identity, pastoral counselors and, 184–87

Pastoral Psychiatry (Bonnell), 73, 136

Pastoral Psychology (journal): annual training directory in, 111; articles in, 124; Ashbrook article in, 174–75; Bonnell article in, 136; "The Consultation Clinic" feature, 133–35; description of, 11, 110; Eckert article in, 163–64; features of, 12, 111–12; on future of the field, 204–5; gender roles and, 166–67, 173–74, 175–77; Hiltner and, 163, 189; Mead article in, 167–68; on Rogerian technique, 186; Rogers and, 114; Rogers on Niebuhr in, 189–92; Thompson article in, 168–69; Wise article in, 138

pastoral technique, 57–58

Pastoral Work and Personal Counseling (Dicks), 170–71

Pastor's Sketches, A (Spencer), 1–2

Paul (apostle), 38–39, 96, 188

Peale, Norman Vincent, 56, 62

Personal Counsel (Frank), 129

personality, views on, 165–66, 169

Powlison, David, 211–12, 238–39

Preface to Pastoral Theology (Hiltner), 203

premarital counseling, 131–35

Progressivism: Boisen and, 22, 39; Holman and, 93; liberal moral sensibility and, 13; pastoral counseling and, 63–70; Social Gospel movement and, 9–10

Protestantism, and healing, 55–58

Psychiatric Interview, The (Sullivan), 113

psychiatric social work, 66–67

psychoanalysis, 64–65, 97

psychology: humanistic, 5, 70, 86; 98–101, 102–3; psychologists and, 65–66; religion and, 242n. 18

Psychology of Counseling, The (C. Narramore), 218–19

Psychology of Pastoral Care (Johnson), 114

psychotherapy, counseling and, 63–64

Psychotherapy and a Christian View of Man (Roberts), 188
Psychotherapy and the Christian Message (Outler), 139
Putnam, James Jackson, 29, 67

Rank, Otto, 73, 98
Reality Therapy (Glasser), 208–9
referral by pastoral counselors, 54–55
Reforming Fundamentalism (Marsden), 213
relationships: "I-Thou," 138, 140; men and, 149–51, 154–55; between ministers and parishioners, 118; therapeutic, 136–38; women and, 144–45. *See also* ethic of relationships
religion: Freud's and Rogers's theories and, 188; health and, 55–58; meaning of, 4; mental health, and, 80, 83; mental illness and, 25–26, 225–26; moral reasoning and, 159; psychology and, 242n. 18;   rituals of, 182; science and, 216–18. *See also* Christianity; salvation; sanctification; sin
Religion and Health (Hiltner), 99, 172
Religion and Medicine (Worcester, McComb, and Coriat), 30
Religion of a Healthy Mind, The (Holman), 76
Rice, Stuart, 18–19
Rieff, Philip, 10, 63
Rioch, Janet, 103
Ritchie, A. D., 18–19
Roberts, David, 188, 235
Rogerian therapy. *See* non-directive approach
Rogers, Carl: Clinebell and, 236; *Counseling and Psychotherapy*, 91, 99, 100; humanistic psychology and, 70, 86; on insight, 101; New York Psychology Group, 103; Niebuhr and, 189–92; theory of, 91–92, 121; training and career of, 66, 90–91; works of, 91. *See also* non-directive approach
Ross, Dorothy, 18

rural past, connections with pastoral counseling, 234–35
Rutledge, Aaron, 112, 178

salvation, 1–2, 83, 199, 227–29
sanctification, 199, 229–30, 232
Sands, Irving, 173
Sane Society, The (Fromm), 113
Scanzoni, Leeza, 222
science: biblical revelation and, 216–18; Boisen and, 18–21, 32–33; Christianity and, 10; and pastoral counseling, 4–6, 47–48
scripture, authority of, 216–23
Search for Reality (Collins), 209, 228–29, 232
secularization, 10–11
Self and the Dramas of History, The (Niebuhr), 189–92
self-realization, 115, 118–19, 127, 177, 260n. 28
Sense and Sensibility (Austen), 7–8
sensibility, 7–8
sex, and self-realization, 118–19
Sex Ethics and the Kinsey Report (Hiltner), 139
Sexually Adequate Female, The (Caprio), 172
Sherrill, Henry Knox, 53
sin: Christian counseling and, 224–25; conservative moral sensibility and, 232; definition of, 189, 192; ethic of relationships and, 140; as leading to sickness, 26, 27–28, 78–80, 185, 226–29; Niebuhr on, 190, 191
Situation Ethics (Fletcher), 219–20
Smith, Mark, 19–20
Snow, Helen, 54
Social Gospel movement, 9–10, 23, 63, 70, 78
social scientists, 19–20
social work, 66–67
Southard, Samuel, 112, 145, 152, 175, 182
Southern Baptist denomination, 212
Spencer, Ichabod, 1–2, 83
Spirit-Controlled Temperament, The (LaHaye), 211

Stewart, Charles, 194
Sullivan, Harry Stack, 86, 96, 103, 113, 235
Szasz, Thomas, 185

theology, return to language of, 187–93
theonomy, 139
therapeutic relationship, 136–38
therapeutic tools: friendship, 57–58, 71; the interview, 59–61
Thompson, Clara, 103, 113, 168–69, 178
Tillich, Paul: Clinebell and, 235; ethic of relationships and, 123; New York Psychology Group and, 103; Niebuhr and, 189; on salvation, 199; theonomy, 139
Tournier, Paul, 210, 218, 225
training in counseling, 69–70, 110–12, 201–2
Triumph of the Therapeutic, The (Rieff), 10
Tweedie, Donald, 210, 214, 215–16, 228

Union Theological Seminary, 18, 22, 23, 41, 71, 234, 235
USO seminars, 88–90, 91, 92–95

values, and Christian counseling, 215–16
Varieties of Religious Experience (James), 18
verbatim method, 58–59
virtue, feminization of, 156–57
virtue ethics, 156
Virtues of Liberalism, The (Kloppenberg), 156

Wallen, John, 91
Weber, Max, 156

Westboro (Massachusetts) Psychopathic Hospital, 24, 28–29
Whyte, William, 107, 120
Wieman, Henry Nelson, 237
Wieman, Regina Westcott, 237
William Alanson White Institute of Psychiatry, 103, 113, 235
Williams, Foster, 118, 132
Wise, Carroll: on Beaven, 57; on Boisen, 42; Council for Clinical Training and, 44–45; as CPE student, 34; gendered moral discourse and, 151; on non-directive approach, 116–17, 118; non-directive therapy and, 125, 127; *Pastoral Counseling,* 114; on pastoral technique, 58; on therapeutic relationship, 137, 138; USO seminars and, 89
women: autonomy for, 165, 166; case for equality of, 162, 166, 175–79; emotional intimacy and, 147–48; as heroines in case narratives, 172–74; moral dilemmas and, 143–48, 152–54, 157–59; purview of, 155–57; and relationships, 143–44, 144–45, 145–47; responsible freedom and, 152–54; stereotypes of, 170–72, 179
Wood, Leland Foster, 119
Woodward, Luther, 131
Worcester, Elwood, 29–31, 34, 64
Worcester (Massachusetts) State Hospital, 16, 31–34, 48–49, 50
World War I, liberal Christianity after, 10–11
World War II, and pastoral counseling, 68–70, 86–90
worm theology, 226

Yoder, H. Walter, 12, 114
Young Men's Christian Association (YMCA), 22, 23, 88–89, 92–95

Zoppel, Richard, 133